In 'Master Negotiator' Diana Negroponte skillfully explains how James A. Baker III helped President George H.W. Bush unravel the Soviet Union. Diana details the power of the personal diplomacy that enabled the Baker-Bush team to achieve the world-changing end of the Cold War, enable the unification of Germany and the assembly of the coalition that expelled Iraq from Kuwait. She has artfully detailed all the small personal interactions with world leaders that made those big diplomatic results possible.

> John H. Sununu, Chief of Staff to George H.W. Bush and author of *The Quiet Man: the Indispensable Presidency of George H.W. Bush.*

'Master Negotiator' sparkles with fascinating insights about how James A. Baker III, with staunch support from his close friend President George H.W. Bush, managed to navigate perilous political and diplomatic currents to help end the Cold War. Diana Negroponte's prodigious research has produced a compelling narrative that recounts how Baker's brief stint as Bush's secretary of state produced a reunified Germany, an end to civil wars in Central America, the expulsion of Saddam Hussein's forces from Kuwait, unprecedented dialogue between Israelis and Arabs and the peaceful dissolution of the Soviet Union. This hinge moment in history will surely be regarded as one of America's proudest eras of diplomatic achievements.

> William Drozdiak. Non resident senior fellow at the Brookings Institution and author of *The Last President of Europe: Emmanuel Macron's Race To Revive France and Save the World.*

A fascinating account of Secretary of State James Baker's skillful diplomacy in ending the last remnants of the Cold War. Important reading for anyone wishing to understand how the Cold War ended.

> Jack F. Matlock, Jr., U.S. Ambassador to the USSR, 1987-91, Professor Duke University and author of *Reagan and Gorbachev: How the Cold War Ended*.

There were times in American history when skills of US statesmanship matched the scale of world's change. Diana Negroponte's biography of James A. Baker, III reminds us of a statesman who could combine steely resolve to win WITH the ability to cooperate with the former enemies by showing respect and empathy.

> Vladislav M. Zubok, Professor London School of Economics and author of *A Failed Empire: the Soviet Union in the Cold War, from Stalin to Gorbachev*

Diana Negroponte has written a compelling account of one of the great American Secretaries of State and a principal architect of the end of the Cold War, James A. Baker, III. From the unification of Germany to the fall of the communist empire in Eastern Europe and the dramatic and peaceful disintegration of the Soviet Union, Baker's masterful diplomacy is chronicled expertly in this fine book.

> R. Nicholas Burns, US Ambassador to NATO, Under Secretary of State and Scholar, Harvard University.

MASTER NEGOTIATOR

The Role of **JAMES A. BAKER, III**
at the End of the Cold War

DIANA VILLIERS NEGROPONTE

ARCHWAY PUBLISHING

Copyright © 2020 Diana Villiers Negroponte.

All rights reserved. No part of this book may be used or reproduced by any means, graphic, electronic, or mechanical, including photocopying, recording, taping or by any information storage retrieval system without the written permission of the author except in the case of brief quotations embodied in critical articles and reviews.

This book is a work of non-fiction. Unless otherwise noted, the author and the publisher make no explicit guarantees as to the accuracy of the information contained in this book and in some cases, names of people and places have been altered to protect their privacy.

Archway Publishing books may be ordered through booksellers or by contacting:

Archway Publishing
1663 Liberty Drive
Bloomington, IN 47403
www.archwaypublishing.com
844-669-3957

Because of the dynamic nature of the Internet, any web addresses or links contained in this book may have changed since publication and may no longer be valid. The views expressed in this work are solely those of the author and do not necessarily reflect the views of the publisher, and the publisher hereby disclaims any responsibility for them.

Any people depicted in stock imagery provided by Getty Images are models, and such images are being used for illustrative purposes only. Certain stock imagery © Getty Images.

The photographs belong to the National Archive and Records Administration (NARA) and are provided to the author courtesy of The George H.W. Bush Presidential Library & Museum and the Baker Institute for Public Policy at Rice, University.

Jacket photograph by Alejandra Negroponte

ISBN: 978-1-4808-9754-0 (sc)
ISBN: 978-1-4808-9755-7 (hc)
ISBN: 978-1-4808-9756-4 (e)

Library of Congress Control Number: 2020920049

Print information available on the last page.

Archway Publishing rev. date: 01/28/2021

To John, who encouraged me through tough times.

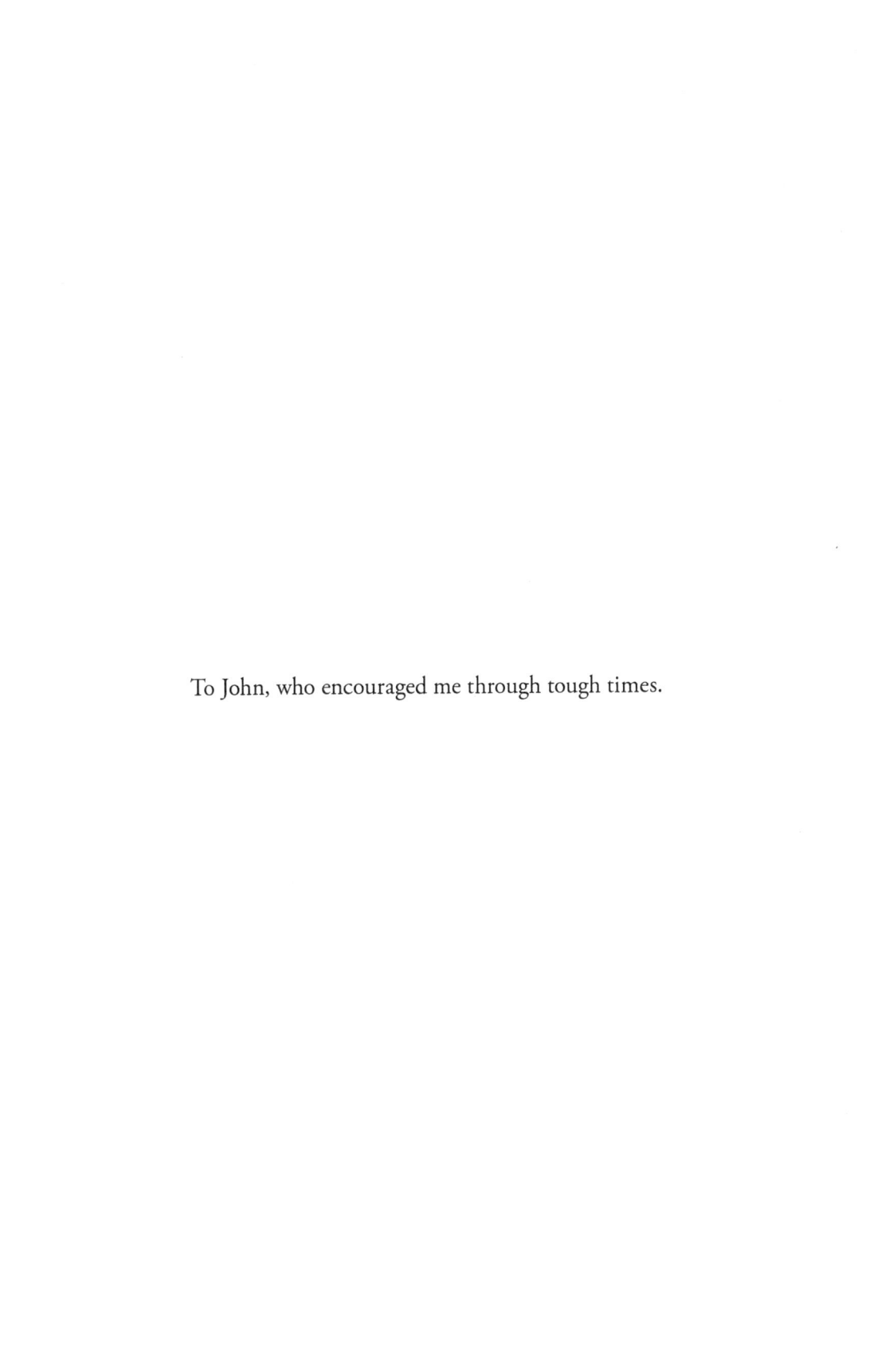

CONTENTS

Foreword ix
Acknowledgements xi
Introduction xiii

Chapter 1   The New Secretary of State 1
Chapter 2   The German Question 37
Chapter 3   Between Idealism and Realism 70
Chapter 4   Efforts to Transform the Soviet Economy 99
Chapter 5   Testing Soviet Intentions in the Americas 132
Chapter 6   Mobilizing Support for the Gulf War 155
Chapter 7   The Arab–Israeli Dialogue 189
Chapter 8   Arms Control 212
Chapter 9   Horror Mirror - the Breakup of Yugoslavia ... 245
Chapter 10   The End Game 265

Epilogue 299
Author's Interviews 307
Bibliography 309
Endnotes 331
About the Author 379
Index 381

FOREWORD

James Baker and I go back a long, long way. In the late 1950s, when Barbara and I and our family moved from Midland out in west Texas to Houston, Jim became one of my very best friends in our new hometown – and our wives were best friends as well. Jim was there when the political bug bit me in the early 1960s. He was at my side when I left the House of Representatives after two terms to run for the Senate in 1970. From our political collaborations, and our many other contacts including tennis, I knew that Jim was competitive and tough. I also saw him face great personal adversity with strength when his first wife succumbed to cancer. (He later was very lucky to find a second perfect partner in his wife Susan.) In whatever he does, Jim is a real fighter and he goes the extra mile. When it came time to choose the person I wanted to serve as my secretary of state, in the golfer's parlance it was a "gimme". Looking back, I was blessed to have him by my side during four years of historic change in our world -- from managing the peaceful end of the Cold War and German unification, to Desert Storm and convening the Madrid Peace Conference, to encouraging democratic and fiscal reforms throughout Latin America. Jim was one of the very finest public servants with whom I had the chance to work -- and he remains one of our most respected "elder statesmen" for his enduring and selfless service to our country. –

G. Bush

George H.W. Bush
November 16, 2014

ACKNOWLEDGEMENTS

Many people have given me their time and energy to help write this book. In particular, I am grateful to Robert Litwak and the staff at the Woodrow Wilson Center who supported this work from the beginning. Christian Ostermann, director of the Cold War International History Project at the Wilson Center guided my early steps. Serious scholars at the Woodrow Wilson Center, Stapleton Roy, Robert Hutchings and David Aaron Miller read chapters that related to their regional expertise and gently corrected my errors. Robert Kimmitt, Vlad Zubok and Nicholas Burns read chapters which related to their specialized knowledge. Eric Edelman provided helpful ideas.

Thanks to librarian Janet Spikes and her specialized team at the Wilson Center, the Library of Congress lent me books in German and French that brought the European perspective to US foreign policy of the period. Enthusiastic interns researched archives for relevant material, notably Paul Mercandetti, Emre Kuecuekkaraca, April Reber, Eric Gorski, Dan Morgan-Russell, Nolan Holl, Jake Roselius and Rose Blanchard. Daniel J. Linke and his staff at the Seeley G. Mudd Manuscript Library at Princeton University opened the archives of James A. Baker III, Daniel Kurtzer and Don Oberdorfer thus giving me access to their original letters and diaries.

Deborah Wheeler and the staff at the George Bush Presidential Library and Museum at College Station, Texas helped me explore the rich presidential archive and whetted my appetite for photographs. Edward Djerejian, director of the Baker Institute for Public Policy at Rice University, Houston led me into Baker's life and Ben Stevenson shared the rich collection of photographs which I have culled to animate the narrative.

Jerrold and Leona Schecter were there at the beginning to advise me how to write a history that would draw a wider public. Alexander Hoyt took up my cause as he shepherded this book in the early years. Their encouragement was invaluable. Rose Blanchard carefully read the whole manuscript, fact checking and ensuring that electronic cites still functioned. William Frucht saw the value of this manuscript and guided me through the early years of the editorial process. His comments were invaluable. Any factual mistakes and interpretations are mine. I apologize if they offend some with whom I have discussed ideas on the end of the Cold War.

Finally, I thank my family who has watched me balance parenting and writing. They have tolerated burned suppers and unmade beds as I focused on writing about a statesman at a critical time of world history.

INTRODUCTION

Scholars disagree about how the 20th century Cold War ended. Some focus on Ronald Reagan's strategy to develop a new anti-ballistic missile system, known as the Strategic Defense Initiative and negotiate through strength with the Soviet leadership.[1] Others emphasize Gorbachev's central role and the radical domestic reforms that he initiated within the Soviet Union. These were well intended but their implementation led to chaos and the dissolution of the Soviet Union. Melvyn Leffler endorses Gorbachev's critical role while recognizing Reagan's emotional intelligence, his empathy and negotiating skills. These characteristics created an atmosphere of trust with the Soviet leader that laid the groundwork for a major arms control agreement.[2] Odd Arne Westad examines broad systemic changes in the United States, the Soviet Union and Europe, arguing that by the 1970s the conflict between capitalism and communism had diminished as nationalism, religions and the rights of people had grown in importance.[3] Adam Roberts identifies the growth of a more stable international framework, the creation of the Commission on Security and Cooperation in Europe (CSCE) and its conclusion in the Helsinki Final Act. Thirty Five nations including the Soviet Union, joined in this agreement, creating consensus on international norms and enabling Soviet leaders to refer to these values when taking otherwise politically risky decisions.[4]

While examining this period of history, this author recognizes the critical contribution of three structural elements: the stagnation of the Soviet economy, the decline of communism and the rise of nationalism, as well as the evolving geo-political configurations of power that explain both the end of the Cold War, and later the dissolution of the Soviet Union. While always considering these factors, this book focuses on the personal leadership of experienced and thoughtful men who enabled the peaceful resolution of the Cold War. It applauds the central role played by presidents and their foreign ministers: Mikhail Gorbachev and Eduard Shevardnadze, Ronald Reagan and George Shultz, German Chancellor Helmut Kohl, Horst Teltschik and Hans Dietrich Genscher, as well as Arab leaders who understood the growing influence of the United States and the declining power of the Soviet Union. In the chapters that follow, I examine the role of James A. Baker III and the small group of policy makers whom he gathered around him. Under their watch, the clash between two ideological systems and the confrontation between two massive military forces decelerated significantly.

James A. Baker III was "a master craftsman of the persuasive and backroom arts at the peak of his powers."[5] He was tough, determined and competitive not only with foreign counterparts but also with colleagues on the home front. Yet, the determination was wrapped in a self-discipline that let few people see the inner man. He was polite, often charming who went out of his way to understand his counterparts. He revealed his inner doubts and dreams to few, among them President George H.W. Bush, his close friend of over 30 years. They were like brothers. Baker had led his presidential campaign in 1988 and the day after the November election Bush chose him to be his Secretary of State. Compared to other foreign policy advisers, Baker knew relatively less about relations with the Soviet Union, but he had a teacher with whom there was total confidence and trust. A more flamboyant character than Bush, Baker made a critical contribution to the peaceful ending of the Cold War.

He was not alone. Working closely with his friend of many years and National Security Advisor retired General Brent Scowcroft they chose to build upon President Ronald Reagan's outreach to Gorbachev, but to contradict many of Reagan's regional policies, especially in Central America. With cautious determination, they supported Gorbachev's reforms aware that he could be ousted at any time and his 'new thinking' seriously jeopardized. By means of hard-ball negotiations from early 1989 to late 1992, together they reduced the threat of nuclear war, supported East European nations seeking freedom, achieved the unification of Germany and anchored it within NATO. Distinct from the previous president's inclinations, they repelled Saddam Hussein from Kuwait, introduced the United Nations to mediate an end to civil wars in Central America, brought the leaders of Israel and the West Bank Palestinians to meet face to face, and actively pursued free trade agreements whose purpose was both economic and political.

Both Bush and Baker had played key roles in the Ronald Reagan administration when Bush was Vice President and Baker was first Chief of Staff and then Secretary of the Treasury. Bush had partnered with Reagan in drafting harsh speeches against the Soviet Union and building up US military strength in the early 1980s. However, in the run up to the 1984 mid-term election and facing a congress that sought to reduce defense spending, Reagan toned down the rhetoric and negotiated with the Soviets over arms control. Both he and Gorbachev dreamed of ridding the world of nuclear weapons. Four years later when Bush campaigned for the presidency, he did not reveal whether he would continue Reagan's engagement with Gorbachev or assert a more combative American posture. The uncertainty was deliberate because both he and Baker were determined not to be seen as Reagan III. Instead, they would forge their own path. To emphasize this independence, Bush chose Scowcroft to be his National Security Advisor, a man who had not served in the Reagan administration, but had been National Security Advisor to President Gerald Ford. Later, Bush appointed Richard 'Dick' Cheney, who had also served in the Ford administration, to be his Secretary of Defense.

Baker was a distinctive man to be Secretary of State: he was so close to the president that each could finish the other's sentence; Bush conferred with him every day and Baker wrote a nightly report that was honest, if not blunt, in keeping the president informed. Baker's Texan drawl may have put off foreign officials, but they grew accustomed to the man known as "Mr. Fix It." Within the State Department, Baker removed Reagan's political appointees and rotated Foreign

Service Officers (FSOs), preferring men and women who would think creatively to face the challenges of 1989 and beyond. In January that year, the end of the Cold War was not assured, divisions among European leaders over Strategic Nuclear Forces (SNF) existed and civil wars in Central America, Cambodia and Afghanistan continued. These were regular problems that any Secretary of State might face. The typhoon came when the citizens of Poland, Hungary and East Germany took to the streets to repudiate Moscow and its handpicked leaders in Eastern Europe. Gorbachev's radical reforms triggered opportunities to oust communist leaders. To understand the changes and anticipate consequences, Baker needed advisers with access to the best intelligence, mental agility and thoughtful recommendations. Dismissive of the bureaucracy, he later came to appreciate talents unseen upon his arrival at the Department of State.

Baker was not a strategic thinker in the school of Henry Kissinger, but he was a deliberative man with a fine grasp of complex facts. He was also a man of action who pursued the logic of his decisions with determination and persistence. This book examines Baker's role in the unwinding of the Cold War. It describes the way in which he negotiated to achieve his goals. It analyzes the accomplishments of the Bush '41 administration, and appraises misjudgments as well as missed opportunities. How might we judge Baker's role as director of US foreign policy in the final years of the Cold War?

There was no playbook on how to react to Gorbachev's domestic reforms and his 'new thinking' on international affairs. His radical changes could have met counterrevolution by Kremlin hardliners determined to maintain Soviet control. In the early months of 1989, Bush and his national security team were uncertain of the consequences of freedom marches in East Germany and Hungary as well as the electoral rejection of the communist leader in Poland. Consequently, they acted cautiously without the time or inclination to develop a grand theory. Baker was less cautious than Bush, but he would not put at risk the steady relationship with the Soviet Union. Stability had preserved a strategic nuclear balance and avoided the threat of direct nuclear conflict since 1945, with the exception of the Cuban missile crisis. But within weeks of assuming office, thousands of men and women in Poland, East Germany and Hungary demanded their freedom and independence.[6] Throughout 1989, revolutionary events threatened the stable bi-polar system that a new president and his secretary of state sought to preserve. How should they respond? Should they further encourage Reagan's cry in 1987, "Mr. Gorbachev tear down this [Berlin] wall," or should they seek to restrain those movements for freedom? It was evident that the US government could not halt the demonstrations for freedom, but what policy toward the Soviet Union should the US pursue?[7]

At the cabinet level, President Bush sought advisers who would work together and not repeat the in-fighting that had characterized the early Reagan years. Together with Baker and Scowcroft he formed a cohesive national security team. They kept their differences among themselves, resolving distinct approaches to policy through internal debate and achieving consensus before communicating the final decision. At a time of revolutionary change in Eastern Europe, this team preferred stable and managed change. It pursued the traditional US policy of working with allies and international institutions to reassure them of US steadfastness. Their goal was to establish the United States as a leader of democratic ideals and influence, a purpose that Bush named a 'New World Order.'

This book raises seven critical questions about Baker's management of foreign policy. First, in the early months following Bush's inauguration, what was the true purpose of the so-called 'policy review'? Initiated by Scowcroft at the National Security Council (NSC), was it a thorough review of US foreign policy, or merely a means to keep the bureaucracy tied up in policy reviews in order to concentrate decision making in the hands of a very small cadre of senior officials? Throughout the revolutionary events of 1989, observers found it hard to identify a clear US strategy. Bush and Baker appeared to react deftly, but without a strategic framework beyond support for liberal democratic and free market forces. Not until October 1989 did the plan for US foreign policy become clear. In two speeches that autumn Baker set out a strategy, but earlier that year and in the face of constant crisis, it was hard to discern a broad US. Few foretold that Gorbachev would resist sending in tanks to suppress freedom seekers stratagem in Eastern Europe, that guerilla forces in Central America would seek peace through UN mediation and that the Soviet Union would disintegrate.

European allies were grumbling over the cost of a seemingly pointless ideological conflict. Several members of the US Congress sought to decrease defense appropriations anticipating a lessening of Cold War tensions. At the NSC, Scowcroft designed a unilateral reduction in US conventional forces in Europe aware of the positive impact that such a decision might have. Thus, Bush and Baker's first strategic decision was to strengthen relations with European allies, thereby creating a firm basis upon which to negotiate with Moscow on arms control and regional issues. They were also concerned that an increasingly united Europe might become more protectionist and thus a trading competitor with the United States. What did the European 'single market' mean for commercial relations with America? Solidifying German and French support for US policies and partnership became Baker's primary task. In his first two years in office, Baker had good reasons to stop off at one or other European capital as he flew back and forth to Moscow. He needed European partnership in improving relations with Moscow and he needed to ensure that a more united Europe did not present a trading competitor.

The second issue was the unification of Germany and its placement within NATO. This was important to Washington, but less to the French president or the British prime minister whose bitter memories of two wars were vivid, affecting their acceptance of a united Germany. In the months after the fall of the Berlin wall in November 1989, Bush supported Chancellor Helmut Kohl's ambition to unite the two Germanys and to place a united Germany in NATO. Baker was instrumental in making that happen, but following an infamous meeting with Gorbachev in the Kremlin on February 9, 1990, the question was raised whether Baker made a commitment on the expansion of NATO to include only East Germany, or was he sufficiently vague to allow for NATO's further expansion eastward. The Russians later claimed that Baker had broken a promise. Many have written on this question and this book analyzes the Soviet and US texts, as well as the remarks of German foreign minister, Hans Dietrich Genscher.[8] We conclude that at that February 9 meeting Gorbachev and Baker's focus was limited to East Germany.[9] Baker neither raised nor committed to NATO's presence elsewhere in Eastern Europe. However, Russian propaganda used that meeting to assert that Baker made a commitment on NATO that the US subsequently broke.

Turning to Asia, a third critical issue is Baker's response to the massacre of students and workers in Tiananmen Square in June 1989. The events created a storm of protest in the US Congress with American citizens demanding a forceful response to Chinese leadership and protection of human rights. Bush, however, sought to maintain his relationship with Deng Xiaoping and not break the long term US economic interests with the Peoples Republic of China.[10] Baker's efforts to achieve a bi-partisan foreign policy in the US Congress were set back as he followed the President's lead. It can be said that Baker ducked for cover, leaving the Deputy Secretary of State, Lawrence Eagleburger to visit Beijing and subsequently explain the president's China policy to an antagonistic Congress. What does Baker's reluctance to associate himself with an unpopular policy tell us about the man?

The fourth question arises in the aftermath of Saddam Hussein's invasion of Kuwait in August 1990. Should Bush's national security team have created a stronger set of security arrangements for the Gulf region?[11] The decision to leave Saddam's army severely weakened, but intact and retaining its helicopters meant that Saddam's resurgence at some future time was likely. The creation of a robust council of Gulf States was debated, but rejected. Instead, Baker moved on from the Gulf war, accepting Gorbachev's request to co-chair a Middle East conference between the Israelis and the West Bank Palestinians. Planning this conference absorbed considerable effort and much time that Baker could have devoted to metaphorically handcuffing Saddam Hussein through strengthened regional institutions. Should he have stayed focused on the Gulf, he might have constrained Saddam from provoking the United States again in 2002.

xix

The fifth issue arose in the late winter of 1990 when problems loomed in the Baltics, Yugoslavia and Ukraine. As the appeal of communism waned, national identification assumed greater relevance, and by 1991, the prospect of 'suicidal nationalism' in the Baltics, the Balkans and Ukraine became critical. In January that year Soviet troops sought to quell violently Lithuanian demands for independence. In June, Foreign Minister Genscher asked Baker to temper Serbian President Slobodan Milosevic's ambitions in the Balkans. In August, Bush agreed to Gorbachev's request to restrain Ukrainian desires for independence. Departing from a summit meeting in Moscow, Bush delivered a speech in Kyiv that recognized their desire for freedom, but refused to equate freedom with Ukrainian independence. As Bush condemned 'suicidal nationalism,' Ukrainian immigrants in the United States rose up in protest. In all three cases, why did Bush bow to Soviet fears of national independence? In speeches, Baker advocated for self-determination, but in practice Baker and Bush acquiesced to Gorbachev's request to maintain the international status quo.

The sixth issue concerns the aftermath of the failed coup to remove Gorbachev and the rise of Boris Yeltsin the president of the Russian Republic. Why was Bush so slow to recognize the changes taking place within the Soviet Union and what they portended for US relations? Both Bush and Baker considered Yeltsin crude and unpredictable, but he had rescued Gorbachev from the hands of the putchists and he advocated serious democratic reform. In the midst of roiling change, Bush was loath to abandon his friend. His strong sense of loyalty and a preference for a stable Soviet Union kept US policy firmly attached to Gorbachev. By October 1991, it was evident that Yeltsin tolerated Gorbachev as President of the USSR only to maintain White House support for his political and economic changes. The bifurcated leadership lasted a few months until Gorbachev declared that the Soviet Union and its institutions would cease to exist by the start of the New Year. Gorbachev's diminished influence was a reality and Baker was not surprised when Gorbachev resigned on Christmas Day.

What role did Baker play in nudging the president to work with

Yeltsin? Despite anxiety over Yeltsin's compulsive behavior, Bush invited him to Camp David in February 1992 to both listen and plan the future US/Russian rapprochement. That meeting was critical in establishing the post-Cold War relationship. It is perhaps the single most important US/Soviet, now Russian, summit since Ronald Reagan met with Gorbachev in Geneva in November 1985. How would Baker execute the decisions reached at that Camp David meeting?

Finally, both Bush and Baker were adamant in their refusal to offer US loans and credits to the Soviet and later Russian government beyond the conditional offer of a trade agreement and a guarantee of commercial loans for the purchase of American grains. Instead, they applauded Chancellor Kohl's willingness to provide credit, grants and gifts in kind. They also asked the Saudis, Kuwaitis and Japanese to support Gorbachev financially. Baker repeated his Gulf War policy of getting others to pay the costs of the Gulf war and the costs of rescuing the economies of Russia and the newly independent states. Baker's advisers were sympathetic to Professor Graham Allison and economist Grigory Yavlinsky's Marshall Plan for Russia, but Baker disagreed. He joined Scowcroft and his successor as Treasury Secretary, Nicholas Brady in refusing financial support to Gorbachev and later Yeltsin, arguing that loans and grants were 'money down a rat hole.' This book raises the question of whether the Russian state at that time had the structural capacity to benefit from grants and new lines of credit. Not only had Russia lost an empire, but its citizens were also impoverished. Humiliated and hungry, they became resentful toward the West. What underlay Baker's reluctance to make a bold effort for Congressional funding? The memory of the Versailles Treaty and its treatment of the vanquished German people should have warned him that a revanchist Russia was possible. Later in the 1990s, the eastward expansion of NATO into the former Warsaw Pact nations and the oligarchs raid on state owned assets, exacerbated Russian political and economic humiliation. The emergence of Vladimir Putin in 1999 should not have surprised observers of Russia.

It is tempting to review the history of the period through the eyes of the next generation, but the role of the historian is to examine decisions made in the context of the time. This book relies on James A. Baker III's papers archives and the National Security archives held at the George H.W. Bush Library at College Station, Texas. Baker's two autobiographies, the autobiographies of President Bush jointly with Scowcroft, as well as autobiographies by Vice President Dan Quayle, Secretary Richard Cheney and CIA Director Robert Gates and William Burns, a young State Department officer enrich our understanding. The recollections of two NSC staffers at the time, Condoleezza Rice and Philip Zelikow further deepen our knowledge of the period. A biography on Brent Scowcroft demonstrates his thinking and delicate management of the close relationship between Bush and Baker. Finally, media coverage and in particular Baker's interviews with the journalists assigned to cover the Secretary of State allow us to appreciate contemporaneous domestic tensions.

The recollection of men and women who worked closely with Baker and at the NSC enable the historian to probe deliberations behind the decisions made in those tumultuous years. The passage of time results in a certain warping of those recollections, but those I interviewed were honest about what they clearly remembered and what was murky. I have had the privilege of spending time with over twenty people who worked with or covered James A. Baker, III as a journalist during his time as Secretary of State. I also interviewed Baker himself: his only reticence was sharing his plentiful dirty jokes with me!

ONE

THE NEW SECRETARY OF STATE

Baker is one of the foxiest of inside operators in American politics when it comes to dealing with Congress. But he is a new boy in the global high-stakes game, and Gorbachev left him sprawled in the dust.

Bob Novak, May 1989[1]

James Baker's skills were attuned to public policy, the economy, and cultivating friends and supporters for Republican presidents. He was a domestic politician whose antennae focused on what he could achieve in the US political arena. No idealist, but with strong Christian values, he selected realistic policies and persuaded others that they were in the national interest. His years as a corporate lawyer in Houston, devoted to absorbing complex details, examining alternative strategies, choosing a course of action and then relentlessly pursuing it, had molded his work style. He mastered his brief, enjoyed hard work, and hated surprises.

The day after the November 1988 elections, George H.W. Bush asked his close friend of thirty-five years to be his Secretary of State. Attendance at National Security Council (NSC) meetings during his four years as

President Ronald Reagan's chief of staff and four years as his Secretary of the Treasury had exposed Baker to the principal foreign policy problems - relations with the Soviet Union and China, Central America's civil wars, South Africa and Cambodia. Furthermore, he knew well the Group of Five finance ministers, and the trade ministers of Japan and Germany with whom he had negotiated more open markets for American automobiles. However, his mastery did not extend to the syllabus of a US Secretary of State. He had much to learn about the complexities of arms control, Soviet internal politics, and the byzantine forces of the Middle East.[2]

During the ten-week transition period following the elections, Baker read the briefs on all the major foreign policy issues including the minutiae of weapon systems, the yardstick of relations with the Soviet Union throughout the Cold War. The Assistant Secretaries of his predecessor, George Shultz, briefed him on the principal issues in their area of responsibility. They faced pointed questions as Baker probed them for possible new foreign policy directions. Irritated, he found these senior officials unwilling or unable to move beyond their policy remit in the Reagan days.[3] Baker was not only absorbing current details in foreign affairs but also seeking out new foreign policy directions. A self-declared man of action, Baker was not a global strategist of the Kissinger school, but he was a thoughtful man who would draw around him advisers who strategically considered the means to achieve US interests.

In agreeing to take the helm at the State Department, Baker understood that he should rely on the knowledge and experience of the incoming president. George Herbert Walker Bush had worked for years on international affairs—as Richard Nixon's permanent representative to the United Nations, as Gerald Ford's chief of the liaison office in China and then as his director of central intelligence, and as Ronald Reagan's vice president. Bush knew personally many world leaders and their political objectives. He combined a thick Rolodex with the personal grace to ensure that his frequent telephone calls – often for social and personal reasons - were answered. He would now share the management of world problems with one of his closest friends, a man he had long called "Bake" or "Jimmy."

Also close to Bush was retired general Brent Scowcroft, a quiet, humble and learned man whose White House experience had begun under President Nixon and continued with President Ford. Scowcroft had been Ford's national security advisor at a time of improving U.S.-Soviet relations, when expectations of a more peaceful world at the end of the Vietnam War had made Congress less willing to support large military budgets. Detente ended with the Soviet invasion of Afghanistan in December 1979 causing Scowcroft, from his position at Henry Kissinger's consulting firm, to advise re-armament. He would be a cautious national security advisor to President Bush, occasionally curbing Baker's bolder proposals and balancing them against the needs of Defense Secretary Richard Cheney and his own deputy at the NSC, Robert Gates. Together, they would act as conservative counterweights to Baker.

Conservatives were skeptical of General Secretary Mikhail Gorbachev's speech to the United Nations General Assembly on December 7 1988. He had repeated his rejection of the Brezhnev Doctrine, committed to reduce the total annual Soviet military spending and withdraw 50,000 men and 5,000 tanks from Czechoslovakia, Hungary and the German Democratic Republic (GDR), known by the shorthand East Germany.[4] Baker preferred to see the Soviet offer as an opportunity for engagement and continued bilateral negotiations, but his conservative colleagues were unconvinced. In their minds, Gorbachev's intent was to widen divisions between European and American citizens who would be less inclined to send the military to defend Europe. Meantime, momentous changes were taking place across Eastern Europe. In Poland, the Soviet-controlled government had begun talks with Lech Walesa's Solidarity. In East Germany, protestant ministers encouraged their congregations to protest the heavy-handed Honecker government. Hungarians were restless and loudly criticizing the communist state. By the end of 1988, opposition to communist rule was reaching a boiling point throughout Eastern Europe. After forty years of Soviet domination, communist ideology had lost its allure and people could imagine freedoms; Eastern Europe had become a volatile mix of grievance, hope, and agitation.

KISSINGER SEEKS A ROLE

That January, Henry Kissinger, who had been national security advisor and then Secretary of State under Nixon, intervened in Soviet relations. Before attending the Trilateral Commission meeting in Moscow that month, he offered to convey a private message from the President-elect Bush to Gorbachev. It should seek to deepen political relations between the Soviet Union and the United States. Bush did not object and Kissinger met with both Gorbachev and Foreign Minister Eduard Shevardnadze on January 17, 1989 indicating that he was Bush's personal emissary. Given the growing freedom movement in Eastern Europe, he suggested that Moscow and Washington might wish to reach a mutual understanding on the region's "special evolution." If left unattended, the place could explode. Kissinger recommended the creation of some form of bilateral deliberative process that would allow a controlled liberalization in Eastern Europe but keep a lid on outbursts of nationalism. "G. Bush, as president," he wrote Gorbachev, "would be willing to work on ensuring conditions in which a political evolution could be possible, but a political explosion would not be allowed."[5] The next day he verbally proposed to Gorbachev that "This confidential channel could be used ... to open up for you somewhat the course of our [US] internal discussions of certain problems so that when we introduce a proposal, you would know what ideas and goals are behind it."[6] He suggested that Soviet Ambassador Anatoly Dobrynin be the Russian point of contact and named Scowcroft whom he knew well from their work together in Kissinger's consulting firm, as the key US interlocutor. In Kissinger's mind, this discreet back channel would permit the US to collaborate with the Soviets and maintain stable bipolar management of global security. It would also ensure him a key role in the new administration.

Baker learned of Kissinger's proposal and promptly squelched it.[7] He had had run-ins with Kissinger as Undersecretary of Commerce in 1976. Campaigning for Gerald Ford that year and knowing that Kissinger was anathema to many Republicans in the South and West, Baker had told an audience at the University of Oklahoma, that were

Ford to be elected, he would not keep Kissinger in his administration. The university's student newspaper picked up the remark and Kissinger learned of it. He complained to Richard 'Dick' Cheney, Nixon's chief of staff, who made Baker apologize to Kissinger. Baker gained two things from this experience: respect for Kissinger's infighting ability, and personal animosity toward him. Because of both men's gentlemanly comportment, however, few knew of their mutual dislike. As the incoming secretary, Baker was not about to concede a special negotiating role to Kissinger, and back-channel discussions smelled of Yalta and the great powers' division of Europe following World War II. The day after he received a copy of the Kissinger memorandum, he hand-wrote an addition to the talking points prepared for Bush prior to a telephone call with Gorbachev: "My channel and the person I have assigned everything to do with foreign policy, and whom you can rely on, is Jim Baker."[8] Scowcroft would not be the key interlocutor with the Soviets. Baker would.[9]

BAKER ASSEMBLES HIS TEAM

As he entered the State Department, James Baker had two incompatible priorities. Bush wanted his presidency to be more than simply Reagan's third term. It should have a distinct outlook with new goals. At the same time, Baker needed a team of advisers with historical knowledge who could guide him in the details of American foreign policy. He faced the challenge of creating a distinctive senior team in the third consecutive term of a Republican administration. Had a change of administration occurred, different people would have thrashed out new ideas during the transition period between the November election and the January inauguration. Baker, however, had to search for noticeable changes from senior officials steeped in Ronald Reagan's foreign policy. Following customary practice, all senior officials had offered their resignations to the incoming president and Baker asked them to remain in office until their successors received Senate confirmation; a process that could take 6 to 8 months. His challenge therefore was to find new ideas from officials who had worked assiduously to carry out Reagan's policies. A defensive posture was inevitable and distinct policies were hard to produce. Furthermore, men and women who had worked closely with George Shultz, expected a promotion. Most were disappointed: Baker kept few holdovers from Reagan's foreign policy team.

Most of the people he chose had worked with him both in the White House and at the Treasury Department. Robert Zoellick, his former Deputy Chief of Staff at the White House and Counselor at Treasury became Counselor and later Undersecretary for Economic Affairs. Margaret Tutwiler continued advising Baker as Under Secretary for public diplomacy.[10] Janet Mullins, campaign manager and later chief of staff to Senator Mitch McConnell joined in March to become Assistant Secretary for legislative affairs. Together with Dennis Ross, his director of policy planning, they would form Baker's inner circle, charged with developing strategies on Europe, the Soviet Union, the Middle East, Africa, and Latin America. These advisers also identified talent within the department, such as Richard Burt, Reagan's ambassador to West Germany, who joined the inner team before heading up the START negotiations in Geneva. Zoellick chose Foreign Service officer (FSO) Stapleton Roy, a China expert, to be the executive secretary charged with controlling paper flow and coordination among the functional and regional assistant secretaries, but Roy was never invited to join the intimate group that ate lunch together whenever the Secretary was in Washington without an official luncheon. Later, Baker added FSO Larry Eagleburger, the Deputy Secretary of State, to the "lunch bunch."

When he first took office, many inside State and in the media questioned Baker's management style. Distinct from George Shultz who preferred a team coach style, delegating policy and implementation to the regional and functional bureaus, Baker was more of a single operator, supported by a very small team. Under Shultz, assistant secretaries had become accustomed to taking the elevator up to the seventh floor to engage with the Secretary and his staff. Now, few FSOs took those elevator rides. Early in Baker's tenure, an acting spokeswoman stopped by his office to tell him about some development, only to be met with stony stares and an instruction to report through Tutwiler, soon known in the building as "Queen Tut." She protected Baker both from critical journalists and from bureaucrats who were accustomed to bringing urgent questions directly to the Secretary's office. They quickly learned that under Baker, management of foreign policy had changed.

Baker did not ask, or want, the White House personnel office to propose names for key positions. He, together with Eagleburger and Robert Kimmitt, his General Counsel at the Treasury Department, sought out talent both from within and outside the bureaucracy. Highly experienced in the working of the National Security structure and known as a lawyer's lawyer, Baker named Kimmitt Undersecretary for Political Affairs, a position customarily held by a FSO. There was little protest from the State Department's labor union to Kimmitt's appointment because Baker had named a long serving FSO, Eagleburger as Deputy Secretary thus ensuring that the professional diplomats had a hard charging and effective spokesman on the 7th floor.

As he entered the Secretary's office, Kuwait was not among the four or five issues that Baker had identified as needing his focused attention, but eighteen months later Saddam Hussein's invasion of Kuwait changed Baker's management style. His preference for relying on a close group of intensely loyal advisers both to develop strategy and to oversee implementation had worked well at Treasury. However, it was a poor match for the breadth and complexity of problems that face a Secretary of State. When Iraq invaded that country in 1990, no one in his inner circle had the regional expertise to respond. Kimmitt stepped into the breach recommending that the US refer the invasion to the UN Security Council and drafting the several US resolutions. The Assistant Secretary for Middle Eastern Affairs, John Kelly, pitched in with a group of experts steeped in regional knowledge. A year and a half into his tenure, Baker recognized that he needed to reach out beyond the lunch bunch. He grew to appreciate the talent throughout his department.

THE STRATEGIC REVIEW

In the transition period after the November 1988 election, Gorbachev had identified the need for radical change in Soviet policy. He had addressed the United Nations General Assembly on December 7, proposing that universal human values should take precedence over the class struggle—a major retreat from Marxist-Leninist ideology. He had also affirmed the freedom of all countries to choose their own destiny, thus renouncing the "Brezhnev Doctrine," by which Moscow claimed the right to intervene in the internal affairs of nations in Eastern Europe and central Asia.[11] His speech was received with praise by many, but some of those who would later form Bush's cabinet remained unconvinced. Gorbachev had expected a warmer response.

As vice president, George Bush had first met Gorbachev in 1985, at the funeral of Soviet leader Konstantin Chernenko. The Vice President had used state funerals and other protocolary events to form friendships with foreign leaders that would serve him well as president. Baker might tease the Vice President with the adage, "You die, I fly," to remind him of his understudy job, but he respected his friend's ability to create a level of trust among world leaders. In December 1988 and following Gorbachev's speech to the UN General Assembly, Bush again met the General Secretary, this time on New York's Governor's Island. Gorbachev was uncertain about Bush: he had a reputation as a moderate Republican and therefore might have to prove his credentials as a tougher negotiator with the Soviets. That December meeting was intended as a farewell gathering for Reagan, and Bush said very little. Baker was not present. On several occasions, Gorbachev turned to Bush to know his opinion, but the Vice President revealed nothing, instead referring to the departing President. Gorbachev left with the impression that Bush might not continue the close relationship that Gorbachev and Foreign Minister Shevardnadze had enjoyed with Reagan and Shultz.

After Bush's swearing in on January 20, 1989, Brent Scowcroft proposed that the State Department undertake a review of Reagan's foreign policy. He recognized the pressure from the conservative wing of the Republican Party and knew that Bush could not merely follow Reagan's path. Baker was a step ahead and had already started to work with Dennis Ross on "big ideas and new initiatives." He understood the need to develop a distinct policy that would strengthen an international environment to support reform and openness in the Soviet Union.[12] From the Soviet perspective, the review reflected divisions within American politics and was pursued for domestic political reasons not for a strategic rethinking of the relationship.[13] To address this concern, Bush had written to Gorbachev on January 17, shortly before he was sworn into office:

> My new national security team and I will need time to reflect on a range of issues - particularly those relating to arms control - central to our bilateral relationships, and to formulate our own thoughts on how best to move that relationship forward. Our purpose is to assure a sound and coherent American approach; it is in no way an attempt to delay or reverse the positive progress that has marked the past year or two.[14]

The impetus was Bush and Baker's determination not merely to continue Ronald Reagan's policies. They would disarm anyone who thought this was Reagan III. Instead, they would strategize and develop alternative policies where needed. While State Department officials worked to review policy, members of the NSC worked hard to write speeches for the president and prepare for his upcoming international meetings. They did not need a 'policy review' to do their work and began to wonder if Scowcroft's initiative was nothing more than a tactic to keep the bureaucracy busy while the White House team moved ahead.[15]

First, they sought to confirm the priority of good relations with Canada. Bush therefore asked Baker to join him on his first foreign trip as President to Ottawa on February 10, 1989, to meet with Prime Minister Brian Mulroney. Mulroney had just seen Gorbachev, and they had discussed developments in the Soviet Union and the General

Secretary's likelihood of success in carrying out his reforms. Baker jotted down Bush's comments to Mulroney:

> The jury is still out on exactly what's going to ultimately happen in the Soviet Union and this means serious communications with our allies - by your friend JAB [Baker] - to see what they think on a whole host of issues, but especially those affecting the USSR. And then, after completing our review we want to take the offensive.[16]

Mulroney understood that the incoming Republican team saw Gorbachev's public relations blitz in Europe as a tactic to reassert Soviet influence and create division between Europeans and Americans. At the same time, he appreciated the fundamental changes Gorbachev was trying to make and thought that Bush and Baker could and should do business with him. However, events in Eastern Europe were moving very fast, and in Mulroney's view, Washington had to grasp the initiative in supporting freedom, democracy, and human rights.[17]

Mulroney was the leader with whom the Reagan administration had negotiated the Canada-US Free Trade Agreement of 1987. There had been some difficult moments when the two sides had failed to find the necessary compromises. Back in October of '87, with the trade talks on the verge of collapse, Ronald Reagan had asked then Treasury Secretary Baker to assume leadership of the negotiations. Baker bargained hard, refusing coffee breaks in order to meet the October 3 deadline with the result that the Canadian delegation had conceded. They had concluded a successful trade accord, but Mulroney did not forget what it had cost him. He admired Baker but was wary of losing his shirt in any future round.

Kissinger's January proposal to create a private back channel to Gorbachev was still on the table when Baker took the Secretary's elevator up to his new office on the State Department's seventh floor. He had asserted his leadership of foreign affairs, but he recognized that Kissinger's proposal merited serious analysis. In exchange for the Soviets allowing the Eastern European nations to liberalize without fear of military intervention, NATO members would agree not to exploit the new freedoms. In March, Baker told *New York Times* journalist Thomas Friedman "it is important that any such idea, to the extent that it is going to be pursued, be pursued carefully, so that you do not send a signal that somehow we are getting together with the Soviet Union and carving up Eastern Europe."[18] By then, Baker had enjoyed his first meeting with the Polish and Hungarian foreign ministers in Vienna and noted how fast the countries of Eastern Europe were moving toward a Western orientation in their economies and political systems. If this was already happening, "why not let the process move forward for the time being?" Nevertheless, Baker noted that if this opening in Eastern Europe was reversed, or if the Soviets sent in the tanks and anarchy ensued then "it would be much more appropriate in my view to look at the possibilities of the proposal that Henry [Kissinger] advanced."[19] The European Bureau at State took its time developing its policy proposals, principally because the Assistant Secretary was defensive about US accomplishments in the face of the unpredictable and fast moving events in Eastern Europe.

The review covered the full panoply of US foreign relations, but principally focused on US-Soviet relations, arms control, regional conflicts, and human rights. Recalling his time as Reagan's chief of staff, Baker sought to maintain the Reagan team's proactive and positive approach. However, both Defense Secretary Cheney and NSC Advisor Scowcroft were more cautious, requiring Baker to argue his case effectively before both colleagues.

The US Ambassador in Moscow, Jack Matlock, believed that there were good reasons for Baker to undertake a strategic review. First, Washington had to understand the serious internal problems that the Soviet Union was undergoing. Second, as the Eastern Europeans shed Soviet control, it became less relevant to debate weapon systems like the Short-Range Nuclear Forces (SNF). But an alternative theme in arms control talks had yet to emerge.[20] Third, the administration needed forward-looking proposals regarding US-Soviet competition in the

Third World. Matlock recommended that Washington test Moscow in various ways to determine if Gorbachev's 'new thinking' was for real.

In February 1989, Matlock sent three cables from Moscow to Secretary Baker, hand-written on legal pads over five snow-filled days at the US Embassy's dacha.[21] He thus imitated, perhaps intentionally, the form in which George Kennan had written his famous Long Telegram from Moscow in 1946. Matlock's first two cables analyzed the internal Soviet situation and foreign policy. They included a proposal that the US consider significant economic aid to support the transition to a free market economy. This would be hard, but Matlock recommended "an urgent, comprehensive study of the steps necessary for the Soviet Union to become part of the world economy," and what the US might do to encourage a transition to a consumer oriented economy.[22] His second recommendation was to hold annual summit meetings so that US and Soviet leaders could keep in touch with each other's thinking. This would aid their negotiations in many areas.[23] Third, In the face of growing ethnic and regional separatism, Matlock recommended opening small offices of four or five Americans in the capital cities of the Soviet republics to provide 'eyes and ears,' in short a US presence. Ten days later, another cable proposed that the US not lighten its pressure on Moscow but rather use its leverage to test Soviet intentions in Central America, Afghanistan and southwestern Africa.[24]

When Bush and Baker failed to respond to these cables, Matlock became disillusioned. He understood that the president was considering a prominent Texan to replace him as Ambassador to the Soviet Union and he and his wife, Rebecca, mentally prepared to leave Spaso House, the US ambassador's residence in Moscow. In March 1989, Matlock came to Washington for consultations. His request to meet with Baker was turned down as the Secretary was out of town, but he enjoyed a twenty-minute private conversation with President Bush in which he advocated for a US-Soviet summit meeting before the end of the year. The president ended the discussion by remarking, ""Well, we'll take a look at it," but his voice indicated that he was not convinced of the need for an early summit.[25] The policy review had not produced anything new and Bush awaited a new perspective from Baker. A second visit in June that year was more productive. In the quiet of the limousine as he drove with Baker to the White House, Baker asked Matlock not to mention his idea of regular summits with Soviet leaders, but on entering the Oval Office, Baker changed his mind and asked Matlock to raise the issue.[26] Regular informal meetings, the ambassador suggested, could accomplish far more than the pomp and circumstance of annual summits. Bush was intrigued. He could not plan a meeting until the strategic review had run its course, but he liked the idea of less structured meetings where the two leaders could discuss critical issues more freely. Matlock succeeded and Bush met Gorbachev six months later.

Despite his misgivings, Matlock was rewarded for his February cables and his straightforward manner. Baker came to recognize his fingertip feel for Soviet reality. Thus, after considering a political appointee, Bush and Baker decided to send a reassuring message to Gorbachev. While the strategic review was ongoing, they would maintain continuity by extending Jack Matlock's presence as US ambassador. Matlock, the most scholarly ambassador in Moscow since George F. Kennan, remained there until August 10, 1991. He became an important adviser to Baker, fearless in contesting the Secretary's opinions in private and respectful in carrying out his instructions. While Matlock was not invited to attend Baker's one-on-one meetings with Gorbachev – an unusual omission for a Secretary of State - Baker briefed him immediately afterwards in the limousine heading back to the Embassy.[27] He did not wish his ambassador to be ill informed.

On March 7, Baker met in Vienna with Shevardnadze and got an earful about the upheavals roiling Eastern Europe as well as the growing opposition to Gorbachev's reforms. Returning to Washington on March 8, Baker told the President and Brent Scowcroft, "We need to move. We need to back Gorbachev. We need big initiatives."[28] Scowcroft urged him to remain steady. He had read the cables analyzing growing weakness in the Soviet Union and he favored quiet support for East European internal reforms.[29] Six days later, the initial policy review yielded National Security Report 3. It justified current policies. Baker was annoyed, describing it as "mush."[30] Bush also was irritated concluding that the report produced little that was new. He shelved the report refusing to place it on the agenda for a NSC meeting.

The president recognized that patience was not a strategy: his national security team needed new ideas. He therefore instructed Scowcroft and his staff to plan events and draft speeches for him to deliver. A sense of urgency took hold at the NSC's European desk.[31] Against the more conservative members of his national security team, namely Gates and Cheney, Bush leaned toward the activist, Baker.[32] He told NSC staff to develop a West European strategy of unity and strength to disabuse those who anticipated American withdrawal from Europe in the face of a weakening Soviet Union. NSC staff received instructions to plan an early spring meeting with French President Mitterrand; to draft an April speech for Bush on developments in Poland; a May speech on US relations with Western Europe; and, to make plans for the NATO summit in June. Despite the talk of a pause, both the NSC staff and Baker's small team of advisers were hard at work developing a policy of engagement with Europe. For them, the pause was an illusion and the calendar of international meetings required the development of strategy and drafting of speeches for the Bush/Baker team. Baker himself had urged support for Gorbachev and action to bolster his reforms, but he had not yet identified how and when this should occur.

MEETING WITH SHEVARDNADZE

The March 7 meeting with Shevardnadze was Baker's first with his Russian counterpart; it occurred while both were attending the Commission on Security and Cooperation in Europe (CSCE). Both men had close personal relationships with their respective presidents, were highly intelligent, skillful negotiators, and were sensitive to criticism. Both came from states with a strong sense of identity: Shevardnadze from the Georgian Soviet Socialist Republic and Baker from Texas. Baker was the son of patrician Houston family, while Shevardnadze came from more humble roots and had lost family members to the Germans during World

War II. Shevardnadze would adamantly oppose the use of military force within the Soviet republics as well as in Eastern Europe, and would remain deeply opposed to German unification. Shevardnadze was also skeptical of his American counterpart. Baker relied on the thick briefing book prepared by his staff and became uneasy when asked questions whose answers could not be found in the binder. Shevardnadze understood that he was dealing with a skillful lawyer, but not a foreign policy expert. He too had been in that position in 1986, when Gorbachev chose him to lead the Ministry of Foreign Affairs. Before that, as First Secretary of Georgia's Communist Party and its de facto leader, he had little knowledge of Soviet policy toward the US and the West. Nevertheless, in the intervening years he had negotiated with George Shultz and West European foreign ministers. By early 1989, Shevardnadze understood the need to lessen competition with the United States in order to harness Soviet resources for the central challenge of economic and political reform at home. He eagerly awaited the policy of the new Bush administration. Gorbachev, for his part, "liked and very much respected President Bush" based on their December 1988 meeting, but he did not know Baker.[33] The Soviet leadership would have little trust in the new Secretary of State until they understood his priorities. Later that March, on the edge of the Cambodia Conference in Paris, Shevardnadze acknowledged that he and Baker would have to work hard to create trust between them.[34]

Gorbachev's ambitious program was centered on two principles of reform: *perestroika* (restructuring) and *glasnost* (opening to new ideas). Their purpose was to enable the Soviet economy to compete in a global economy and take advantage of the technological changes resulting from electronic communication. These principles introduced both the elements of a market economy and the freedom to speak without restrictions—but their interaction may have been unexpected. *Glasnost* allowed the Soviet people and media to criticize openly, and among the things they criticized most were the effects of *perestroika*. Citizens argued publicly over food shortages and rising prices, as well as the perennial complaints of government incompetence and corruption.[35]

Baker and Bush welcomed Gorbachev's reforms, but they were not naive. The restructuring of a command economy was a long and painful process that was likely to produce both unemployment and inflation. *Perestroika* threatened the well-entrenched interests of apparatchiks who could derail the reforms and oust Gorbachev and his team of reformers. In its backing of criticism, *glasnost* encouraged citizens to challenge the communist party, risking the election not of reformers but hardline conservatives. Intelligence reports suggested that both the military and the KGB were uneasy with Gorbachev and his associates. It was evident to Baker that the reforms could be reversed at any time. They depended on one man's continued hold on power. US policy should be to support the man and his commitment to reform the Soviet system.

Few within the Bush Administration believed that Gorbachev would actually succeed in changing Soviet structures and culture. Baker therefore had to exercise restraint in his support for Gorbachev's reforms. In a speech delivered at the Center for Strategic and International Studies (CSIS) on May 4, 1989, he described the Soviet changes as both "promising and problematic."[36] The positive developments, such as the democratic openings in Poland and Hungary, had to be balanced against the recent production of 3,500 new Soviet tanks and continued support for the Sandinista government of Nicaragua and the revolutionary forces in El Salvador. This speech clearly indicated that Baker would not be passive in the face of changes in the Soviet Union. He welcomed the early signs of democratization, free markets, private initiative, and Gorbachev's desire to participate in the global economy. He rejected the advice of those within the administration who sought to sit tight and await Soviet concessions.

Five days later as he left for Moscow, he told the accompanying journalists, "… the goal of this trip in one sentence is to make clear to the Soviets that we are seeing an active, constructive, positive and expanding relationship with the Soviet Union. We want to test the new thinking across the whole range of our relationship … Our policy must be to press forward with our agenda, to test the application of Soviet 'new thinking' again and again."[37] Barely four months into his new job, Baker sounded aggressive. He could point to testing the reality of Gorbachev's new thinking. Should it succeed he could expand the relationship. Should it fail he could withdraw that constructive relationship. While offering an olive branch to Gorbachev, he was assuring conservative Republicans that he was tougher than Reagan. He was learning how to balance outreach to Moscow and at the same time assure the right wing of his party that he was no romantic. Testing would be the leitmotif of that first year. Later that May, Baker told a group of journalists "We want to test the new thinking across the whole range of our relationship. If we find that the Soviet Union is serious about new global behavior, then we will seek diplomatic engagement in an effort to reach mutually beneficial results." [38] Policy planning director Dennis Ross explained that the purpose of testing the Soviet Union was to give Gorbachev a push to "do the right thing and overcome their bureaucracy."[39] In English, "testing" sounded assertive and active. It required the Soviets to take actions that Americans could judge, but in reality it was a passive form of engagement that placed Washington as the responder. It had the advantage of preserving Washington's option to step back should Gorbachev's reforms fail, or should he resign under pressure as Nikita Khrushchev had done in October 1964. Nevertheless, "testing" did not remain the principal policy for long. By August 1990, the word was gone from Baker's lexicon.

DINNER WITH NANULI AND EDUARD

In Moscow for his first meeting with President Gorbachev and a third meeting with Shevardnadze, the Foreign Minister and his wife, Nanuli, invited Baker and his wife, Susan to dinner. They should gather a Georgian meal of roast lamb, wine and vodka in their small apartment behind the foreign ministry. This evening repeated the dinner that the Shevardnadzes had enjoyed with George Shultz and his wife, Obie, resulting in the development of a new level of trust between the two foreign ministers. Once again, the Shevardnadzes and their two American guests rubbed knees around the small table while interpreters stood behind them, scribbling in their notepads. Baker told the Shevardnadzes about his years in law practice and in the Reagan government, about his youth and a Russian-born history teacher who had influenced him greatly. To Pavel Palazchenko, the Soviet interpreter, Baker appeared fascinated with the Russian soul as well as with Shevardnadze, the Georgian. It was evident that behind the cool and sober-minded politician, Baker had a genuine empathy for both Shevardnadze and Gorbachev.[40]

Susan Baker recalls that despite their need for interpreters, Eduard, Nanuli and the Bakers "developed a deep and trusting relationship." She was struck by Nanuli's outsize personality and elegant bearing.[41] Baker recalled the passion with which Nanuli spoke of Georgia and her desire for freedom. Susan was amazed that freedom might be possible, later writing, "Jim believes progress on ending the Cold War could have been much slower and, perhaps, less peaceful."[42] Shevardnadze later wrote that had that relationship of trust not existed, the divisions between the two countries might have continued to spark conflict and hostility.[43] After forty-five years of Cold War, both the American and Soviet leaders were determined to create a cooperative relationship that would reduce tension and prevent further decade-long proxy wars. In the privacy of his own apartment, the foreign minister talked freely and at length about domestic issues, particularly the restiveness of various nationalities within the Soviet Union. Baker listened carefully. It was evident that Shevardnadze wanted his American counterpart to understand both the need for *perestroika* and the challenges of implementing it. Gorbachev's priority was to put the domestic reforms into action, but in order to do so he needed improved relations with Washington. As the former Treasury Secretary, Baker strongly recommended the rapid reform of both the currency and freeing up prices, but Shevardnadze considered this unworkable in the politically volatile Soviet context.[44]

The next morning, May 11, Baker drove to the Kremlin for his first meeting with President Gorbachev. The two met alone in St. Catherine's Hall with their note takers and interpreters. Gorbachev had just emerged from a raucous gathering of the Communist Party of the Soviet Union (CPSU), and Baker expected him to be tense or tired. Instead, he was energetic and alert. Shevardnadze had already briefed Gorbachev on the Secretary's economic recommendations, which led to Gorbachev's detailed explanation of why he could not free up prices at that time. Instead, the Soviets needed a new international climate to conduct the "huge and vitally important task of transforming itself...." Gorbachev also repeated something he had said before to foreign visitors, namely that his reforms were moving more slowly than he hoped: "in a big and complex country like ours, no one can expect the process to be easy, especially in a period of revolutionary change. Perhaps we are now passing through the most difficult moment."[45] Baker reassured him that President Bush did not wish *perestroika* to fail. To the contrary, "we would very much like it to succeed."[46] Gorbachev was relieved. He had not known the extent to which President Bush would empathize with his reformist agenda. Now, the president's alter ego had emphasized the American government's desire to witness Gorbachev's success.

The two men moved on to discuss improving US-Soviet relations, a prime test of which could occur in Central America. Would Mr. Gorbachev be willing to announce that the Soviet Union was cutting off arms shipments to Nicaragua? This proposal put Gorbachev on his guard; he responded that Washington should negotiate this issue directly with Fidel Castro in Havana. If Baker was willing to enter into such negotiations, then the Soviets could publish a Soviet arms cut off. Baker had no instructions regarding negotiations with the Cubans, and the subject remained unresolved. It was time for advisers to join the two principals.

Baker's advisers, led by Dennis Ross of the Policy Planning staff, entered the room to find that Gorbachev's personal military advisor and former chief of the General Staff, Marshal Sergei Akhromeyev, had joined the meeting. Seeing the much-decorated Marshal, the US team readied itself for a surprise move on arms control. Gorbachev told Baker's team that the Soviet Union would reduce its short-range nuclear force in Eastern Europe by 500 missiles. This unilateral gesture, he hoped, would lay the groundwork for the elimination of all remaining short-range nuclear forces and prevent the deployment of the new American Lance II missiles.[47] Gorbachev would also announce these concessions at the upcoming Conventional Forces in Europe (CFE) talks in Vienna. Baker's advisers groaned. This was clearly a publicity stunt designed to soften Western European opinion. Baker believed that Gorbachev had thrown him this "wonderful propaganda initiative" in order to cut his legs out from under him. Several years later, Baker exclaimed, "Five hundred! That's great, they have thousands of them, we had eighty-eight [short-range ballistic missiles in Europe]."[48] He saw Gorbachev's offer as an effort to drive a wedge between the US and Western European allies. "Frankly, that set us back a little bit in terms of our being a little bit more forthcoming and a little bit more trustful."[49] Gorbachev asked Baker to keep this news confidential and hold back on any US announcement, as he had not yet advised the Warsaw Pact leaders. On that note, Baker and his team departed.

On the flight home, Baker learned that Shevardnadze, at that moment, was holding a press conference in Moscow and announcing the proposed unilateral cuts to the assembled press. In his private cabin, Baker fumed that Gorbachev had "ambushed... sandbagged me." Later, he accepted the headline "Gorbachev Rolls Baker."[50] However, at the time, he composed himself and walked to the back of his plane to meet the press corps. Feigning unconcern, he briefed reporters in detail on Gorbachev's proposal and admitted that it was a surprise. "We expected something from him, but I can't say we expected this."[51] The public relations coup had succeeded. Gorbachev had gained further popularity in Western Europe and made Baker look unprepared. The American political fox had been left sprawled in the dust.[52] Baker had also made another mistake: he and the President had intended to move the discussions away from arms control, but Gorbachev's move had made arms control once again central to the bilateral relationship.

CENTRAL AMERICAN POLICY

Back at State, Baker searched for creative voices that could amend Reagan's policy of supporting the Nicaraguan Contras against the communist leaning Sandinista government. The issue had created deep political divisions among US citizens as well as within the Congress. If Baker hoped to pursue a bipartisan foreign policy, he had to resolve the several

Central American wars through a policy that could gain support of both Republicans and Democrats. The illicit sale of weapons to Iran through Israel, in exchange for cash that was then given to the Contras, had been run through Colonel Oliver North at the NSC and CIA Director Bill Casey. It had created the worst scandal of Ronald Reagan's presidency. North's effort to circumvent congressional restrictions provoked deep political divisions in both Congress and the American public. Baker was fortunate that the NSC and Director Casey had deliberately kept Reagan's Treasury Secretary in the dark.[53]

In search of someone who would earn support from both sides of the aisle, Republican Congressman Henry Hyde recommended Bernie Aronson, a Democrat speechwriter for former Vice President Walter Mondale, who had advocated strongly for the Contras during the Reagan administration on condition that they respected human rights. A man knowledgeable about Central America's civil wars and keenly attuned to the political vibrations in Congress, Aronson was well placed to lead the administration's Central American policy through shoals of political critics. He was quick and smart, producing a policy paper for Baker by early February 1989.[54] It focused on a multilateral approach, supporting Costa Rican President Oscar Arias and his policy of strengthening democracy and regional solidarity against Cuban, Soviet, and US interference in the region. This policy deliberately broke with the Reagan administration's policy of military support for both the Salvadoran government and the Contra forces.

Aronson proposed to Baker that the US accept UN mediation to broker a peace between the warring parties in El Salvador and hold free elections in Nicaragua. Introducing the United Nations into "the US backyard" was bound to provoke criticism from conservative Republicans, but it offered a way out of the political quagmire in Congress. Consequently, early in the administration, Baker began to work both the Democratic majority and the ranking Republican members on Capitol Hill. He would build on his reputation as an honest but tough negotiator to move past the bitter political rancor over the Contra scandal. On March 24, the President and the congressional leadership signed a Bipartisan Accord on Central America.

Baker also relied on Aronson to negotiate with the Soviet foreign ministry over Cuba and develop a new diplomatic approach towards resolving civil wars in El Salvador, Guatemala and Nicaragua. He had taken Aronson with him to the Soviet Union on May 9, knowing that Moscow and Havana played important roles in stirring the national revolutionary movements in these countries. Both Baker and Aronson appreciated that testing the Soviet commitment to Cuba was distinct from testing Fidel Castro's commitment to revolutionary forces in Central America. Baker was determined to test Moscow's willingness to end its support for communist-supported movements by seeking a pledge to end Soviet military backing for the Sandinista government. He never obtained that commitment publicly, but Moscow did not object to free elections. The following year Violeta Torres de Chamorro, widow of the assassinated publisher of *La Prensa* and the leading opposition candidate, was elected president of Nicaragua. Baker and Aronson proved the polls and pundits wrong. Pressure on the Soviets resulted in a democratic outcome in Central America. However, there was more pressure to come from American conservatives.

CHENEY & GATES

Serious divisions existed within the Bush administration over its emerging policy toward the Soviet Union. Conservatives within the Pentagon and the CIA had objected to Ronald Reagan's warm relationship with Gorbachev. They feared that in seeking his place in history, the naïve president had led the United States on a disastrous course. A lessening of Cold War tensions appealed to an electorate tired of high defense expenditures, but Congressional demands to reduce the Pentagon's budget could cause the postponement, or outright cancellation, of more advanced short-range nuclear weapons such as the Lance II. Baker called this school "the 'status quo plus' crowd who felt that the Soviet Union was disintegrating at a rapid rate and all we really had to do was wait for the apple to fall from the tree and pick it up."[55]

The Defense Department was leaderless until March 21, 1989, because the Senate rejected Bush's first nominee for Defense Secretary, Senator John Tower. By the time Dick Cheney was confirmed, several weeks had been lost in developing a new strategy. Cheney had been Gerald Ford's chief of staff and retained deep suspicion of Soviet intentions dating back to the height of the Cold War. Deputy National Security Advisor Robert Gates was an expert on Soviet affairs, having written his doctoral dissertation on the Soviet Union's relations with China.[56] Back in the spring of 1985, he had advised Shultz that Gorbachev remained a committed communist, cunning and highly dangerous.[57] Four years later, he remained highly suspicious of Soviet capacities to change. In a speech delivered on April 1 in Brussels, Gates had said of Gorbachev, "He is pulling all the levers of change in a society and culture that historically has resisted change….The outcome is by no means clear, and prolonged turbulence seems certain."[58] Cheney endorsed this position on the Evans & Novak show of April 22. He said he doubted that *glasnost* and *perestroika* would succeed and predicted that Gorbachev would be replaced by a man far more hostile to the United States.[59] Mediating between the proactive Secretary of State and the two skeptics was Scowcroft, who sought to dampen expectations of a peace dividend from improved US-Soviet relations.[60] Until consensus was achieved, Baker asked the White House to distance itself from Cheney and Gates's public statements. This would help assert the President's determination to support Gorbachev's reforms in the face of opposition from within his own cabinet.

Upon returning from Moscow in mid-May, Baker told Don Oberdorfer, the *Washington Post*'s foreign correspondent that the Soviets had agreed to cut back military aid to Nicaragua.[61] When questioned further by State Department correspondents, the bureau with responsibility for Latin American policy contradicted the Secretary. They had not seen a diminished flow of military equipment to Nicaragua. On the contrary, they noted that a recent State Department review of Eastern bloc and Cuban military aid to Nicaragua found that the socialist Sandinista government had recently taken delivery of a shipment of helicopters, military supplies and other equipment.

Realizing that this information contradicted Baker's story, Margaret Tutwiler ordered the bureau not to release its report. Baker's staff was trapped; they had released a story favorable to the Kremlin and then suppressed the facts prepared by the bureaucracy. Tutwiler employed considerable persuasive skill in distinguishing between "a temporary increase in the delivery of Soviet-bloc weapons" and a decreased supply of weaponry in the future.[62] Gates, however, was quick to point out the contradiction, arguing from within the White House that the Soviets were sending mixed signals and Baker had succeeded in amplifying them. The truth was that during Gorbachev's April 1989 visit to Cuba, he had proposed cutting off supplies to the Nicaraguan government, and through them to the guerrilla forces in El Salvador, but Fidel Castro had resisted the idea.[63] Cuban support for Marxist forces in Central America would continue until mid-1990, despite mild entreaties from Gorbachev.

Meantime, in the public's view, the strategic review of relations with the Soviet Union dragged on. In addition to his January 17 note to Gorbachev,[64] Bush had warned him about the review process in a telephone call the day after he assumed the presidency, and Gorbachev appeared to understand. However, as months went by, the Soviet leadership chafed at the leisurely pace of the review.[65] Not only Moscow but London and Paris were anxious for the administration to announce its conclusions. Baker disingenuously commented that five months "was not an inordinate amount of time for a new administration and for a new president to put his imprint upon foreign and security policy."[66] He was aware of the intense work at the NSC to draft four policy speeches for Bush, but he was also determined to show that the new administration was developing its own initiatives, not just warmed-over Reagan policies. That might have been a sound tactic in normal times, but events in Eastern Europe were changing so rapidly that Washington's absorption with process and the President's delay in calling a NSC meeting on the subject provoked adverse reaction. Public criticism of lackluster American leadership annoyed both Bush and Baker. Baker, the politician ever sensitive to press criticism, ultimately urged the President publicly to complete the review.

On May 12, Bush finally declared the review finished, announcing in his commencement address at Texas A&M University.

> Our goal is bold, more ambitious than any of my predecessors could have thought possible. Our review indicates that forty years of perseverance have brought us a precious opportunity, and now it is time to move beyond containment to a new policy for the 1990's - one that recognizes the full scope of change taking place around the world and in the Soviet Union itself.[67]

Having observed the changes within the Soviet Union, Bush believed that "we are approaching the conclusion of a historic postwar struggle between two visions." This was pure Reaganesque poetry. Observers looking for specifics could find only two. First, the revival and expansion of President Eisenhower's 1955 "Open Skies" proposal to build mutual confidence by allowing unarmed aircraft to fly over each other's territory. Second, an offer temporarily to suspend the Jackson-Vanik amendment, which denied the Soviet Union Most Favored Nation (MFN) status in trade with the United States until the Kremlin opened up the emigration of Soviet Jews. Neither policy charted a bold new path. Nor did the President address the cuts in short range nuclear forces and troop levels that Gorbachev had proposed two months earlier. The press was skeptical. David Hoffman wrote in the *Washington Post*, "If President Mikhail Gorbachev was looking to President Bush's maiden speech on superpower relations for specific clues to the direction of US policy toward Moscow, he did not find them."[68] Not only Gorbachev but also European leaders were frustrated at having to wait still longer for the new US policy toward the Soviet Union.

THE NATO SUMMIT

That June's NATO summit in Brussels presented an opportunity for Baker and the President to capture the diplomatic high ground. Both men were determined to move relations with the Soviet Union beyond arms control toward discussions over central and Eastern Europe.[69] Meanwhile, the months leading up to the summit were dominated by fierce wrangling over the modernization of Strategic Nuclear Forces (SNF). British Prime Minister Margaret Thatcher remained focused on deterrence, seeking to upgrade the Lance II strategic nuclear missile system in order to maintain an effective defense against continued Soviet tank production. On the other side, German Chancellor Helmut Kohl, his Foreign Minister Hans-Dietrich Genscher, and the majority of West Germans argued strenuously that an enhanced nuclear presence on West German soil made Germans more vulnerable to a nuclear exchange. The German and British positions were irreconcilable.

Thatcher was particularly critical of James Baker, whom she found less congenial than George Shultz. Charles Powell, her principal foreign policy advisor, had told the Prime Minister to expect a Secretary of State with a "problem solving approach" to US foreign policy,[70] but Thatcher considered this a mixed bag.[71] Beneath her personal skepticism of the two Texans who preferred leather boots to lace-up shoes, lay a deeper concern. Having decided not to pursue further integration in the European Economic Community, Thatcher put great importance on solidifying the Anglo-American alliance, and she worried that for both men, the British-American relationship might become a lesser priority than it had been for Ronald Reagan. The prospect of losing the "special relationship" and the ear of the American president who had supported her over the Falkland Islands, among other occasions, was worrisome for the Prime Minister.

President Bush and his team looked for a creative alternative to prevent a split within NATO. As the summit approached, Scowcroft proposed that their focus should be on conventional forces, troop levels, tanks, and, if possible, aircraft. But there was much dispute within the administration on the size of the cuts, and whether they should include aircraft capable of delivering both conventional and nuclear weapons.[72] Baker argued for a 25 percent reduction below current levels. Defense Secretary Cheney argued for 15 percent. The President split the difference and proposed a 20 percent reduction, which would require the US to withdraw approximately 30,000 troops, and Moscow to withdraw roughly 325,000 troops from Eastern Europe.[73] He considered this large enough to satisfy both NATO allies and the international press.

To underscore the importance the administration attached to solving the impasse over SNF, two emissaries were sent in mid-May to European capitals: Baker's deputy, Larry Eagleburger and Scowcroft's deputy Robert Gates. In European capitals, senior officials contacted the U.S. ambassadors to learn the purpose of this visit, but the Assistant Secretary for European Affairs Ray Seitz was clueless, leaving the embassies in the dark. Upon learning from the British Foreign Office that Eagleburger and Gates were planning to meet with the Prime Minister at 10 Downing Street, Seitz raced up to the seventh floor and demanded to know 'what the heck' was going on. Stapleton Roy, the State Department's executive secretary, firmly told Baker that he should keep his regional Assistant Secretary informed. Only after Baker briefed Seitz could US embassies in London, Paris, Bonn, and Rome send cars and staff out to airports to meet the two senior officials. Without institutional support, both would have stood curbside flagging down a cab!

The NATO ministerial meeting opened on May 29. As the foreign ministers droned on through dinner, Baker listened attentively, only occasionally resisting changes that Foreign Secretary, Sir Geoffrey Howe was asking for. At one point, Dennis Ross, seated behind Baker, asked why he had become so passive. Surely, this was the moment to advance the case for reducing conventional forces. Baker demurred. As the President's subordinate, he was "managing up," preparing the groundwork for his superior to make the deal. He knew that later that night, the President would have to telephone the Prime Minister and seek a compromise. "I want him to be able to say to her, 'Jim stayed with Geoffrey the whole way. There was no daylight between Britain and America. This is the best we can do.'" Baker was also thinking ahead to the next day. If Bush failed to persuade Thatcher to compromise, she might bring up the short-range missile question before the heads of state, thus bringing the British-German disagreement into the open and risking a failed NATO summit. "The closer I stayed to Howe, the harder it would be to argue that there was more to be gained."[74] By staying with the British Foreign Secretary throughout the night's negotiations, Baker left little room for Thatcher to ask more of Bush. Shortly afterwards, Baker called Bush to make sure they agreed on negotiating tactics. It worked. Thatcher agreed to negotiate conventional forces first and to postpone SNF modernization for a later time.

When President Bush unveiled his conventional forces proposal the next morning, Thatcher told her team that it transformed the discussion.[75] Baker recalls that "it caused a massive stir in the room."[76] French President Francois Mitterrand, who normally remained silent at NATO meetings to avoid undercutting his nation's unilateral military position on NATO participation, took the floor to congratulate the Americans: "the president of the United States has displayed imagination – indeed intellectual audacity of the rarest kind."[77] The international press, which days earlier had criticized Bush as hapless, now hailed him as a leader. Baker had served him well.

IN WYOMING WITH SHEVARDNADZE

In pursuing his prime interest, the US relationship with the Soviet Union, Baker needed an original way to talk informally with his Soviet counterpart, Eduard Shevardnadze. Why not invite him to the Jackson Lake Lodge in Wyoming? This broke the territorial limit of 25 miles beyond which Soviet officials were prohibited from traveling outside Washington, New York City, and San Francisco. Surrounded by the Tetons and with only a small group of advisors, the two men could discuss a wide range of bilateral issues. Shevardnadze was delighted to see the United States, as was his aide Sergei Tarasenko.

To get to the nearest airport, Baker offered Shevardnadze a ride in his official plane, upsetting his Russian handlers but giving the men the chance to talk quietly, each with only a note taker and an interpreter. Dennis Ross, who acted as Baker's note taker, sat uncomfortably on a pile of satchels for the four-and-a-half-hour flight. Shevardnadze had eaten before boarding the plane, but Baker and Ross had not. Two hours into the flight, a very hungry Ross interrupted the foreign ministers' conversation to suggest a break. Baker responded, "You think so?" but Shevardnadze answered, "Dennis is just always hungry." The two continued discussing the nationalities question for another twenty minutes, until Ross, like a dog needing to pee outside, scratched enough to gain Baker's attention. "I think Dennis really wants to have a break," said Baker, and finally Shevardnadze conceded: "We'll give in to Dennis this one time."[78]

In the conversation, Shevardnadze had shared with Baker the Soviet dilemma over the nationalities issue. As a Georgian subject to Moscow's central control, he spoke in great depth about the difficulty of keeping USSR unified. The unusual trip seemed to have banished the traditional Soviet fear of revealing vulnerabilities that US leaders might exploit. He talked of the pent up desire within each republic to express their own culture in the face of a central authority that repressed all dissent. The decades of central control, he allowed, were "unnatural and that was unhealthy."[79]

Overlooking Jackson Lake and the majestic Teton mountains, the Jackson Lake Lodge offered Baker the opportunity to get to know his Soviet counterpart without a flock of advisers and the protocol of bilateral meetings in capital cities. September was not the season for hunting elk, antelope, or deer, but it was a good season for trout. Once there, Baker took Shevardnadze down to mountain-fed streams to fish; something his friend had never done before. Shevardnadze's failure to catch a single trout did not upset the collegiality, but NBC's Tom Brokaw chided Baker for not giving his Soviet friend a better line and fly. Baker sent a handwritten reply "No worms – probably why Shev didn't catch anything… Had never fished before at all! So the fly rod was out. The spinning rod was even too tough. But only the true sportsman like you noticed."[80] Baker was sensitive to Brokaw's criticism, but he responded with wit and a compliment.

Over two days of formal meetings at the lodge, walks in the shadow of the Tetons, and steak dinners, the ministers discussed chemical weapons, arms control, Nicaragua, and other regional issues. During their walks together, Shevardnadze informally shared details of the economic difficulties confronting the Soviet Union. It was clear to Baker that the transition to social democracy and market capitalism was a serious challenge that would take a very long time. As a thank-you gift, Shevardnadze gave Baker an enamel picture of Jesus Christ's resurrection. "You see, even we Communists are changing our worldview," he said.[81] In exchange, Baker gave Shevardnadze a pair of Texan leather boots, standard gear for men who moved truculent cattle and could easily slip on the muck of a cattle pen. He would need those boots, Baker told him, to keep his footing amid the political upheavals rocking the Soviet Union.

According to Ross, this unprecedented visit created a new level of trust and confidence that enabled the two men to talk openly about other themes on the bilateral agenda.[82] The mountain air and their personal chemistry encouraged solutions to once difficult problems. After they returned from Wyoming, they instructed their respective teams to make progress on the transition to democracy in Afghanistan, environmental issues, and technical economic cooperation—issues on which they had seemed blocked just a week earlier. They also made progress on arms control and, of greater significance, dropped the linkage between negotiations on the Strategic Arms Reduction Treaty (START) and Reagan's Strategic Defense Initiative, known colloquially as Star Wars.

From his career in US politics, Baker understood the importance of personal friendship, and it proved invaluable over the coming months as dramatic changes rocked the superpowers' relationship. Shevardnadze's candor allowed Baker to understand how unprepared both the Soviet leadership and the people had been for the political and economic changes required by *perestroika* and *glasnost*. He also told Baker that Gorbachev failed to understand what was happening in Eastern Europe: the Soviet leader clung to the belief that the Soviet republics and Soviet dependent satellites would voluntarily seek to retain a union among socialist nations. The reality was that Gorbachev and Shevardnadze were losing control over Eastern Europe.

Washington too would be blown forward by the pace of change. President Bush might try to stabilize revolutionary forces, but liberalization was inevitable. Scowcroft remained the cautious member of the team, and Gates the critic of real change in the Soviet Union – to the point that Baker asked the President to personally order Gates to cancel a speech that Gates planned to give in October at Georgetown University. Bush did so but admitted that the request "caused some heartburn over here."[83] Baker had used Cheney's appearance on the Evans & Novak show to demonstrate to the Soviet leader that Bush also faced domestic opposition, but he knew that an administration cannot have conflicting voices on foreign policy, or it creates confusion. Years later, Baker acknowledged that the unified voice came from the fact that he and the President were close friends. "I would submit to you," he told me in an interview, "that H.W. and I were forty-year friends. I ran all of his campaigns. He relied on me. The statutes say the Secretary of State is going to be the foremost foreign policy advisor to the president and the implementer of foreign policy. Bush made sure that was how it worked. That's I think one of the reasons why his foreign policy was so successful."[84]

Increasingly confident in his responsibilities and with growing trust in the Soviet and European leadership, Baker sometimes took the initiative and acted on his own authority without first checking with Bush. Scowcroft did not protest, knowing that Baker and the President shared lunch together every week, met whenever Baker chose to walk into the White House, and talked on the telephone nearly every day. They were said to finish each other's sentences. Scowcroft was not offended, recognizing that in the Bush-Baker friendship, "Bush always had the upper hand."[85] By late 1989, Baker had acquired significant foreign policy skills and learned the subtleties of diplomatic communication. He had emerged the leader in Bush's foreign policy team, and although relations with Scowcroft and Cheney remained cordial neither doubted that Baker's close relationship with President Bush gave him an ability to speak with authority that no one else within the administration possessed. Scowcroft did not vet Baker's speeches, and Baker tested most of his policy proposals directly with the President. There was no daylight between them. Only one exception arose, when Baker leaned too far in favor of Foreign Minister Genscher's formula for the two Germanys. Swiftly, the White House moved to correct him, and Baker fell into line without a murmur.[86] Foreign leaders should hear a single voice and policy from American leaders. Baker's only gripe against his boss erupted at the President's summer home on the Maine coast. Then Baker yelled, "Goddammit, I've told him a thousand times, don't be photographed taking friends out in that cigarette [speed] boat. Americans managing their limited family budget don't understand your idea of fun."[87]

On the international stage, Baker understood that the changes taking place demanded a US response aimed at preserving stability yet encouraging self-determination among the Eastern European nations. His attitude was "let's get what we can now and lock in as much change as possible."[88] In October 1989, addressing the bilateral relationship in a speech before the Foreign Policy Association of New York, he urged Americans to act realistically and to engage Moscow in the search for mutual interests. He then laid out his five pillars of US policy:

- Europe whole and free;
- Resolution of regional conflicts, i.e. Central America and Afghanistan;
- Expansion of arms control;
- Institutionalization of *glasnost* and democratization; and
- Provision of technical assistance to support economic reform.[89]

In setting priorities among these areas, Baker placed Europe and regional conflicts ahead of arms control, stressed democratization over human rights, and shifted the bilateral relationship with the Soviet Union into a US effort to see economic reform succeed.[90] These pillars of foreign policy would endure through the end of his term. Ten months into his tenure as Secretary of State, Baker had developed a pragmatic and realistic set of goals.

THE FUTURE BELONGS TO FREEDOM

On October 18, two days after Baker's New York speech, the East German [aka German Democratic Republic, GDR] leader Erich Honecker resigned in a bloodless coup. On October 23, the Hungarian parliament formally renounced communism and established a republic. Its first act was to tell the Soviet troops to return home. On November 4, half a million people gathered in the Alexanderplatz in East Berlin to demand the right to travel. Five days later, Gunter Schabowski, the media spokesman for East Germany's Politburo mumbled through new travel regulations, which he had not read, but permitted "leaving the GDR... possible for every citizen ... exit via border crossings." In response to questions of when the regulations would come into force, the bewildered high ranking official uttered the phrase "immediately, right away."[91] Within hours, an estimated 20,000 East Germans were climbing over the shattered concrete that had divided East from West Berlin. On November 10, Bulgaria's longtime leader Todor Zhivkov resigned, and the Bulgarian Communist Party was defeated in free elections the following spring. On November 28, the Communist Party of Czechoslovakia announced that it was giving up power, and a month later they elected Václav Havel as president. On December 21, an angry crowd turned on the Romanian leader Nicolae Ceauşescu and his wife. Three days later, they fell before a Romanian firing squad.

Every day that Baker arrived to work, he confronted new developments in Eastern Europe and the developing world. The principle of self-determination and the reduced fear of Soviet military intervention energized people to seek freedom. Shevardnadze had started to draft his book entitled *The Future Belongs to Freedom,* which would be published two years later.[92] In the meantime, the leaders should meet. [93]

THE SEASICK SUMMIT

Ambassador Matlock had asked President Bush to meet with Gorbachev before the end of the year. Bush had finally agreed, but the President loathed the formalities of holding a summit meeting where the host country could wrap the conference in fanfare and protocol. He needed quiet time to get to know Gorbachev and to talk over a wide range of issues. Looking at a date in December, Gorbachev had proposed Italy, following his meeting with Karol Wojtyla, the Polish pope. The president's brother proposed Malta, having enjoyed a recent vacation on the island. The compromise was Malta's Valletta Harbor. The location and timing were closely held while Baker worked out the details with Shevardnadze. Baker called Matlock to inform him of the summit's place and dates, but warned him not to inform any of the Embassy staff.[94] He wanted no leaks, no Maltese government receiving line and no press frenzy.

The weather in Malta may have been balmy for the Bush family vacation, but as the Soviet and US delegations arrived on December 2, 1989, Valletta Harbor was enduring the storm of the century, including twenty-foot waves. To avoid the formalities of being guests to a foreign leader, Baker and Scowcroft had proposed that Gorbachev and Bush meet on their respective flagships, the USS Belknap and Soviet cruiser, Maxsim Gorkiy. The latter was docked portside while the Belknap rode the 10-12 foot waves inside the harbor, the crew trusting that its two anchors would prevent it from heaving onto the port's retaining rocks.

Unlike Bush, Baker was no sailor. Turbulent seas were not in his comfort zone. He, Chief of Staff John Sununu, and Brent Scowcroft were bunked on board the Belknap while the rest of the US delegation stayed in hotels ashore. Calmed by a patch against sea sickness, Baker knew not to eat. He and Scowcroft had arrived with a twenty-point program for discussion with the Soviets. Originally intended only as an "interim" meeting to prepare for a full-scale summit the following year, the meeting in Malta acquired a life of its own. For the senior Soviet officials, it symbolically closed the Cold War.[95] In the face of the cascading events, Gorbachev insisted that US troops should stay in Europe, that both the Soviet Union and the US be equally integrated into European problems, and that both should work together to keep those problems from exploding. Bush was more reticent. Toward the end of the first day's meeting aboard the Maxsim Gorkiy, Gorbachev mentioned his concern over the ideological basis for self-determination in Eastern Europe. Baker intervened, "I would like to clarify our approach to self-determination. We agree that each country must have the right to free elections. But all this makes sense only when the people in the country are really in a position to choose freely. This also falls under the concept of "Western values."[96] Gorbachev seized on the reference to "Western values," asking whether there were not also "Eastern values." Swiftly, Baker the lawyer intervened: "By way of compromise, we will say that this positive process is happening on the basis of 'democratic values.'" This wording satisfied both sides.

At dinner that night onboard the Soviet cruiser, Baker spoke about essential economic reforms to ensure *perestroika's* success. Gorbachev's senior foreign policy advisor, Anatoly Chernyaev, recognized him as "acting as a professional economist" with the ability to address these aspects of the reform program.[97] What impressed the Soviet delegation was the Americans' sincerity in wishing *perestroika* to succeed. They had heard it from Reagan, but were unsure whether his successor was a committed to the domestic restructuring program. After the first days' discussions, Gorbachev came away with the strong belief that "on an emotional level the US president, the Secretary of State, and Scowcroft had made a choice to support the reforms."[98] Nevertheless, Baker did not see the Malta meeting as the end of the Cold War. He needed tangible action that would demonstrate both nations' capacity to work together: this would come eight months later. Meantime, he recognized that Bush had now reached the same level of trust and respect for Gorbachev that Baker had reached three months earlier at his Wyoming meeting with Shevardnadze. A working partnership was in place that would carry Bush and Gorbachev through the stresses and challenges of 1990.

One week after Malta, Baker was ready to publish the strategic plan for the administration's new Atlanticism. Before the Berlin Press Club on December 12, he laid out the steps that Bush and he would take to endorse the US commitment and give a new collective purpose to Europe. He cited the European Community as a model for "drawing [countries] together while also serving as an open door to the East."[99] He gave support to the thirty-five member body, CSCE despite his cynicism for this unwieldy body and he advocated a new mission for NATO. It should now focus on confidence building measures. In short, NATO should become less of a military alliance and more political in nature. He went on to confirm US support for German unification and the European Community. He made no mention of trade competition, but rather the higher goal of political and economic unity. At a time when conflict with the Soviet Union was receding, Baker spoke of a future in which the US would "remain a European power… as long as our Allies desire our presence as part of a common security effort."[100] The so-called pause was over, and maybe the Cold War was over too. Baker had set out the priorities that the Bush administration would take over the next three years. Meanwhile, Baker had to focus on German unification.

TWO

THE GERMAN QUESTION

The Iron Curtain once cut through the entire continent of Europe, dividing it not only physically but ideologically: Communism and Soviet domination in the East, liberal democracy in the West. Germany alone had a 96-mile wall, constructed in 1961, that cut off East from West Berlin. Over the years 68 people had lost their lives trying to scale the twelve-foot barrier. Europeans had lived under these opposing ideologies for more than a generation, and the nuclear weapons intended to protect each side instilled in both the fear of mutual destruction. Americans had neither the threat nor the living memory of a war fought on their soil, but they fought the Cold War in the far-off lands of Korea and Vietnam, and proxy wars closer to home in Central America. In the name of deterrence, both great powers developed weapons of mass destruction and produced sophisticated strategic missiles. With the possible exception of the Cuban missile crisis of 1962, American presidents acted cautiously toward Moscow, and risk avoidance characterized the US response to Soviet military repression of East Germany in 1953, Budapest in 1956, Prague in 1968, and Afghanistan in 1979. Washington broadcast its views and ideals through the Voice of America, but it made little effort to dislodge the Soviets from their control of Eastern European nations.

In his second term, Ronald Reagan changed this cautionary posture to engage with Mikhail Gorbachev and promote freedom in Eastern

Europe. Having worked closely with Reagan as both chief of staff and Treasury Secretary, Baker believed that Gorbachev's reforms vindicated Reagan's policies. But Reagan faced opposition, and his successor George H.W. Bush even more so from conservative Republicans who criticized them for naïve behavior toward the Soviet leader. Some of these critics had read Russian history and concluded that periods of westernization were followed by retraction and withdrawal.[1] Baker never disregarded those conservatives, who included Secretary of Defense Dick Cheney and deputy NSC adviser Bob Gates. But as an optimist and man of action, he leaned toward the hope that Gorbachev could carry forth *perestroika, glasnost* and "new thinking" in Soviet foreign policy.

As Baker took office in January 1989, he was fully aware that Eastern Europe had entered a period of economic decline, social unrest and dwindling respect for communisms. Furthermore, uncertain succession plans for aged leaders presented opportunities for political change, if not distance from Moscow. Gorbachev had discarded the Brezhnev Doctrine, stating publicly that he would not use force to repress these nationalist movements, and Baker's advisors watched carefully to ensure that Gorbachev kept his word. But they knew that old-time Kremlin apparatchiks viewed liberalization as weakness and a threat to Soviet socialist power. To balance hard-liners against his reforming instincts, Gorbachev had made statements in Poland that "socialist achievements could never be reversed, nor could this or that country be ripped out of the socialist community."[2] Observers in the West could not be certain that Gorbachev would not repress freedom movements in the satellite republics, despite his apparent commitment to 'new thinking."

Washington was also aware that "Gorby-mania," the exuberant adulation for the reformist Soviet leader, partly grew out of a desire to see American boys go home. Gorbachev's reforms and personal charisma lulled many Europeans into thinking the Soviets had fundamentally changed. On this issue, West European leaders stood firmly against their citizens, explaining that the American military presence was the best deterrence against any Soviet effort to repress their democratic way of life and standard of living. But as the Soviet threat eased and the chronic weaknesses of the Soviet system became apparent, European citizens increasingly questioned the need for American deterrence. Why should they continue to live in fear of a nuclear exchange while the Soviet leader smiled as he toured European capitals and declared his commitment to reduce the number of Warsaw Pact troops in Eastern Europe? Prime Minister Margaret Thatcher was not alone in seeking to retain an American presence through NATO in Europe. French President François Mitterrand and West German Chancellor Helmut Kohl also sought to strengthen the indispensable link across the Atlantic. Together, they supported early efforts to gain freedom and democracy in Poland, Hungary, and the German Democratic Republic (GDR) known in the West as East Germany, while also seeking assurance that the American presence was firm. Even as they supported liberalization, they needed American commitments to NATO's collective security.

The cascade of liberalizing events had begun in 1980, when shipyard workers in the Polish city of Gdansk demanded higher wages and the right of the *Solidarność* trade union to participate in government decision making. Under orders from Moscow, President Wojciech Jaruzelski violently suppressed this uprising and arrested its leaders. Eight years later, a new wave of strikes and labor unrest spread across Poland, with workers insisting once again on recognition as a legitimate trade union. This time, Jaruzelski did not crack down. Instead, in April 1989, *Solidarność* won recognition and the right to participate in elections to a bicameral parliament. That same month, the Hungarian government ordered the electricity in the barbed-wire fence along the Hungary-Austria border turned off. In June, *Solidarność* – now a political party – won ninety-six out of one hundred seats in the new Senate. By autumn, demonstrators in the East German cities of Leipzig and Dresden were openly protesting against Erich Honecker's authoritarian but incompetent rule.

Throughout 1989, the US pursued a policy of restraint, hoping to ensure that freedom movements were led by homegrown national spirits, not US policy. Baker did not comment in April 1989, when Hungary began to remove the electric cable along its 150-mile border fence with Austria, enabling East German citizens to escape through Hungary to

Austria and thence to the West. He was on vacation in the Tetons on August 19, when nine hundred East Germans rushed the Hungarian border after a summer picnic organized by pan-European pro-democracy groups and escaped into Austria.[3] He remained silent when two hundred thousand protestors gathered in Leipzig in the autumn demanding free elections and the end of one-party rule.

However, he was forced to act in early October, when eighteen East Germans entered the US embassy in Berlin seeking asylum and refused to leave. Baker sought advice from James Dobbins, the former deputy chief of mission at the US embassy in Bonn. Dobbins advised Baker to turn out the asylum seekers from the embassy on condition that the East German authorities promise not to arrest them.[4] He reminded Baker that Cardinal József Mindszenty had sought refuge in the US embassy in Budapest in 1956 and remained there for fifteen years. Baker listened to Dobbins, then called Shevardnadze and worked out an arrangement by which the eighteen were permitted to travel to the West, provided the US embassy closed its doors to future asylum seekers. This arrangement solved the immediate dilemma but infuriated the human rights community in the United States, which sought active government support for asylum seekers from the GDR. One month later, the issue became moot. East Berliners would climb over the wall into the West setting the stage for eventual reunification.

At the National Security Council, Robert Hutchings made a tepid case for American support of changes in Europe: "Today the top priority for American foreign policy in Europe should be the fate of the Federal Republic of Germany.... Here we cannot promise immediate reunification, but we should offer some promise of change."[5] Not all NSC advisors shared this optimism. Philip Zelikow and Condoleezza Rice recalled that in the spring of 1989 they had no reason to think German unification was about to make its way onto the international agenda.[6] An April 1989 survey actually showed a decline in the number of Germans who believed that reunification should remain a goal of West German policy.[7] There was no such survey in the GDR, but the size of the protestant protest marches against the Honecker regime suggested that its citizens were becoming more audacious in their demand for freedom. All these events alerted the White House to the unpredictable nature of freedom movements. One agonizing question was whether the Soviets would try to hold onto their European republics. With 370,000 troops in the GDR, they retained the capacity to do so.

THE STEP-BY-STEP APPROACH

Together with Baker and Scowcroft, Bush recognized the importance of addressing the German question without forcing Gorbachev to bend so far that Kremlin apparatchiks would force him out. In the spring of 1989 the White House began cautiously supporting Polish moves for freedom, followed in July by a presidential visit to Warsaw and Gdansk. Bush and Baker's quandary was the appropriate time-frame for independence from the Soviet Union. Listening to *Solidarnośc* leaders in Poland, NSC official Hutchings projected a five to ten year transition for the East Europeans to reach full independence and democratic governance. He was more awake than others in the Bush administration to the fervor for freedom in Eastern Europe, but less confident about what it meant.[8] At odds with most in Washington was retired general Vernon Walters, the US ambassador to West Germany, who predicted the unification of the two Germanys without setting a timeline. Walter's rambling anecdotes led listeners to understand that unification was coming soon, but his inability to be brief irritated Baker, who excluded the polyglot Walters, with his seven languages, from the decision making process. He had no time for long stories, even if the conclusion was correct.

Baker remained concerned that the flowering of democracy might provoke Soviet retaliation. He remained skeptical of the advice from foreign policy experts who told him that by permitting the Poles to hold free elections and choose their prime minister, Gorbachev was sending a message to *all* Eastern Europeans that he would not suppress their national movements. Conservatives within the Republican Party continually reminded him that he and the President were being too accommodating to Gorbachev.[9] Ever the politician, Baker was careful not to alienate an important wing of the Republican Party.

While Washington deliberated, East Germans were fleeing to Hungary and Czechoslovakia. The expectation of change was vibrant and President Bush sought to catch this spirit as he flew to Mainz, West Germany, for NATO's 40th Anniversary. In his speech there, he described the United States and Germany as "partners in leadership" and suggested that Central and Eastern Europe, where the Cold War had begun, should be where it might end: "As President, I will continue to do all I can to help open the closed societies of the East. We seek self-determination for all of Germany and all of Eastern Europe. And we will not relax, and we must not waiver."[10] The speech did not directly endorse a reunified Germany, but Bush's emphasis on the value of self-determination left little doubt that should the citizens of the two Germanys decide to unite, America would stand behind them.

NO DANCING ON THE RUBBLE

The breach of the wall at Bornholmer Straße in Berlin happened on the night of Thursday, November 9, 1989, and an estimated three million East Germans crossed on foot and by car through the several openings in the wall over the next three days. Their numbers startled Baker and Bush. By 3 a.m. on November 10, East German border guards using water cannons cleared an area between the wall and the Brandenburg Gate. They also tried to drive people off the wall with water hoses, but failed to prevent thousands from clambering up and over.[11] Many crossed out of curiosity, to taste the bananas and sex shops of West Berlin before returning home.[12] Others sought out relatives and a safe place to remain. By dawn, guards had successfully restored border controls at Berlin's Invalidenstraße. A motorized East German division trained in urban warfare with air support went on alert, but orders to deploy never came, and the units never left their barracks.[13] Gorbachev chose not to give the command, and no one in the disorganized GDR government was willing to risk ordering the slaughter of their own civilians.

Baker was hosting a luncheon for Philippine President Corazon Aquino in the Benjamin Franklin room on the State Department's eighth floor when Stapleton Roy, the State Department's executive secretary, passed him a note: "The wall dividing East and West Germany has been breached and the East Germans have announced that border points are being opened." It took a moment for the news to sink in.[14] After being divided by ideology, concrete and barbed wire from their countrymen for 28 years, East Germans were now asserting their freedom to travel. After bidding farewell to President Aquino, Baker rushed over to the White House to join Bush in watching live television coverage of citizens dancing on top of the wall. It vindicated Ronald Reagan's engagement with Mikhail Gorbachev, but it also made the question of reunification, which had been turning ever less abstract for months, suddenly very real. As he watched the dramatic events on television, Baker called Ambassador Walters in Bonn and US Principal Officer Harry Gilmore in Berlin to ensure that American forces did not undertake their usual motorized patrol along the wall in the American section, but kept their distance from events in and around Berlin. He also took a call from Chancellor Kohl, who requested a US aircraft to fly him from Poland to Berlin. Kohl wanted to be there and not leave the victory solely to his political opponent, the Social Democrat mayor of West Berlin, Walter Momper.[15]

A few days after the wall fell, Soviet Foreign Minister Shevardnadze warned against "the attempt of some circles in [West Germany] to place the question of reunification … on the agenda."[16] Gorbachev went further, declaring that unification was not "an issue of current policy."[17] Both men advised French Foreign Minister Roland Dumas that talk of unification was causing "great anxiety." They also sent messages to Western capitals calling for consultations among the Four Powers—the USSR, US, Britain and France—that had ruled Berlin since World War II. Moscow's official line was that German reunification was "not on the agenda."[18]

Mitterrand did not support unification, and at the gathering of the EEC heads of state in Paris nine days later to discuss the ramifications from the fall of the wall, reunification was not mentioned. Instead, the twelve leaders emphasized European unity, stability, and their willingness to provide economic and financial help to Poland and Hungary. In response to a question, the press spokesman said that unification was a matter for the "distant and indefinite future."[19] Thatcher stated both publicly and in a private letter to Bush that "there must be no question of changing borders ... Any attempt to talk about either border changes or German reunification would undermine Mr. Gorbachev."[20]

Bush and Baker understood the dilemma facing Gorbachev and Shevardnadze. Should Washington support unification too enthusiastically, Gorbachev might be ousted by the apparatchiks. The exodus of thousands of East Germans to the West, and the problem of absorbing and housing hundreds of thousands of Soviet soldiers returning from Eastern Europe, justified keeping these troops in the GDR for another three to four years. Baker understood that the cascade of liberating events in Eastern Europe throughout 1989 had put the Soviet leadership in a difficult and tenuous position. Gorbachev's warning, "A chaotic situation may emerge with unforeseeable consequences," now sounded less like a threat than a warning: the stability of the region, and of the Soviet Union itself, were at risk. Baker would therefore follow the President's decision to respond in a deliberate and low-key manner.[21] They would not dance rhetorically on the rubble.[22] When Ambassador Walters heaved himself up onto part of the destroyed wall, he drew a reprimand from Baker.[23]

On Friday, November 10, Margaret Tutwiler brought Baker reams of press reports from around the world. On top, he wrote in his customary thick black felt pen: "Something we've wanted for 40 years. Eur that's whole + free."[24] On ABC Primetime Live, Baker reminded the audience: "It has been the policy of the NATO Alliance and the policy of the United States of America to support reunification for over forty years." When interviewer Chris Wallace suggested that this sounded boilerplate, Baker responded, "That is our policy."[25] There should be no gloating over a western victory.[26]

In Moscow, Gorbachev called Horst Teltschik, Chancellor Kohl's senior foreign policy advisor, and other Western leaders to say that the events of that night "could create a chaotic situation with unpredictable consequences."[27] He personally conveyed the same warning to Bush, Kohl, Mitterrand, and Thatcher. On Saturday, November 11, Bush, Baker and the national security team pondered whether Soviet troops in the GDR would stay in their barracks. Would the hardline apparatchiks in the Kremlin remove Gorbachev from power? Would citizens in other Warsaw Pact countries demonstrate their desire for freedom? Would there be a rush of migrants toward Western Europe, and would social welfare systems be able to absorb these new refugees? In short, how should NATO respond to these events? The fall of the Berlin wall was a turning point, but few understood the consequences.

The next day, Baker had lunch with Soviet Ambassador Yuri Dubinin, who emphasized Gorbachev's concerns. Baker's notes from that meeting recall his reply: "We said we understand [the] imp[ortance] of keeping order."[28] Caution remained the leitmotif. In the tumult of events, a steady hand was needed. It was also essential to maintain close consultation with allies, as well as with the Soviet leadership. Bush agreed to meet with Gorbachev, but both sought a low-key meeting where they could talk freely without the pressure of a publicized agenda. That meeting in Malta's harbor happened three weeks later.

THE UNIFICATION QUESTION

The question of German unification had been rising quietly all year. In March 1989, the National Security Council predicted that the "Roundtable Agreement" in Poland foretold radical change in the GDR.[29] Polish President General Jaruzelski's agreement to sit with leaders of *Solidarność to* discuss open elections indicated a crack in the façade of authoritarian rule. With no disapproval from Moscow, Jaruzelski was on his own to seek accommodation with Lech Wałęsa and his coalition of independent trade unions. Wałęsa was hesitant to share power with Jaruzelski, but the leaders of *Solidarność* were eager to negotiate a share of political power and help stop the collapse of the Polish economy.

Hutchings, focused on Eastern Europe at the NSC, suggested that if elections were held as scheduled in June 1989, they would bring an end to communist rule in Poland. And if it ended in Poland, Hutchings concluded, it was finished everywhere in Eastern Europe, including the GDR.[30] However, he did not think trends toward greater liberalization in Eastern Europe meant German unification. It was more likely that an independent, socialist East Germany would emerge.

Soviet and European leaders remembered well that the last time Germany was unified, it had launched two world wars that caused the death of more than fifty-six million people. Baker had none of the anti-German phobia prevalent in Europe. Americans had more-vivid memories of Soviet tanks rolling into Berlin, Budapest, and Prague to suppress democracy and freedom. Would the Soviets again use force to suppress popular outpouring for freedom in Poland, and to retain control over East Germany, the industrial crown jewel of the Soviet Socialist Republics? Prime Minister Thatcher was the firmest in rejecting reunification. Earlier in the year when Baker visited London, he found the prime minister disdainful if not hostile to his proposals on both German unification and strategic nuclear forces (SNF). Thatcher accused Baker of placing America's relationship with Germany over the "special relationship" with Great Britain. In her determination to maintain that longstanding relationship, Thatcher would go to great lengths to assert its indispensable nature, even as she confronted Washington directly over the Lance II missile. Baker knew that Thatcher had grown increasingly unpopular within her own Conservative party, and opinion polls suggested that the British public thought she was out of touch. Nevertheless, the Iron Lady had been a staunch ally of Ronald Reagan, and Baker was not about to ignore her despite her theatrical, if not autocratic manner. Baker tempered her and her hardening European skepticism, aware that her own back-benchers might force her resignation.[31]

Bush and Baker thus had to navigate between Helmut Kohl, the new standard bearer of Germany's longstanding promise of unification; a hostile Margaret Thatcher; and François Mitterrand, who had no great enthusiasm for unification and was more focused on greater European integration. Thatcher had lived through the German Blitz as a teenager in London in 1940 and '41. Mitterrand had supported the Vichy government in his mid-twenties before joining the French resistance against Nazi Germany in 1943. Neither he nor Thatcher welcomed a unified Germany that might once again dominate Europe. The way ahead was not clear, and the German question remained a persistent and divisive issue between Washington, London, and Paris. It would require careful strategic planning and tactical preparation to achieve Kohl's dream of a united Germany without alienating its historical foes.

Perhaps the greatest of those historical foes was the Soviet Union, which had lost more than 20 million soldiers in the Second World War. Five months before the fall of the Berlin Wall, Kohl and Gorbachev held three meetings in Bonn to discuss the unfolding situation in Eastern Europe. Both agreed on the right of peoples to self-determination,[32] but left unsaid was whether this principle should apply to the GDR. Instead, they commiserated about Honecker's behavior, his personal ambition, and his avoidance of economic and political reforms. The two men agreed to telephone each other on key issues rather than rely on their respective bureaucracies.[33] Their ideas about when reunification might take place differed widely. Back in 1983, Gorbachev had estimated that it might happen in fifty years[34]—long enough after he had left the scene that he had no need to worry about it. In 1987, journalist Timothy Garton Ash, covering both East and West Germany for the Financial Times, remembered that the eventual end of divided Germany was privately discussed "at a high and even at the highest level in Moscow."[35] But he had no evidence that these talks became operative policy. Instead, when he asked them, Soviet leaders would deny any thoughts of German unification. Later, in the face of Polish elections, the opening of the Hungarian border with Austria, and hundreds of thousands of East Germans protesting in Dresden and Leipzig, these leaders hardened their stance: unification would not happen.

As citizens destroyed the concrete wall with their own hands, it was necessary for Washington to become more active diplomatically, both with Gorbachev and with European leaders. Bush and Baker met with

West Germany's Minister of Foreign Affairs, Hans-Dietrich Genscher, in Washington on November 21; with Thatcher at Camp David on November 24; with Gorbachev at Malta on December 3 and 4; with NATO allies at a second Brussels summit immediately thereafter; and with Mitterrand on the Caribbean island of Saint Martin on December 16. In the face of European alarm at the speed of events in Germany, and the danger that the Europeans could delay or stop unification, Bush and Baker decided to make it a priority. They would encourage Kohl while trying to avoid a chaotic breakdown of order that could give the Soviets reason to deploy their still considerable forces in Eastern Europe. They needed a process of controlled self-determination.

A TEN-POINT PLAN AND A FOUR-POINT RESPONSE

West Germany was growing uneasy over the huge influx of refugees. The East German economy was in sufficient turmoil to threaten its very existence,[36] and it was up to Chancellor Kohl to restore some kind of political stability. But after Kohl and the Christian Democrats could not agree with their coalition partners, Hans-Dietrich Genscher and his liberal Free Democratic Party (FDP), on how to respond, Kohl announced to the West German Bundestag on November 28 a Ten Point Plan. This plan, drafted by National Security Advisor Horst Teltschik, instructed the Four Allied Powers that the West German government would play a lead role, and called for humanitarian and economic assistance to the GDR and the development of "confederative structures" between the two Germanys after free elections in the East.[37] The eventual goal was the "regaining of German state unity" within the context of European integration.[38] With this plan, Kohl set the terms and pace of German unification and preempted objections from the Four Powers.

The text of Kohl's speech reached the White House only a couple of hours before he presented it, and the President, Baker, and Scowcroft had to wait for it to be translated. In Moscow, Paris, and London, none of which received an advance copy, Kohl's plan came as a surprise. It was also a surprise to Genscher.[39] Kohl had asserted primacy on the German question and would defer neither to the Four Powers nor to his coalition partner. While he was irritated at the lack of advance consultation, Baker admired Kohl's move and admitted that in similar circumstances he might have done the same thing.[40]

Now he responded quickly. In order to reassure Kohl of Washington's support and at the same time offer some reassurance to Moscow, Baker offered "four principles" on German unification that he thought Bush should deliver to Gorbachev at the December summit meeting in Malta, and to NATO leaders at the subsequent gathering of foreign ministers in Brussels.

1. Self-determination should be pursued without prejudice to its outcome;
2. If there is to be unification, it should occur within the context of Germany's continuing alignment within NATO and the European Community;
3. The process should be peaceful, gradual and step-by-step; and
4. Following the principles of the Helsinki Final Act, the inviolability of existing borders should be respected (meaning the existing Polish-German border).[41]

Perhaps in retaliation for Horst Teltschik's failure to provide Washington with an English-language advance copy of Kohl's Ten Points, Baker did not inform Bonn before publishing his own 'four principles." His presumption irritated Kohl's advisor, who recognized that Washington had superimposed its own agenda on Kohl's.[42] But Baker also had a message for NATO allies. The US administration proposed that the two sets of principles could work together: unification could take place within a broader geo-political context; and self-determination could be pursued through a controlled, gradual process. There would be no gallop to the finish line.

While the December summit in Malta established good personal relations between Bush and Gorbachev, it did not resolve their differences over German unification. Shortly after his return to Moscow, Gorbachev announced to the Central Committee of the Soviet Communist Party (CPSU) that he would maintain the status quo in the GDR.[43] His statement was intended to calm the Central Committee members, who were alarmed that the Warsaw Pact might be collapsing. In the weeks following the Malta summit, Gorbachev also cracked down on nationalist protests in Baku, Azerbaijan. Was he trying to pre-empt the Kremlin apparatchiks who were sure to push back against cascading liberalization in the Soviet Republics, Eastern Europe and elsewhere? To dampen speculation about potential Soviet repression, Baker held a press briefing in which he revealed the content of a classified cable from the US Political Office in East Berlin which stated that despite the "disorder born of change…demonstrations continue peacefully amidst rumors of potential violence."[44] His purpose was to calm international financial markets.

FROM CAUTIOUS TO ACTIVE SUPPORT

After their deliberately low-key response to the fall of the Berlin wall, Bush and Baker gave unequivocal support to Kohl's determination to unify the two Germanys.[45] Ambassador Walters had predicted that unification would come early. Henry Kissinger thought it was inevitable. Scowcroft hesitantly agreed: it might be inevitable, but it would not come quickly.[46] Washington's support for Kohl was genuine and based on careful consideration of US interests. Robert Hutchings recalled that "the US could not be seen as opposing German unification, or even showing hesitancy. If it were coming, as we believed likely, it would come whether we willed it or not."[47] Members of the State Department's European bureau, mindful of Soviet hostility to German reunification and the growing criticism of Gorbachev's leadership by conservatives on the CPSU, urged caution. Still, these differences within the Washington bureaucracy were mild compared to differences within Europe and the Soviet Union. Bush recognized that only by actively supporting German reunification could the US ensure that it took place without destabilizing Europe's economic integration.[48] But the British and French governments remained to be convinced that a unified Germany would not re-emerge as a threatening power in the heart of Europe.

Following the Malta summit, Bush and Baker had agreed to Shevardnadze's request for a meeting of the Four Allied Powers, so long as it was at the ambassadorial level and not at the foreign minister level. On December 10, for the first time in decades, Ambassador Walters and his colleagues from the Soviet Union, Britain and France met in Berlin at the Kommandatura building from which the Four Powers had once governed Berlin. Baker instructed Walters to keep the meeting low key, but the four ambassadors let themselves be photographed standing in front of the building, which represented the Four Power victory in World War II. This greatly upset the Germans – who had not received an invitation – as well as Baker, who arrived in Berlin the same day.[49]

After dinner on December 11 with Chancellor Kohl, Baker called his advisers to let them know that he was considering a visit to East Germany the next day. Only the US Ambassador to the GDR, Richard Barkley, welcomed his proposal. Baker listened to the warnings from Walters and his other advisers but concluded that he would go ahead. It would be a first by an American Secretary of State: none had ventured outside Berlin to visit the GDR. He notified Moscow, anticipating Gorbachev's support, but received no reply.

The following day, the American motorcade drove across the Glienicke Bridge, also known as the Bridge of Spies, where US pilot Gary Powers was swapped for Soviet Colonel Rudolf Abel in 1962, and Natan Sharansky was swapped for Karl Koecher in 1986. On the eastern side of the river, Baker entered Potsdam, the site of the 1945 conference that set conditions for the division of Europe. By crossing this bridge, he made a publicity splash. More than his advisors, he understood the scope and speed of the changes underway. Later, he would be the first Secretary of State to visit Albania and would receive a rock star's welcome.

In Potsdam, he met for an hour with the new premier, the communist Hans Modrow, and emphasized Washington's commitment to "self-determination." He welcomed Modrow's decision to hold multi-party elections the following May (the elections were later moved up to March). Modrow shared his concern that East Germans, once free from Soviet overlords, might take revenge on fellow citizens who had worked with the Soviets, and he requested that care be taken to prevent that sort of retaliation. Baker outlined the economic help the US was preparing for Poland and Hungary, and offered it to the GDR. Afterwards, at a press conference with Modrow, Baker emphasized "the importance of moving forward peaceably in a stable way."[50] Modrow stood rigidly beside his American visitor and said nothing.

Baker then drove to a nineteenth-century church where he met with Lutheran ministers, whose Monday marches had galvanized the process of liberalization. They assured Baker that they would continue to press peacefully for reforms and try to avoid political upheaval. This was the first of several times that Baker broke with tradition and risked visiting places and people unaccustomed to meeting senior US government officials. In so doing, he sought to emphasize America's decision to support those changes in a peaceful and controlled manner.

EUROPEAN RESISTANCE TO UNIFICATION

From the night of November 9 through the formal declaration of a reunified Germany the following October, Baker devoted much time and effort to the German question, which had become the most critical issue in the Soviet relationship. The President consulted Gorbachev with the goal of maintaining the stability of the Warsaw Pact while emphasizing the importance of no-military intervention. Both he and Baker understood the need to strengthen Gorbachev's role in international affairs to counter the growing criticism he faced back home. Later, Baker would discreetly assure Gorbachev that a strong Germany would be a financially generous neighbor. West Germany ultimately contributed between 50 billion and 80 billion deutschmarks (US $78.5-125.6 billion) to support the Soviet economy and pay for the repositioning of Soviet troops formerly stationed in the GDR.[51] (The range of financial aid is perplexing until one understands that much of the financial support came in government credit guarantees to West German banks, as well as donations of coal and potatoes that did not show up as financial aid.) Washington was ready to provide the political leadership while Chancellor Kohl provided the financial means to make German unification within NATO acceptable to the Soviet leader.

Beyond Gorbachev and Shevardnadze, opponents to unification were many and vocal. British Prime Minister Margaret Thatcher, French President François Mitterrand, as well as the Italian and Polish leaders, each for different reasons, sought to prevent, or at best delay unification. All remembered the consequences of a powerful and expansive Germany in the center of Europe. It would take months of intense diplomacy to convince all parties that a unified Germany within NATO was the best way to ensure a responsible and constructive Germany anchored in western institutions. Looking back that outcome seems logical, but in the second year of the Bush administration, that prospect seemed a long way off at best, and was probably unachievable. It would require consistent work with America's allies.

Bush had arranged for French President Francois Mitterrand to give the 1990 commencement address at Boston College, and he combined the speech with an invitation to his vacation home in Kennebunkport, Maine. Barbara Bush, knowing that the weather was still cold in late May, was anxious that the stern and formal French president might feel awkward in the coastal simplicity of the Bush compound. She went to great lengths to refurbish a bedroom, bringing in a new king size bed and plentiful blankets. To her relief, Mitterrand was delighted: this was true hospitality and he relished the time spent with the President, although he avoided riding in Bush's speedboat. Instead, he preferred long discussions with his American counterpart, as well as Baker and Scowcroft. When the subject of German unification arose, he said to his American hosts, "As long as the Soviet Union is strong, it will never happen… Since 1917, the Soviets have had a major hang-up about encirclement. Since their Civil War, they have had a siege mentality. Now they have Eastern European problems, Baltic problems, etcetera.

They won't take a chance on reunification."[52] Asked at a press conference where he stood on reunification, Mitterrand replied, "If the German people wished it, I would not oppose it, but not enough has changed since World War II to permit it … the Soviets will never yield on the German problem.[53]

Mitterrand's priority was to strengthen the twelve-member European Economic Community through closer economic and political integration. At that time, the EEC was largely a trading partnership, but Mitterrand was determined to negotiate a treaty that would grant every citizen of the member states the right to vote and run for office in a European Parliament. He hoped the treaty would also create a single European currency, a European Central Bank, and common policies on social welfare, the environment, foreign affairs, and security.[54] In a more united Europe, Germany would never again battle its European neighbors. To make this vision a reality, Mitterrand needed to consolidate the European project and preserve Western values in the face of a Soviet Union whose leader, Mikhail Gorbachev, called for reform but whose control over the Kremlin apparatchiks might be tenuous. The West could not ignore a potential crackdown by Soviet troops to repress liberalization in Eastern Europe. Honecker could have sent in troops to repress the large demonstrations against his regime, and then justified his actions by telling Moscow, "This was necessary to preserve stability."[55]

Bush and Baker were committed to supporting Mitterrand's vision, even though they saw the prospect of a single European market as "a major challenge." Would the European Union be inward looking and impose tariffs on US goods and services, or would it continue to look outward? Baker recognized that it would take a well-coordinated, consistent, active effort to ensure that Europe retained its Atlantic outlook.[56] For the people of Eastern Europe, a single European market would offer both a political and economic opportunity: an organization that could help them leap forward commercially and technologically. It would be an impetus for Eastern Europe to develop closer ties with prosperous Western Europe.[57]

TWO PLUS FOUR

Baker sought a framework that would let East and West Germany plan their own future. James Dobbins had written a note to Dennis Ross on January 1, 1990, proposing a dual track by which the two Germanys took the lead on domestic issues while the Four Powers oversaw the external aspects of unification. Dobbins recommended that Washington steer well clear of a 'super power condominium.' "We should avoid setting a US blue print for change in Europe, keep the emphasis on German self-determination, stay away from Four Power intervention and begin to work with Bonn, Paris and London on guidelines for channeling movement toward German unification."[58]

Baker read the memo, but it was his two closest aides, Ross and Zoellick, who pursued the idea and prepared a draft framework, details of which were still in flux when British Foreign Secretary Douglas Hurd arrived in Washington on January 28, 1990. Hurd had two items on his agenda: conventional forces in Europe and German unification. Despite Thatcher's preference to prioritize SNF and deployment of the Lance II missile, the two foreign secretaries easily reached consensus on conventional forces. But they left the German issue unresolved. To the Americans, the British seemed unwilling to commit to an approach that gave the lead to the two Germanys. That night, following his one-on-one meeting with Baker, Hurd wrote in his diary: "To Baker. Brisk, intelligent. 15 minutes alone and we agree on the need for a framework for NATO and German unity."[59] This implied agreement on the Two plus Four framework, but the official record contains no reference to this. We may assume that Baker shared the plan in the private meeting and that Hurd did not oppose it.

That evening, Hurd's advisors Sir Peter Wright and Andrew Wood met with Zoellick and NSC advisor Robert Blackwill at a small dinner hosted by Sir Anthony Acland at the British embassy. Zoellick told his British counterparts that he had had a formula in mind for some time, but it was not the current position of the Administration to involve the two Germanys in the Four Power talks.[60] The British guests displayed interest but made no commitment.[61]

Under Zoellick's formula, the two German leaders would determine the internal elements of the new state, namely the new Germany's legal, political and economic structure. This might occur after the East German elections, now brought forward to March 1990. Both German leaders would then join the Four Power leaders to discuss the external aspects of unification. Zoellick argued to his bosses in the White House and at State that the big advantage to this framework was US inclusion throughout the process. The State Department and the NSC both agreed on the framework and the need for close coordination with Kohl and Genscher.

Upon returning to London, Hurd and the Foreign Office recognized that the Americans had a workable formula, but it lacked important details that they could contribute. Hurd and his advisors decided to support Washington's plan with further ideas on how the GDR might relate to the European Economic Community (EEC), as well as ways to resolve the problems of the Polish/German border.[62] Thatcher was not consulted, except to tell her that the Americans were developing a framework which would take into account the Four Powers' responsibilities.

In late January 1990, and after his surprise meeting with Baker, GDR Premier Modrow flew to Moscow to seek Gorbachev's help. The economy was spiraling downward, with industrial production slowing and shortages appearing in the state-run shops. Modrow warned the Soviet leader that unless the GDR and the Soviet Union took the initiative now, "the process that has begun will continue to unfold in an uncontrolled manner at a breakneck pace."[63] To slow it down, the Soviet Union should reaffirm its legal rights under the Four Powers accord: Modrow recommended summoning a conference of the Four Powers to stabilize the current situation. Shevardnadze agreed and told Modrow that he had requested such a meeting three times in recent weeks, but Baker had demurred each time. The American did not wish to undermine German leadership by letting the Soviets, French, British and Americans determine the next steps.

GENSCHER'S SPEECH AT TUTZING

Hans-Dietrich Genscher first raised German unity and security when he spoke at the Evangelische Akademie Tutzing on January 31.[64] He had written this speech alone and did not clear it with Kohl. Caught off guard by Kohl's ten-point speech, Genscher now sought to distinguish his position from Kohl's and put his own stamp on German foreign affairs. Since the beginning of his career as foreign minister, Genscher had sought to resolve the German problem in an all-European context in a way that would avoid offending Soviet sensibilities.[65] In his speech, presenting what became known as the Tutzing formula, Genscher proposed that the GDR and the FRG (West Germany) alone negotiate "a treaty charting the course toward German unity in Europe."[66] Negotiations could start after the East German elections and move the countries in a gradual, stepwise path toward a new confederation, starting with an economic and monetary union. This plan was in lock step with the measures proposed by Modrow. Modrow and Genscher differed significantly, however, on German membership in the EEC and NATO. Modrow rejected both. Genscher's formulation suggested harnessing a uniting Germany to a benign all-European security framework that would emerge out of the structures of both NATO and the Warsaw Pact. He made no mention of US nuclear weapons or Western troops in Germany.

To address East German concerns about neutrality, Genscher proposed that there be "no expansion of NATO territory eastward." NATO's military structure should not extend to the GDR, nor should foreign troops or nuclear weapons be stationed there. Genscher barely mentioned a role for the Four Allied Powers. Instead, the decisions of the two Germanys would be ratified by the Conference on Security and Cooperation in Europe (CSCE), a gathering of thirty-five countries including Europe's neutral nations. This group, Genscher suggested, could help design a new cooperative security structure to cover all of Europe. Summit meetings of the CSCE would become the key European diplomatic forum for considering the "future structure of Europe."

Genscher's Tutzing formula would also ensure that German unification was locked into a broader European framework.

Baker was alarmed. The CSCE was an unwieldy organization, and relying on it could stall unification as envisaged by Kohl and Teltschik, as well as Bush. Baker also knew that Genscher's speech represented his personal views and did not have Kohl's approval. It was therefore unlikely to fly. In the two days between the Tutzing speech and Genscher's arrival in Washington, Zoellick talked at length with Genscher's key advisor, Frank Elbe. Zoellick previewed the Two plus Four framework with him and also agreed to study Genscher's proposed military restrictions for NATO in the GDR. Elbe, in turn, agreed to the Two plus Four mechanism, including its commitment to German unification. Meanwhile, other policy options were brewing in Washington.

Robert Blackwill at the White House urged a "rush toward *de facto* unification along lines worked out between the United States and the Federal Republic"[67] that would present Moscow with a *fait accompli*. Condoleezza Rice agreed on the pace but "preferred to try to achieve rapid reunification through a six-power negotiation that would include the two German states."[68] She calculated that in the face of such momentum, the Soviets would eventually capitulate. The third option, from Assistant Secretary for European Affairs Ray Seitz, claimed that the Two plus Four draft would slow the unification process, alienate the Germans, and give the Soviets too great a voice in negotiations.

After listening to all three options, Baker vigorously promoted Zoellick's Two plus Four framework when he met with Genscher in his seventh-floor office on a frigid February 2. Baker asked that the fireplace be lit, not so much to warm the large room as to create intimacy. By now, he had taken the lead in developing the strategy for unification, but it required German endorsement of Two plus Four. He thus spent two hours with his West German colleague.

Baker warmed to Genscher, recognizing in him another skilled politician from a party that played a critical role in German politics, but who needed to be moved away from neutrality. Genscher, born in the

GDR, was more interested in peace and reconciliation than US nuclear deterrence. But neutrality was not acceptable to Washington, and after listening carefully, Baker was both firm in his insistence on NATO membership and careful to respect German sensibilities. He understood that Genscher, in his Tutzing speech, had presented a formula intended to make unification acceptable to the Soviets. Based upon the principle of self-determination, it would limit NATO's jurisdiction and military structure to West Germany. Baker appreciated the goal of the Tutzing formula and did nothing to dissuade Genscher from discussing it further in Washington. But on the two other key matters, he was emphatic: Genscher's pan-European security system to replace both NATO and the Warsaw Pact was a non-starter, and he opposed Genscher's idea that the CSCE oversee unification.

At the joint press conference following the meeting, Baker agreed to go along with the Tutzing formula "for the time being."[69] Genscher told the press that he and Baker "were in full agreement that there is no intention to extend the NATO area of defense and security toward the East." When asked by a journalist what he meant, Genscher insisted that he was "not talking about a halfway membership [for a united Germany] this way or that. What I said is there is no intention of extending the NATO area to the East."[70] The vagueness of these sentences left journalists and others bewildered.

Genscher now appeared to suggest that membership in NATO's political councils should apply to all of Germany, but NATO troops would not be stationed within the former East German territory. Baker was relieved that Genscher had accepted the principle of a unified Germany within NATO and spoken against German neutralization, but he did not contradict or seek to clarify Genscher's remark and so seemed to consent to this formula. The question of how to implement Genscher's two-part formula was not raised, and NATO expansion beyond Germany was not yet a political concern.[71]

NSC staffers were not happy with Genscher's proposal. They had neither endorsed the Tutzing formula nor developed a policy regarding NATO's extension beyond the GDR. Given Baker's closeness to the

President, no member of the NSC questioned the public position that he had taken, but his apparent acceptance of Genscher's formula caused anxiety within the confines of the NSC. On the brighter side, Bob Blackwill, the NSC Director for Europe and Soviet Affairs, and Philip Zelikow, his deputy, recognized that Genscher's statement had taken into account Soviet sensibilities, and soothing Gorbachev might make him more willing to accept a unified Germany in NATO. The challenge lay in implementing such a plan. Would the Eastern part of Germany be included within NATO's collective security guarantee? Would NATO have authority over the GDR's National People's Army? Was the French model of political but not military membership of NATO replicable to the GDR? Baker appeared not to have thought through these critical questions.

Baker was willing to use a version of the Tutzing formula when he travelled to Moscow a few days later. He was not overly concerned about Genscher's formula, knowing where Chancellor Kohl stood on reunification and full incorporation into NATO. To smooth over any differences between the US and German positions, Baker constantly repeated that the issue would have to be settled in the Two plus Four framework. He told Tom Friedman of the *New York Times*: "We were in full agreement that there is no interest to extend the NATO area of defense and security toward the East." He also "agreed that a unified Germany would have to continue to be aligned with NATO, but that no NATO troops would be extended into what is now East Germany."[72] In Baker's mind, the GDR was as far as NATO extension should reach, but he was sufficiently vague to allow others to interpret his words differently. He also needed the support of the French and he was in a hurry.

On February 6, during a one-hour refueling stop in Shannon at 5:20 a.m., Baker met with French Foreign Minister Roland Dumas, who was in Ireland for an EEC meeting. Dumas claimed interest in the Two plus Four framework and promised to consult with President Mitterrand, but he made no firm commitment, nor did he wish to see the Americans leading this process. Soon afterwards, Dumas suggested that Mitterrand ask Kohl to propose Two plus Four, rather than Paris or Washington, to avoid the impression that it was being foisted on the Germans. Flying out of Shannon that dark morning, Baker went on to Prague to meet with the new, pro-Western Czech president, Vaclav Havel, and his foreign minister. Both supported Genscher's policy of a unified Germany within the EEC but were less interested in a united Germany within NATO. Instead, they hoped that both Cold War alliances – NATO and the Warsaw Pact – would transform into something new and not overtly military. Recognizing that Bush and Baker were the leaders of the western alliance, Havel used the meeting to press his priority: he urged Baker to press Gorbachev on the withdrawal of Soviet troops from Czechoslovakia.

BAKER'S MEETINGS IN MOSCOW

When he met with Shevardnadze at 8 p.m. on February 7, Baker found his friend energetic and relaxed despite having just left a meeting of the CPSU at which Gorbachev had come under fierce criticism for recommending a multiparty system and ending the Party's monopoly of political power. Baker assumed that Shevardnadze would have little ability to make concessions, but he wanted to explain what the US government was seeking with regard to Germany, and to argue that it was also in the Soviet Union's interest. Shevardnadze took a harder line on German unification than his boss due to the sufferings of Georgian citizens during German occupation in the "Great Patriotic War" (as the Soviets called World War II). Furthermore, his brother had been killed by German troops in 1941, leaving him with a deep hostility toward Germans.

On February 8, Shevardnadze and Baker discussed the full range of Soviet-US issues, from Afghanistan and Cuba to the Conventional Forces in Europe (CFE) Treaty and the Strategic Arms Reduction Treaty (START). Baker also inquired about rumors that pogroms against the Jewish population were about to begin. Shevardnadze dismissed this concern. Ethnic problems existed, he admitted, but the Jews were not being singled out. The anti-Semitic ultranationalist organization said to be mounting the pogroms was a fringe group with little ability to threaten the Jews.[73] He then told Baker about a new problem.. Questions were raised as to "why did you and Gorbachev lose Eastern Europe? Why did you surrender Germany?"[74] Shevardnadze's bleak assessment of Gorbachev's problems shook Baker. To his close advisors, Baker reported "The odds have got to be against his survival... The freedom genie is out of the bottle. They're not on track to cure their economic problems or their ethnic problems, so it'll come from below... We should help Gorbachev *when it is in our mutual advantage* [emphasis original]... We don't risk anything by hitching our star to Gorbachev. As long as he's there, he's the one we should be focused on."[75]

Later that day, Baker told Shevardnadze that NATO would transform itself into a more political organization and that the Soviet Union would be more secure if a united Germany was firmly anchored in NATO, which would provide a crucial check on its power.[76] In a session with only Dennis Ross and Sergei Tarasenko as note takers plus their interpreters, Baker opened with a careful presentation. First, he addressed the need for the Two plus Four formula by which the two Germanys should determine their own internal arrangements. The Four Treaty Powers would manage the external aspects of unification to ensure stability. They could announce this formula after the GDR elections on March 18.[77] Second, Baker rejected Premier Modrow's proposal for a neutral Germany. He argued that this would be more dangerous for Moscow than a unified Germany within NATO. A neutral Germany might seek nuclear weapons to ensure its own security, whereas a Germany firmly anchored in a more political NATO would have no need for them.

To calm Shevardnadze's fears, Baker referred to Genscher's Tutzing formula. Turning Genscher's "no extension of NATO" language into a more lawyerly formulation, he promised that if a united Germany was included in NATO, there would be ironclad guarantees "that NATO's *jurisdiction* or *forces* [emphasis added] would not move eastward."[78] US troops, however, would remain in Europe as long as America's allies wanted them there. Baker repeated his pledge that NATO would evolve into a more political and less military-oriented alliance. Despite the intimate nature of the meeting, Shevardnadze expressed strong reservations about the danger of a united, militarized Germany. A weakened Warsaw Pact would leave no counterweight to NATO. Therefore, German neutrality was the only acceptable solution.

Shevardnadze knew personally the dangers of war with Germany and he urged upon Baker, once more, the need for a meeting of the Four Powers to discuss a peace treaty to end World War II. He could support German unification, but only in phases because there were so many problems to address. Shevardnadze knew that the British, French, Dutch, and Poles shared his concerns, and he argued that ten years hence a unified Germany could challenge a hypothetical non-nuclear world. Furthermore, an extreme right-wing party already had 20 percent of the West German vote. What would happen if it grew into a serious force? Baker responded "In effect it suggests that the risk comes not from the United States, which for a long time you've seen as your enemy, but instead it suggests that greater risk could come from a neutral Germany that becomes militaristic."[79] This was why the United States wanted Germany in NATO, which would provide a continued American troop presence. If a united Germany was included in NATO, the US and its allies would guarantee "that NATO's *jurisdiction* or *forces* would not move eastward."[80] Later in the conversation, and to make it easier for Shevardnadze to concede, Baker repeated that if a united Germany were securely rooted in NATO, the US government could guarantee that no NATO forces would be deployed on the territory of the former GDR. Shevardnadze was unconvinced, but Baker had laid out the line he would pursue with Gorbachev the next day. He gave himself some wiggle room by adding that Two plus Four was an American proposal and he could not guarantee the Germans would agree to it. He had discussed the formula with Genscher and heard no objection, but neither had he received an explicit agreement. The meeting ended with Shevardnadze unconvinced.[81]

Genscher, meanwhile, had complicated his commitment to limit NATO's expansion in his discussions with Foreign Minister Hurd. After he left Washington, he had stopped in London to gain the British support for his Tutzing formula. In talking with Hurd, he repeated that the CSCE would be "an important vehicle for helping the Soviet Union to come to terms with the erosion of the Warsaw Pact." Furthermore, "the Russians must have assurance that if, for example, the Polish government left the Warsaw Pact one day, they would not join NATO the next."[82] Inexplicably, the West German transcript of the meeting gives the example as Hungary, not Poland[83]—but the important point is that Genscher was willing to contemplate NATO's expansion to nations beyond the GDR. We do not know whether these remarks, made at the British Foreign Office on February 6, were relayed to Washington or Moscow. Given the shortness of time, it is doubtful that Baker knew of these reports when his plane landed in Moscow on February 7, but Soviet intelligence might have collected either the British transcript or the West German transcript, or both.

BAKER MEETS WITH GORBACHEV

On February 9, Baker met with Gorbachev in the Great Hall of St. Catherine's, seated each side of the long, ornate table. While he proposed the Two plus Four framework, Gorbachev said he preferred to refer the problem to the CSCE, not the Four Powers. Baker argued that the CSCE was "far too unwieldy and cumbersome." Gorbachev admitted that Two plus Four was realistic, but he was unwilling to make a commitment. According to the Soviet note taker, Baker responded,

> We understand that it is important not only for the USSR but also for other European countries to have guarantees that – if the United States maintains her military presence in Germany within the NATO framework - there will be no extension of NATO's jurisdiction or military presence one inch to the East.[84]

Implied in this sentence was that NATO's Article 5, with its common defense guarantee, would not extend to GDR territory. Baker offered this in exchange for Soviet acceptance of the continued presence of US troops in West Germany. He elaborated,

> We are of the opinion that the consultations and discussions in the framework of the Two plus Four mechanism must give guarantees that the unification of Germany does not lead to the extension of NATO's military organization to the East.[85]

Gorbachev claimed to share Baker's view of the situation and agreed that German unification was the reality to which they all had to adapt. Before leaving, Baker made a final comment. It was surely preferable that a unified Germany remain in NATO, with the guarantees that the alliance's "*jurisdiction* and *forces* will not extend to the east beyond the current line."[86] He had now gone further than Genscher, excluding not only NATO's military structure but also its jurisdiction from the GDR.

Back in Washington, that restriction provoked a sharp outcry from the NSC. Baker had leaned too far forward on his skis. Blackwill went to Scowcroft, who went to the President. Bush was sending a letter to Kohl that very night, in which he would correct Baker. Limiting NATO *jurisdiction* to West Germany was untenable in a unified Germany. For the first and maybe only time in Bush's administration, a difference appeared between the President and his Secretary of State.[87] When Baker and Dennis Ross received the draft of Bush's letter to Kohl, with the question of whether NATO *jurisdiction* should or should not shift eastward from its present position, both realized that Baker had gone too far. They fell into line without a murmur.[88]

There followed an exchange that has become the basis of intense debate and the grist of Russian propaganda. Did Baker make an informal promise not to expand NATO eastward? He and his immediate advisers are emphatic that he gave no broad commitment about this: the whole conversation centered on Germany. But six years later, the US ambassador to the Soviet Union in 1990, Jack Matlock, testified before the House Committee on International Relations: "Gorbachev did get an informal, but clear, commitment that if Germany united and stayed in NATO, the borders of NATO would not move eastward. All right, that wasn't a legal commitment, but it was made."[89]

In an article in *Der Spiegel* in 2009, Gorbachev alleged that there had been a promise not to expand NATO "as much as a thumb's width further to the East."[90] Russian President Dmitry Medvedev also weighed in, arguing that assurances had been made and broken.[91] The problem is that neither Matlock nor Medvedev was in the meeting on February 9, 1990. Ambassadors normally accompany the Secretary of State in meetings with senior foreign officials in order to inform themselves, ensure follow up, and demonstrate the US secretary's confidence in his ambassador. On that day, Baker chose not to follow this practice, preferring to brief his ambassador afterwards in the quiet of the limousine driving back to the Embassy.[92] As for Dmitry Medvedev, in 1990 he was a graduate student at Leningrad State University.

In 2006, the Gorbachev Foundation released a book co-authored by Gorbachev's foreign policy advisor and confidant, Anatoly Chernyaev, purporting to provide a wealth of materials on "the German question," including transcripts, recordings, and news clippings. Chernyaev claimed to have been in the Great Hall for the meeting with Secretary Baker on February 9, 1990, and his transcript of the meeting with Baker reads:

> JAB III: I want to ask you a question, which you do not necessarily have to give an answer to now. Assuming that the merger [between East and West Germany] does take place, which do you prefer: a united Germany out of NATO, fully independent, with no US troops; or a united Germany, preserving the link with NATO, but with guarantees that the NATO jurisdiction or troops will not be expanded to the East of the current line?
>
> M.S. GORBACHEV: We will have to think about all of this. We will thoroughly discuss all of these questions at the managerial level. Needless to say, clearly, the expansion of the NATO zone will be unacceptable.
>
> JAB III: We agree with that.[93]

Baker's words were sufficiently vague that subsequent readers have interpreted his language as they preferred. Did that exchange constitute a promise not to expand NATO into former Warsaw Pact countries? With the exception of Gorbachev himself, who has wavered, all those who heard it have denied that they understood it that way.

However, Genscher's remarks to the British foreign minister three days earlier raise the question of whether Genscher anticipated that the Poles and the Hungarians might someday seek NATO membership. Twenty-five years later, Baker confirmed that his words, as he understood them, meant only extension to the GDR. He asserted that he and Gorbachev did not discuss the Warsaw Pact at the February 9 meeting.[94]

The issue arose in 2001 and 2002 when NATO extended membership to the three Baltic States, and in 2008 when NATO offered steps toward membership for Georgia and Ukraine. At that time, Russian Foreign Minister Sergei Lavrov claimed that in the 1990s, the US had "made a commitment not to expand NATO" and had "repeatedly broken this commitment."[95] The question of what was said in the Great Hall continues to reverberate.

CHANCELLOR KOHL TAKES THE LEAD

After his talks with Gorbachev, Baker sought to reassure Kohl that the US and the Soviets had cut no deal on Germany. He asked Ross to write a report of his meeting with Gorbachev for Kohl, who was due to meet with the Soviet leader the next day. Baker also suggested to President Bush that he write a letter to the Chancellor assuring him of US support at this critical time. (This is the letter in which Bush corrected Baker on NATO jurisdiction.)[96]

Kohl was pleased with the letter, which allowed him to assert confidently that only the German people had the right to decide whether they wished to live together in a single state. When he met with Gorbachev and Shevardnadze on February 10, Kohl asked about their attitude toward a united Germany in NATO and received an ambiguous answer. Gorbachev said he would prefer that the GDR remain within the Warsaw Pact, but he needed financial support. He asked for a donation of coal and potatoes: a recognition that the Soviet people were suffering from lack of basic products that winter of 1989-1990. Gorbachev also sought a loan of DM 5 billion.[97] Kohl had no doubt that his deutschmarks were necessary to striking a bargain with Moscow over Germany's future security arrangements.[98]

The critical meeting came in July that year, when Kohl accepted Gorbachev's invitation to meet first in Moscow and then at his summer home in the hills above Stavropol. In his memoir, Teltschik wrote that Kohl would not have travelled to Stavropol had Gorbachev not already accepted the German right to be united within NATO.[99] Historian Andreas Roedder concludes that the meeting was an achievement in itself. Gorbachev needed financial aid and Kohl needed Soviet approval for unification in NATO. The elements of a grand bargain existed, although no explicit quid pro quo was ever expressed. Both men knew that any sale or purchase of patrimony for cash would be unacceptable to their citizens. Therefore, Kohl agreed to pay the costs of withdrawing Soviet troops as well as part of their resettlement costs in the Soviet Union.[100] He also agreed to provide goods, grants and credits to stabilize Soviet finances. The West German contribution to the Soviet Union has never been precisely calculated, but estimates range from DM 50 to 80 billion (US $78.5 to 125.6 billion). It included credit guarantees to West German banks as well as raw materials – coal, potatoes, meat – whose cash value was not specified.

THE FINAL SETTLEMENT

On September 12, 1990, the Treaty on the Final Settlement with Respect to Germany was signed by the Four Powers and the two Germanys. It ratified much of what had been agreed upon between Germany and the Soviet Union, as well as between the US and its allies. Among these agreements were a German commitment to respect its eastern border with Poland at the Oder—Neisse line; Germany's renouncement of atomic, biological and chemical weapons; the withdrawal of all Soviet troops by the end of 1994; and the commitment that no permanent West German military units - integrated in NATO – would be stationed in the (now former) GDR until all Soviet troops were withdrawn. The treaty terminated the rights of the Four Powers, and Germany became sovereign and free to choose its alliances.[101]

By the autumn of 1990, Shevardnadze was a different man. He was tired and deeply disturbed by Gorbachev's increasingly authoritarian tendencies. Pressure from Kremlin apparatchiks had forced Gorbachev to withhold self-determination to the Baltic States and violence had erupted in Vilnius, resulting in the death of fifteen men. Tensions were also rising in Azerbaijan and in Shevardnadze's home state of Georgia. Under these pressures, he reneged on previously agreed troop withdrawals in the CFE talks. Baker became exasperated before recognizing that his friend was on the verge of resigning. Pressure from hardliners and Gorbachev's turn to the right had made his job unenviable. For Shevardnadze, it was a question of timing so as not to undermine his comrade, Mikhail Gorbachev. When his resignation came in December 1990, both Gorbachev and Baker were saddened. Baker had lost a true friend.

THREE

BETWEEN IDEALISM AND REALISM

The tension between idealism and realism was familiar to James Baker from his time at Princeton, when he wrote his senior thesis on two British parliamentarians of the early twentieth century: Ernest Bevin and Aneurin Bevan. The distinctions between the two men reflected the tension within Baker's life and his preference for achieving his goals through purposeful and pragmatic steps.

Bevin had founded the Transport and General Workers Union, which became the largest trade union in Britain and a strong supporter of the Labour Party. His rejection of pacifism and his strong work habits led Winston Churchill to invite him to join his World War II coalition government as Minister of Labor. Bevin firmly opposed communists, whom he regarded as "workshy intellectuals," and he worked to prevent their infiltration into the trade union movement. He never forgot his trade union roots, and his socialism was marked by a strong dose of realism. As foreign secretary in the postwar Labour government of 1945, Bevin remained staunchly anti-Soviet, feeling that Churchill was too susceptible to Stalin's flattery at Potsdam.

Aneurin Bevan, sixteen years Ernest Bevin's junior, was a lifelong champion of social justice, the rights of working people and democratic socialism who, as Minister of Health, helped establish the national welfare system. In World War II and on domestic issues, he sided with the Soviet Union against fascist Germany. His passion for socialism earned him the enmity of both Ernest Bevin and Winston Churchill, a fight that Aneurin relished. He entered the postwar Labour government but resigned in protest when National Insurance funds were cut to pay for rearmament. A contemporary said of Aneurin Bevan, "he wasn't cut out to be a leader; he was cut out to be a prophet."[1] In his senior thesis, Baker concluded that Aneurin Bevan's idealism kept him from achieving his own goals, while Ernest Bevin's focus on producing results was the preferred route. "Those who know me will not be surprised that I favored the approach of the realist," wrote the twenty-year-old Baker.[2]

The balance between idealism and realism confronts every Secretary of State, but Baker's speeches and responses to journalists' questions did not reveal his preference for the realist option. Those who heard him advocate self-determination or promote democratic values, and who saw him meet repeatedly with Soviet human rights activists might think he leaned toward idealism. He strongly favored holding democratic elections in Nicaragua even though the democratic opposition was not assured of winning. He favored elections in Eastern Europe even though polls suggested that the Socialist Party in East Germany would win. More troublesome and significant for Baker were two situations that began early in his tenure at the State Department: the slaughter of workers and students around China's Tiananmen Square, and Lithuania's efforts to rid itself of Soviet control. In both cases, Baker had to weigh the Wilsonian principles enshrined in the United Nations Charter against the pragmatic pursuit of national security and economic interests. Well after his retirement from government, he said, "you can pursue human rights so long as national security is assured."[3]

From his early days at the State Department, Baker had shown the ability to both pursue the President's foreign policy priorities and persuade reluctant senators on both sides of the aisle to agree to pragmatic solutions, or at least not protest too loudly. With the acumen learned as Ronald Reagan's chief of staff, he persuaded the Republican minority leader of the Senate Foreign Relations Committee that negotiations with Marxist Leninist guerillas were more likely to achieve peace than continuing military support for the anti-communist Salvadoran government. Baker's skill in persuading legislators to accept his pragmatic foreign policies grew, but he was sensitive to criticism and pushed back against accusations that he was abandoning American ideals and values. This may explain why he frequently concealed his pragmatism behind idealistic speeches.

CONFRONTING CHINA AFTER TIANANMEN SQUARE

From the summer of 1989 to early 1991, Baker and his deputy Larry Eagleburger had to confront hostile critics in Congress over his policy toward China and the Baltic States. Faultfinding letters rained down on Baker for his "business as usual" style with the Chinese leaders. The conservative columnist William Safire disparaged Baker's "pusillanimous evenhandedness" in not standing with the Baltic democrats who pursued reform.[4] In letters and opinion pieces and on television and radio talk shows, commentators heaped scorn on President Bush and his Secretary of State for not standing firm for American values. Freedom of the press, freedom of religion, freedom of association, and the right to self-determination appeared to have been sacrificed for the sake of other foreign policy interests. In an interview with Morton Kondracke, Vice President Dan Quayle cast doubts on Baker's toughness, even calling him an appeaser for supporting Gorbachev's reform programs. The article, published in the Washington Times, prompted Baker to send an annotated copy to Bush with the note, "Mr. P__ We have successfully avoided this kind of crap for 9 months… Please have it knocked off. JAB III"[5]

On June 3, 1989, Baker's plans for a golf game with his eldest son were overtaken by Jamie's recommendation that Dad switch on the television. Baker watched heavily armed units of the People's Liberation Army (PLA) fire on demonstrators in the vicinity of Beijing's Tiananmen Square. It was night time in Beijing, and the Chinese leaders had sent in tanks to clear the four thousand workers and students who had occupied the central square and surrounding streets of Beijing since March.

Two weeks earlier, US Ambassador James Lilley had sent cables to the State Department describing the Chinese government's "probable" use of force, an action he upgraded to "imminent" on May 26.[6] The mild response from Washington, whose leaders doubted that the reformist Deng Xiaoping would harm US-China relations, led Lilley to suspect his cables were not being forwarded by lower-level members of the National Security staff.[7] They were in fact passed on to Secretary Baker, but neither he nor his staff responded.[8] However, once the TV pictures hit Washington early on Saturday, June 3, Lilley and his staff finally found attentive officials at the most senior levels of government. Bush had the lead, and having been chief of the US Liaison Office in China in the mid-seventies, he had developed a fondness for the Chinese people and a close relationship with Deng Xiaoping. Consequently, he did not want to jeopardize that relationship. Recognizing the President's knowledge and leadership on China, Baker ensured implementation of the president's preference.

Baker had not relied on cable traffic alone to keep him informed of events in China. After Mikhail Gorbachev's visit to Beijing in May 1989, foreign journalists, including CNN and ABC, had remained in Beijing to cover the widening protest movement and the hunger strike in Tiananmen Square. There were plentiful warnings that conservative Premier Li Peng would suppress the protests on Deng's behalf. It was only a question of time. American viewers became enraged against the Chinese leadership after seeing TV coverage of a lone armored personnel carrier careening through crowds of demonstrators with no care for the humans in its way. During Saturday afternoon, Chinese citizens edged toward a line of soldiers backed by jeeps with machine gun turrets. The calls of "don't shoot your own people" and "Chinese don't kill Chinese" were to no avail. These soldiers were not from Beijing itself but from distant provinces, instructed to impose order in the Imperial City. They opened fire on unarmed people, cutting them down with bursts of automatic weapons fire that lasted up to forty-five seconds. Students rushed forward to pick up the fallen, only to be met with another hail of lethal fire. Hideous bonfires in Tiananmen Square followed as the authorities sought to burn and hide the human wreckage scattered throughout central Beijing. That weekend found the Bush family up at Walker's Point on the Maine coast, their escape from the pressures of Washington. But there was no escape from these events. Before retiring for the night, Bush asked Baker and Scowcroft for options.

Bush's friendship with then-Vice Premier Deng Xiaoping had begun in October 1974, when he became chief of the US Liaison Office in Beijing. They conversed often during Bush's ten-month posting in Beijing, and later, as a private citizen, he had received Deng in Houston, calling him "an old friend."[9] Bush recognized in Deng, a man who sought to modernize and integrate the Chinese economy into the global economy. Consequently, US/China friendship was critical to China's new willingness to work with capitalist countries.[10] In Bush's mind, a personal relationship existed which enabled the two men to telephone each other. As the sun rose on Sunday, June 4, Bush called Deng but got no answer. He called again throughout the day, but was not able to speak with the Chinese leader. The rebuff frustrated Bush and advisers feared that Deng had been pushed aside, or worse, had suffered a heart attack.[11] It was unheard of to refuse a telephone call from the President of the United States. For his part, Baker communicated with Ambassador Lilley and the Chinese Ambassador in Washington, Han Xu. Using the embassy's well-established contacts with the foreign ministry, he too failed to get through. The Chinese leadership had isolated itself. (Both Bush and Baker chose to ignore long-standing Chinese practice that no leader would respond to an incoming telephone call unless he both knew the content of the call and had an agreed upon response.) All Baker could do was to stay apprised of developments through the US embassy and consulates in China, as well as TV journalists. The news was grim.

In April 1989, thousands had come out to remember the late General Secretary of the Chinese Communist Party (CCP) Hu Yaobang, who had died on April 15, and to support his successor, the reformist Zhao Ziyang. Students and workers called for greater democracy and freedoms but they confronted soldiers recruited from the capital city who had been ordered to impose order. In response, Beijing residents and demonstrators swarmed around their military buses with elderly women berating the soldiers verbally and stopping the buses from moving forward. Elsewhere in the city, several thousand citizens surrounded another busload of forty soldiers. Students climbed on top of the bus posing for photographs while holding rifles and wearing PLA helmets. The People's Liberation Army seemed to wilt in the face of people power. At one point, ordinary citizens repelled a column of five thousand unarmed soldiers who, in retreat, seemed more like a children's crusade than a military strategy.[12] Unnerved by the growing protest, Deng and Premier Li Peng declared martial law on May 18. Instead of relying upon Beijing troops to confront local citizens, they ordered the dispatch of military detachments from distant parts of China to impose order upon the demonstrators.

The overwhelming sentiment among the elders on the CCP Standing Committee was that the government must get tough with the protestors. Li Peng insisted, "No government in the world would tolerate this kind of disorder in the middle of its capital city." Another close confidant of Deng said, "If we retreat any further we're done for."[13] On June 2, aircraft unloaded new troops with armored vehicles at Nanyuan Airfield. They joined tanks, armored personnel carriers, and trucks lined up in a convoy on the main road into Beijing. Their instructions were to crush the spontaneous flowering of an incipient democracy movement in Beijing. In other parts of China, authorities began to arrest and put on summary trial students and sympathizing workers.

One of Baker's closest advisers, Margaret Tutwiler had a keen feel for the political pulse of the nation. Now, she urged Baker to do more. She had worked with him since his early days as Reagan's Chief of Staff and her political antennae had helped Baker make astute decisions on several occasions. After seeing the television footage of unarmed students mowed down by advancing tanks, she told Baker that Monday morning that she could not brief the press. Events were just too horrible. Baker gave her no leeway. Sternly, he instructed her to brief the press because it would send the wrong signal if she failed to do so.[14] She read to herself the President's statement, delivered the day before as he got off the helicopter on the White House lawn, and then repeated his sentiments to the assembled press: "Our intentions are not to harm the Chinese people."

She could say that with conviction. Meanwhile, American citizens and their representatives in both the Senate and House of Representatives demanded sanctions, disengagement, and withdrawal of Most Favored Nation (MFN) status.

Early on Monday, June 5, Bush announced a ban on new weapons sales to China and the suspension of military contacts. American citizens, their congressmen, and press clamored for more. On June 7, Ambassador Lilley met with the Chinese Vice Foreign Minister who had stonewalled an earlier request to meet. Lilley had received instructions from Baker to gain landing rights for chartered United Airlines flights in order to evacuate non-essential embassy personnel and US citizens, including many American students at Peking University. There was a clear and present danger, but the Chinese government was unwilling to face the reality on the ground. Instead, in their meeting the Vice Minister told Ambassador Lilley "the situation in China is complex… It is not easy to understand events at a single stroke."[15] Back in the United States, the national press called for a strong government response. Baker remained in sync with the President, who recalled that the Chinese leadership was clearly in an embattled frame of mind. In his opinion "It was important not to respond in a way that played into the hands of the hard-liners who were pushing for even more repressive action, which would inevitably lead to more bloodshed.[16] They had to find the right balance.

In the days that followed, the President suspended all military contracts, including a new F-8 avionics package worth $550 million and contracts for torpedoes, large-bore artillery shells, helicopters, and artillery radars. US diplomats were instructed not to attend diplomatic events hosted by the Chinese, and the Fulbright program in China was terminated. Both Commerce Secretary Robert Mosbacher's forthcoming trip with American businessmen to China and Treasury Secretary Nicholas Brady's proposed visit were halted. Yet Congress wanted more: the US should revoke its offer of MFN status.[17] Bush counted on his fifteen-year friendship with Deng to restore relations, and Baker respected the President's desire to take the lead. Bush wrote in his diary "I take this relationship very personally and I want to handle it that way"[18]; Baker did not try to dissuade him. Bush did not want Chinese leaders to succumb to those within the CCP who sought to withdraw "the middle kingdom" from growing participation in the global economy. On the contrary, he sought ways to keep the outward and more modernizing Chinese leaders in the ascendency.

Over the next few days, the White House called Deng's office repeatedly, only to be told that requests to talk with the chairman had to come through the Chinese Embassy in Washington. Few leaders had ever turned down a US President's request to speak by phone. An irritated Bush asked Baker if Deng could be ill. Finally, Bush sat down at his electric typewriter to write Deng a four-page letter "from the heart."[19] He sent it on June 20.

> Dear Chairman Deng: I write this letter to you with a heavy heart. I wish there was a way to discuss this matter in person, but regrettably that is not the case. … I write in a spirit of genuine friendship, this letter coming as I'm sure you know from one who believes with a passion that good relations between the United States and China are in the fundamental interests of both countries… I also recall your unforgettable words about the need for good relations with the West, your concerns about "encirclement" and those who had done great harm to China, and your commitment to keeping China moving forward… The wonder of TV brought the details of the events in Tiananmen Square into the homes of people not just in "Western" countries but worldwide. … The people of the world saw the turmoil and the bloodshed with which the demonstrations were ended … The actions that I took as President of the United States could not be avoided. As you know, the clamor for stronger action remains intense. I have resisted that clamor, making clear that I did not want to see destroyed this relationship that you and I have worked hard to build.[20]

The letter included a request that Deng meet with the President's confidential envoy. On June 25, communicating through Chinese Ambassador Han Xu, Deng agreed to receive such an emissary.

Baker was reluctant to engage the Chinese leadership in this manner. He believed such a meeting would not persuade the Chinese to stop executing pro-democracy men and women, and if the President's emissary pressed the point, the executions would only continue privately. Baker, however, agreed that although the mission would not save students' lives, the personal emissary might defuse the current tension in the relationship.[21] He therefore asked that Deputy Secretary of State Larry Eagleburger accompany NSC Advisor Brent Scowcroft to Beijing. Without informing their families or staff of their real destination, and with only an interpreter and secretary each, they flew straight to Beijing, refueling in mid-air to avoid questions during a refueling stop. At the meeting in Beijing on July 10, Scowcroft found the Chinese leadership guarded, but also well disposed to deal with the Bush administration.[22] Nonetheless, the visit made no difference to the Chinese leadership's determination to rout out "counter revolutionaries" and restore order. Not only those who had gathered in Tiananmen, but other students throughout the nation, as well as Tibetans, were arrested, beaten and jailed. Hundreds of thousands were believed to have died.

SANCTUARY FOR FANG LIZHI AND LI SHUXIAN

A few days after the assault on Beijing, and without telling the East Asia Bureau so as not to divulge to Chinese authorities his absence from the embassy, Baker called Lilley back to Washington for consultation. He left Raymond Burghardt, the political counselor, as chargé d'affaires. Burghardt, a Foreign Service officer with deep knowledge of China, focused on two priorities: first, the evacuation of US citizens, including Ambassador Lilley's wife and his own wife, Susan; and second, the delicate issue of caring for the renowned astrophysicist Fang Lizhi and his wife, Li Shuxian, a material physicist.[23] Both had fled to the US Information Agency building some distance from the US Embassy on June 6 after learning that Fang was on the Chinese government's black list.

The question was how to handle their need for protection. The US policy was to avoid offering refuge to people seeking asylum, but this time Baker intervened personally. He was concerned about the bad press that would result if the United States rejected an asylum request, an action that would place Fang and his wife in considerable danger. Baker therefore instructed Burghardt to ask the scientists whether they sought asylum. He also talked with Bush, who favored protecting the couple but wanted to know how long would that protection be offered.[24] Would they be like Cardinal Mindszenty, holed up in the US Embassy in Budapest for fifteen years? On June 7, Burghardt jumped into the Marine Embassy Guards' van and headed out to a hotel where Fang, his wife and son cowered in one room. As he opened the door, Burghardt knew they wanted American help. Their bags were already packed and stacked beside the door. Bundling all three onto the floor of the van, Burghardt drove at top speed to the embassy compound that housed both the ambassador's residence and the embassy health unit. Fang Lizhi and Li Shuxian spent the next thirteen months in a room off the health unit before they could travel safely to the United States.

On June 6, Presidential Spokesman Marlin Fitzwater announced that Fang and his wife had taken refuge in the US embassy, thereby informing the Chinese authorities of their whereabouts. "The Chinese government went ballistic," Lilley later wrote, accusing the US government of interfering in China's internal affairs and violating its sovereignty.[25] Even though it further damaged Sino-US relations, Baker told Lilley to keep them safe within the Embassy compound. US Marine Embassy Guards were now armed with automatic weapons to defend the Americans and their Chinese guests.

Reports that Chinese security forces were planning to storm the embassy compound to extract Fang and Li seemed all the more credible after June 7, when sharp shooters stationed in a nearby building targeted a different compound that housed many foreign diplomatic families. Thanks to a tip the night before, the compound was evacuated except for a few families who hid from the bullets. The Chinese government's purpose was to "close the door to beat the dog," that is, fire on the foreign diplomats to chase out the photographing foreigners and then crack down on Chinese citizens to restore order.[26] Chinese authorities continued to arrest students and others considered "counter-revolutionaries." Bishop Fan Xueyan and eleven other religious leaders others were seized and taken away, after which, the Senate Foreign Relations Committee reported, "hundreds of priests, ministers of the gospel, church administrators and other Christians just vanished, as if they had never existed."[27] It was a period of considerable confusion in Washington and widespread terror in China.

After months of mass arrests and secret trials that resulted in the summary shooting of those found guilty, Scowcroft and Eagleburger quietly returned to Beijing on December 10, hoping to keep the lines of communication open. The US media learned they were there when Chinese television recorded Scowcroft's speech at the banquet that night. His words of appreciation for the host government were pounced on immediately by critics in the United States, who asked why "business as usual" had resumed. Two months later, in early February 1990, Eagleburger was called to testify before both the Senate and House foreign relations committees. The Senate hearing on February 7 began as James Baker's plane was landing thousands of miles away in Moscow, where he would spend the next two days meeting with Shevardnadze and Gorbachev. With the President personally handling the China problem, Baker chose to focus on the Soviet Union and Eastern Europe, leaving his deputy Eagleburger to face congressional grilling. In the current hostile atmosphere, defending the administration's China policy was a herculean and unrewarding task. Baker left that to Eagleburger.

MEDIATING CONGRESSIONAL PRESSURE

The scorn and criticism directed at the administration by both Republicans and Democrats in Congress reflected the public concern that economic interests and geopolitics had taken priority over American values. In his opening statement, Congressman William Bloomfield (R-MI) said "The overwhelming revulsion in Congress and among the American people to the actions of the Chinese leaders should not be mistaken."[28] Eagleburger was excoriated for his two unpublicized visits to Beijing, and his judgement was called into question. Senator Helms compared him to Neville Chamberlain, the British Prime Minister who, upon returning from Munich after signing an agreement with Adolf Hitler in September 1938, claimed to have achieved "peace for our time."[29] Others were more generous, recognizing Eagleburger as an exemplary public servant, "a skilled policy maker as well as a real straight shooter."[30] In both the Senate and House, the full blame fell on "the team": the President, Scowcroft, and Baker.

Eagleburger was faithful to the administration's policy, and in his prepared statements he raised the central question: "Do we seek to isolate China and cause it to turn inward or do we seek to facilitate its return to reform and openness by continuing to pursue the contacts and ties that encouraged such reforms in the first place"?[31] President Bush, he argued, was committed to managing the US-China relationship as his predecessors had done since 1971. The President knew that "we had only limited leverage on the Chinese leadership. The challenge was to make clear American revulsion at and condemnation of the bloodshed at Tiananmen, yet express it in a way that would maintain, to the extent possible, our ability to influence events within China and encourage a return to reform of the economy and the society."[32]

Senator Joe Biden (D-DE) suggested that the administration was making the effort to get the China relationship back on track when blame lay squarely with the Chinese leadership. He used the metaphor of a wife shouting and kicking her husband out of the house. Should the husband creep home with a bunch of red roses to ask forgiveness, or should the wife begin the process of reconciliation? Biden thought the administration was acting like the humiliated husband. Why, he asked, was the "China card," the strategic counterweight to the Soviet Union, so important? Was it the principal reason for seeking to reset relations?[33] Eagleburger replied that the "China card" was still marginally important, but that changes in the Soviet Union and Eastern Europe were so fundamental "that it [China] was no longer the dominant or controlling factor."[34] Henry Kissinger had sought to establish diplomatic relations with China in order to provide a counterweight to the Soviet Union, but in 1989 China's role as "a major player on the world scene" was diminished. Biden remained unsatisfied, asking whether the Chinese repression would cause eastern European countries to say, "we'd better hurry up and get Soviet troops out of our country... because we are worried about Gorbachev and whether he can last, as we are worried further that things may unravel as we try to put together democracies in these countries."[35] Massive repression against critiques of the Chinese leadership had sent signals throughout Europe and the movement in Eastern Europe and the Baltics to free themselves from Moscow's grip accelerated.

Biden was not alone in seeing the connection between US policy toward China and the independence movements in the Baltic States. In both cases, American values of self-determination, democracy and freedom of expression were pitted against pragmatic national security interests. Could American pressure for human rights endanger the global strategic balance? By breaking away, would Lithuania and the two other Baltic States undermine Gorbachev's leadership? In both cases, would the backlash from conservative forces undo the reforms that Gorbachev and Deng Xiaoping had introduced and America had welcomed?

THE EASTERN EUROPEAN DEMOCRACY MOVEMENTS

The crisis in China coincided with Bush and Baker's announcement that they had completed their strategic review of US foreign policy. They had outlined a policy of cautious step-by-step support for liberalization in Poland, Hungary and Czechoslovakia. Baker thought each nation had a good chance to achieve independence from Moscow, but only with the Soviet Union's acquiescence. He supported the President's decision not to exploit the changes taking place in Eastern Europe. Washington's caution would help Gorbachev remain in power and thus keep his "new reforms" on track by avoiding words or actions that could inflame hardliners in the Kremlin. There should be no gloating or triumphant declarations from Washington as Eastern European countries broke free of their old restraints. In July 1989, President Bush told Polish and Hungarian leaders, "We're not here to make you choose between East and West." Instead, he quoted Gorbachev on freedom of choice and told reporters that "we're not there to poke a stick in the eye of Mr. Gorbachev: just the opposite - to encourage the very kind of reforms that he is championing, and more reforms."[36]

Baker conveyed the same message to Shevardnadze on July 29, 1989 at the Paris Conference on Cambodia. He and the President were impressed by what they had seen in Poland and Hungary and would continue to support reform to the extent they could. Neither he nor the President was trying to create problems for the Soviet Union. Nevertheless, he added a warning: serious problems in the US-Soviet relationship would occur if Moscow used force to stop peaceful change.[37] Shevardnadze responded that to use force in Eastern Europe would end *perestroika* and that Moscow saw the reforms in Poland and Hungary not as a threat but as consistent with *perestroika*. "The pace, the movement, the process" in those countries was up to them.[38] Baker listened carefully, unsure if this tolerance would extend to the Baltic States. He was also unsure if Shevardnadze, the man now responsible for foreign affairs, was sidelined from the struggle between Gorbachev and hardliners in the Soviet military.

THE BALTIC STATES

Eighteen months earlier, in February 1988, the Lithuanian parliament had passed a declaration of sovereignty, and Vytautas Landsbergis had founded *Sąjūdis*, a political organization to lead the independence and pro-democracy movement. That June, thousands had demonstrated and demanded that their delegates to the forthcoming 19th CPSU advocate for greater Lithuanian autonomy. In the US, Lithuanian Americans called upon their congressmen, wrote editorials advancing independence for Lithuania, and pressed the case for their nation's freedom from the Soviet Union. Two years later, Baker reiterated the State Department's traditional position, responding to Dan Rather of CBS Evening News, "It's the position of the US that their [Baltic States'] forcible incorporation into the Soviet Union was illegitimate in the first instance. We continue to refuse to recognize their incorporation into the Soviet Union and, in fact, we continue to fly the flags of these republics in the hall of our State Department."[39] This message was directed to the Kremlin: your occupation was illegitimate and remains so. However, we shall do little if anything to change that fact.

Baker's State Department covered the three Baltic States from an office that was separate from that of the Soviet Union, and US ambassadors posted to the Soviet Union avoided visiting the Baltic States to emphasize their distinctive status. It was both unusual and a first occasion when Ambassador Matlock met with representatives from the Baltic States during the June 3, 1989, meeting of the newly elected Supreme Soviet in Moscow. Matlock justified his meeting on grounds that these representatives were democratically elected Baltic deputies to the Soviet Congress of People not merely Socialist Soviet representatives.[40] Washington had no objection. During the meeting with Matlock, the Baltic members asked how Washington would respond to a Lithuanian declaration of independence. He replied cautiously, "If Lithuania remained under effective Soviet control, the American government could probably not recognize its government as independent, no matter how much it might sympathize."[41] Matlock was issuing a warning, but the Lithuanian delegation interpreted these elliptical words as encouragement to rid themselves of "effective Soviet control." Their determination was courageous, coming just as the Chinese army was crushing the democracy movement in Tiananmen. Provoked to speed up the process of self-determination, *Sajūdis* joined with national fronts from Estonia and Latvia to form a Baltic Council, which would fight for Baltic recognition in the Soviet Congress of People. Baker could see clearly that Baltic leaders were determined to press for self-determination, but he was uncertain how far the people would press for independence.

On August 22, 1989, the Lithuanian parliament declared the 1940 Soviet annexation of the Baltics illegal, and the next day, two million people joined hands to form a human chain some 420 miles long connecting the three Baltic capitals. *Sąjūdis*, together with the independence movements in Latvia and Estonia, had succeeded in mobilizing this massive popular force despite Soviet claims that "extremist elements with narrow nationalist positions" had organized this "hysteria."[42] Russian television devoted nineteen minutes to reading the Central Committee statement on "the virus of nationalism." In Moscow, a few hundred people attempted a sympathy demonstration in Red Square, but the police detained seventy-five of them for breach of the peace. It was clear that Soviet acquiescence to democratic forces in Eastern Europe was not to be equated with an independence movement in the Baltic States. Neither Gorbachev nor the Soviet military were ready for breakaway republics. Baker had read those tea leaves and one of his advisers told reporters "the Soviet leadership at the highest levels is of the opinion that it can't let Lithuania go."[43] The question was what should the United States do about this?

Upon his return from vacation in September, Gorbachev summoned the entire Lithuanian leadership to Moscow for a joint meeting with the CPSU, but he could not persuade them to abandon their pursuit of independence. Instead, the Lithuanian Communist Party broke ranks with the CPSU. Alexsandr Yakovlev, a close ally of Gorbachev and the godfather of *glasnost*, sent Washington a warning. He told the visiting Zbigniew Brzezinski, the former US national security advisor, that the Kremlin saw Lithuania's movement toward independence as a threat, if not potentially "the end of *perestroika*."[44] Yakovlev did not elaborate, but after Brzezinski's report to the White House, Bush and Baker knew they had to tread carefully. Moscow had drawn a red line and confrontation should be avoided.

In early December, the seaboard summit in Malta created much anxiety among the leaders of the Baltic States, who feared that the

Americans had made a deal with the Soviets over their heads. This was not the case, but Matlock chose not to reassure the Lithuanians by meeting with them, as he could not protect them if Moscow cracked down. On its own, the Lithuanian parliament moved to abolish the leading role of the Communist party, and on December 20, 1989, the Lithuanian Communist Party Congress endorsed the motion to separate from Moscow.

1990, THE BALTIC STATES' CRITICAL YEAR

Early in the New Year Gorbachev flew to Lithuania's capital, Vilnius, to be met by more than two hundred thousand angry Lithuanians standing outside the Catholic cathedral chanting "independence!" [45] This January 11 encounter was the first time a Soviet leader had set foot in Lithuania, and he dived into the crowd calling for independence at the workplace, in the cities, "in the republics, but *together*!" Gorbachev hoped for a willingness to listen, but instead the citizens of Vilnius were hostile and abusive as they argued with him. Irritated, Gorbachev responded by warning them that if they were to secede, the Russian minority would lose their rights and Lithuania would have to pay back the money the Soviet central government had invested in Lithuanian housing and factories. Without Soviet oil, gas and other resources, he warned, Lithuania would fall into a "mud puddle." From the Soviet point of view, Lithuania was the site of crucial ports and communication lines: "our security lies here."[46] The crowd in Vilnius appeared ready to tolerate the cost of secession.

Despite Gorbachev's pleas, the newly elected Lithuanian parliament declared independence on March 11, 1990. Four days later, Gorbachev issued an ultimatum, giving the Lithuanian leadership three days to retract their declaration of independence. He was ignored, and on March 18, Soviet armored vehicles drove through Vilnius. They fired no rounds, but a warning had been issues: the Soviets had the capacity to crack down militarily on the movement for freedom and democracy should *Sąjūdis* leader and now head of state, Vytautas Landsbergis not suspend the declaration of independence and return to the position before March 11. Ten days later, the Kremlin issued a second ultimatum, demanding that the citizens of Lithuania turn in their firearms to the Ministry of Internal Affairs within seven days. A third ultimatum, two days later, demanded that the Lithuanian government turn in hundreds of army deserters, surrender private weapons, and protect Soviet property. Despite the increasing psychological pressure, Landsbergis and his government remained firm, refusing to accede to any of these Soviet ultimatums. With the example of Berlin clear in their minds, Lithuanian citizens were willing to ignore the Soviet threats and instead press on for independence. Moscow had not ordered East German troops to fire on those leaving for the West. Surely, Soviet pressures would not overwhelm Lithuanians. They could withstand the pressure, but Washington's help would make a significant difference.

Throughout March, Baker and the President urged Gorbachev and Shevardnadze to respect the will of the Lithuanian people, "we hope that all parties will continue to avoid any initiation or encouragement of violence."[47] At their backs were 743,000 Americans of Lithuanian descent, nearly all of them passionate about independence from the Soviet Union.[48] Some of America's best-known journalists and TV commentators joined them, including George Will, Bill Keller, A.M. Rosenthal, David Brinkley, Sam Donaldson, and Patrick Buchanan. Former President Reagan, former Secretary of State George Schultz, and AFL-CIO President Lane Kirkland also endorsed Lithuanian independence.[49] It was clear where Republican sympathy lay, and Baker could have used the clamour as leverage in his calls to Gorbachev and Shevardnadze. But both and Baker and Bush temporized. They had only one solution, rhetoric, patience and hope the confrontation would die down with time. They knew that direct confrontation would place Gorbachev in an impossible situation; one in which the reforming Secretary General might be ousted. It was better to wait and see.

On March 20, Baker met Shevardnadze in Namibia, where both were celebrating Namibian independence. During the meeting, Baker warned Shevardnadze that the use of force would affect American-Soviet relations: "If you use force or coercion, there would be all sorts of consequences. We wouldn't be able to control them." Shevardnadze replied, "We have taken note of the nuances in your public statements, and we appreciate them." Baker was firm: "We can't continue these nuances forever. If you ratchet up the pressure on this issue, we can't sustain them."[50] Shevardnadze remarked that the Soviet military was taking a tougher stance on Lithuania. The KGB and Soviet generals now demanded that no concessions be made to the Baltic States.[51] Despite the calm in Vilnius and the ability of Lithuanians to go about their daily business, the potential for violence was high. In Moscow, state television raised tension by reporting chaos and unrest in Vilnius.

Baker raised the warnings. On March 20, the State Department sent a tougher public warning to the Kremlin not to use force against Lithuania. The statement carried the implicit warning that bloody conflict in Lithuania could affect US–Soviet relations and the prospects for a summit meeting in Washington planned for late May.[52] When the Soviets did not reply, Bush sent a letter to Gorbachev on March 22 with a similar message.[53] On March 26, Senator Ted Kennedy met with Gorbachev for seventy-five minutes, during which the Soviet leader complained bitterly that US criticism was undermining his attempts at moderation. The movement for independence in the Baltic States, he said, had spread to Soviet Georgia, Azerbaijan, and Armenia, and he was under intense domestic pressure to impose an economic boycott that would crush Lithuania's rebellion.[54] Kennedy returned to Washington deeply concerned with Gorbachev's inability to control his generals and the fear that events in the Baltics had created a looming crisis for the Soviet leader.

On March 14 1990, Mikhail Gorbachev was elected President of the Soviet Union. Ten days later, he ratcheted up the pressure on the Lithuanians.[55] At 3 a.m. on March 24, more than one hundred tanks and trucks as well as more than 1,500 solders armed with automatic weapons thundered past the Parliament building in Vilnius, startling legislators who were working through the night to create an independent government. On March 27, Soviet troops stormed a psychiatric hospital on Vilnius's outskirts and arrested about two dozen young Lithuanians who had taken shelter after deserting from their Soviet army units. On the same day, heavily armed Soviet troops took control of Lithuania's Communist Party headquarters and seized several other party buildings in the capital. US and other foreign diplomats and journalists were ordered to leave Lithuania when their Soviet visas expired. The State Department's historian reminded Baker and his advisers that these actions were reminiscent of the prelude to the Soviet invasion of Czechoslovakia in 1968. Officials in the East Asia Bureau added that it was reminiscent of the tank and troop movements in Beijing some nine months earlier.

Soviet Foreign Ministry Spokesman Gennadi Gerasimov said that interference from abroad in the crisis would not be tolerated, adding, "the Lithuanians could have given the first Soviet President [Gorbachev] a quiet first one hundred days. They didn't. Too bad!"[56] Soviet tanks surrounded the radio station in Vilnius and the nuclear power plant. It was becoming evident that the KGB, the generals, and conservative leaders had gained the upper hand and rejected concessions for the Lithuanians and other republics which might follow. If Gorbachev hoped to hold onto his presidency, he had to demonstrate the ability to project Soviet power in Lithuania.

By the spring of 1990, the Soviet military was emerging as a major independent player in negotiations between Moscow and Washington. The generals were increasingly concerned that civilian overlords were making too many concessions at their expense.[57] The primary focus of the military was on negotiations for a START treaty, but their immediate task was to avoid the breakup of the Soviet Union. The challenge was significant. On April 3, the Estonians expressed their desire to be an independent nation, followed by the Latvian parliament on May 3.

In response to this show of force, Bush and Baker changed their position and tone. Facing the probability of violence as well as overwhelming pressure on Gorbachev from hardliners, Baker reiterated US support for a peaceful resolution of the dilemmas in the Baltic republics. He stepped back from the previous harsher warnings of consequences to US-Soviet relations should the confrontation in Lithuania turn violent. Instead, he urged negotiation. While Bush corresponded with Gorbachev, Baker sent similar messages to Shevardnadze: "I want to be sure that the Soviets understand our position and understand that we are not trying to make things difficult for Lithuania or for the Soviet Union or anybody else."[58]

Aware that their retreat from the Baltics was causing significant domestic problems, Baker compensated for the President and his backpedaling on Lithuanian independence in a speech on the value of democracy. Delivered to the World Affairs Council in Dallas on March 31, Baker spoke of his commitment to democratic principles:

> The time of sweeping away the old dictators is passing fast; the time of building up the new democracies has arrived. That is why President Bush has defined our new mission to be the promotion and consolidation of democracy. It is a task that fulfills both American ideals and American interests... American foreign policy abroad must reflect democratic values.... There are others who argue for a realpolitik that has a place only for economic or military or political interests and leaves our values at home....America's ideals are the conscience of our actions. Our power is the instrument to turn those ideals into reality.[59]

He focused on Nicaragua, where US insistence on presidential elections, held only a month before, had brought Violeta Chamorro and her democratic opposition party to power. He chose not to mention China, Lithuania, or the Baltic States, exclusions that puzzled many in the audience. The omission implied that there were limits to the advancement of democracy. The US had not responded to the Soviet crackdowns in East Germany in 1953, Hungary in 1956, and Czechoslovakia in 1968, or to the Soviet invasion of Afghanistan in 1979. Nor would the administration provide military support to Lithuanian freedom fighters in 1990. Baker knew that Bush wanted to avoid raising expectations: "I am not going to be the President who gives subject peoples the false impression that if they rebel, they are going to get help."[60]

Baker's speech was not directed so much to his Texan audience as to the Kremlin leadership. Washington might temporize to avoid violent conflict in the Baltic States, but the Kremlin should recognize America's commitment to democratic values. Baker also asked Prime Minister Thatcher, President Mitterrand, and Chancellor Kohl to talk to Landsbergis and try to persuade him and the Lithuanian parliament to suspend its declaration of independence. Instead, they should negotiate with Moscow. As they sought to calm the Lithuanian crisis, the Western leaders should also emphasize that the issue was not whether the Baltic States should be free, but when.[61]

On April 3, Shevardnadze flew to Washington to finalize preparations for the forthcoming summit. This time, Baker wrote that he "seemed utterly distracted" and sometimes fell back on formal, ideological arguments or left it to the hard liners in his entourage to state the Soviet position.[62] Lithuania was the only subject on the first day's agenda, and Baker expressed genuine worry: "We do not want to see this deteriorate because it is going to have a direct effect on our relations. We have come so far in the last fourteen months. I do not want to see that undermined."[63] Shevardnadze pointed out the political constraints he faced on the Baltics. Baker retorted that the US Senate had just voted 93-0 to condemn Soviet actions in Lithuania. Both men were under considerable domestic political pressure, with little flexibility to reach a compromise. Shevardnadze had harsh words for Landsbergis, describing him as the man who played the piano rather than a true democratic leader. Baker was in a jam. Were he to persuade Landsbergis to travel to Moscow to negotiate with Gorbachev, he risked the accusation of carrying water for the Soviets. He was already considered overly protective of Gorbachev, and further pressure on the Lithuanians would surely backfire domestically.

President Landsbergis was helpless in the face of US wavering on the Lithuanian question. "This is Munich," he declared. "We feared that America might sell us [out]… I don't understand whether it is possible to sell the freedom of one group of people for the freedom of another. If that is so, then of what value is the idea of freedom itself?"[64] The

Lithuanian leader believed Baker might have told Shevardnadze that the US would overlook a limited degree of Soviet military intervention, but Baker's spokeswoman, Margaret Tutwiler denied that there was any such agreement: "Any suggestion of such is absolutely and totally false."[65]

With Lithuania refusing to suspend its declaration of independence, Gorbachev issued yet another ultimatum: over the Easter weekend, Lithuania must annul its independence declaration within forty-eight hours or face economic sanctions. On April 18, Moscow stopped the flow of oil to Lithuania's only refinery and shut off 84 percent of its natural gas. Only the minimum required for essential services would continue. Gorbachev also ordered the blockade of food and industrial spare parts.

CONGRESS INTERVENES

Not only congressional leaders but also conservative opinion leaders turned up the heat on Baker and the President to stand up to Gorbachev. William Safire, the *New York Times* columnist, kept up a stream of criticism against the administration's policy and its implementers.[66] He called on both Bush and Baker to stand up for freedom and respect for human rights: "We are playing out one of the great moral moments in modern history."[67] Members of the Senate and House demanded immediate diplomatic recognition for Lithuania, and moderate Republicans insisted on recognizing independence. The administration held a key bargaining tool: a trade agreement with the Soviet Union. Gorbachev badly needed this commercial agreement to prove to his domestic critics that he could bring economic benefits to the Soviet people. The US Congress now placed that agreement in serious doubt. The administration might negotiate a trade deal, but Congress made clear that it would not approve it. On April 16, the House of Representatives passed a nonbinding resolution by a 416-3 vote urging the President to recognize Lithuania's independence "at the earliest possible time."[68] The resolution was useful to Baker, who used it to pressure Gorbachev and Shevardnadze on the importance of a negotiated outcome with Landsbergis. But Baker was unwilling to risk cancellation of the Washington summit: too many other issues were at stake with the Soviets. In the end, the President presented the concluded trade agreement to Gorbachev, with the stern words that only Congress could approve it and grant the USSR Most Favored Nation status.

On April 27, nine senators denounced Bush's Lithuania policy, calling on the administration to renounce the trade agreement as ill timed. The senators, many of whom had backed Bush's foreign policy stands were unusually critical though they were careful not to attack the President personally. "I am appalled at the lack of sensitivity by the White House towards the Lithuanian people as they desperately struggle to reassert independence," said Republican Senator Gordon J. Humphrey. "To announce an agreement liberalizing trade with the Soviets, two days after the President revealed he would assess no penalty against the Soviets for their bullying of Lithuania, is callous and unfeeling in the extreme."[69] Baker had worked hard to maintain a bipartisan foreign policy, but the administration's perceived weak response to the crackdown in China, followed by the lackluster support for Lithuanian independence had legislators on both sides of the aisle hammering the State Department. The proposed trade agreement, to be signed in Washington at the May summit with the Soviets, galvanized both Democrat and Republican lawmakers to strongly criticize the President's foreign policy.[70]

Meanwhile, Baker needed time. For him German unification demanded priority over the Baltics. He called repeatedly for dialogue between Moscow and the Lithuanian leaders, but he had to walk the finest of fine lines. Despite his recent election as president, Gorbachev politically was much weaker. He was also increasingly vulnerable to the KGB, the generals, and apparatchiks, for whom *perestroika* had provided neither political nor economic benefits. Baker and Bush knew that if they pushed Gorbachev too hard, those hardliners would oust him on grounds that he was a puppet of the Americans. Despite Baker's insistence that he negotiate with the Lithuanian leaders, Gorbachev refused to see the delegation from Vilnius. Both sides understood the unspoken threat that the Washington summit might be canceled. Baker flew to Moscow for his final preparatory meeting to the summit. Laser focused and tough, Baker met with Gorbachev on Friday, May 18: "You must negotiate your way out of the Lithuanian crisis."[71] Gorbachev agreed, but postponed his meeting with the Lithuanian leader until June 12—after the Washington summit.

On that same visit, Baker met at Ambassador Matlock's residence with fifteen Soviet Jews 'refuseniks' who had been refused exit visas.[72] Sitting with them in a circle to avoid any suggestion of hierarchy, Baker listened carefully and assured them that he would bring up their individual cases with Gorbachev. But he knew that Kremlin hardliners were resisting the issuance of exit visas to Soviet Jews, who were likely to find brand new apartments in occupied territories seized from Palestinians. Arab allies of Moscow complained bitterly about this migratory pattern, which undermined years of Soviet diplomacy in the Middle East.[73] Nevertheless, it was important for Baker to listen to the 'refuseniks' complaints and to demonstrate that he was more than a hardnosed Texan lawyer. He had made a point of meeting with 'refuseniks' on many of his visits to Moscow. Now, more than ever, he needed to demonstrate that he had heart and a commitment to human rights. It failed, however, to convince Americans back home.

Back in Washington, Bush met with Lithuanian Prime Minister Kazimira Prunskienė on May 18, hoping she would be more flexible than Landsbergis. To assure the Soviets that Prunskienė was not receiving the protocol due to the prime minister of an independent country, the White House made her park outside the White House grounds, submit to a security inspection, and walk the hundred yards to the West Wing entrance. Prunskienė never complained publicly about this treatment, but after the meeting she criticized the President for doing nothing to help Lithuania. "Simply making statements that there should be cooperation and urging Lithuanians to sit down at the bargaining table is not sufficient at this time, when the Soviet Union is interfering in Lithuania's relationship with Western countries," she said.[74] She bitterly resented being told that Lithuania must suspend its declaration of independence before it could even start negotiations with Moscow.

Pressure to support the Lithuanians intensified in the United States. In May, George Will wrote "sealed borders, MiG overflights, journalists expelled, coordinated media disinformation, beatings, tanks rumbling through streets at 3 a.m., economic blockade; that is the sort of force – not gunfire – that Brezhnev primarily used in Czechoslovakia in 1968."[75] Will was influential within the Republican Party, and the criticism hurt Baker and the administration. The Baltic-American Freedom League found a supporter in Representative Steny Hoyer (D-MD), who argued for diplomatic recognition of the Baltic States' independence as he campaigned to be co-chairman of the US Commission on Cooperation and Security in Europe (CSCE).[76] Both the Lithuanian American and Estonian American communities lobbied Congress ferociously on behalf of the states' right of self-determination. Over the next few months, the Lithuanians agreed to discuss a transition to full separation from the Soviet Union in an effort to get Gorbachev to lift the economic embargo. On June 29, the Lithuanian parliament suspended the laws passed since its March 11 declaration of independence, and the Soviets lifted the embargo the following day. Conditions returned to a more tolerable level, while the Baltic States insisted on their independence as a *de jure* fact.

SHEVARDNADZE RESIGNS

From August 1990 onward, as Baker grew preoccupied with mobilizing a coalition against Saddam Hussein's invasion of Kuwait, developments in the Baltics slid to the bottom of his inbox. Nevertheless, the resignation of his good friend Eduard Shevardnadze on December 20 was a blow. The two of them had developed a friendship in addition to a close professional relationship. When Baker sought reasons for Shevardnadze's departure, his friend justified his resignation by saying that authoritarian tendencies had returned to the Kremlin. He did not have to be explicit: Baker understood that Gorbachev, to survive, had become dictatorial. Furthermore, Shevardnadze had never forgotten his Georgian roots. The intimate dinner they had enjoyed with their wives in Shevardnadze's Moscow apartment the previous year had impressed upon both Susan and James Baker the depth of Shevardnadze's nationalist sentiment.[77] If Gorbachev could send in tanks and embargo fuel and food in Lithuania, what might he do in Georgia? The Washington policy of supporting Gorbachev so long as he did not use force against the Soviet republics was becoming less tenable. On the day of Shevardnadze's resignation, the Soviets began military patrols on the streets of several Lithuanian cities to round up draft dodgers and enforce conscription laws.

In the US Congress, Senator Robert Byrd (D-WV) charged Baker with looking the other way while Gorbachev did as he pleased in the Baltics. Senator Bill Bradley (D-NJ) said "it would be a sad irony if the price of Soviet support for freeing Kuwait was American acquiescence in Soviet aggression against another illegally annexed country."[78] The only people with wry smiles were Deputy National Security Adviser Robert Gates and Defense Secretary Dick Cheney, whom Baker had criticized early in 1989 for their warnings about Soviet authoritarian behavior. The egg was now on his face, but Baker focused elsewhere.

ASSAULT ON THE VILNIUS TELEVISION TOWER

Whether Gorbachev himself, or the KGB together with military officers, decided to send armored tanks and military detachments with live ammunition to impose Soviet rule in Vilnius is open to debate, but at 2 a.m. on Sunday, January 13, 1991, their forces opened fire with live rounds. Thirteen people died, including a young woman who was crushed under a Soviet tank. Later that night, a technician from the Lithuanian television station broadcast ongoing events to European listeners. Landsbergis telephoned Gorbachev, but to no avail. Soviet soldiers took over critical infrastructure. Earlier that month in Latvia's capital, Riga, communist forces eager to return to Soviet rule took control of the Ministry of the Interior, but ordinary Latvians built barricades throughout the city center, determined to resist. In the protests at barricades, five people died. Baker refused to be distracted. He was focused on the looming military campaign to repel Saddam Hussein from Kuwait.

Five days earlier, he had been in Geneva talking to Iraqi Foreign Minister Tariq Aziz, giving Iraq a last chance to withdraw from Kuwait before the UN-approved deadline of January 15 for military action. Either to take advantage of Washington's focus on Iraq or seeking to push off the American deadline, the Soviets chose that time to do what they had done in Hungary in 1956, shortly after the Suez crisis.[79] Just the US and its allies were about to unleash missiles on Baghdad, Gorbachev chose to send Soviet military units into Lithuania. Was this meant as a distraction? Did the Soviet generals seriously believe they could delay the onset of the Iraq war? Did they underestimate the American ability to focus on two security threats at the same time?

Baker's staff described events in Lithuania as a sideshow that might have been considered a major crisis had there not been a larger crisis in the Middle East. The principal European expert at the NSC said, "This is a classic challenge to us as a superpower. We've got to prove to the world that we can walk and chew gum at the same time, that we can deal with two crises at once."[80] Bush gave a firm statement on Sunday, January 13, as he stepped off a helicopter to address the White House press pool. Resorting to violence "threatens to set back or perhaps even reverse the process of reform which is so important in the world and the development of the new international order."[81] He seriously considered rescinding the package of economic assistance programs he had promised only a month before to Gorbachev, but the need for a unified front on the eve of coordinated military action against Saddam Hussein took priority. Bush and Baker remained pragmatic and hard-headed. Despite the opprobrium of the Western world against the Soviet leaders, they would not allow events in the Baltic States to distract them from the major offensive against Saddam's forces. A secondary consideration was that Soviet generals would be watching the show of US firepower in Iraq. Twelve years later, Shevardnadze's successor as Foreign Minister, Aleksandr Bessmertnykh, admitted "the performance of the US technology was enormously effective and impressive."[82] Soviet anti-aircraft defenses placed in Iraq were blown away in the first few hours. The display of American military superiority impressed upon Soviet leaders the fact of their relative decline.

"PRAGMATIC IDEALISM"

It might be tempting to think that in this complex web of crises, President Bush was the realist and Baker the idealist. Bush left it to Baker to rescue the Chinese dissident Fang Lizhi and deliver a speech on democracy and human rights to the Dallas World Affairs Council. That distinction would be wrong. The two saw eye to eye on the need to find pragmatic solutions to international problems.

It is doubtful that Baker would have publicly stressed the principles of democracy and human rights without the strong pressure from Congress. Checks on authoritarian behavior, domestic or foreign, are often expressed through congressional statements and critical inquiries into executive action. Bush anticipated the outrage against China, and Baker ducked the verbal blasts by sending his deputy both to Beijing and then to Capitol Hill. In the first six months of the administration, he was still learning on the job. But as a skilled politician and knowing that Congress would again criticize the State Department for its lackadaisical support of democratic ideals—in Lithuania—Baker used congressional pressure as leverage in his talks with Soviet leaders. If Gorbachev was under pressure from hardliners in the Kremlin to prevent secession by the Baltic States, Baker was under pressure from Congress to stand up for their right of self-determination.

Baker upheld that principle but delayed its effect as he put other goals ahead of it: a unified Germany in NATO, and a global alliance against Saddam Hussein. Much later, in testimony before the Senate Foreign Relations Committee, Baker devised a new term to avoid the "cynicism of realism and the impracticality of idealism." He called it "pragmatic idealism." As Americans, he said, "we are a practical people less interested in ideological purity than in solving problems."[83] "Pragmatic idealism" took into account the complexity of the real world as well as the painful trade-offs that have to be made. There are no quick fixes or easy answers but only "the real world in which we must live, decide and act with due regard, of course, for our principles and our values."[84] Baker showed that he remained a follower of Ernest Bevin.

FOUR

EFFORTS TO TRANSFORM THE SOVIET ECONOMY

As the former Treasury Secretary, Baker was aware of the challenges facing the Soviet leadership as it sought to reform its centrally planned economy. The Soviet economy was a catastrophic failure with the centrally planned economy breaking apart.[1] GOSPLAN used outdated information and often misleading orders to command production levels at factories and farms throughout the USSR's eleven time zones. Consequently, any real gains in the socialist economy productivity were largely a statistical illusion.[2] General Secretary, Nikita Khrushchev had sought to introduce economic reforms by allowing decisions to be made at the factory and farm level, but his reforms had met with defiance from members of the Politburo. In 1964, Leonid Brezhnev forced Khrushchev out of power and furthered the central administrative-command-style government. His successors had approached reform tendentiously, conscious of the power of the CPSU who administered top down commands and frequently accepted gifts for waivers issued to 'mafia' friends. During the height of the Cold War, the US government viewed the corruption and poor economic performance as synonymous with a communist dictatorship, but the election of a Soviet reformer, Mikhail Gorbachev presented an opportunity.[3] He had announced measures to encourage productivity in the Soviet Union and needed to reduce international tensions with the United States and Western Europe in order to transform the Soviet economic system.[4]

The question for the Bush administration was how to respond? Should American entrepreneurs take advantage of Gorbachev's deregulation of foreign trade? Should they join the rush to invest in key Soviet industries as the European business community was doing? Should the US government offer Most Favored Nation (MFN) status and expand bilateral trade? Should it offer technical advice on financial matters? Baker understood that the Soviet economy presented an enormous challenge for both Western Europe and the US with implications for national security. Should Gorbachev stumble in his economic reforms, *perestroika* and *glasnost* would probably end. Kremlin apparatchiks who preferred the stability and personal benefits of the old system would surely bring the reforms to a grinding halt. Baker, therefore, had a direct interest in US policy toward engagement with the Soviets on economic and financial matters.

MIKHAIL GORBACHEV

Ending the stagnant Soviet economy was the reason behind the Politburo's choice of 54-year-old Mikhail Gorbachev when Premiere Konstantin Chernenko died on March 11, 1985: Gorbachev's intelligence, determination and energy made him the right man to introduce significant reforms to Soviet society. His claim to leadership depended on his ability to convince the younger generation of Soviet leaders that he could do something about the rigid structural problems and stagnation that beset the USSR. Gorbachev was highly educated, well travelled and in comparison to his fellow party leaders intellectually sophisticated. But as the longtime Soviet foreign minister, Andrei Gromyko noted Gorbachev "might have a good smile, but he has iron teeth."[5] As Central Committee Secretary in charge of Agriculture, he had shown those teeth when he ruthlessly dismissed party officials who failed to meet their annual production targets. Also, as a rising member of the communist party, Gorbachev said or did nothing to indicate that he was a radical reformer. He adulated party bosses as he climbed up within the Politburo structure, and he never challenged Premieres Brezhnev, Andropov or Chernenko. To them, he was a young, energetic and highly educated party member who would bring about reform, but not such radical change that would break the Soviet system. Back in March 1985, when Gorbachev assumed the post of General Secretary of the Communist Party no one dared to think of dissolving the system.

Gorbachev had plans. He would decentralize the state system and liberalize on the margins.[6] He would not succumb to bourgeois capitalism, but move toward a socialist market economy, whatever that meant. To do so, he gathered economists around him to learn how he might make the Soviet economy more productive. His focus in those early years was on transferring decision making down to the farm and factory level. The Cooperative Law turned managers into decision makers and entrepreneurs. Power over enterprises swung from ministries to local Communist party committees which organized "elections", but local managers ensured their own success despite loud criticism from workers. By 1989, local managers had effectively become quasi-owners of state enterprises.[7] They proceeded to buy from state subsidized enterprises at low prices and sell to the emerging private sector at high prices. Under Gorbachev, the dream of a workers democracy never became a reality.

Gorbachev himself was a neophyte in free market economics and struggled to determine what was politically acceptable. In July 1989, he established a Reform Commission headed by a leading reform economist, Leonid Abalkin whom he appointed a deputy prime minister. In January 1990, he named Nikolai Petrakov, a leading reform economist to be his personal economic advisor and two months later, he appointed a Presidential Council which included Stanislav Shatalin, another prominent reform economist. Within the space of a year, he had launched three distinct groups of economists to strategize: the Abalkin program which was radical, Prime Minister Nikolai Ryzhkov's program which was conservative and rejected private ownership and Grigori Yavlinsky's '400-day program' (later to become the '500-day' program) that was inspired by Poland's radical market reform. All three programs met strong criticism from members of the Supreme Soviet and Gorbachev did nothing. Then in September 1990, Gorbachev requested two alternative reform programs and members of the Congress of People's Deputies expected Gorbachev to adopt the more radical reform program. Instead, he criticized all the economic programs because they threatened financial stability. Then he asked a respected liberal academician Abel Aganbegyan to produce a synthesis of the various programs. When that synthesis coincided largely with Shatalin's program, Gorbachev criticized it roundly. In the end, the Supreme Soviet failed to adopt any economic program.[8] Gorbachev had good intentions, but he had no firm idea on how to transition the Soviet economy to a socialist market system. For many in the Politburo, macroeconomics was a bourgeois and unacceptable concept. Thus, Gorbachev would cherry pick from economists who had little exposure to western economic theories. Baker watched as Gorbachev listened to diverse economic plans, then jettisoned them to keep political peace. On June 29, 1989, Gorbachev told his Politburo colleagues "We have two years, maximum" to fix this. "Otherwise, we shall have to resign."[9]

Meantime, the nationalities question with growing ethnic tensions in the Baltics and the Caucuses complicated Gorbachev's management of the Soviet Union. He concluded that little could be gained in economic policy without profound political reform. Gorbachev's strength was his political acumen and ability to seek compromise. His skills were those of a man who could instigate change from within the system and in all major policy decisions from 1985 until 1990, Gorbachev identified the winners and avoided siding with losers.[10] The drawback was that he never made a clear-cut choice or formulated a lucid strategy. Boris Yeltsin, his nemesis, later gave this description to Newsweek, "He wanted to combine things that cannot be combined – to marry a hedgehog and a grass snake – communist and a market economy, public-property ownership and private-property ownership, the multiparty system and the Communist Party with its monopoly on power."[11] Rather than joust with Soviet politicians, Gorbachev preferred to tilt with a new American leader, George H.W. Bush and his national security team. He might also seduce US investors through his deregulation of foreign trade. With sales of American washing machines, televisions, perfumes and razor blades, he might dampen the growing Soviet dissatisfaction with his leadership.

US ENTREPRENEURS SEEK OPENINGS IN THE SOVIET MARKET

As Treasury Secretary, Baker had known that American businessmen were looking for opportunities to expand their enterprises in the Soviet market of close to 249 million people. Armand Hammer, whose cordial business relations with the USSR went back to the 1920s, had signed an agreement in April 1988 for Occidental Petroleum to help the Soviets build two plastics factories. Hammer hoped that this would provide Russia with consumer goods and improved living standards.[12] Baker was also acquainted with James Giffen, a New York investment banker with longstanding ties to Soviet officials. Giffen had used his investment bank, Mercator Corporation, to create an American Trade Consortium, which included Chevron, Del Monte, Eastman Kodak, Johnson & Johnson, and Archer Daniels Midland, in an effort to start joint ventures with Soviet industries. (Another member, Ford Motor Company, dropped out when it could not resolve its concerns over convertibility of the Soviet ruble and other issues.) Under Giffen's leadership, the consortium had signed a trade pact in March 1989 to manufacture up to $10 billion in consumer and industrial goods then in short supply.[13]

Over many years, Jim Giffen had cultivated relationships at the highest levels of the Politburo. The prospects were exciting, but when they tried to negotiate actual deals, corporate leaders discovered that discussions with factory managers still needed the approval of officials within the relevant Soviet ministries. Despite Giffen's cabinet-level contacts, frightened mid-level officials still fought to keep control of favorite "state orders" for goods.

Still, there were some successes for US and West European investors. Between 1987 and 1991, the world's largest McDonalds opened in Moscow, followed by a Pizza Hut. Gulfstream Aerospace negotiated to develop a new line of high-priced corporate jets with Sukhoi, the Soviet maker of the SU-27 Flankers and other fighter planes. Fiat built a new plant to manufacture 300,000 cars a year, and the Italian Ferruzzi Group developed 1.5 million acres of prime farmland. Five of Europe's largest banks joined with Soviet partners and launched the Moscow International Bank to finance new trade and investment as well as to train new Soviet bankers. Even Robert Haldeman, Richard Nixon's former chief of staff, showed up in Moscow as the developer of a new hotel. Despite bureaucratic hurdles, corporate managers and their lawyers found ways to develop joint venture partnership and gain a foothold in the Soviet market. However, as the Soviet economy deteriorated and challenges to Gorbachev rose in the winter of 1990, foreign investors grew skittish.[14]

Leaders of Giffen's Trade Consortium kept Baker's advisors at the State Department informed about what they heard and saw in their negotiations with Soviet leaders. But the bureaucratic maze involved in gaining any official permit doomed many hopes of profitable ventures and sustainable enterprises. Many in the GOP listened to these business leaders and sought to help them by proposing a trade agreement and granting the Soviets MFN status, but they remained deeply skeptical of the climate for business in the USSR. The American concept of the rule of law did not exist there, and transactions were undertaken with no assurance of fair rules to resolve disputes.

Gorbachev's economic reforms had loosened both wages and profits. Profitability became a mantra and industries freed from many former bureaucratic restraints quickly learned to behave like capitalists. Confronting strong demand for their products, they raised prices and guaranteed profits. The loosening of wages in order to buy social peace resulted in rising salaries and newfound purchasing power. However, this new demand for consumer goods, formerly out of range for ordinary citizens, created shortages. Consequently, anticipating empty shelves, men and women began scooping up goods and hoarding them.

The soap scandal was the perfect example of these colliding concerns. Fears arose in 1989 that soap producers would shift from cheap soap to fancier brands as the new economic rules came into effect. Soviet citizens therefore bought up the lower-priced soaps fearing shortages. When the self-fulfilling prophecy of shortages came true, citizens searched for any soap they could find and the Kremlin had to confront angry women who could not find soap at any price in the stores. Moscow introduced rationing of essential products and in 1989 striking Soviet miners in the Arctic Circle made soap one of their demands. Meantime, co-ops were discovered selling soap at six times the regular price, while doctors in Tajikistan reported patients whose tiny homes were so full of stockpiled soap that their children were suffering allergic reactions.[15] The Soviet economy was halfway between the old command economy and a pre-capitalist system trying to respond to market signals. How might Western governments respond?

BAKER GRAPPLES WITH SOVIET REFORMS

To guide him, Baker needed to understand whether the Soviet economy was, or was not collapsing. Just how bad was the Soviet economy? On his first visit to Moscow as Secretary of State in May 1989, he had sought Shevardnadze's advice. As the Bakers dined privately with the Shevardnadze in their official apartment, Baker raised questions about the Soviet economy. Shevardnadze seemed to dismiss these problems, focusing instead on the ethnic issues and the nationalities problem. Gorbachev's *perestroika* was entering its fourth year, and official Soviet statistics showed Soviet economic growth at 3 percent,[16] including a significant increase in agricultural production of meat, milk and egg outputs. Production of consumer goods, a measure of Gorbachev's economic plan, were up by 10 percent and overall industrial production had increased by 14 percent. The former Treasury Secretary was aware of the illusory basis on which Soviet statistics were issued and he remained highly skeptical of Shevardnadze's numbers. Only days before his departure for Moscow, he had listened to former Soviet ambassador Anatoly Dobrynin warn him "People are worried. Their biggest concern is the economy."[17]

By the spring of 1989, there existed shortages of basic foods and household necessities causing Susan Baker to wonder how Nanuli Shevardnadze had managed to find such succulent fares. She learned of a "second economy" that lay outside the realm of Soviet statisticians. It covered a generous greasing of palms for obtaining hard-to-find food. Nanuli could barter the recent gift of a French headscarf for the olive oil and garlic that flavored her meat. She could grow vegetables in her garden beside the dacha offered to Shevardnadze as a senior Communist Party official. In Moscow, half of the apartment repairs, 40 percent of auto maintenance, one third of appliance repair and 40 percent of all tailoring and shoe repair occurred beyond the sight of Soviet statisticians.[18] A Soviet economist calculated that approximately 20 million people made their principal living in a secondary economy and millions more moonlighted in it.[19]

Only four months after Shevardnadze's homely dinner, his focus had shifted. Now he was consumed by economic problems and their consequences for Gorbachev's *perestroika*. On the flight to Wyoming in September 1989, and with only Baker, Dennis Ross, Sergei Tarasenko, and their interpreters around him, Shevardnadze described a number of serious challenges. The price of oil had fallen, hovering between $16 and $19 a barrel diminishing the return on the USSR's major export commodity. Moscow's efforts to shift investment priorities was a herculean task. The economic structure required that 60 percent of capital investment support the production of fuel and raw materials. With a further 20 percent dedicated to the military, This left only 20 percent to invest in machine tool industries as well as the consumer sector. Meantime, citizens found employment in one of the 300,000 construction projects, way more than was needed, but reducing that number by two-thirds presented a real danger of mass unemployment. The ruble had only minimal value, with Soviet citizens holding overall 400-450 billion rubles, but they had nothing to spend it on; store shelves carried few consumer goods.

In March, the coal miners in the Arctic Circle had begun their strike for better living conditions, including soap, fresh foods and vegetables.

Earlier in July, a work stoppage in the Kuzbass city of Mezhdurechensk sparked 158 other strikes involving 177,862 miners in the same region.[20] Miner's strikes continued through the autumn. Land privatization was postponed and the budget deficit had grown exponentially. By December 1989, Soviet citizens were roiling with discontent. Gorbachev was well aware of the need for far reaching reform, but he believed that first he should establish a democratic political structure so as to gain public support for the private ownership of property that his economic reforms entailed. Gorbachev relied on advisers for economic policy, but he remained the master of political maneuvers and he trusted his own instincts to establish the right sequence of when and how to introduce the economic reforms. In retrospect, his political aptitude reflected Gorbachev's ignorance about economics. This would become clear the following year.

The year 1990 saw a Soviet economy slip from low growth rates to negative growth in all key indexes. CIA estimates showed a decline in GNP from annual growth rates of 2.25 percent in the years 1986-1989 to between -2.4 to -5% in 1990. Industrial output during the same period fell from 2.4 to -2.8 % and agricultural output fell from 11.2 to -3.6 percent.[21] Instead of focusing on the deteriorating economy, Gorbachev focused on the growing political divide between the Union of the Soviet Republics (USSR) and the stirring nationalities problem in the several republics, including the Baltic States. Rather than focus on economic problems, Gorbachev reverted to what he knew best, exerting political control over the Union.

In a congressional hearing early that year, Baker observed that Gorbachev "uses obstacles to further consolidate his authority. Then he takes steps to press political and economic reforms further. He does not fold; he does not call. He raises the stakes."[22] Baker also had to raise the stakes. Merely watching the degradation of the Soviet economy was not enough. The president had to do something and Baker favored a trade agreement. Bilateral negotiations to achieve this could facilitate discussions on pricing and value of the rubble. Besides, Congress was interested in a trade agreement with the Soviet Union as well as economic support for Eastern Europe. Immigrants from Poland, Hungary and Lithuania had become influential constituents.

However, a blockage existed to expanded trade with the Soviet Union. The call for increased emigration of Soviet Jews in the Jackson-Vanik Amendment of 1974 remained a lynchpin of US foreign policy, despite the fact that it violated the rules of the World Trade Organization (WTO) and impeded the grant of MFN status to the Soviet Union. Back in December 1989 at the Malta summit, Bush had offered important trade, investment and tax agreements, but all remained conditional on the Soviet codification and implementation of a new emigration law, a necessary condition under Jackson-Vanik. Baker therefore raised the question, should Congress terminate Jackson-Vanik, or should it continue to grant annual waivers?

APRIL 1990, BAKER TESTIFIES BEFORE THE HOUSE COMMITTEE ON WAYS AND MEANS

As the movement for freedom grew in the Baltic States and Gorbachev retaliated by threatening economic sanctions, the likelihood of a successful Washington summit at the end of May 1990 became increasingly doubtful. What could Washington offer Moscow, and under what conditions would they complete a trade deal? To clarify the administration's position, Baker accepted an invitation to testify before the House Committee on Ways and Means to discuss US policies toward the Soviet Union, including Soviet economic reforms.

Both in his written testimony and in his answers to questions on April 18 1990, Baker reiterated the phrase used since October 1989: "we want *perestroika* and *glasnost* to succeed. But we also recognize the limits of our influence." Now he expanded on his earlier testimony to provide a political explanation for Gorbachev's inability to carry out market reforms:

> These are practical and determined men, whose aim is not freedom for freedom's sake, but the modernization

of the Soviet Union. They are not the heirs of Locke and Montesquieu, but of the great Russian modernizers, like Peter the Great and Alexander II... He went on

Gorbachev and his allies must operate as members of a collective leadership with very different notions of what reform means . . . so the decisions are often compromises. This ad hoc policy development process is a severe handicap when the objective is to overhaul a society's basic attitudes toward economic life.[23]

Underlying the rationale for a restrained bilateral response was the recognition of limited US influence.

Chairman Dan Rostenkowski (D-IL) was eager to know the status of the Soviet trade agreement and receive confirmation that it would be submitted to Congress for its approval in spite of the restrictions imposed by the Jackson-Vanik Amendments. Committee members appeared more willing to trade with the Soviet Union and to seek waivers to Jackson-Vanik, but in the course of the hearing, Congressman Bill Archer (R-TX) went beyond Jackson-Vanik in cautioning his colleagues. While the Soviet Union maintained an aid program of approximately $15 to $16 billion to support Communist objectives in the world, including Cuba and Nicaragua, should not the US prioritize economic support to Poland and Hungary? Both had asserted their own independence from Moscow and were charting an independent course.[24] Archer typified those Republican members of the Ways and Means Committee who sought to restrict economic support for the USSR.

Baker's response was clear. The US does treat Eastern and Central Europe differently from the Soviet Union. He insisted that human rights issues remained a focus of US policy, among them the right to emigrate. The Soviets should recognize the right to self-determination and support the movements toward freedom and democracy in Eastern Europe. The Bush administration's policy was that the Soviet Union should both enact and implement their emigration laws before the US granted MFN status and passed the trade agreement.[25]

Throughout the hearing on April 18, Baker's willingness to listen and engage with congressmen on both sides of the aisle with courtesy and honesty won him applause. Thomas Downey (D-NY) captured a general sense when he congratulated Baker, "at a fulcrum point of history... I think you are really in a position and have been doing it of establishing, for the first time since the end of World War II, a bipartisan foreign policy vis-à-vis the Soviet Union."[26] Baker worked hard to sustain bipartisanship as he prepared for the forthcoming summit with Gorbachev.

MAY 1990 SUMMITRY

During his preparatory meeting in Moscow in mid-May 1990, Shevardnadze had warned Baker that that the Soviet Union needed $20 billion in credits and other aid to cushion Soviet society against the shocks of *perestroika*. It was clear that the Soviets had upped their demands since the Malta summit, the previous December. Baker replied that the only aid he could expect was in the form of expertise and technical training. Shevardnadze responded that the situation was dire and that hardliners, exasperated at the slow pace of reform and lack of consumer goods, were grumbling publicly.

On his second day in Moscow, Baker met for five hours with Gorbachev. In addition to the prime topic of German reunification, Gorbachev raised the Soviet economic problems. He complained to Baker that the conditions imposed on Soviet participation in the newly formed European Bank for Reconstruction and Development (EBRD) reflected US efforts to block west Europeans from helping the Soviet Union. Gorbachev went on, "As I watch the critical points in our relations, sometimes I have a sense that you want an edge, you may seek an advantage. In the past, I would note this, and I would watch this. Now I think our relations are such that I have an obligation to share my view with you."[27]

It was clear to Baker that Gorbachev faced deep troubles and did not need the US to complicate his life further. Baker made it clear that US taxpayers would not willingly finance Soviet loans so long as the Soviets were still subsidizing countries such as Cuba, Vietnam and Cambodia "to the tune of ten to fifteen billion dollars a year." He also noted that the Soviets continued to have 'very high defense expenditures.' Furthermore, on the domestic front Gorbachev needed to present a credible economic reform program. Gorbachev insisted that in carrying out his economic reforms he faced a significant gap in funding over the next few years. He reiterated Shevardnadze's request for $20 billion in loans and credits. The symbolic participation of the United States was important for him. He needed to cushion the impact of these reforms and acquire the means both to buy consumer goods and to convert defense installations into civilian production plants. Baker inferred from this request that Gorbachev needed to show that his policies had succeeded in getting the US to contribute to Soviet needs.[28] He was willing to offer expertise and technical training, but he had no loans or credit beyond the agricultural commodity guarantee program that had existed since the 1970s.

When the summit gathered in Washington on May 30, Gorbachev told Bush that he needed a trade agreement as a symbol to show the Soviet people that he was making progress with the west: "I need this."[29] Baker supported Gorbachev's request, knowing that opposition within the Senate would prevent ratification of the trade agreement. At Camp David the following day, Gorbachev repeated his request for the money and Bush understood that "when everything around [him] was falling to pieces" he would try to help, but "we couldn't hand them the $20 billion of financing they wanted unless they made deep economic reforms – and even then we didn't have the money."[30] Meantime, the President's signature on a trade agreement would save face for Gorbachev back home, where grumbling over empty shelves was rising. In Washington, members of the Soviet delegation who accompanied Gorbachev were criticizing him with no effort to be discrete. The American guests at a Soviet Embassy reception were astounded to encounter ridicule from the very members of the Soviet delegation accompanying Gorbachev. He was in trouble and needed to show his critics a US-Soviet trade deal, despite the lack of assurance that the Senate would ratify the accord. The May summit passed and more international meetings lay ahead.

SUMMER OF SUMMITS

In preparation for the NATO summit due on July 5, Gorbachev sent a letter to NATO leaders requesting long-term credits and other help. NATO members interpreted this as a means to enable a reunified Germany to join NATO. Bush was not willing to contribute financially, but Chancellor Kohl indicated his willingness to make significant contribution toward the costs of returning Soviet troops home.

Five days after the NATO summit, the leaders of the G-7 met in Houston at Rice University. When the question of financial support for the Soviet Union arose, President Bush responded that the US could provide technical assistance to the Soviets but no money so long as the Soviets continued to spend vast sums on their military and on support for Cuba.[31] To hearten Gorbachev, Bush joined his six fellow heads of government in issuing a brief statement that supported and encouraged Gorbachev to move toward a free market economy. The leaders also accepted Bush's proposal that the IMF study Soviet economic needs. This would allow IMF economists to advise the Soviet leaders, despite the fact that the Soviet Union was not a member of the multilateral institution. At Houston, the intervention in support of Gorbachev was minimal and reflected only the shortest period of summit deliberation. Nevertheless, the G-7's request that the IMF study Soviet economic woes indicated a path forward. To those who viewed the IMF study as a delaying tactic, Bush replied that he wanted "to make clear to President Gorbachev that he ought to view this outcome very positively." But he further noted, "I think Mr. Gorbachev understands that at this juncture sending money from the United States is not in the cards."[32]

KOHL CONTRIBUTES

Earlier, on May 4 that year, Shevardnadze had asked Kohl for financial assistance, assuring him that the Soviet Union was a good credit risk with massive resources. He requested a Deutsche Mark (DM) 20 billion credit line with a five-to-seven year payback term. Chancellor Kohl decided to be forthcoming. Recognizing that Germany would need to leverage its economic weight to gain Soviet acquiescence to unification and NATO membership, he was ready to negotiate trade and economic issues as part of the international recognition of a reunified Germany and the renouncement of all rights by the Four Powers.[33] He also promised to talk to his partners in the G-7 about a significant international commitment to the USSR, but he feared that other European leaders would be less generous. That May Kohl was ready to leverage German financial weight, recognizing that the price would be high. Nine days later, Teltschik flew secretly to Moscow with two prominent private bankers, Hilmar Kopper of the Deutsche Bank and Wolfgang Roller of the Dresdner Bank.[34] Teltschik's purpose was to secure credits for Gorbachev in exchange for his agreement on a unified German membership in NATO.[35] The deal was a tall order as both ordinary Soviet citizens and Kremlin hardliners opposed a united Germany in NATO. Memories of the Great War were still vivid and the prospect of a strong Germany allied to the West on its western flank remained objectionable to most Soviets.

In that May 14 meeting with the German bankers, Shevardnadze reiterated Gorbachev's request for DM20 raising it to 25 billion credit line. Due to the government's inability to pay interest on various outstanding debts, the Soviet government could no longer access the international credit market, a fact endorsed by Kopper and Roller. Recognizing that he would need Gorbachev's support for the next steps in the unification of the two Germanys, Kohl asked the two bankers to extend credit to the Soviet government.[36] They offered Gorbachev credits of DM5 billion as part of the overall German settlement.[37] In addition, the government offered DM730 million to pay for Moscow's 380,000 troops still stationed in the GDR.[38] Unspoken was the quid pro quo that the Soviets would accept the Two by Four framework for a united Germany.

By July 1990, the DM5 billion credits had been spent in part to repay old debts and Gorbachev needed more money. However, the chancellor's willingness to extend further credit conflicted with the bankers who were reluctant to expand business ties or extend loans to the Soviet Union because "its credit worthiness is impaired" and "the Soviet Union has stopped paying its bills." In their opinion, before extending further credits, the Soviet Union had to acquire the reputation as a reliable debtor.[39]

Kohl's offer of yet more credit arose when he and Gorbachev met in Moscow on July 14 before flying to Gorbachev's birthplace in the mountains above Stavropol. Foreign policy advisor, Teltschik joined the gathering. At that meeting, Kohl offered Gorbachev a total package of DM8 billion, most of which would go toward building houses and retraining Soviet soldiers upon their return home from the GDR. Gorbachev was visibly irked at the offer and insisted that Soviet calculations of the costs amounted to DM11 billion. This amount increased to DM16-18 billion when transportation and stationing costs were included.[40] The harshness of Gorbachev's tone surprised Kohl and Teltschik, but they recognized that tough bargaining was necessary to both ensure Soviet support for unification and keep Gorbachev in power. His successor might be even more demanding.

Two days after the meeting at Stavropol, Kohl telephoned Gorbachev to say that he could not offer the DM16-18 billion, but that Germany was willing to give DM12 billion. Gorbachev did not relent. He continued to bargain hard, implying that Germany unification might still be in doubt if more assistance was not forthcoming. Said Kohl, "That was the clear message. I realized I was obliged to offer the Soviet Union an additional DM3 billion interest-free credit."[41] The telephone negotiations had been extremely difficult, but when Baker learned of the plan, he was relieved that both leaders had struck a deal.[42] His focus on the Soviet Union and the German questions changed abruptly when Saddam Hussein invaded Kuwait on August 2, 1990. Swiftly, he turned his attention to the Gulf and mobilization of support within the UN Security Council, leaving it to others to follow economic troubles in the USSR.

GORBACHEV CONFRONTS GROWING CRITICISM

Despite the five economic plans presented to him, Gorbachev remained dissatisfied and scolded legislators in a September 21 meeting of the

Supreme Soviet for dragging their feet on an economic rescue plan. He asked for sweeping new emergency powers to stabilize the economy. Three days later the Supreme Soviet voted to give preliminary approval for a plan to transform the Soviet economy into a free-market system. However, the plan barely got off the ground before Gorbachev on October 16 submitted a scaled-back economic plan to the same legislature. It drew an angry response from Boris Yeltsin, his former ally on *perestroika* turned political rival.[43] Yeltsin called the program nothing more than an attempt "to preserve the administrative bureaucratic system."[44] He announced that he would ignore the Soviet Union's economic plan and set up for the Russian republic a currency, customs service and army. Furthermore, he would instigate a '500-day' transition to a free market economy beginning on November 1.[45] It was clear to observers in Washington that knives were drawn in Moscow's political battles, but Baker needed Gorbachev's continued support as he mobilized the international coalition to repel Saddam Hussein from Kuwait. The situation in the Soviet Union was becoming increasingly tenuous and the US government could not afford to get involved in the Gorbachev/Yeltsin dogfight. As their leaders squabbled, the lives of ordinary Soviet citizens deteriorated.

The Soviet economy was crippled with growing budget deficits and soaring inflation that dampened plans for rapid free-market innovations. Economists drafted economic reforms, some more radical than others, only to meet the reaction of legislatures who no longer accepted Gorbachev's will. The concepts of private property and a currency valued by market rates were heretical to many members of the Politburo. It was no wonder that Bush and Baker observed the efforts to reform the Soviet economy with a high degree of skepticism. Prospects of gradual economic reform were slim and budget deficits, inflation, and shortages of children shoes, winter leather gloves, and other consumer goods had made Soviet citizens increasingly angry.

Political reform was also in danger with Gorbachev under increased pressure from hardliners and military leaders to impose order on the economy and reject pressure for Lithuanian independence. The problems were monumental and there was a clear danger that the population would lose faith in Gorbachev and his reforms. Baker continued to listen to Shevardnadze's economic concerns; the corporate lawyer and former treasury official thinking through ways in which the US government might help. Beyond pursuit of a trade agreement, he proposed to the president that Secretary of Commerce, Bob Mosbacher lead a business delegation to Moscow. Clearly, a visit by leading American businessmen would demonstrate confidence in Gorbachev's leadership. At the same time, successful corporate leaders might identify where their investments could yield profits and where they would meet bureaucratic rotten eggs.

US BUSINESS DELEGATION SEEK OPPORTUNITIES IN MOSCOW

On September 9, 1990, Baker and Mosbacher led a business delegation to Moscow. The delegation included CEO's of major US corporations as diverse as Don Kendall, the veteran investor who had brought Pepsi and Pizza Hut to the Soviet Union and Ken Derr of Standard Oil of California to two younger entrepreneurs, eager to establish a YPO chapter in Moscow.[46] Others came from Texaco, Sealand Service, Dresser Industries and Dwayne Andreas from Archer Daniels Midland, one of the world's largest grain companies. One of the YPOs, Jim Jamieson recalls the excitement of participating in an entrepreneur-led economic revolution that would transform the communist world. Discussing his hopes with Ann Daud of Fortune Magazine, Jamieson shared his vision that "entrepreneurs were the true foundation of economic development."[47] There had to be thousands of opportunities for an entrepreneur of modest ambitions to make money and help resuscitate capitalism in the reopening of the Soviet Union.[48]

Led by both Baker and Mosbacher, the delegation attended a meeting with Gorbachev and his economic team in the Kremlin on September 13. Gorbachev dominated the discussion, confronting Baker with the Jackson-Vanik Amendment that prevented the grant of MFN until leaders allowed Soviet members of the Jewish faith to emigrate. At that meeting, Gorbachev was combative, challenging Baker, "Will you find a way to take care of our many immigrants? I'll tell you what, if I release the Jews, I will do it only on one consideration. You take them all. You give each one a visa to come to the United States. Mr. Secretary it would ruin you."[49] Baker refrained from answering. He might push back on arms control, but now he sought to encourage this delegation in their search for business opportunities. He, therefore, avoided a fight with the man upon whom so much reform depended.

Meantime, the delegation had questions: should they partner with the central government or with the republics? Who were the contact persons needed to get things done in a country without adequate procedures for private business? In a subsequent meeting with Moscow's mayor, Gavril Popov advocated the buying and selling of raw commodities in order to earn hard currency. He lamented that half of agricultural production was lost for lack of grain storage and suggested that American investors construct temperature controlled storage facilities. The future lay in new technology and economy wide reforms. Two days later, in a meeting with Gorbachev's chief economist, Leonid Abalkin outlined his economic plan: one year to move to a market economy, approval of a new union treaty and review of a 50 million ruble budget deficit. The back-to-back meetings had left many in the delegation worn out and irritable. Their Soviet interlocutors had contradicted each other; there was no single plan, only projects on paper. The price of transition to a market economy was mind-boggling, but the price of doing nothing was already too high. 50 million people in the Soviet Union were unable to meet basic needs; there were chronic shortages of milk, meat and other staples. The problems were greater than optimistic entrepreneurs could solve. Only the US government, in coordination with other nations could help Gorbachev out of his economic catastrophe.

BAKER APPEARS BEFORE THE SENATE FINANCE COMMITTEE, OCTOBER 4, 1990

Three weeks after the meeting in Moscow with Gorbachev and the business delegation, Baker made the unusual move of testifying before the Senate Committee on Finance. This committee exercised no oversight over the State Department, but Baker knew its members from his days as Treasury Secretary, and he sought to emphasize the consequences of a failing Soviet economy.

With his written testimony submitted for the record, Baker delivered his remarks orally, capturing the attention of the committee members. Here was the nation's foremost diplomat demonstrating his familiarity with economic issues, born of his three and a half years at the helm of the Treasury department. Senator Lloyd Bentsen buried the hatchet of a bitter 1988 presidential campaign in which he had run as the Democratic vice presidential candidate to make peace with then GOP campaign chair, James A. Baker III. Baker would not focus on the US economy, as in previous years, but analyze the Soviet economy since 1985 when Gorbachev came to power with a mandate to reform. He explained to the committee the effects of Soviet economic reform programs on the United States and how US trade and economic policies could affect the fundamental changes underway in the Soviet Union. Despite a competing event—a joint session of Congress to listen to the President of Mexico—both Democratic and Republican senators stayed to hear the Secretary of State. His underlying message was that the Bush administration would be cautious, mindful that US national security interests guide any response to Soviet economic troubles. He knew, as well, that many of his listeners were reluctant to give economic aid to an enemy of forty-five years.

Gorbachev's reforms were staggering tasks requiring not only new laws but a rethinking of social attitudes by millions of people accustomed to living by the familiar Soviet phrase, "they pretend to pay us, and we pretend to work."[50] The Soviet economy had been stagnant since Khrushchev's time, and previous reform efforts had made little difference. The underlying problem was that comprehensive reform was politically difficult to implement because many in the Soviet leadership remained ideologically resistant to change. The reforms were piecemeal. Designed in committees by Politburo members holding distinct opinions, the proposals sometimes contradicted each other. For example, the reform of cooperative enterprises should allow private ownership in the cooperative, but because there was no real competition, the reform led to plentiful opportunities for monopolistic behavior. Profits were not reinvested in the cooperative but were siphoned off and shared among the new owners. Areas where competition might arise, such as printing and medical cooperatives, were excluded from the reforms. Furthermore, the wide latitude on taxation of cooperatives allowed favored arrangements and invited corruption. These piecemeal efforts led to bottlenecks, higher budget deficits, and the printing of more rubles at increasingly less value.

In his opening statement, the former Treasury Secretary laid out the steps the Soviet leadership needed to make in order to transform their economy. These included the introduction of market prices, stabilization of the currency and backing it with gold, fiscal restraint, and market competition. Baker's purpose was to support Soviet efforts to achieve a more open society with a transformed economy that would produce greater stability on a global stage. But he knew this transformation could not be magically accomplished all at once. In his testimony, he recommended practical steps the Soviets could take that would demonstrate their seriousness in moving toward a more open system.

To support Soviet reforms, he recommended the following US policies:

- A more stable international environment in which regional conflicts were resolved. Meantime, Baker remained dismayed by ongoing Soviet support for Cuba, Nicaragua, and other regional conflicts;
- Appropriate arms control, such as the Conventional Forces in Europe Agreement (CFE), a mutually beneficial strategic arms reduction treaty (START), a Chemical Weapons Accord, and verification measures to all agreements in order to reduce the risk of a surprise attack;
- Peaceful reform in Eastern Europe, allowing for self-determination and fundamental freedoms, human rights, and the rule of law.

- Working together as partners in addressing the scourge of drugs, the challenges of environmental damage and the threat of terrorism;
- Some technical and economic assistance as the Soviets restructured their economy; and
- The possibility of Soviet membership in the World Bank and International Monetary Fund, if it made sufficient progress with its reforms.

Elements of this policy were already in place, but Baker was clear that the US offer of help must depend on the Soviets restructuring their own economy. He concluded his remarks stating, "the jury is still out… on whether he [Gorbachev] will ultimately succeed or fail."[51]

A persistent line of questioning from the senators was on the trade agreement then under negotiation and the proposed grant of MFN.[52] In response to Senator Bentsen's question on what the US stood to gain from this trade agreement, Baker responded that expanded commercial relations in nonstrategic products could benefit both sides, so long as Soviet trade was no longer subsidized. Senator John Chafee (R-RI) reminded Baker that the Europeans were galloping ahead of American businessmen to take advantage of the vast Soviet markets, and he urged him to lose no time in taking up the economic opportunities. Senator Max Baucus (D-MT) urged Baker to use the waiver provision in the Jackson-Vanik amendment. At that time, the United States was the only country that had not yet offered MFN to the Soviet Union.

Both Senators Moynihan (D-NY) and Danforth (R-MO) raised other issues. Why should the US support the Soviet economy while its leadership continued to build up its military establishment? Baker responded categorically that the US government should avoid throwing money at this Soviet problem. However, we should work closely with our allies to encourage the development of the private sector. He was more supportive of assistance to Poland and Hungary, which he described as "democratic governments seeking to survive," than to the Soviet Union. The way forward was through the development of commercial relations. As the hearing ended, Moynihan thanked him "for essentially an interesting morning."[53] Baker had gained the senator's support, but with no prospects for US grants or loans, he needed potential foreign donors. He would approach the Saudi King. After all, he had protected the Saudi kingdom against a probable Iraqi invasion.

SAUDI ASSISTANCE TO THE SOVIET UNION

In October 1990 and with the intent of raising US$2 to 3 billion, the Soviet minister for foreign trade had led a delegation to Riyadh. According to the Saudi official, the Soviets had pleaded poverty and said they had lost $20 billion in trade with Iraq because of the Gulf crisis.[54] Baker followed up the Soviet request. With the goal of holding the anti-Saddam coalition together, Baker was willing to ask Saudi Arabia to lend the Soviet Union $1 billion with additional financial aid likely from other Gulf countries. Coupled with similar pledges of assistance from other Gulf States, the Saudi loan would help Moscow at a time when popular unrest was growing. The timing of the public announcement on November 28 coincided with the upcoming UN Security Council debate on the use of "all necessary means" to repel Iraqi forces from Kuwait. The Saudi funds ensured that Moscow would remain allied with Baker's coalition.

The Saudis were not alone in their support for Moscow. Kuwait's ambassador to Moscow announced that Kuwait was prepared to lend the Soviet Union $1 billion as part of a total $6 billion package from the Gulf States. Furthermore, Qatar's finance minister also visited Moscow. It was clear to all that Soviet participation in the anti-Iraq coalition was crucial to its success.

US RECESSION OF 1990-91

Meanwhile, beginning in July 1990 (and lasting for 8 months), the US economy entered a mild recession which also affected the US capacity to provide financial support for the Soviet leader. The recession was caused by a real estate collapse, turbulence in the stock market, and failures in the Savings & Loan industry. Also, with Bush's determination to defend Kuwait against the Iraqi invaders, oil prices had spiked and the prospect of war made the markets jittery. Would taxes have to rise? It seemed that everybody was deleveraging at once. Compared to previous recessions, that of 1990 to 1991 was mild, with GNP declining by 1.3 percent, unemployment rising to 7.8 percent and inflation rising to 6.5 percent. The greatest impact from rising inflation, the threat of war in the Persian Gulf, and a rise in gasoline prices was the fall in consumer confidence.[55]

The absence of cable TV business networks and the government's steady management of the economy led investors to maintain confidence in the US ability to respond to world events wisely. After all, Bush and his economic team were children of the Depression, veterans of World War II, and people who had exhibited steady hands during the Cold War. Their soundness avoided uncertainties in the market and avoided an investment and consumption freeze. But the recession was significant enough that the President's team could not be seen offering financial aid to the Soviet Union while employment and consumer confidence fell in the United States. Throughout the deliberations over the form of support for Gorbachev, the domestic economic context remained a critical factor. Baker was keenly aware of the internal constraints, but he had one program that he could expand: agricultural credits.

COMMODITY CREDIT CORPORATION (CCC)

Since the height of the Cold War in 1974, the United States had extended commercial credit guarantees to the Soviet Union. This enabled the Soviets to access private financing for the purchase of US agricultural commodities on a commercial basis. American farmers benefitted from these credit guarantees as they kept prices high for US farmers, and at the same time enlarged the market for American grains in Brazil, Algeria as well as the Soviet Union.

In October 1990, President Bush (with Baker's strong concurrence) raised the commercial credit limit for the Soviet Union to $1 billion. In June 1991, the credit limit rose to $1.5 billion before falling to $1.25 billion in November 1991 and $1.1 billion in April 1992.[56] This additional economic support for the Soviet Union did not have a serious impact on the US budget because the increased price for farmers reduced their federal price support. Baker argued that it was a win-win situation. A higher credit ceiling meant increased sales of wheat to the Soviet Union with mutual benefit to US farmers. Senators from farm states welcomed the proposal and only a few grumbled about the risk of nonpayment and probability of calls upon the federal government to pay the guaranteed price.

From December 1990 until October 1992, the United States offered $5.6 billion in Department of Agriculture credits guarantees to the Soviet Union and its successors, Russia and the newly independent states.[57] Apart from the CCC, Baker was cautious in using other financial instruments at the government's disposal. Pressure was building upon both him and Bush to provide grant aid to the Soviet Union. Both demurred. Gorbachev had good intentions, but he did not know how to transition to a market economy. They watched as a series of economic plans was tried then jettisoned to keep political peace.

THE "GRAND BARGAIN"

In November 1990, Professor Graham Allison, the Douglas Dillon professor of government at Harvard's Kennedy School met Grigory Yavlinsky, the prominent Soviet reform-minded economist and former first deputy prime minister of the Russian Federation. Together, they drafted a joint program for the Soviet Union's transformation to democracy and the market economy.[58] They presented their plan to US, Soviet and European leaders ahead of the 1991 G-7 meeting in London. Baker received Allison's report in June that year while negotiating with Israeli and Arab leaders for a Middle East conference. He was fully aware that Soviet prices were rising rapidly, output had fallen by close to 10 percent and foreign trade had plummeted with imports falling by more than 40 percent in the first quarter of 1991.

Yavlinsky and Allison wrote that the US had an opportunity to spearhead an international effort "that will, over a decade lead to democracy and a market economy in the Soviet Union." There was a "grand bargain" to be achieved in which international technical assistance, credits, loans and grants would enable the democratic reforms to succeed. They reminded the President and Baker, as well as listeners in Congress, that economic chaos after World War I had bred extremism in which Nazism took root and brought Hitler to power. They argued that Western nations spend more than $250 billion annually in military defense against Soviet threats, a sum that could be reduced by investing in the successful transformation of the Soviet system. Their grand bargain argued that a failure of the Soviet economy would lead to a failure of political reforms:

> The principal reason why Soviet reform efforts strike such sympathetic notes in the West is not promised slow-down in Soviet tank production ... [but] the prospect of nearly 300 million more human beings having the opportunity to enjoy the freedoms of a democracy and the prosperity of a market economy must be in the West's enduring interests.[59]

In Allison's words, the US faced a choice. It could provide assistance to the Soviet Union in its reforms or it could "attempt to sit on the sidelines." He believed that the US could not escape "a game in which its vital interests are at stake."[60] The report recommended that international donors provide significant grants and the IMF, World Bank and the newly created European Development Bank provide the technical assistance as well as loans and credits. Disbursement of aid would begin in 1992 and continue through 1995. The authors also hoped that with institutional support, significant private sector capital would begin to flow in during this period, with the energy sector leading the way.

In testimony before the US Senate Committee on Commerce, Science and Transportation, Allison stressed that the "grand bargain" was a step-by-step process, strictly contingent on the Soviet Union delivering on the recommended economic reforms.[61] Poland, Hungary and Czechoslovakia were complying with the conditions imposed on its aid program and the Soviet leadership should do the same. In his testimony, Allison stated that the US should not put any money down on the table: "No bag of billions up front, at all, none." Instead, the Soviet leadership had to comply with IMF and World Bank recommendations in order to access loans and assistance "which would then be backed by governments."[62] The next step was for the Soviet leadership to reveal its gold and dollar reserves which information was not shared with the IMF or the World Bank.

Baker considered that Yavlinsky was a serious economist and did not push aside the report. However, he knew that the president was adamant in his rejection of grant aid to Gorbachev. Both Scowcroft and Treasury Secretary Nicholas Brady responded that giving money to the Soviet government was "like throwing money down a rat hole."[63] Baker's challenge therefore was how to respond to the grave economic deterioration in the Soviet Union in the absence of any practical Soviet program. Furthermore, any program should avoid negatively affecting the US economy and congressional support for his foreign policy. Baker juggled several complex problems on his plate.

JULY 1991, THE G-7 MEETING

In the summer of 1991, The new Secretary of State was focused on getting Syrian President Hafez al-Assad to attend the Middle East conference and the G-7 summit was somewhat of a distraction, except for the encounters with heads of government whose support he needed to bring both Palestinian and Israeli leaders to the negotiating table. The Soviet Union was not a member of the G-7 and two months before the gathering in London, the White House had stated that Gorbachev would not receive an invitation. It was a "non-starter."[64] Bush and Baker wanted to avoid Gorbachev taking advantage of the world stage and forcing western leaders into making early commitments of enormous financial aid.[65] However, as the date approached, the

President changed his mind, becoming both more flexible and more generous. Economic issues had now become as important as arms control in bilateral relations. Thus, Gorbachev received an invitation, but Baker stressed at a June speech in Copenhagen that the US had ruled out "the big bang" approach.[66] In other words, Baker rejected Allison and Yavlinsky's "grand bargain."

Gorbachev had talked to Professor Graham Allison before leaving Moscow and showed him the latest iteration of his economic plan that called for a Western promise to assist the Soviet Union in exchange for a Soviet pledge to accelerate reforms. Yavlinsky had drafted the latest plan, but remained skeptical that Gorbachev would stick with it, fearing that he was doing nothing more than give G-7 leaders the impression of greater Soviet willingness to undertake necessary reforms.[67] Western leaders expected Gorbachev to arrive with a comprehensive package of specific reforms, sufficient for them to instruct the IMF and World Bank to begin extending loans. The seven governments had ruled out an immediate large-scale infusion of cash and they remained divided on their willingness to help the Soviet Union. Gorbachev's principal supporter, Germany kept pushing for more technical assistance. France and Italy stood with the Germans, but others were less enthusiastic, including the Americans. As one senior British official said, the US delegation was "behaving in a most obstinate way, making it hard to assemble a package."[68]

Bush and Baker were cautious. US intelligence had informed them that Gorbachev was under considerable domestic pressure to deliver consumer goods, impose order and resist calls for independence from the Baltic nations. However, Gorbachev was their friend and loyalty was important. At a minimum, G-7 leaders could agree on giving the Soviet Union associate membership to the IMF and World Bank with instructions to develop programs that would assist the Soviet transition to a market economy.

Beyond that, Baker offered a few proposals to ensure that Gorbachev "will not leave empty-handed," but he offered few specifics beyond reiterating promises made at the CSCE conference in Berlin one month earlier. The US could provide expert advice and small grants from the West to help the Soviet Union reform its food distribution system, attract investments in oil and gas and convert its defense industries to civilian use.[69] Nevertheless, Baker held serious concerns that Gorbachev continued to avoid providing specifics on his plan for property rights, the legal framework to underpin a market economy and the relations between the central government and the Soviet republics. He knew that Bush and Gorbachev still had a private luncheon at the US Embassy in London to follow the formal G-7 meetings and a forthcoming Summit meeting in Moscow at the end of July. There was still time for Gorbachev to provide them with specific plans on key economic issues, but further challenges lay ahead. Yavlinsky, having drafted the June version of the comprehensive economic plan, resigned rather than be associated with Gorbachev's economic generalities and half measures.[70] Gorbachev presented no comprehensive economic plan to the G-7 leaders and failed to answer questions on how European loans had been spent. Some suggested that they had been diverted to North Korea.[71] The White House was resigned to Gorbachev's inability to deliver market reforms.

Meantime, Baker had problems closer to home. In Central America, Cuba remained a menacing interventionist in El Salvador, a Contra-Affair had damaged the Republican Party's reputation and General Noriega, the Panamanian leader had thrown out the election results to remain in power. While not a priority for Baker, he nevertheless could not be seen to ignore problems so close to home.

Baker consults President Bush, Oval Office. *NARA, courtesy of the George H.W. Bush Presidential Library.*

Golf game with President and Scowcroft, Andrews Airforce Base. *US government photograph, courtesy of the Baker Institute for Public Policy.*

Mikhail Gorbachev greets Baker, Kremlin, May 1989.
US government photograph, courtesy of the Baker Institute.

Baker and Mexican Foreign Minister Solana sign
agreement in the presence of both presidents, June 1990.
NARA, courtesy of the George H.W. Bush Library.

President confers with Baker, Scowcroft and Chief of Staff John Sununu in the Oval Office, 1990. *NARA, courtesy of the George H.W. Bush Library.*

Toasting Shevardnadze at Jackson Lake Lodge, September 1989. *US government photograph, courtesy of the Baker Institute.*

Consulting with Hans Dieter Genscher, June 1990.
US government photograph, courtesy of the Baker Institute

Consulting with PM Thatcher and Foreign Secretary Hurd, Downing Street. *US government photograph, courtesy of the Baker Institute*

FIVE

TESTING SOVIET INTENTIONS IN THE AMERICAS

One of Baker's priority as Secretary of State was to restore a bipartisan approach to foreign policy within the US Congress. In his efforts to restore mutual trust between the parties over foreign policy, the challenge came not only from Democrats but also from Republican conservatives, many of whom considered President Reagan's outreach to Moscow romantic and unsustainable. To these conservatives, Baker had to demonstrate that the incoming Bush administration would make hard-nosed calculations to protect US national security. At the same time, he had to convince the Democrats that the Bush administration considered diplomacy a genuine option in resolving international conflicts. He decided that Central America, known as the 'holy grail' of both Democrats and conservative Republicans, should become the first test case.

The civil wars in Nicaragua and El Salvador had dragged on for close to a decade, representing two of the proxy wars through which the US and USSR fought the Cold War. Baker recognized that Soviet withdrawal of support for the Sandinista government of Nicaragua and from Marxist inspired guerilla forces in El Salvador would demonstrate Gorbachev's commitment to improving relations with the United States.

Openly making these countries a test case for Gorbachev might also convince Republican conservatives that the Bush administration was tougher in dealing with the Soviets than Reagan had been.

Central America had been a running sore in Congress since the early 1980s. The region's civil wars pitted those supporting liberal democracy and capitalism against a Marxist-Leninist alternative. In El Salvador, the government's failure to reign in death squads against civilians had made the conflict highly contentious in national media, in churches, and on college campuses. These divisions had spilled over into heated debate in the US Congress, whose members were divided on the issue. Republican Senator Jesse Helms supported the Salvadoran right-wing party created by Roberto d'Aubuisson. From the other side of the aisle, Democratic Senator Chris Dodd accused d'Aubuisson of masterminding the assassination of Archbishop Oscar Romero in 1980; a charge later confirmed by a UN investigation. Confronted by guerilla forces who espoused Marxist ideology and received material support from Warsaw Pact countries via Cuba, both the Carter and Reagan administrations had provided significant military and financial aid to El Salvador's government. That aid had not led to victory for government forces, but to a stalemate. For Baker, the issue was how to resolve that impasse because it affected broader relations between Washington and Moscow.

Meantime, Fidel Castro was eager to maintain his influence in Central America and sustain revolutionary movements that he hoped would pin down, if not defeat, the imperialist power to the north. Contesting this policy in the 1980s was President Reagan, whose administration, in addition to supporting El Salvador's government, had provided substantial military support to the Nicaraguan Contras. When Congress imposed a ban on further financial and military support for Contra leaders, National Security Advisor John Poindexter, his deputy Robert McFarlane, and Lt. Col. Oliver North searched for alternative sources of funds. With the active encouragement of CIA director Bill Casey, they created an ingenious but illegal sale of US arms to the embargoed Iranian regime in exchange for cash to buy weapons for the Contras. Too clever by half in its effort to circumvent congressional oversight, the infamous Iran-Contra scandal scarred the final years of Reagan's presidency. At the time, Baker was Secretary of the Treasury and deliberately sidelined from this scheme within the NSC. While he knew that Congress had prohibited US support for the Contras, he could rightly claim to be ignorant of the trade of Iranian arms for Contra cash until the scandal hit the press.

Both the Nicaraguan and Salvadoran civil wars had clouded any effort to improve relations with the Soviet Union. However, Gorbachev's focus on *perestroika* and *glasnost* required better relations with Washington in order to lower defense expenditures and devote resources to internal reforms. Therefore, in August 1987, the Soviet Foreign Ministry urged Nicaraguan President Ortega to seek a negotiated solution to the conflicts in both Nicaragua and El Salvador, and the following year the Soviets reduced their delivery of oil to the Sandinista government. The most significant break came in December 1988, when Gorbachev announced to the UN General Assembly that the Soviet Union would no longer support wars of revolutionary nationalism.[1] His speech raised the expectation that Moscow would stop supporting both the Sandinista government and the FMLN in El Salvador. Moscow would still support Cuba, but American officials believed Gorbachev's 'new thinking' might change that too. President-Elect Bush met with Gorbachev on New York's Governor's Island shortly after his UN speech and quietly decided to add Central America to his review of foreign policy toward the Soviet Union.

Baker did not attend that meeting, but he agreed with Bush's shift in policy. If President Bush hoped to improve relations with the Soviet Union, he and Baker had to create trust on Capitol Hill and restore a bipartisan approach toward resolving the proxy wars that had pervaded Soviet-US relations since the 1950s. Later, at Aronson's recommendation Baker persuaded the President to make Central America the first test of Gorbachev's "new thinking" Gorbachev should demonstrate his need to improve relations with the United States by ending support for revolutionary forces in El Salvador and Nicaragua. Baker knew that Moscow's actions in Central America ran through Havana. While Washington supported El Salvador's government and Nicaragua's paramilitary opposition (the Contras) against Daniel Ortega's government, Cuba supported the Salvadoran guerrilla opposition, the *Frente Farabundo Marti' de Liberación Nacional* (FMLN) and the Nicaraguan Sandinista government (FSLN).[2] To both, Fidel Castro provided political advice, logistical support, radios and arms shipments from the Soviet Union.[3] He also offered rest and recreation for wearied leaders on Cuban beaches.

Early in 1989, Baker told the President that the US should "subject the Soviets to Chinese water torture on this subject. We'll just keep telling them over and over – drop, drop, drop – that they've got to be part of the solution in Central America, or else they'll find lots of other problems harder to deal with."[4] Bush endorsed this approach, writing to Gorbachev on March 27 "It is hard to reconcile your slogans… with continuing high levels of Soviet and Cuban assistance to Nicaragua. There is no conceivable military threat that justifies that assistance. And now, at a point when we are clearly charting a new course, your assistance is almost certain to be used to undercut [our] diplomatic effort…"[5].

To carry out this new policy, Baker needed an outsider with knowledge of the area and a fresh perspective on possible solutions. He sought someone with credibility for both Democrats and Republicans in Congress. At the suggestion of Republican Congressman Henry Hyde, he recruited Bernard Aronson to be his Assistant Secretary of State for Inter-American Affairs (ARA). Aronson was a former White House speechwriter and Director of Policy for the Democratic National Committee. He had become involved in the region on a human rights mission to El Salvador in the early years of its civil war, after which he worked with centrist Democrats in both House and Senate such as Les Aspin, Chuck Robb, and Sam Nunn to forge a bipartisan policy towards U.S. assistance to the Contras. Both the newly minted Secretary of State and his counselor, Robert Zoellick believed that Aronson could reach out to centrist Democrats and support the creation of a bipartisan policy in Central America.

Baker tasked Bernie, as he was known, to draft policy recommendations for the region. In a "confidential and highly sensitive" memorandum drafted in late January 1989, Aronson wrote "The level of aid flows from the Soviet bloc to Nicaragua, the FMLN and to Cuba and the expectations of future levels of aid will significantly, and I believe, decisively influence the leverage we can bring to bear in a regional diplomatic initiative and its prospects for success on terms acceptable to the United States."[6] He went on "I believe the only way we can develop that degree of leverage is by making the Soviet bloc role in Central America the first and initially most important issue in our bilateral relations with the Soviet Union."[7]

In Aronson's analysis, the solution to Central America's conflicts lay in supporting regional diplomacy based on the Esquipulas Treaty, which in the words of its author President Oscar Arias made democracy the key to peace. Instead of arming their preferred parties, the Soviet Union and the United States should withdraw from direct involvement in their civil wars and use their collective leverage to press for negotiated solutions to the conflicts in Nicaragua and El Salvador. The principles enunciated by the five presidents at the colonial Guatemalan town of Esquipulas should guide US policy. Diplomacy, rather than military solutions, should become the preferred policy. Consequently, Baker asked Aronson to join him when he visited Moscow in May 1989. He would follow Aronson's advice and make the withdrawal of Soviet arms and other support for the Sandinistas and the FMLN the first test of Soviet intent to improve relations with the United States.

Calling for the Soviets to cooperate in Central America was nothing new. Since 1987, Reagan and Secretary of State George Shultz had sought Gorbachev's cooperation on Nicaragua and El Salvador. Aronson's predecessor, Elliot Abrams, had met twice with his Soviet counterparts: Vladimir Kazimirov, the head of the Latin American division at the Soviet Foreign Ministry, and his successor, Yuri Pavlov. He had taken a confrontational stance with both officials, demanding the withdrawal of Soviet support for the Nicaraguan Sandinistas as well as pressure on Fidel Castro to cease support for the FMLN in El Salvador. That approach had not worked. Baker chose instead to work with the five Central American Presidents. They would approach the problem in a regional forum while maintaining Washington's commitment to support the Salvadoran government, and to a lesser extent the Contras.

US SECRET MEETINGS WITH CUBANS

Relations with Cuba required a distinct strategy. Castro did not dance automatically to Moscow's tune, and Gorbachev's efforts to convince him of the necessity of *perestroika* and *glasnost* fell on deaf ears. Developing a new US policy with Cuba required a new approach.

Since the Ford administration, US secretaries of state had initiated secret contacts with the Cuban government with a view to normalizing relations, usually meeting in New York hotels or at La Guardia airport. Exit permits for US citizens living on the island, release of CIA agents in Cuban jails, family reunification, fishing rights, and migration had filled the agendas of these secret talks.[8] Even Reagan's firm anti-communist stance tolerated quiet outreaches to Havana in order to resolve migration issues after Castro allowed 120,000 Cubans to leave the island in what became known as the Mariel boatlift. The problem for Reagan was how to persuade Castro to take back 2,746 "excludables" who had joined the boatlift but were unacceptable in the United States because of their criminal records. Reagan refused to discuss lifting the US economic embargo, and the bilateral talks failed to resolve any conflicts. If anything, they hardened the US confrontation with Castro. "There could be no talk about normalization," wrote the Reagan official, "no relief of the pressure, no conversation on any subject except the return to Havana of the Cuban criminals and the termination of Cuba's interventionism."[9]

Baker was unaware that secret talks had also taken place during the Ford administration, and he claimed to be ignorant of the meetings during the Reagan administration.[10] Instead, he believed there was a good chance that Moscow might leave Castro to determine Cuba's future on his own. Cuba was an important asset to the world communist movement, but Moscow's ability to sustain the island's economy had declined significantly. The Cuban government would have to become more independent, economically, from Moscow. Baker knew that Castro was no poodle of the Soviet Union. With no encouragement from Moscow, he had initiated military support for Agostinho Neto's socialist government in Angola, sending 36,000 Cuban soldiers to Africa in boats and aircraft. Castro last Moscow meeting of heads of communist and worker's party governments in 1987 had left him singularly unimpressed by Gorbachev's "new reforms." He proclaimed that *glasnost*'s freedom of press and free speech would be the downfall of the communist system. As for *perestroika*, political and economic openings might be necessary for the Soviet Union, but Cuba's revolution required sustained authoritarian control and maintenance of the command economy.[11] Baker recognized that he would gain nothing from reaching out to the island's leader, so he maintained a hardline stance. Republican politics in Florida and New Jersey also required holding a firm anti-communist line. Cuba policy should remain related but distinct from US policy toward Nicaragua and El Salvador.

CENTRAL AMERICAN POLICY REVIEW

In the first two months of Baker's leadership at State there was no consensus within the Bush administration on how to address the Central American civil wars. The strongest opposition to change came from right wing Republicans who had championed the defeat of communism in Latin America under the Reagan administration and now sought to stall any move toward conciliation. As Reagan's chief of staff, Baker had gained the enmity of many hardliners for leavening Reagan's conservative instincts with a dose of political realism. On the Democratic side and influenced by the Catholic Church and the human rights community, Baker was under strong pressure to end US support for the Salvadoran army and its security forces. He knew that Reagan's policy to defeat Salvadoran guerillas had failed, and he had endured a front-row seat for Reagan's political battles with Congress over aid to the Contras. It was time to change course.

Baker faced a stark choice: either seek additional congressional funding to defeat militarily the Salvadoran guerillas and the Sandinista government, or pursue a negotiated political outcome. It was clear to him that the Democrats, with majorities in both the House and Senate, were unlikely to pass further military funding for the Contras which was set to expire in March 1989. The Chairman of the House Foreign Affairs Committee, Lee Hamilton, warned Baker that a request for additional funding "would precipitate one helluva fight."[12] Baker was prepared to negotiate with them in order to achieve a bipartisan policy toward Central America.

Early that March, the Deputy Assistant Secretary for Central America, Cresencio Arcos, accompanied Baker, Margaret Tutwiler, and Janet Mullins, his congressional advisor, to the office of House Minority Leader Robert Michel. Their purpose was to persuade the Republican leadership of the need for a political solution. In Michel's office they met with him and the House Republican leadership: Congressmen Robert Lagomarsino, Robert Dornan and Duncan Hunter and Henry Hyde. Baker laid out his strategy: his primary focus was to get the Soviets out of Central America and contain Cuban influence. In Nicaragua, he would not abandon the Contras but would seek a negotiated solution. He would pursue the same goal in El Salvador.

House Republican leaders, already suspicious of Baker, were reluctant to accept his policy towards Central America. Knowing this, Baker had brought Cresencio Arcos to the meeting, not just for his detailed knowledge but also to demonstrate that Baker had corralled one of the bureaucracy's conservative assets to pursue a negotiated political solution. If Arcos, a former supporter of the Contras, could accept the reality of the new policy, conservatives on the Hill could follow. Arcos recalls that the Republican leaders "were not won over, but agreed not to stand in Baker's way."[13]

The following day, Arcos accompanied Baker to the Senate. In the office of Senate Minority Leader Bob Dole, Baker argued that the administration would not get the authorization for additional funding and in its absence; they should give peace talks a chance. As the meeting drew to a close, Dole rose and said, "I think we all support Jim [Baker]." At that moment, the senior Republican on the Foreign Relations

Committee, Senator Helms, who had been absent from the meeting, entered the room and angrily asked Baker if he was turning his back "on our boys," meaning the Contras.[14] Baker, put on the defensive, threw his arm around Arcos' shoulder and asked, "Cris, you're with us, aren't you?" Cresencio, knowing that any hopes for promotion would end immediately if he did otherwise, nodded in agreement. Helms stormed off unsatisfied. He knew he could not muster sufficient votes in the Senate to continue funding the Contras.[15]

Baker and Aronson spent 9 days meeting with all factions of the Congress to draft a bi-partisan policy. On March 24, 1989, President Bush, with the congressional leadership from both parties at his side announced the Bipartisan Accord on Central America. It stated that the Contras had the right to reintegrate into Nicaragua's political process with full civil and political rights. They would exercise these rights by participating in presidential elections on February 28, 1990, one year earlier than previously scheduled. In exchange, the US would provide the Contras with humanitarian assistance conditioned on them observing a cease-fire. The neighboring Central American governments would enforce the agreement through a concerted diplomatic effort, and the Soviet Union would demonstrate that "its proclaimed commitment to 'new thinking' is more than a tactical response to temporary setbacks, but represents instead a new principled approach to foreign policy."[16] Furthermore, the State Department agreed to consult extensively with the various congressional committees over the nature and amount of US support to the Contras through the February 1990 elections. The United States would also respect the results of these Nicaraguan elections. Bush and Baker had created a bipartisan foreign policy and tested Soviet intentions in the Americas. Nevertheless, in a White House briefing shortly after announcing the Bipartisan Accord, Baker asked rhetorically "Does it mean an end to the war? Let's hope so." The administration had no plans to request further military aid, but if the Sandinistas stole next year's election, Baker warned "there is no bar or prohibition to that in this agreement in the event that conditions should deteriorate substantially."[17] He kept his options open.

SOVIET OUTREACH TO CUBA

On April 2 1989, Gorbachev arrived in Havana and warned Castro that he was rethinking Soviet policies toward the Third World. In a speech to the Cuban National Assembly, Gorbachev said he opposed theories that justified the export of revolution and all forms of foreign interference.[18] These changes and the Soviet support for a democratic solution in El Salvador spoke loud and clear: there would be no resupply of Soviet hardware and communication equipment to sustain an insurgency. Castro extended courtesies and the platform of his National Assembly for the Soviet leader, but his dislike of Gorbachev was evident.

That May, in his first visit to Moscow, Baker raised the question of Central America with Shevardnadze. He stressed the importance of ending the conflicts in Nicaragua and El Salvador and moving toward regional disarmament. With Soviet Foreign Ministry officials, Aronson found that senior advisors accepted the concept of partnership in Central America, but not necessarily on the terms Baker and Aronson proposed. Washington's idea of partnership required the Soviets to instruct both the Cubans and Nicaraguans to terminate arm shipments to the FMLN. Aronson made it clear that failure to abide by the agreed terms of the partnership would have negative implications for US–Soviet relationships saying, "I trust that your government will act on this information as your government has pledged it will do."[19]

Aronson also shared with Baker his belief that the Soviets were willing to reduce their support for the Sandinista government. Gorbachev had promised to end shipments of "heavy weapons" to Nicaragua while the electoral option was tested, but would make no commitment to reduce or end Soviet support for Cuba. At any time, Cuba could thus replace the Soviet Union as the principal supplier of armaments and funds to the Sandinistas, and through them to the FMLN. In his meetings with both Gorbachev and Shevardnadze over the next several months, Baker continued to raise Soviet support for Nicaragua and especially Cuba, knowing that Soviet subsidies and armaments from the GDR and

Bulgaria enabled Castro to promote socialist revolutions in the Western Hemisphere, including El Salvador.

NOVEMBER 1989 OFFENSIVES

The FMLN guerrillas made one last push to assert that they still had strength. Beginning on November 11 and lasting for three weeks, they mustered their men and women for a violent attack on the capital city, San Salvador. They broke into houses belonging to prominent families and held the inhabitants hostage, but never harmed or stole from their captives. The Salvadoran armed forces responded, but they owned the city only by daylight. At night, the FMLN crept out of hiding to battle for control. When ammunition ran out, they retreated into the surrounding hills. The FMLN had demonstrated that they could carry out a major assault, but it was a final heave.

Five days later, a US-trained brigade from the Salvadoran armed forces marched into the Jesuit *Universidad Centro Americana* (UCA), forced six Jesuit priests to lie face down on the lawn of their rectory, and shot them at point blank range. To prevent there being any witnesses, they also shot the housekeeper and her daughter. Unbeknownst to the brigade, the housekeeper's sister watched the executions from a window overlooking the lawn. Her tale contradicted the official version, which blamed the FMLN for the assassinations. Washington was horrified. On November 18, Aronson was scheduled to testify before the House of Representatives on the budget for Central America. In his testimony, he stated his belief that the killers of the Jesuits were right wing death squads not the FMLN. The atmosphere in the hearing was electric leading Congressman Jim Moakley to introduce a bill that withheld 50 percent of US military aid to El Salvador absent the arrest and prosecution of the murderers.[20] Baker and Aronson realized that they were in a tragic logjam with no possible military solution to Salvador's civil war. They had to pursue a negotiated solution supported not only by the five Central American presidents, but also by the United Nations. That December, a Peruvian UN diplomat met with a delegation from the

FMLN in Montreal and reported that they were ready to start talking. Baker gave Aronson the task of monitoring and, where possible, assisting those talks. Meanwhile, a problem adjacent to El Salvador affecting US national security interests in the Panama Canal continued to deteriorate.

THE REMOVAL OF MANUEL NORIEGA

Throughout the Reagan administration, officials had sought to negotiate with Panamanian President Manuel Noriega over his drug trafficking, money laundering, and treatment of political opponents. Noriega had been on the US payroll for decades, receiving more than $162,000 between 1959 and 1986 from the US Army, and more than $160,000 in the years 1971-1986 from the Central Intelligence Agency.[21] The Drug Enforcement Agency also had a close partnership with him. Nevertheless, even as he profited from close relations with the Americans, Noriega worked his connections with the Colombian drug cartels. A skilled manipulator, he was willing to deal with anyone who would pay him.

After months of negotiations, the Reagan administration suspended military and economic assistance to Panama in July 1987, and in December it halted humanitarian and scholarship aid. It also reduced Panama's sugar quota. In February 1988, the Justice Department indicted Noriega on drug trafficking and money laundering, but nothing was done to bring him to justice. The suspension of economic assistance and humanitarian aid hurt Panamanian citizens, and the indictment appeared to do little other than increase political pressure on Noriega. Panama did not have an extradition treaty with the United States and Noriega did not intend to defend himself in a US court. Three months after the indictment, Deputy Assistant Secretary Michael Kozak held a secret negotiation with Noriega's Miami based lawyer, offering to drop all charges against him if he would step down and then stay out of politics. Part of the deal was that presidential elections would choose his successor. When Vice President Bush learned of these negotiations, he told Treasury Secretary Baker to quash them. Running for president, he would not be associated with any negotiations with a drug dealer.

Baker called in Deputy National Security Advisor John Negroponte and instructed him to end the talks ASAP.[22]

Upon assuming office, Bush and Baker embarked on a hardline policy toward Noriega: they would not drop the indictment. Meantime, Noriega continued to provoke Washington by illegally entering US controlled airspace around the canal and by detaining US soldiers without charges. From the NSC, William Pryce, the senior official dealing with Panama and Central America reported that "Noriega had no intention of losing the [forthcoming] May 7 elections. They are his vehicle for achieving legitimacy and putting pressure on the United States to normalize relations."[23] Bush considered trying to seduce Noriega with a $3 million financial aid package for "adherence to civil and political rights."[24] However, a CIA-funded program of $10 million to support Noriega's political opponents counterbalanced any official US aid.[25] Bush also appointed an electoral observer group led by Presidents Jimmy Carter and Gerald Ford. Such was the importance of returning stability to Panama and secure passage through the canal that Bush and Baker were prepared to risk alienating supporters in Latin America by interfering in Panama's affairs. An important deadline underlay this policy: under the terms of the Panama Canal Treaty of 1977, the next chairman of the Panama Canal Commission should be a Panamanian citizen. The President's national security team refused to accept that "Noriega's patently illegitimate government" might manage and operate the canal.[26]

Until May 1989, Washington's escalation of pressure had little impact on Noriega, who manipulated nearly every situation to his advantage. There appeared to be no quick means to remove him except by force, and Bush prided himself on using diplomacy. Following the Panamanian presidential election on May 7, Noriega announced the victory of his candidate, Carlos Duque, in a blatantly fraudulent vote. Former President Carter called on Noriega to respect the actual winner, opposition leader Guillermo Endara who had gained three times as many votes as Duque.[27] Pictures of Endara's vice presidential candidate bloodied from beatings by Noriega's thugs, together with his murdered bodyguard, were broadcast on American television.

Baker recalled Ambassador Arthur Davis, withdrew dependents not living on military bases, and reduced embassy staff by two-thirds. Hoping to prevent more violence and assert the United States' legal right to defend the canal's operations, President Bush dispatched an army brigade to bolster US troops already stationed in the Canal Zone. They should undertake unlimited training exercises to increase the frequency and presence of US troops within Panama. He and Baker were ready to escalate the situation and force Noriega to yield.[28] In response to US entreaties, the Panamanian Defense Force (PDF) refused to abandon Noriega and his government did not collapse. Noriega continued to dodge Washington's traps.

Following the fraudulent election outcome, Baker approached Latin American and other world leaders to denounce Noriega. At the Organization of American States (OAS), Baker and Aronson argued for a tough resolution, but both knew that Latin American governments were wary of US intervention. "We recognize," wrote NSC Counsellor Nicholas Rostow "that many countries in Latin America will be reluctant to take firm action against a neighbor, even one with a repugnant dictator like Noriega, and we must be prepared to go it alone, while seeking the understanding and tacit support of others."[29]

At an emergency session of the OAS one week after the Panamanian elections, Baker and Aronson lobbied for a tough resolution. A majority of the members condemned Noriega for abusing Panama's electoral process, but in return, the United States had to accept language that "no State or group of States has the right to intervene, directly or indirectly, for any reason whatever, in the internal or external affairs of any other State."[30] Clearly, this limited US options to remove Noriega. Baker understood that the OAS, which made decisions through consensus, not majority vote, was incapable of condemning Noriega. However, in order to retain US congressional support, he made every effort to work with that organization. Should force become necessary, he had to show that he had exhausted every diplomatic alternative.

Three weeks after the election, Baker instructed the US embassy in Panama to deliver an unequivocal message: "The President is receiving detailed reports of every act of violence and harassment your people undertake. The message for you is 'lay off.' The President said the crisis will not end until you give up power. The President meant what he said." [31] US embassy officials delivered the same message to their respective contacts in the PDF.

Meanwhile, Nicaragua, together with Cuba and the Soviet Union, accused Washington of interfering in the Panamanian elections. Cuban government officials claimed that the US had paid $100 million to the opposition (versus the $10 million appropriated by Congress), and Nicaraguan President Ortega placed his military on combat alert in anticipation of American military action.[32] Baker was testing Soviet "new thinking" in Nicaragua and El Salvador, but Panama was a different ball game. This was a test of Washington's resolve to defend its national security interest in assured and continued passage through the transoceanic canal.

In the face of a stolen election and evidence of Noriega's relationship with the Cali and Medellin drug cartels, Baker asked Mexican President Carlos Salinas and Brazilian President Jose Sarney to help him isolate Noriega. The OAS had a reputation as a vacuous institution, but it was the only hemispheric body that could bring pressure upon a member state which had breached its democratic principles. The State Department used its ambassadors throughout the hemisphere to call attention to Noriega's flagrant theft of the election.

President Salinas was in Washington for an official working visit, including an address before a joint session of Congress, when General Moises Vega led a mutiny of PDF officers. On October 3, they entered the Panamanian *Comandancia* and arrested Noriega. US soldiers at their base half a mile away documented events minute by minute but did not move. As the coup progressed into the afternoon, soldiers loyal to Noriega rushed to the *Comandancia*, suppressed the mutinous officers, and rescued the president.[33] US soldiers never intervened. There were several reasons for the stand down of US troops. Baker contended that the timing was not right: "If you're going to risk American lives, it's the President's view that you do so on your own timetable. You don't do so on the basis of someone else's plans and in response to rapidly changing circumstances."[34] Bush justified nonintervention as deference to other Latin American countries' sensitivities.[35] But In Washington, the Mexican president found himself caught in between welcoming a Panamanian effort to rid themselves of Noriega and concern over the credibility of his White House host. Diplomatic efforts to isolate Noriega without the willingness to take relatively straightforward military action in support of the mutineers suggested an irresolute administration. In a gesture of solidarity with Bush, President Salinas agreed to suspend Mexican oil shipments to Panama as well as technical cooperation. Brazil recalled its ambassador to Panama, leaving the nation more isolated but Noriega more resolute.

Senior officials in Washington, including Baker, endured public criticism and serious soul-searching. Senator Helms called the national security team "a bunch of Keystone cops, bumping into each other."[36] Congressman Hyde complained that the President looked "indecisive, vacillating and weak."[37] Baker and his team recognized that the NSC had failed to coordinate and make timely recommendations to the President. Despite the claim of a closely integrated national security team, the reluctance of the Defense Department (DOD) and its Southern Command to take military action conflicted with Baker and his state department's willingness to use military assets based in the Canal Zone. In response, NSC Advisor Scowcroft strengthened the crisis-management process to assure better coordination among the appropriate agencies; steps that would serve the White House well the following year, when Saddam Hussein invaded Kuwait. This was a watershed moment for US policy toward Panama: Baker and the President's team vowed never to let another opportunity pass them by.[38]

On December 15, Noriega declared war on the United States, citing harassment, unfair sanctions, international humiliation, and open aggression against Panamanian citizens. It was evident to Baker and other observers that in any military confrontation US forces would easily defeat the PDF. But Noriega calculated that Bush would not risk war and the loss of his reputation as a master of diplomacy.

The next day, PDF soldiers manning a roadblock near their

headquarters in Panama City detained two cars with US license plates. In the first car were four off duty US Marines. A US Navy officer with his wife drove the second car. Both had lost their way in the maze of narrow downtown streets. The Navy officer and his wife watched the PDF soldiers stop the car with the Marines, cock their weapons and approach the car with the probable intent of shooting through the car windows. The Marines accelerated through the roadblock, but not before shots were fired at them, killing one Marine and injuring another. Then the PDF soldiers turned to the Navy officer and his wife. They blindfolded both of them and took them to an unknown place, believed to be the PDF headquarters, where they were interrogated and beaten.[39] When he learned of the incident, President Bush was particularly incensed by the abusive treatment of an unarmed lady.

Southern Command raised the alarm immediately, and Baker recognized that the confrontation with Noriega had reached a boiling point. The President now possessed the justification for US military action, and this time the DOD and the White House did not delay. Bush accused Noriega and the PDF of intentionally conducting the violent assaults. State Department spokeswoman Tutwiler said that the United States was taking Noriega's declaration of war more seriously after the injury and killing of the Marine: "Noriega's irresponsible declaration of a state of war last week, followed only hours later by indiscriminate and unprovoked violence against Americans clearly increases tension in Panama. We find the unwarranted use of violence against Americans by the Noriega regime unacceptable."[40]

Whatever the cost to US relations with Latin American governments, Bush, Baker and Scowcroft had decided that safeguarding the lives of Americans, defending democracy in Panama, combatting drug trafficking, and preserving the Panama Canal Treaty justified the dispatch of military forces. On December 20, the 82nd Airborne Division parachuted into combat for the first time since World War II. Members of the 3rd Battalion reinforced the 12,000 American troops already stationed in the Canal Zone. That night the President addressed the nation to explain the invasion. At Baker's recommendation, he stated that

Noriega was a dangerous drug trafficker who posed a grave threat to the American public and its values.[41] That Christmas, Noriega sought refuge in the Vatican's Apostolic *Nunciatura* (the Embassy of the Holy See). The Nuncio to Panama refused to expel him, claiming, "An embassy is only empowered to deal with the government of the host country."[42] Baker called the Nuncio in Washington, asserting that Noriega's stay at the *Nunciatura* threatened additional lives and the US government would not allow Noriega to travel to any country other than the United States.[43] That same evening, after getting no commitment, he called Pope John Paul II,[44] ignoring the fact that Rome lay six hours ahead of Washington. The Pope took the call late at night. The President's Chief of Staff, John Sununu also woke up the pontiff with the same message. At that hour, both men could let off steam, but they should not have expected a swift response. Meanwhile in Panama City, US forces surrounded the *Nunciatura* and blasted loud music. Both in Rome and Panama City, the Americans interrupted a good night's sleep.[45]

On December 27, the President ordered the withdrawal of US troops, and on January 3, 1990, US forces removed Noriega under cover of night. He was flown to Howard Air Base in the Canal Zone, where DEA agents arrested him. Twenty minutes later, he was on a C-131 transport plane to southern Florida, to be arraigned on federal drug charges. To assure citizens and officials throughout the hemisphere that the United States had not invaded a sovereign country without cause, General Maxwell Thurman, commander of American troops in Panama, stated that Noriega had surrendered of his own accord: "The decision was his."[46] This was blatantly untrue: US forces had taken him. Whatever degree of duress he endured, more than two years of negotiating had come to an end. A jury found Noriega guilty, and he served seventeen years of a forty-year term in a US prison.

Noriega's surrender and the outpouring of support for his removal from thousands of Panamanian citizens enabled Baker to go on the moral offensive. He instructed Luigi Einaudi, the US Ambassador to the OAS, explicitly to tie events in Panama to the wave of democracy movements then sweeping Eastern Europe: "Today we are living in historic times. A time when a great principle is spreading across the world like wildfire. That principle, as we all know, is the revolutionary idea that people, not governments, are sovereign."[47] The rhetoric of democracy was juxtaposed against the President's willingness to use force to protect national security interests. He and Baker were also downplaying a military disaster that occurred during the December invasion. The pilots of two Stealth bombers received confusing instructions from their base in Nebraska and erroneously dropped their load within meters of a PDF army barracks causing loss of both military and civilian lives.[48] The operation was poorly coordinated and threatened to derail Bush and Baker's focus on support for democracy. Baker was grim when he heard the news and thereafter assumed control over US policy toward Central America. No longer would the State Department pursue one course of action and the NSC and the Defense Department pursue another. Strategy and action regarding the Western Hemisphere would be concentrated under one roof—his.

NICARAGUA'S PRESIDENTIAL ELECTION

The immediate test was the presidential and legislative elections in Nicaragua. Daniel Ortega was well ensconced as president, with the Sandinista party exercising control over the country through a well-trained police system and intelligence apparatus that resembled those of East Germany (GDR). Amid a civil war that had claimed 30,000 lives in a nation of 3.5 million, the Sandinistas ruled with help from Cuba, the GDR and Bulgaria. The government was well entrenched and only a few commentators expected it to lose the election. Aronson, however, was confident that if Nicaraguan citizens were assured that their votes would be secret; they would oust the oppressive Sandinista government. The State Department counseled unity among the fourteen political parties, who represented both the right and left of the political spectrum. They should join under the banner of UNO, *Union Nacional de Opositora*. In the days before the election, it remained unclear that UNO could dislodge the Sandinista regime. In Washington, Aronson was in a minority in trusting the electoral outcome so long as international observers were present and the Soviets and Cubans allowed Nicaraguan citizens to vote freely. In his view, Nicaragua sensed the winds of freedom blowing through Eastern Europe.

On February 27, 1990, the electoral tribunal announced that UNO's leader, Violeta Chamorro, had won 55 percent of the vote, beating Ortega by 14 points. A well-known figure whose family owned the national newspaper, *La Prensa*, she was also renowned as the widow of the newspaper's publisher, Pedro Joaquin Chamorro. He had been assassinated in January 1978 by supporters of the dictator Anastasio Somoza. In her acceptance speech, and conscious of the deep divisions within the country, Chamorro announced, "this is an election that will never have exiles, or political prisoners, or confiscations… Here we have neither victors nor vanquished."[49] The 10,000 members of the opposition Contra forces were part of a general amnesty for all crimes committed during the civil war. In granting that amnesty, Violeta gained the support of both the Contras and the Soviet-trained Nicaraguan army, which had also carried out brutal assassinations against its enemies. To consolidate peace, President Chamorro chose Ortega's brother, Humberto Ortega, as her Minister of Defense. This was risky, but she knew that the country needed compromise after its decade-long civil war.

In the months following the election a relative peace descended on the nation. Baker's pursuit of a free and fair election was vindicated, and he and Aronson were widely praised for pursuing a policy that removed the Soviets from Central America, installed international observers, and allowed national citizens to decide their own leaders. The victory was short lived as subsequent corrupt governments amended the constitution making it easier for Ortega to run again and win as president in 2007. Then, he undermined democratic institutions and determined to hold onto power.

The democratic outcome of the Nicaraguan election affected the guerrilla forces in El Salvador, whose supply route was now shut off. FMLN combatants continued to fight in the hills while their *comandantes* sat around green baize tables seeking a negotiated outcome with the Salvadoran government. After two years, the UN-mediated peace process reached an agreement that destroyed the role of the armed forces in Salvadoran politics.[50] The FMLN became a political party that actively took part in the democratic process despite the fact that *comandantes* who confessed to war crimes were excluded from politics for ten years. Baker attended the signing of the peace agreement on January 16, 1992, in Mexico City, a reflection of the role the Mexican government had played in hosting several negotiating sessions and nudging the FMLN to make difficult concessions. Mexico became more important in the eyes of the Bush administration as it sought to enter into a regional trade agreement with its neighbors to the north.

NEGOTIATING A NORTH AMERICAN FREE TRADE AGREEMENT

Throughout the resolution of both Central American conflicts, Mexico had played a significant role. Once an active participant in the non-aligned movement whose pleasure was to irritate the United States, the Mexican government adapted its foreign policy to the times. Presidents Reagan and Miguel de la Madrid recognized their common interests in transforming Mexico from a poor agricultural nation to a manufacturing hub. De la Madrid's successoral, Carlos Salinas de Gortari, reinforced that trend. Returning from a meeting of the World Economic Forum in January 1990, he announced that he sought to modernize Mexico and use its low labor costs as a competitive advantage in a regional North American market.

President Salinas therefore asked US Ambassador to Mexico John Negroponte to transmit a message directly to Bush and Baker: he was ready to begin negotiations for a free trade agreement. Both Bush and Baker were Texans who appreciated the importance of good relations with their neighbor to the south. They were receptive to the idea. However, there was one caveat: Baker obdurately refused to expand the negotiations to include Canada. He supported a bilateral agreement, but not a regional trading arrangement.[51]

His reason was the difficulty of negotiating with Canadians. He had experienced tough bargaining in October 1987, when a bilateral US-Canada trade agreement met a roadblock.[52] The Canadians had rejected the Reagan team's insistence that US national courts decide US/Canadian commercial disputes. Clayton Yeutter, the US trade negotiator at the time, had exhausted his remit and talks were on the verge of collapse when Reagan asked the toughest negotiator in his cabinet, Treasury Secretary Baker, to resolve the problem. Baker played hardball. He let negotiations wallow until the moment when Congressional fast track authority to undertake trade agreements was about to lapse. With only hours to go, he summoned Derek Burney, the Canadian trade negotiator, to Washington. They met at the Treasury Department throughout the night with no meal breaks. Exhausted, they reached a compromise and clinched the trade agreement. Baker emerged triumphant, but two-plus years later he had no desire to repeat the experience.

In June 1990, as Salinas came to Washington for an official working visit and preliminary talks on a bilateral free trade agreement, Canadian Prime Minister Brian Mulroney moved into high gear. He foresaw that two bilaterals—a US-Canada agreement and a separate US-Mexico agreement—would place Washington in the driver's seat with an overwhelming advantage. Mulroney therefore called Bush and began a persistent effort to override Baker's preference. They should begin talks for a North American free trade agreement. Salinas sided with Mulroney, and Baker adjusted. This was important to his friend, President Bush, so he would go along.

The negotiations to create NAFTA began in 1991, were completed in 1993, and the treaty went into effect on January 1, 1994, a year after Bush left office. Throughout the negotiations, Baker's priorities lay elsewhere, but he kept himself informed of progress and setbacks. Robert Zoellick, his counsellor and close advisor was now the Under Secretary of State for Economic Affairs. He was Baker's point man on trade negotiations, having opened the Japanese market to US cars and trucks. The chief negotiator was Carla Hills, the US trade representative, but when talks faltered in August 1992, Baker became concerned that the approaching presidential election might lessen US bargaining power.

With the Democrats ahead in the polls and reliant on the trade unions, which vehemently opposed free trade agreements, Baker sought to accelerate the negotiations. He recommended to Bush that Zoellick intervene to resolve the outstanding issues. However, the President, ever loyal, refused to undermine Carla Hills. He agreed that Zoellick could strengthen the US negotiating team, but not override Hills.

That same August, Baker knew that his close friend, George Bush would ask him to leave the management of US foreign policy and move to the White House as Bush's campaign chief for the upcoming November elections. Together they sought to turn the several foreign policy successes into an electoral victory for George H.W. Bush. The nation, however, was not convinced, preferring a president who would focus on domestic problems.

SIX

MOBILIZING SUPPORT FOR THE GULF WAR

James Baker was focused on the Soviet Union and the inclusion of a unified Germany within NATO when Iraqi leader Saddam Hussein's bellicose rhetoric grew louder. The Iraqi leader had become more aggressive toward his neighbors with fierce anti-Israeli and anti-Kuwaiti tirades. Saddam's failure to demobilize the million-man Iraqi army and the estimated $30 billion war debt resulting from his eight-year war with Iran should have put Washington on notice that real threats lay behind the menacing words. However, Baker's principal advisor on the Middle East, Dennis Ross, was preoccupied with Soviet issues, making the circle of close aides too tight to focus on a growing menace in the Persian Gulf.

Assistant Secretary of State John Kelly, the senior diplomat dealing with Iraq, was not a member of Baker's inner circle of advisors and lacked immediate access to the secretary's office on the seventh floor. Kelly was a career Foreign Service officer who had recently served as principal deputy in the European bureau and deputy director of the Policy Planning staff. His knowledge of the Persian Gulf was relatively new and he spoke no Arabic. Several months after his appointment, Kelly, carrying the new Bush policy towards Iraq, visited the region and met for the first time with Saddam Hussein. The Iraqi president's ambition to lead a pan-Arab movement was well known, as well as his determination to recoup some of the $70 billion spent on the costly war with Iran. Saddam Hussein was no friend of the United States, but he provided a buffer against Iran and the Reagan administration considered him a partner in the region.

CONDITIONAL ENGAGEMENT

In October the previous year, National Security Directive (NSD) 26 set out the Bush administration's policy toward the Gulf States.[1] This endorsed the US commitment to defend its vital interests, namely, "access to Persian Gulf oil and the security of key friendly states." The US would pursue this interest through "the effective support and participation of our western allies and Japan." Regarding Iraq, "normal relations… would serve our longer-term interests and promote stability." The US government "should propose economic and political incentives for Iraq to moderate its behavior and to increase our influence with Iraq." In pursuit of this and "as a means of developing access to and influence with the Iraqi defense establishment, the United States should consider sales of non-lethal forms of military assistance, e.g. training courses and medical exchanges, on a case by case basis."[2] In short, NSD 26 called for "conditional engagement" with Iraq. The US would seek 'a normal' relationship with Iraq on the condition that Saddam's treatment of the Shia population, the Iraqi Kurds, and other domestic critics complied with international law and human rights. President Bush approved this policy and Assistant Secretary Kelly sought to carry it out when he met with Saddam Hussein in Baghdad on February 12, 1990.

Commercial opportunities was a further incentive for the US to maintain good relations with Iraq. Commercial credit guarantees permitted the Iraqi government to purchase American rice which benefited US farmers and had the support of agricultural constituencies in Congress. American businessmen were also eager to export to Iraq with the help of Export-Import Bank financing. Thus, despite the knowledge that Iraqi had used mustard gas and other chemical weapons against Iranian forces, Kelly carried out the NSD 26 policy of "conditional engagement." He stressed the condition of improved treatment of Saddam's critics, and warned the Iraqi leader that the annual State Department's Human Rights report would be sharply critical of his record.[3]

The radio program Voice of America (VOA) also criticized Saddam in an editorial published on February 15. The opinion piece criticized secret police abuses in Iraq as well as seven other countries: "The rulers of these countries hold power by force and fear, not by the consent of the government… the tide of history is against such rulers."[4] Saddam's fury now turned against Washington, leading Baker to question whether he had lost control over policy in the Gulf. The VOA editorial irritated him and he demanded new procedures that would require State Department clearance of all VOA editorials that concerned sensitive subjects, such as Iraq. This interference with the VOA's independent editorial policy irritated many in Washington, but Baker was justified in curtailing VOA's freedom given the delicate situation between Iraq and its neighbors.

A month after Kelly's meeting with Saddam, US intelligence detected the construction of six fixed launchers for long-range Scud missiles at an Iraqi base near the Jordanian border and within range of Israel. Also, there were unconfirmed reports on misuse of the commercial credit guarantees from the purchase of rice to the acquisition of military weapons. At the NSC, there was increasing disquiet over Iraq's behavior. The senior staffer for the Middle East and Persian Gulf, Richard Haass, reported that US policy was failing to work as expected. He gathered mid-level officials to discuss whether the policy of limited cooperation with Iraq needed adjustment.[5] Meantime, at the State Department, two junior analysts in the Policy Planning staff sent their paper with its criticisms of Iraq to their boss, Director Dennis Ross. The paper asserted that Iraq had emerged from its war with Iran stronger than formerly assessed and argued that Saddam Hussein's regime was the main threat to stability in the area and should be contained.[6] Ross found the argument persuasive, but failed to act upon it.[7] He was Baker's principal advisor on both the Soviet Union and the Middle East. With so much happening between Moscow and Eastern Europe, Iraq failed to receive sufficient attention.

On April 2, Saddam criticized Israel directly and announced that Iraq had developed binary chemical weapons previously possessed only by the US and the Soviet Union. If Iraq is attacked, "by God, we will make the fire eat up half of Israel."[8] He went on to assert that Iraq possessed a new chemical arsenal that was as powerful as nuclear weapons. "We do not need an atomic bomb," he said. "We have the dual chemical. Whoever threatens us with the atomic bomb, we will annihilate him with the dual chemical."[9] He gave no details on the nature of these chemical weapons.

Four days later, Saddam received a delegation of US senators in the city of Mosul. Angrily, he criticized the Bush administration for furnishing Israel with Patriot missiles. Senate Minority Leader Bob Dole remarked that President Bush wanted better relations with Iraq, consistent with "conditional engagement," but Saddam ignored the conditions. His impulsive behavior was driving him to action. How should he recover monies spent, land lost, and higher oil prices? Baker's response was harsher than that of Senator Dole. Through his spokeswoman Margaret Tutwiler, he called Saddam's remarks "inflammatory, irresponsible and outrageous."[10] However, the force of Baker's public statement was muted by the failure both to end the commercial credits for the purchase of American rice and continued Export-Import Bank credits. Without leadership from Baker and other cabinet level officials, their deputies could not reach agreement on ending US programs that would hurt rice producers and American companies looking for new markets. US policy toward Iraq floundered.

On May 30, 1990, Saddam chaired the Arab League Summit meeting in Baghdad and complained of Kuwait's economic warfare against Iraq. He claimed that Kuwait and other Gulf States had given him $30 billion as a grant, not as a loan, and that excessive oil production had resulted in a significant fall in oil prices.[11] Saddam warned the Kuwaitis: "You are wrecking our means of sustenance and if you cut people's means of sustenance, it is equivalent to cutting their neck and killing them."[12] Threats accompanied a sharp confrontation between him and Sheikh Jabir al-Ahmad al-Sabah, the emir of Kuwait, who rejected the demand for billions of dollars and territorial concessions. Saddam's drive for supremacy in the Arab world threatened not only Kuwait, but other Arab neighbors who feared that the freedom movements then transforming Eastern Europe could spread to the Middle East.[13] The difference was that their reformer was an aggressive Iraqi with a powerful military machine, an army of nearly a million men, chemical weapons, battlefield missiles, and a history of breaking the accepted rules of modern warfare. In a stinging tirade, Saddam said that only a revolution that swept aside the corrupt, pro-Western regimes of the Arab world could liberate the Arabs to fulfill their historic destiny. Among the Arab leaders, few took his words seriously.[14] This exchange, filled with bombast was carried out behind closed doors, but only the Saudis suspected that it was a precursor to serious invasion plans. King Fahd approached Washington for a show of strength with which to deter the Iraqi leader and met a response from Defense Secretary Cheney. Otherwise, few in Washington paid attention. Baker and his advisors were focused on the forthcoming Washington Summit with Gorbachev, and the national media mentioned neither the Arab League meeting nor Iraqi threats. When reports of Saddam's meeting with Sheikh Sabah reached Washington, they met only passing interest.[15] No one called for a meeting of the NSC.

In June, US Permanent Representative to the UN Thomas Pickering visited Baghdad and Kuwait. Meeting with Sheikh Sabah and the energy minister, Pickering learned that Saddam's vocal demands for repayment of outstanding debts, as well as reduced oil production in order to raise oil prices had become more outlandish. In response to Pickering's question whether the Sheikh would like a response from Washington, the Kuwaiti leader shrugged his shoulders and responded that Saddam's bullying was well known, but would not result in military action.[16] Pickering reported this back to Washington. Reassured that he did not have a crisis in the Gulf, Baker continued to focus on Moscow, the German question, arms control and fast moving events in Eastern Europe.

IRAQI MILITARY BUILDUP AND A US REFUELING EXERCISE

On July 20, a foreign military attaché travelling from Kuwait City to Baghdad encountered hundreds of Iraqi military vehicles filled with troops and weapons moving south toward the Kuwait border. Within hours, US satellites focused their lenses on the border area and analysts estimated that thirty thousand Iraqi troops were positioned close to Kuwait. In the following days that number grew to more than one hundred thousand troops. In plain sight, Iraqi tanks were loaded onto railroad cars. Was the intention to intimidate the Kuwaiti leadership or preliminary to an invasion?

As a precautionary measure and fearful that Saddam might also move against Saudi Arabia, the Pentagon in July agreed to carry out aircraft refueling exercises with the United Arab Emirates. Their purpose was to send the message that the US was a serious force whose word should not be ignored, but Saddam interpreted the refueling exercises as a provocation. He used sophistry, charming Senate staffers who were on an investigatory mission to Baghdad while lashing out publicly against the United States and Israel. Now fully engaged in the nature of the Iraqi threat, Under Secretary of State Bob Kimmitt and Director for Policy Planning Dennis Ross favored standing up to the Iraqi leader and supported the refueling exercise. However, the Senate staffers, influenced by Saddam's charm offensive, believed that reason would persuade Saddam to stand down. They failed to understand the nature of the man who had built up the Ba'athist party and ruled by means of patronage to his supporters as well as brutal repression of his enemies.

In late July 1990, Baker was enjoying a fishing trip on Siberia's Angara River with Shevardnadze. It was Shevardnadze's way of paying Baker back for the unusual visit to his Wyoming ranch the previous September. While out on the river, he received news from Kimmitt that Iraqi forces had mobilized on the Kuwaiti border; the CIA for the first time concluded that an invasion was more likely than not. Baker asked

Shevardnadze to restrain Saddam Hussein, a Soviet client since 1972, but the foreign minister assured Baker that Saddam did not plan to invade.

However, on August 1, Kimmitt called Baker to report that Kuwait was under attack. Baker again talked to Shevardnadze, who related that the Iraqis had assured Yevgeny Primakov, the member of Gorbachev's Presidential Council and principal handler of Saddam Hussein that they would not attack. As he spoke, Iraqi troops were rolling into Kuwait and heading toward the capital. Shevardnadze was deeply embarrassed: Iraqi leadership and Soviet intelligence had misled him and he had to face the facts through Baker and CNN. Baker realized immediately that he had gained leverage based on better intelligence. With that, he instructed Dennis Ross to work on a US-Soviet statement while he flew on to Mongolia for a previously scheduled visit. (The country was geopolitically strategic because the vast Mongolian territory lay between the Soviet Union and the People's Republic of China.) Meantime, Baker sent Ross to Moscow with one instruction: he should draft a joint US-Soviet statement that would demonstrate unequivocal common purpose. At the same time, he instructed Kimmitt and Pickering to seek a UN Security Council resolution calling for unconditional withdrawal. Resolution 660 passed unanimously at 4 a.m. on August 2, 1990, only hours after the invasion.

Later that day, Ross called Baker to suggest that the joint declaration should not only condemn the invasion, but also call for joint action against Iraq. Ross proposed that Baker fly back to Washington through Moscow and make that statement with Shevardnadze. He would do his best to arrange this. With this offer, Baker called the president at his summer home in Kennebunkport who readily agreed to a joint US-Soviet statement so long as the wording was strong.

Gorbachev was on vacation at his dacha in Crimea. Away from Moscow, he allowed Shevardnadze to take the lead in negotiating with the Americans. Thus, Ross began to draft a text with Sergei Tarasenko, Shevardnadze's senior policy advisor. Baker's first item of business was to seek Soviet leadership in jointly condemning Saddam's action. The second item was to ask the Soviets, as the principle suppliers of military equipment to Iraq, to suspend arms sales. Baker knew the critical importance of seeking Soviet collaboration in repelling an invasion which broke international law and the sanctity of international boundaries. After eighteen months of constant dialogue with Gorbachev and Shevardnadze, Baker was ready to test the degree of newfound partnership. Together, the US and the Soviets should condemn the invasion, suspend weapons sales to Iraq, and seek a strongly worded UN resolution urging Iraq and Kuwait to begin talks.

JOINT US AND SOVIET STATEMENT, AUGUST 3, 1990

In his autobiography, Baker underlines the importance of obtaining Soviet collaboration. Baker claims that the joint statement condemning Saddam Hussein's invasion of Kuwait ended the Cold War on grounds that it was a pragmatic step clearly marking a new level of trust and common purpose not seen since World War II. Had the Cold War still lingered, the US would have stood behind Kuwait and the Soviet Union would have stood with Iraq. They would have drawn hostile lines in yet another proxy conflict. Instead, Cold War enemies committed to work together. Since the latter days of the Reagan administration, Soviet and American leaders had built up confidence in each other. A degree of personal trust developed slowly between Gorbachev and Reagan, as well as between Shevardnadze and George Shultz; this confidence spilled over to their successors. However, that level of trust was tested on several occasions throughout the Gulf crisis.

Back in Moscow Ross and Tarasenko drafted a common text. The Arabists in the Soviet Foreign Ministry watered down the language, dismaying Ross. He rejected their amendments. Tarasenko went back to redraft and emerged with yet another weak text. It was clear to Ross that a tepid statement would send the wrong message to Saddam: the US and the Soviets were not together on Iraq. Tarasenko went back, this time to Shevardnadze. He returned with an acceptable text, except for the brackets around phrases calling for an arms embargo. Ross and

Tarasenko could not resolve those critical issues. It needed Baker and Shevardnadze's personal intervention to remove the brackets. Baker was on his way to meet Shevardnadze.

Baker was fully aware of the risk of landing at Moscow's Vnukovo Airport only to face Soviet rejection of a recently drafted UN Security Council resolution or, worse still, a refusal to join him in condemning Iraqi action. Ross and Tarasenko had reached a satisfactory conclusion except for the bracketed text. Gorbachev's willingness to give Shevardnadze the lead had helped them manage the response to the US request. Baker's only request was that the statement have teeth! Thus, together, Baker and Shevardnadze announced the unconditional Iraqi withdrawal from Kuwait…

> We take the unusual step of jointly calling upon the rest of the international community to join with us in an international cut-off of all arms supplies to Iraq…In addition [we] call on regional organizations, especially the League of Arab States, all Arab Governments, as well as the Non-Aligned Movement and the Islamic Conference to take all possible steps to ensure that the UN Security Council Resolution is carried out.[17]

Gorbachev's "new thinking" and the trust established between foreign ministers made possible this unprecedented statement. Nevertheless, Shevardnadze made it clear to Baker that the Soviets were not agreeing to gunboat diplomacy. Baker assured Shevardnadze that the president planned no unilateral military action unless American citizens were harmed, but Shevardnadze remained wary of a US military move.

On August 6, the Soviet Union joined the United States in a UN Security Council vote that imposed a worldwide economic embargo on Iraq. At the same time, Defense Secretary Cheney was in Riyadh offering King Fahd military support through the stationing of US military forces in the kingdom. Cheney shared overhead photographs of Iraqi troops deployed on the former Saudi-Kuwaiti neutral zone and convinced the king that the Iraqi challenge could not be stopped by financial pay-offs. It required a swift military response. Baker received instructions to inform the Soviets of Cheney's offer to the Saudis. He assured Shevardnadze that this military positioning was not intended to take advantage of the situation and enhance US influence in the region. However, Shevardnadze was not pleased: "Are you consulting us or are you informing us?"[18] Baker replied that he was informing the Soviets. On his own reasoning and without instructions from Washington, he suggested that the Soviets might wish to contribute naval forces, or ground forces. Baker asked, "How can we work together on this? . . . Is there something else that we can do to cooperate on this?"[19] Shevardnadze proposed that they resurrect the moribund UN Military Staff Committee, which had lain dormant during the Cold War.[20] Baker promised to consider it. After consulting with Bush and Chairman of the Joint Chief of Staff General Colin Powell about Soviet involvement in the Gulf crisis, he called Shevardnadze to inform him that the president was ready to pursue the matter. Baker's proposal to welcome Soviet naval or land presence in the Gulf was now official: it was a first-time offer.

His proposal met with considerable concern from the State Department's Middle East bureau. For over forty years, US policy had focused on keeping the Soviets *out* of the Middle East. Now the secretary was throwing out that policy for short term gain. There was a huge sigh of relief when Gorbachev rejected the offer, but meantime Baker had made a good faith offer to work with the Soviets. Said Ross, identified only as an unnamed State Department official, to the accompanying journalists, "It was a major step for the Soviets to break with an old ally [Iraq] to issue a joint statement with the United States condemning that ally.... It was an equally major step for the United States to invite the Soviet Union to become militarily, as well as politically, involved in the Gulf."[21]

On August 8, Saddam officially annexed Kuwait, strengthening the Soviet and US resolve to condemn the annexation and impose sanctions. The UN Security Council passed the resolution unanimously. On August 12, Saddam presented a peace initiative which remained the official Iraqi peace plan for the next six months. The initiative offered to consider "the formulation of arrangements for the situation in Kuwait" *after* the withdrawal of Israel from the Occupied Territories and Syria from Lebanon. The linkage to a resolution of the Palestinian issue struck a sensitive chord with many Arabs and was embraced warmly by Jordan and the Palestinians. For the Soviet Union and France, the proposal offered each of them the opportunity for a more pro-active policy towards Palestine. The linkage, however, was unacceptable to the White House and Baker rejected it outright. There should be no linkage between Iraq's annexation of Kuwait and Israel's occupation of the West Bank and Gaza. Consequently, tension over linkage to the Palestinian problem persisted among the members of a potential anti-Saddam coalition. Baker was maneuvering a complex situation with his support for Gorbachev tempered by the need to assert the sanctity of international boundaries and reject Iraqi occupation of Kuwait. To observers in Washington, he appeared in full control, never ceasing to entertain with his customary litany of jokes - many of them unfit for feminine company - that hid his irritation at losing his vacation days up in the Teton Mountains.

IRAQI OIL TANKERS SAILS SOUTHWARD

In the first three weeks of August, talk of war was widespread. The threat to Saudi Arabia and the prospect of Saddam wringing a chokehold over oil supplies resulted in broad support from western leaders, seeking to stop Iraq's aggressive action. Initially, Bush justified the American position in pragmatic terms, namely the security of oil supplies from Saudi Arabia and the Gulf. This contrasted with Britain and France, which placed greater focus on upholding international law. Prime Minister Thatcher declared that the international community must defend the principle that aggression shall not be rewarded: "If we let [Iraq's invasion of Kuwait] succeed, no small country can ever feel safe again. The law of the jungle would take over from the rule of law."[22] On August 5, Bush announced that the overriding objective was that "this will not stand, this aggression against Kuwait."[23] He thus placed US prestige on the line. The US could not afford to lose this challenge and the degree of Soviet-American coordination strengthened the resolve of the UN Security Council members to support the anti-Iraq coalition. But problems lay ahead.

On August 17, two Iraqi oil tankers steamed southward toward Yemen, where the CIA feared that they would unload their cargo of oil. The US navy was ready to interdict, board, and if necessary sink the ships. Secretary Cheney, NSC Advisor Scowcroft, and General Powell recommended taking military action. It would demonstrate seriousness in carrying out the Security Council embargo. They had the ear of President Bush who was still on vacation in Kennebunkport. Baker demurred. He argued that the UN resolutions did not support military action to enforce the sanction regime and that unilateral action risked a Soviet bolt out of the coalition, "I was sure that unilateral action would be disastrous... We're going to be much worse off losing the Soviets than losing that ship."[24] Baker urged Bush to delay naval action until the UN Security Council approved the use of military force to enforce sanctions. He urged Soviet support for such a resolution, but Gorbachev needed extra time. At Baker's instruction, US Permanent Representative to the UN Thomas Pickering sought delay of the Security Council's meeting in order that the Soviets might impress upon Saddam the need to withdraw unconditionally from Kuwait and release all foreign nationals. Shevardnadze asked Baker for five days to persuade Saddam. The Americans gave him three days.

On August 22, Shevardnadze replied that the Soviets would support a UN Security Council resolution by Saturday, August 25 if Saddam refused to yield. Baker called him: "We'll give you your three days, but will you promise me now that if we do move on Saturday, we will have your support?"[25] Baker did not receive a specific Soviet commitment, but Shevardnadze understood that Baker could not hold back forever and would act with, or without a Security Council resolution. On the afternoon of Friday, August 24, Shevardnadze sent the Soviet reply: "Saddam's answer was not worth commenting upon."

Now he instructed the Soviet's Permanent Representative to work with Pickering at the UN to make certain amendments, but not change the substance of Security Council Resolution 665. At 4 a.m. on Saturday August 25, the Security Council voted thirteen to zero with only Yemen and Cuba abstaining. The vote endorsed the use of force to uphold the UN embargo against Iraq. It was troublesome for the Soviets, whose chief Arabist in the Kremlin, Yevgeny Primakov had lost this battle. One month later, with the Soviets holding the chair of the UN Security Council, Baker gained approval of Resolution 670 that expanded the naval blockade against Iraq. The Soviet joint agreement with the United States softened up all five permanent Council members for the next round, namely UN approval of "the use of all necessary means" to force Iraq out of Kuwait.[26]

THE TIN CUP TOUR

Soviet support was essential, but not sufficient. Significant funds were needed to offset the cost of the US military enterprise, called *Operation Desert Shield*. Military operations around the Arabian Peninsula to protect Saudi Arabia cost the US approximately $1.5 billion a month and Baker knew that American voters did not wish to see their tax dollars used to protect Saudi Arabia. Added to this, UN Resolution 660 impacted Turkey, Egypt and Jordan who saw a major fall in commercial relations with Iraq, as well as the return of their citizens fleeing from Kuwait. Both governments therefore sought financial assistance to weather the consequences of the UN trade embargo. Treasury Secretary, Nicholas Brady raised funds from Japan and South Korea for these so-called 'front line states,' while Baker raised funds for the US military effort, known popularly as the "Tin Cup Trip."

On September 6, he arrived in Jeddah to meet with King Fahd and Foreign Minister Saud, both grateful for the US commitment to station troops as a deterrence in their country. They were also determined to rid the region of Saddam Hussein. Minister Saud pledged $15 billion on condition that the emir of Kuwait pledged the same amount.

The next day, Emir al-Sabah agreed. Baker flew onto Cairo, where President Hosni Mubarak urged President Bush to continue his hard line against Saddam. Mubarak went beyond the occupation of Kuwait to express concern that Saddam could remain a regional threat even after resolution of the immediate crisis. He agreed to send more troops as well as an army division with tanks and artillery to Saudi Arabia. In their one-on-one meeting at Mubarak's summer palace, Baker stressed that there should be no deals contemplated with Saddam until he complied with UN resolutions calling for Iraq to withdraw from Kuwait and restore the legitimate government. Said Baker, "We agree strongly with you… there should not be any settlements or agreements that in any way minimize or diminish the content and substance of those resolutions."[27]

Baker was trying to guard against any temptation for deal making that could weaken the resolve of Arab leaders to stand firm against Iraq. He directed this message primarily at Moscow to ensure that Gorbachev remained committed to the full and complete enforcement of UN Sanction, and avoid the Soviets trying to compromise the content of those resolutions.[28] Baker was dogged in his determination to discourage any diplomatic moves in that direction while continuing to apply pressure on Baghdad with the UN embargo and military build-up.

After three hectic days in the Middle East, Baker flew north in early September 1990 to join the president at Helsinki where Bush and Gorbachev would seal their friendship and cooperation in a joint statement. For the first time, both men referred to each other by their first names. They also agreed that after repelling Saddam Hussein, they would jointly seek to bring Israel and the Palestinians together in the search for peace. Baker was not convinced that this could succeed, but he was determined to keep the Soviets on board this joint effort in the Gulf. He, therefore, did not object, but sought the task of drafting the final communique with Shevardnadze.

Immediately afterwards, Baker called on NATO members to send ground-based military units to join US deployed forces against

Iraq. His intent was to expand west European participation in the American-led drive to force Iraq to end its occupation, but he met no firm commitment for ground troops. However, several NATO members agreed to provide aircraft and ships to transport Egyptian combat troops to Saudi Arabia, and to help evacuate foreigners from Iraq and Kuwait. Fundamentally, NATO members were determined to keep their formal alliance structure aloof from conflicts that did not involve an attack on the territory of a member state. They made small contributions, more out of a desire not to offend the Americans than out of any perceived threat to national security. Belgium agreed to send twenty thousand tons of wheat to Egypt. Greece volunteered "sea lift" ships, and Denmark offered two large "garage ships" to move troops and heavy equipment. Baker preferred the dispatch of ground troops, "even if they were only symbolic" in number.[29] It was important that the United States not be seen as the sole military power, but rather a leader of an international coalition with strong NATO participation in addition to Arab presence. Later, Baker would return to European capitals with a plea to increase their contributions after President Bush had doubled the number of US troops readied to liberate Kuwait.

ENGAGING WITH SYRIAN HAFEZ AL-ASSAD

From Brussels, Baker returned to the Middle East, this time to Syria and a meeting with President Hafez al-Assad. Ross argued against this visit on grounds that the secretary would gain nothing new. Longstanding US policy had been to isolate Syria because of its support for terrorism. Secretary Shultz had written off Assad based on his alleged sabotage of a US sponsored peace plan for Lebanon in 1982.[30] Baker was more audacious; in addition to a Syrian commitment to send one hundred thousand troops, he sought credible Arab solidarity against Saddam, and an opening for a Middle East peace effort to pursue *after* Saddam's withdrawal from Kuwait. To his advisers, he argued that peace talks with Israel provided Assad with the possibility of regaining the Golan Heights.

Assad was a difficult customer, but he appreciated Baker's strength and decisiveness. He liked the frankness of the discussion and assured Baker that they could "accomplish more in the future."[31] Baker recognized that Damascus and Washington remained far apart on Syria's support for the Liberation of Palestine-General Command, a splinter group within the PLO. Furthermore, Syria was on the State Department's list of outlaw nations that sponsored terrorism and remained under US sanctions. Foreign Minister Farouk al-Sharaa was not prepared to concede on matters of national security and he insisted that any attacks against Israel or Israeli interests should not be considered terrorist attacks.[32] It was clear that the two sides remained far apart on terrorism, but there was a more immediate challenge, namely increasing the pressure on Saddam Hussein. Said Baker, "We share a common purpose with respect to problems in the gulf… but we make no secret about the fact that there are still problems revolving around this question of terrorism."[33] Baker did not let the problem of support for terrorism get in his way of ensuring that Syria joined the international coalition. Other Arab states would join, knowing that Assad had accepted the American invitation, and Gorbachev could feel relief in knowing that an Arab ally had taken an anti-Saddam stand. In Baker's opinion, his calculated risk of going to Damascus had worked out.

From Damascus, Baker flew to Rome where he met with Prime Minister Giulio Andreotti, the president of the European Economic Commission, and Foreign Minister Gianni de Michelis. Here, Baker had friends with whom there was no divergence of opinion. Italy was ready to deploy Tornado Fighter aircraft to Turkey, a battalion of commandos and helicopters to Saudi Arabia, as well as fuel and rear area support for US forces. In addition, the Italian government committed to cash transfers of between $90-120 million for the 'front-line' states of Egypt, Turkey, and Jordan. De Michelis remained a close friend of the Bush administration. As Baker emerged from his meetings, he was exhilarated that a "new world order" had emerged. However, beyond recognition of predominant US power and shared values, it was unclear what responsibilities were expected from America's allies.

SEEKING GERMAN SUPPORT

Meantime, back in Washington there was mounting congressional criticism that Germany was displaying reluctance to commit resources to the multi-national effort. Why should the US be the sole guardian of freedom, and where were Germany and Japan? Baker knew that he had to persuade Chancellor Kohl to increase its contribution, but the timing was sensitive. Kohl had three significant problems. First, German unification was less than one month away and the cost of integrating the East into West Germany was estimated in the billions of deutschmarks. Second, the Soviets remained against unification and Kohl had to manage a most delicate negotiation with Gorbachev. Finally, opinion polls in Germany showed little, if any enthusiasm for extensive involvement in the Gulf crisis as Germany received only 0.3 percent of its oil from Iraq, relying instead on the North Sea and Norway.[34] In the midst of these essential German problems, Baker was asking for German help "out of the European theatre." To Kohl, this was a distraction, but one that could not be ignored. The US president had fully supported unification, despite Soviet opposition and European skepticism. Kohl, therefore, had to find some way to respond to Baker's request.

They met for ninety minutes at Kohl's country home at Ludwigshafen in south-central Germany. There was no question of German forces participating due to the constitutional restraints on military action outside NATO, but Germany could help financially as well as transport Egyptian troops and equipment to the Gulf. Recognizing Baker and Bush's extraordinary assistance in gaining German unification, Kohl agreed to contribute support in the form of military equipment and economic assistance, valued at $1.87 billion. For several members of Congress, the German contribution was inadequate and stood in stark contrast to Britain, who had committed eight thousand combat troops, and France's promise of four thousand troops as well as naval forces. Those traveling with Baker made little effort to disguise their extreme disappointment with West German behavior. "They felt that Bonn, America's richest European ally, has been remarkably unforthcoming in the gulf crisis."³⁵ Baker understood Kohl's predicament as he prepared to unify the two Germanys and he was relieved that the Germans were on board, if only for symbolic support.

The visit to Ludwigshafen ended Baker's twelve-day tour of Europe and the Middle East which in total had raised $16 billion in financial help for the multinational coalition, as well as extensive commitments of military support. By January 1991, Baker and Bush had raised pledges of over $70 billion and 670,000 troops from thirty-four countries, of which 425,000 were from the United States. Baker could rightly claim that we paid fewer direct costs of the Gulf War than any previous war in which the US engaged as a nation. When the final accounts were prepared, he had raised more monies that the actual costs incurred by the United States.

PURSUING US GOALS THROUGH THE UNITED NATIONS

By mid-October, Baker and Bush had concluded that Saddam would not withdraw uncondition-ally without the use of force. It therefore became necessary to prepare the justifications for a continued international stand against Iraq so that the coalition remained intact. Baker tasked Kimmitt to manage the UN effort in collaboration with Assistant Secretary for International Affairs, John Bolton and UN Permanent Representative Pickering. Together, they would drive the policy to force Iraqi withdrawal. From the conclusion of UN Resolution 660 on August 2 through passage of UN Resolution 678 on November 29, 1990, Pickering would not let a day go by without focusing on Kuwait and Iraqi aggression.³⁶ No other issue would dominate discussions within the Security Council. Twelve resolutions on Iraq were passed after August 2, each needing Soviet and Chinese support or acquiescence. To achieve this, Baker worked his counterparts in capital cities and Bush worked the telephone with his presidential colleagues, building upon the friendships formed over eight years as vice president. Pickering worked his fellow ambassadors at the UN, as well as the international press at the UN "stake out," where he explained positions taken in Security Council meetings to the international press.[37] Pickering's frequent use of this pulpit earned him the resentment of those around Baker, who would have preferred that the Secretary alone communicate to the press corps.[38]

Baker needed more than Soviet support for UN resolutions, trade embargoes and the use of force against Iraq. He also needed Chinese support, and US relations with Beijing were delicate after the repression of Chinese workers and students the year before. Bush could count on the British, but the French had significant arms business with Iraq and could complicate coalition building. Beyond the Permanent 5 members, there were 10 members who rotated through the UN Security Council, each for a two year term. They did not hold veto power, but their votes counted and influenced the Chinese who did not want to find themselves among the minority on any vote. Baker knew that he needed to work with each of these members through their respective capitals and through the UN. Having made the decision early on to build a coalition against Saddam and demonstrate that Iraq was isolated against world opinion, Bush and Baker had to work furiously to hold that coalition together and prepare allies for a military offensive should Saddam not withdraw unconditionally. Bush, knew the working of the UN Security Council from his time as President Ford's Permanent Representative to the UN from 1971-73. Now he worked closely with Baker, Bolton and Pickering to use the UN Security Council to advance Washington's interests, despite the fact that the Pentagon was skeptical of the UN's usefulness and Prime Minister Thatcher considered it was a useless body.[39] Bush and Baker were determined to make the UN work in defense of universal values, the rule of law and their determination to support a small, friendly state in the oil-producing Gulf. In their opinion, it was the first test of "the new world order."[40] Could the United States exercise its pre-dominance in the world to regain the territorial integrity of Kuwait?

In the midst of the UN debates over Iraq, on October 8 Israeli security forces killed seventeen Palestinians on the Temple Mount in Jerusalem. This action could not have come at a worse time for

Washington. Just as the anti-Saddam coalition, including Arab nations, had come together, the Israeli response diverted attention to the Israeli-Palestinian conflict. Baker called Israeli Foreign Minister David Levy and warned that he would not use the American veto to defend Israel in the upcoming UN debate and any resolution condemning Israeli action. Kimmitt instructed Pickering not to veto UN Resolutions 672 and 673, which condemned Israeli action. Relations with Israel remained tense, and Baker warned Jerusalem: do not jeopardize US efforts to maintain the anti-Saddam coalition. Iraq is the gravest threat that you face, so control your security forces and refrain from provocative actions.

SOVIET EFFORTS TO ESTABLISH LINKAGE

Relations with Moscow did not remain as clear as they seemed when Shevardnadze appeared at Vnukovo airport with Baker on August 3. Gorbachev was eager to find a face-saver for Saddam Hussein, with whom the Soviets had a twenty-seven year-long relationship. A commitment to an international conference between the Israelis and the Palestinians might provide Saddam with the justification for his withdrawal from Kuwait. Baker had listened to the idea of a regional peace conference at his first meeting in Moscow in May 1989, but interpreted it as an effort by Gorbachev to remain a relevant power in the Middle East. Baker did not follow up. For a second time, Gorbachev raised the idea of a peace conference jointly chaired by the US and the Soviets at the Malta Summit in December 1989, eight months before the Iraqi invasion. Neither Bush nor Baker pursued the idea, knowing that the Israelis disliked intensely UN conferences that historically had been highly critical of Israel.[41]

Gorbachev raised it a third time on September 9, 1990 when the two leaders met in Helsinki for a summit focused on the Iraqi invasion. At that time and at subsequent meetings, Baker insisted that there could be no linkage between Saddam's removal from Kuwait and an Israeli-Palestinian peace conference. They should respect the UN Security Council resolutions, which called for the unconditional and immediate withdrawal of Iraq. Despite Soviet requests, Baker believed that it would be a mistake to deal with Palestinian problems thus giving Saddam an Arab justification for his unprovoked aggression. President Bush had a "rather tough discussion" with Gorbachev over linkage with the latter claiming that Saddam should not be driven into a corner and should be given a minimum opportunity "to save a little political face."[42] However, in a separate room Baker and Shevardnadze drafted their own communique. When it came time to deliver the summit meeting communique, Baker succeeded in presenting the foreign ministers' text as the final document. It made no reference to an Israeli-Palestinian peace conference despite the effort of Primakov, to slip the words into Gorbachev's draft. Later, Baker admitted, "we had made some commitments to our Soviet friends that we would be interested in addressing the problems of the Middle East in the aftermath of Iraq's withdrawal from Kuwait, however that withdrawal took place."[43] In his view, a US and allied victory provided a "window of opportunity to maybe break an old taboo between Arabs and Israelis, the old taboo being that they would never sit down face to face and negotiate peace, save for the single exception of Egypt."[44]

As the likelihood of military action to remove Iraqi forces grew, the French and the Soviets repeated their efforts to link Iraqi withdrawal to Israeli withdrawal from the West Bank, Gaza, and the Golan Heights. Linkage represented their separate and sometimes combined effort to seek a political way out of using military force. On each occasion Baker and his colleagues insisted on respect for UN resolutions calling for unconditional and immediate withdrawal. They rejected any direct link.

GROWING DOMESTIC OPPOSITION

Back in August, the president had gathered congressional leaders at the White House to explain his policy. Baker came away from the meeting irritated by the accusation that he had failed both to explain adequately the reason for troop deployments to Saudi Arabia and not done enough to obtain financial aid from Japan and Germany. As time passed and sanctions appeared to have little impact on Saddam's behavior, American public support for *Operation Desert Shield* waned. By November, opinion polls indicated that a narrow majority of Americans did not find Saddam's invasion of Kuwait sufficient cause to go to war.[45] Indeed, sending five hundred thousand troops to fight the fourth largest army in the world was a recipe for heavy duty body bags coming home in their hundreds.

On October 24, the President with Baker and Cheney held a closed briefing for congressional leaders. Both Senate and House leaders asked that the president obtain UN approval for military action before he ask them to vote on the use of force.[46] They also requested more time for economic sanctions to work. Baker warned the members "we and our partners will use force if nothing else works."[47] He knew that Bush and his national security team had made the decision that same day to use military force should the Iraqis not withdraw unconditionally from Kuwait. He was a straightforward man who did not believe in dissimulation. The congressional leaders should understand that the president was determined to eject Saddam Hussein from Kuwait.

In the campaign leading to the midterm elections that year only one campaigner from the traditionally isolationist Midwest sought votes by attacking Bush's policy in the Gulf. Democratic Senator Tom Harkin criticized the decision to call up the reserves and led Senate action to threaten Germany and Japan if they refused to pay their fair share of *Operation Desert Shield*. Other politicians chose to stay away from the crisis in the Gulf and focus on domestic issues. Due to the pending mid-term election on November 6, Bush did not communicate his decision to call up further troops and prepare for military action against Saddam. He waited until November 8 to inform the Congress that he was doubling the number of troops in the Gulf. Both that decision and the delay created apprehension that the administration sought to go to war without congressional authorization. This aroused the suspicion that a small cabal around the president had decided to send thousands of troops to war without any serious political debate.[48]

Baker was out of town when the White House decided to delay the presidential announcement on doubling the troop force, but immediately he realized the error. He knew that it would take several weeks of hard work to restore the trust and confidence of congressional leaders. As he flew from Europe to the Gulf, to Moscow, and on to Colombia, Baker called key Senate and House members from his plane to explain what was happening. He believed that only a concerted and bipartisan commitment to eject Iraqi forces would convince Saddam that US resolve was unshakable. In his telephone conversations, Baker noted that Saddam was trying to split the international coalition and was releasing foreign hostages on a partial basis with the intent of dividing the anti-Iraq coalition.

On November 14, the President convened another meeting of the congressional leadership. It was evident that support for the administration's policy was evaporating.[49] House Speaker Tom Foley represented a majority of House members seeking more time for sanctions to work.[50] Democratic Senator Sam Nunn was concerned that the US was preparing for a different kind of war and that it had abandoned reliance on sanctions. These arguments from congressional leaders frustrated both the president and Baker because both believed that they were doing the right thing morally. However, their justifications varied from the moral defense of a small nation to the pragmatic. Baker suggested that American jobs would be lost if we lost secure access to the energy supplies of the Persian Gulf.[51] To the Episcopalian Bishop Edmond Browning, Baker showed pictures of the Iraqis cutting people's tongues out and raping women held in Kuwait to emphasize the immoral nature of Saddam's occupation and its violation of the laws of war.[52] Bush emphasized that Iraq might be close to acquiring nuclear weapons, giving the US "a real sense of urgency."[53] The absence of a single, straightforward explanation raised public concern that the administration was looking for justifications to take the nation to war. The secrecy surrounding the decision to develop an offensive capability against Iraq and the lack of clarity in explaining the reasons for military action against Saddam Hussein led to political disquiet and anxiety.

Both the president and Baker continued their concerted effort to convince Congress that, should economic sanctions and an embargo fail to remove Saddam, military force might be necessary. The issue of US credibility was on the line, but there was no assurance that Congress would give the President the authority to use military force. Constitutionally, the president as commander in chief might not need a War Powers Act, and Defense Secretary Cheney opposed seeking congressional authority on grounds that the risk of losing the vote was simply too great. However, Baker and Scowcroft favored seeking and gaining both congressional and public support. They would go "the extra mile" to avoid war, but if it became necessary, they would seek congressional backing. Republicans were supportive of the president, but sought to avoid a public debate that would send a message of political divisiveness to Saddam Hussein. The White House meetings of November 14 ended with a request that Baker return to the region and continue to gather allies in support of the US cause. This should not be Saddam versus Bush, but Saddam versus the world. Continued pressure against Iraq from the UN Security Council was essential.

THE MARATHON TO REACH UN RESOLUTION 678

By mid-October, it had become evident that sanctions alone would not oblige Saddam to withdraw from Kuwait. The threat of war was needed. Baker was convinced that the administration, working through the UN Security Council, could achieve a Security Council resolution authorizing the use of force. Cheney and Scowcroft were skeptical. Prime Minister Thatcher was adamantly opposed. If you fail to get the resolution, she argued, you would find yourself alone against Iraq with perilous long-term consequences for the US and its western allies.[54] Baker stood firm. He believed that a concerted effort to persuade ALL members of the Security Council could result in a favorable vote. He persuaded Bush and offered to meet with every president or foreign minister from the fifteen nations on the Security Council, as well as those nations providing troops. He would ask them to support a UN resolution, authorizing the use of force for the first time since Korea in 1950. The issue was too important to leave to

UN ambassadors; it should be addressed at the highest level. With the additional leverage of the US month-long presidency of the Security Council in the month of November 1990, Baker would do his very best to achieve the desired outcome. As he later admitted, he used "an intricate process of cajoling, extracting, threatening and occasionally buying votes."[55]

Beginning on November 3, he visited twelve countries on three continents in a matter of eighteen days. The marathon began in Jeddah where in addition to meeting with King Fahd, Baker took the helicopter out to the military base near Dhahran where 4,200 American troops were stationed. Their high morale impressed Baker who talked about their defense of American values. He emphasized that aggression against a small nation should not pay, unlike Hitler's actions in the 1930s. He spoke of a new world order of peace and freedom. Finally, he thanked them and their families for their service.[56] For Baker, the meeting was emotional and reminded him of his two-year service in the Marines. Also, his son William Winston, though not yet called up, was in the Army Special Forces.

When Baker reached Moscow on November 7, Shevardnadze could no longer support the use-of-force. The apparatchiks in the Kremlin had gained strength and directed their attacks against the foreign minister who, they claimed, was acceding to the Americans both in Europe and in the Middle East. Shevardnadze no longer had freedom to maneuver and he now asked Baker for more time. Gorbachev called Baker to his dacha outside Moscow where he proposed two resolutions: the first would authorize the use-of-force after a six-week period and the second would order the commencement of hostilities. Baker hated the idea. It sent a weak message to Saddam and he doubted that they could get the second resolution. He left Moscow believing that Shevardnadze was more sympathetic with the US position, but that Gorbachev remained opposed.[57] The Soviet leader sought to resolve the crisis through negotiation and invited Tariq Aziz, the Iraqi vice president and chief spokesperson for Saddam Hussein, to Moscow on November 21. Only when those talks failed to show any Iraqi sign of moderation despite the

Soviet leader's harsh talk with Saddam Hussein, did Gorbachev agree to support the Security Council resolution.

Perhaps the most challenging meeting was with the Chinese Foreign Minister Qian Qichen, who was on his way to meet Saddam in Baghdad. Baker met him at Cairo airport on November 6. Qian expressed firm commitment to uphold all Security Council resolutions, but he resisted the prospect of a use-of-force resolution. China believed that the sanctions were beginning to work and therefore talk of force was premature. "War would alter the balance of power in the Gulf and must be averted at all costs," he argued.[58] Baker countered with the importance of a united front to convince Saddam that the international community was serious. Regretfully, he told Qjan he did not expect Saddam to leave Kuwait peacefully. The two men negotiated for a while before Baker departed, leaving Qian to understand that a Chinese veto would seriously harm Sino-US relations. Several days later on November 24, as he landed in Bogota, Colombia to gain that country's Security Council vote, Baker spoke by phone with Shevardnadze. His Soviet counterpart had just met with Chinese leaders whom he believed would support the proposal, now identified as Security Council Resolution 678. In Shevardnadze's words, despite cautious Chinese pronouncement he believed that "They are ready, along with others to cooperate on additional measures in order to reinforce the prior resolutions."[59] In the end, the Chinese abstained from voting on Resolution 678. That was sufficient for Baker. He had avoided a Chinese veto.

Resolution 678 permitted the use of force under the terminology "use all necessary means." Kimmitt had drafted the language with the intent of both creating latitude on what specific means to use, as well as using a euphemism for military force. It did not oblige military action, but it established a credible threat. The international community now held the authority to use force unless Saddam withdrew completely, immediately and unconditionally from Kuwait by January 15, 1991.[60] The Security Council members debated the deadline, with the Soviets seeking January 30 and the US preferring January 15.

SEEKING CONGRESSIONAL SUPPORT FOR THE USE OF FORCE

The persistent effort to win multilateral support at the UN was intended not only to isolate Iraq, but also persuade the US Congress to act as resolutely as the international community. On December 5 and 6, Baker testified before the committees on foreign relations in the Senate and House, respectively. On both occasions Baker stressed "We are making every attempt to resolve it [Gulf crisis] peacefully without appeasing the aggressor... [but] no one can tell you that sanctions alone will ever be able to impose a high enough cost on Saddam to get him to withdraw... [Therefore] we need continued support for our military preparations to make credible an offensive option to liberate Kuwait."[61]

Baker laid out the consequences of a failure to continue preparations to use force. The Congress should understand that the United States had vital national interests at stake. A dangerous dictator, armed to the teeth with the sixth largest army and fifth largest tank army in the world, controlled Kuwait. He could dominate the oil-rich Gulf States who would stand up to him only reluctantly, for fear that they too would suffer the Kuwaiti fate. In short time, Saddam would add nuclear weapons to his arsenal of biological and chemical weapons. Consequently, he would threaten Israel and the economies of Europe and Asia would suffer from excessive increases in the price of oil. The United States was the only nation that could do the job: "We must stand with the world so that the United Nations does not go the way of the League of Nations."[62] The debate was fierce: nearly half of those in Congress opposed going to war, or at least opposed resorting to military action in January. Baker recognized that the country was "overwhelmingly opposed" to "the idea of going to war in the Persian Gulf."[63]

On December 20, Eduard Shevardnadze wrote to his friend James Baker to inform him that he was resigning from Gorbachev's government. The last months had been increasingly stressful with Gorbachev listening more to the hardliners in the Kremlin to preserve his authority. Direct verbal attacks on Shevardnadze were cheaper than attacks on Gorbachev. Shevardnadze was blamed for losing East Germany. Now a Soviet ally, Iraq faced the brunt force of an international coalition. There was a limit to how much he could withstand, and by Christmas 1990 Shevardnadze had retreated to his native country, Georgia. With his departure, Baker lost a much trusted colleague and a personal friend. Their relationship had started frigidly in May 1989, but after the flight to Wyoming and the talks alongside the trout stream that September, the formality had gone and genuine friendship had developed. It deepened over the next twelve months, resulting in their successful drafting of both the final communique at the Helsinki summit and the joint statement at Moscow's Vnukovo airport.

Shevardnadze's departure was a blow for Baker. Fortunately, his successor Aleksandr Bessmertnykh was a known figure who had recently served as Soviet Ambassador in Washington. Although there would never be the same intimacy between these men, both sought to create a constructive relationship. Baker worked with Bessmertnykh at the Berlin meeting of the OSCE in June 1991 to forestall the breakup of Yugoslavia, but they held stark differences over independence for the three Baltic States.[64]

ONE LAST DIPLOMATIC EFFORT

That December, Defense Secretary Cheney and National Security Advisor Scowcroft were pursuing military preparations, but the president and Baker were determined to make one last try at diplomacy. They had not yet gained congressional approval for military action to repel Iraq and both knew that they must demonstrate to Congress that they had made every effort to achieve Iraqi withdrawal from Kuwait through negotiation. Both recognized the necessity of bringing the American people along if their president was going to send men and women off to fight. Vietnam had demonstrated what happens to the war effort when a president lacks the support of American citizens. Both Bush and Baker had to survive the judgements of history and prove they had not gone to war precipitously. There were not Texan cowboys. Instead, Baker would show that "we've left no stone unturned in a search for a peaceful resolution of this, albeit an unconditional withdrawal."[65]

Thus, early in the New Year and only days before the January 15 deadline, Baker flew to Geneva to meet with Iraqi Vice President Tariq Aziz. They met on January 9. Allies were alarmed at the prospect that the US might waver at this last minute thus leaving them exposed to Iraqi retaliation, but Baker was determined to remain firm and not dilute any of the twelve Security Council resolutions on Iraq, not least Resolution 678. Nevertheless, back in Washington, National Security staff bit their nails.[66] They feared that the skilled lawyer and determined negotiator might obtain a political outcome thus negating the need for military force. Baker presented Aziz with President Bush's letter for Saddam Hussein. Aziz asked for a copy, which he read quietly for ten minutes, or so before responding, "I cannot accept this letter, it's not written in the language that is appropriate for communications between heads of state."[67]

Baker replied, "All right I'm sorry that you choose not to take the letter, but … it seems to me, Minister, that you're taking a rather large burden on your shoulders because you're the only person on your side of the table." At that moment, Dennis Ross noticed Tariq Aziz's hands tremble. He was under close watch from Saddam Hussein's brother-in-law on his right and Saddam's personal interpreter on his left, whom Baker assumed were there to ensure that Aziz did not stray from his instructions. Baker then warned that Iraqi forces had to leave Kuwait unconditionally and if not overwhelmingly superior force would be used against them: "[You] should not make the mistake of assuming that [you] will control the terms of the battle, as perhaps [you] might have in [your] war with Iran. … This would be a totally different situation, that our technological superiority was overwhelming."[68] Aziz did not buy this argument: "You haven't fought in the desert before. Your Arab allies will turn and run, they will not fight their brothers. You will be surprised at the strength and the determination and the force and the courage of the Iraqi military."⁶⁹ It was clear that there was no compromise and at the end of six and a half hours, Baker stated that he had nothing more to say. He had stayed close to his talking points and reached the end. Nevertheless, he was willing to extend the talks and listen to his Iraqi interlocutor. At no point did Tariq Aziz present an opening – he offered nothing to suggest a compromise.⁷⁰ With nothing more to discuss, the two men shook hands, as did their advisors. The talks ended and Baker called Bush to relate that US Iraqi relations had reached an impasse. Back at the White House, that deadlock gave rise to relief mixed with the sobriety; war was now inevitable.

On January 12, 1991, the Senate voted fifty-two to forty-seven to authorize the president to go to war. Those senators who had opposed most aggressively the use of force said that in the aftermath of the Tariq Aziz-Baker meeting in Geneva, opposition to the US use of force eroded.⁷¹ Bush had sought and obtained congressional support for the war. There was a solemn recognition that US credibility was on the line. Military plans were ready and the allies, including the Soviet Union remained with the United States. To reassure allies of the president's intent to repel the Iraqis from Kuwait, but not to occupy Iraq or rid the country of Saddam Hussein, Baker visited US troops and the emir of Kuwait. He then went onto reassure the Saudi, Egyptian, Syrian, and Turkish leaders that the war was a limited one. He had failed to avoid military conflict, but had succeeded in consolidating the international coalition, upholding UN Security Council resolutions and establishing a new partnership with the Soviet Union.

Early on January 17 stealth bombers, cruise missiles and infrared night bombers attacked Iraq airfields, communication networks, weapon plants and bridges over the Euphrates. The purpose was to assert air control before the ground offensive began. On February 24, 540,000 troops from the US, Saudi Arabia, Egypt, France, and Great Britain encircled and defeated the Iraqi army and liberated Kuwait. Four days later a ceasefire went into effect, and on February 27 President Bush declared the war over.⁷²

AFTERMATH OF THE GULF WAR

On March 8, Baker flew to Riyadh to meet with the emir of Kuwait and the foreign ministers of the Gulf Cooperation Council.[73] He came to thank them for their critical contributions and emphasize the positive cooperation among allied military forces in their joint defense of Kuwait. To his interlocutors, the power of US technology was evident, but more important to Baker was US credibility. President Bush had carried out the goals agreed upon with US allies and not more. The US army had not moved onto Bagdad to remove Saddam Hussein, nor had it created safe havens in the South to protect opponents to the regime. However, the fight with Saddam was not over. As the Iraqis withdrew taking massive casualties on the Highway of Death leading back to Baghdad, Generals Schwarzkopf and Powell recommended to the president that the Revolutionary Guard keep its helicopters to ferry the wounded to hospitals and military officers back to Baghdad. It proved to be a colossal mistake, but its origins were the respect for the soldiers of a defeated nation.[74]

In early March, the Shia opposition in the south and the Kurds in the north rebelled against Saddam Hussein. Kurdish forces captured Irbil and other population centers. From Damascus, Iraq's historical nemesis, the Syrians encouraged Iraqi opposition groups and urged Iraqis to take up arms against the Baghdad government. Saddam retaliated with vengeance, using his helicopter gunships to target his opponents. The revolts in the south and north had strengthened Saddam's grip on the Revolutionary Guard. Baker and others had hoped that disgruntled members of the Guard would topple Saddam after his devastating defeat, but they underestimated his enduring power and ability to use the revolts to stress his invincibility. Demanding loyalty, he confronted the Shia and the Kurds. In the south, he drained the marshlands between the Euphrates and the Tigris to force ancient Shia tribes to leave. In the north, the Kurds faced repression forcing them to flee toward the Turkish border. Approximately half a million Kurds – including the elderly, infirm, and children – ran with the little they could carry to mountains and valleys where Saddam continued to strafe, bomb, and drop napalm. Huddled on the side of mountains, they called upon the governments of the coalition forces that had liberated Kuwait to help them.

On April 8, Baker landed in Turkey close to the border with Iraqi Kurdistan to see for himself and to awaken the conscience of the western world to the plight of these refugees. He brought television crews and correspondents of national newspapers to record the plight of these people and to gain the support and sympathy of the international community. Baker spent ten minutes on the ground before Turkish security hustled him away, fearful that the refugees would overwhelm the American delegation. But in that short time, Baker listened to desperate men ask why the coalition had not continued to fight for two more days and thus defeat the dictator, Saddam Hussein himself.

Others asked for humanitarian relief, "Mr. Baker," cried a young man in English, "I want to talk with you… You've got to do something to help us… Our children are suffering from hunger and starvation," pleaded Sam Timathwes, who managed to get within a few feet of Baker. "We don't have enough water supply… We need medicines, we need food."[75]

"We know that," Baker said quietly. An ocean of anxious faces turned his way from the hillsides and broad valley below. Gamely, Baker attempted an adequate reply, "We have a rather large, big airlift going on right now, hoping to help many of you people, both on the Turkish side and on the Iraqi side of the border. But what's really needed, as you just point out, is a massive international relief effort…"[76]

"That's right," Timathwes said, and a few who could hear Baker's words nodded their heads.

Then Baker marched back to his motorcade and sped north into Turkey. The meeting moved him emotionally. He was taken aback by the alarming scenes of families camped out in the frigid air without cover, food or clean water. He had experienced life in the Teton Mountains and knew how cold nightly temperatures were at high elevations in early spring.[77] Families would spend hours scraping for firewood and food. It was a desperate sight and the memory remained with Baker for many years.

On his flight onto Jerusalem, he called both the president and Cheney persuading them to undertake this humanitarian mission. "I'd never seen anything like this and a lot of people were going to die if we didn't do something and do something quickly."[78] Baker urged action that became the genesis of *Operation Provide Comfort* and the acceptance of a British plan to create safe havens in northern Iraq. Cheney had made it clear to Baker that the US military should not take on the responsibility for creating and enforcing a safe haven, but Baker knew that it wasn't going to be enforced by others. "It was going to have to be enforced by Uncle Whiskers and we really didn't want to do it, but when you saw the magnitude of that humanitarian nightmare building there, we really ended up providing a safe haven."[79] He had persuaded the president that the US could not ignore the plight of thousands of families exposed to Saddam Hussein's helicopters and the ravages of weather. The British plan could assist in protecting the displaced families from Saddam through a quasi-no-fly zone. Furthermore, together with the coalition partners, he could mobilize humanitarian aid. However, there were diplomatic consequences that Baker was hesitant to pursue.

LINGERING UNANSWERED QUESTIONS

Later in 1991 and for his work in persuading international partners to support the UN Security Council resolutions that upheld the sovereignty of Kuwait, authorized the use of military force to repel the invading forces and upheld American values, Baker received the Presidential Medal of Freedom from a grateful president.[80] However, despite this most notable recognition, there was a regional security issue that Baker had not yet achieved. How might the US reinforce regional security through the strengthening of the Gulf Cooperation Council (GCC)? Should he have persuaded the GCC leadership to develop the capacity to monitor and constrain Saddam from further aggressive behavior in the region? US Ambassadors accredited to each of the Gulf States advocated for greater regional effort, but none had the clout of an American Secretary of State. Were he, personally, to persuade the leaders of the Gulf States to strengthen information sharing and to hold combined military training exercises, an effective regional shield might have constrained Saddam Hussein from acquiring Weapons of Mass Destruction, known as WMD. Secretary Cheney could well have undertaken this task, but Baker had the personal reputation and star-like quality to persuade, to cajole and if necessary to buy their agreement.

Less strategic issues persisted. Covered fully by the international press in the months following the withdrawal of coalition forces from Iraq, three questions lingered: should the US have permitted Saddam Hussein to keep his helicopters; should the coalition forces have maintained a buffer zone in the south, or occupied some little part of southern Iraq; and, should the coalition have eliminated Saddam Hussein's leadership. In the light of the second Iraq war of 2003, the answers are different from those that Baker gave in the years following the 1991 war to free Kuwait. Closer to that time, Baker defended the Bush administration on grounds that they had no intention to occupy Iraq or any portion of Iraq, nor was there a political aim to eliminate Saddam Hussein. On the contrary, he claims that *had the US remained* to ensure safe havens and thus viewed as an occupying power, the potential for Middle East peace would have disappeared.[81] Bush and Scowcroft have claimed that they gained the support of a coalition of willing partners to eject Saddam from Kuwait, not to destroy Saddam. Bush kept his word.

Nevertheless, his national security team might have anticipated that Saddam would assert his power once again in the region and the best defense was regional solidarity through a stronger and effective GCC. Baker did not give that policy sufficient attention. Instead, he recalled Bush's commitment to work with Gorbachev to seek peace between Israel and the Palestinians. Baker had avoided this quandary since assuming leadership at State, but his personal prestige, as well as that of the US government were so high that now might be the time to bring the parties together. He had few illusions. From his frequent trips to the region Baker understood the complexities that lay ahead

SEVEN

THE ARAB–ISRAELI DIALOGUE

B aker was physically drained but mentally invigorated. His effort both to maintain the anti-Saddam coalition and convince the US Congress that war in the Gulf was necessary had left him tired, but convinced that the United States had a special role to play in maintaining international order.[1] By late February 1991, coalition forces had liberated Kuwait and the US could rightly claim 'mission accomplished.' President Bush would not commit the US to regional entanglements, leaving containment of Saddam Hussein to the United Nations. As coalition forces drove the Iraqi army out of Kuwait, the opportunity arose to share the administration's options with Congress. In the interests of advancing a bi-partisan foreign policy, Baker addressed the Democratic led House Foreign Affairs Committee and the Senate Committee on Foreign Relations. He had two fundamental questions for them: should there be a permanent, locally stationed ground force made up of local troops under UN auspices; and how could the international community reinforce deterrence in the Gulf, whether by contributing forces or through other political arrangements such as resolutions or security commitments.[2]

The challenge was how to transform the outlook for the Gulf region with US and Western encouragement, but without US funding or military forces.[3] Baker's advisers knew that the continued presence of US forces in Saudi Arabia was unacceptable to Pan Arabs and Islamic sentiments.[4] Instead, local states and regional bodies should assume the responsibility for maintaining national sovereignty and inviolate borders. In the President and Baker's mind, the Gulf Cooperation Council (GCC) was best placed "to lead in building and reinforcing a network of new and strengthened security ties in which no regional state should be excluded." Implicit in this phrase was the inclusion of Israel.

The last and maybe the hardest of Baker's challenges for future regional security was "the search for a just peace and real reconciliation for Israel, the Arab states, and the Palestinians."[5] In the aftermath of the Iraq war, there "may be opportunities for peace if the parties are willing... and... we are committed to working closely with them to fashion a more effective peace process."[6] To carry this out, Baker would consult closely with allies in the region. Mentally, had he just packed his bag and once more climbed onto his plane to travel throughout the Middle East? Should he use these visits to strengthen regional institutions and create a cooperative environment to consolidate security arrangements? More broadly, could he both strengthen regional security and discuss whether the time was right for Arab states to engage with Israel?

Ross, as Director of Policy Planning and longtime advisor to Baker reminded him that the time was ripe for US mediation between Israel and the Palestinians, but in February and March 1991 Baker was unsure. He had avoided personal involvement and travel to Israel in order to protect his reputation on a problem that had evaded US mediators for decades.[7] However, there was a commitment that he had made to Shevardnadze at the Helsinki Summit back in September 1990. There, he had agreed that once the Iraqis had withdrawn from Kuwait, he would be ready to consider a dialogue with the Israelis and the Palestinians under the joint chairmanship of both the United States and the Soviet Union. Despite the warning of Egyptian President Mubarak NOT to initiate an international conference on the Middle East because "its going to look like Saddam Hussein delivers and we can't,"[8] Baker believed that Saddam's resounding defeat avoided that connection. But he never underestimated the difficulty of unlocking that riddle and achieving that dialogue.

Years before, Richard Nixon had warned him against getting ensnared in Middle East peace negotiations. The problems, Nixon said, were insoluble and could burn Baker politically.[9] For a man inclined to avoid losing causes, the prospect of dedicating time and energy to a problem that had long eluded any solution was not compelling. Nevertheless, Baker had made a commitment and Bush had also expressed interest in finding a resolution to the Israeli-Palestinian problem. Sufficient reasons existed to engage with the Middle East as a logical follow up to the Gulf War.

US influence was at its zenith in the months following the Gulf War. The anti-Saddam coalition comprised nearly every Arab state as well as the Soviet Union and NATO. Japan had contributed $2 billion.[10] The Soviet Union was absorbed with its own internal economic problems and had few resources to support its long-time ally, Syria. The Arab world recognized that only the US the sole remaining superpower, could muster the military and financial means to cajole the Israelis to enter a dialogue.

Baker's success in creating and maintaining the anti-Saddam coalition and repelling Iraqi forces created an aura around him. Wherever he landed in the Middle East, he was treated like a head of state.[11] Baker was not Bush, but their friendship was well known, and the success of the American coalition was attributable in large part to both men. In 1989 Baker had deliberately avoided travel to Israel and involvement in the Arab-Israeli conflict, but in 1991 his personal influence was considerable. Could he bring about an international peace conference to address the Israeli-Palestinian dispute?

EARLY DAYS: BAKER'S APPROACH TOWARD ISRAEL

The Israeli-Palestinian conflict has been an issue from the very start of Baker's tenure. At his confirmation hearing, before the Senate Committee on Foreign Relations on January 17 and 18, 1989 Baker had reiterated his commitment to Israel's security in his opening remarks. He noted the nation's "enduring support for the state of Israel… We are determined to build upon the achievements of our predecessors. ...As President-elect Bush has described it... the purpose of the negotiations... is, above all, a just, enduring peace that ensures Israeli security."[12] Senator Rudy Boschwitz of Minnesota sought to confirm Baker's commitment to Israel by asking if the administration "will continue the policies of the Reagan administration with respect to the Middle East." Baker replied that, "generally speaking... that is correct,"[13] an answer that left him room to maneuver. Senator Connie Mack of Florida suggested bilateral talks between Israelis and Palestinians. Baker agreed to study whether such talks should become part of US policy towards Israel.[14] While agreeing with Senator Helms that the PLO had to refrain from acts of terrorism before any meeting with US officials could take place, he acknowledged Shultz's meeting with the PLO in Tunis the previous month, and he kept open the possibility of future meetings to discuss the PLO's announced "abstinence from terrorism."[15] In short, days before the Bush administration took office; Baker expressed a more flexible approach toward meeting with the PLO.

The strategic review of key foreign policy issues that Bush and Baker undertook upon entering office also included examination of the extent to which they could move away from Reagan's unequivocal support for Israel. Recognizing that the Middle East was vital to US interests, Bush was ready to hold peace talks between Israel and the Palestinians, but his challenge was to find Palestinians with whom Israeli Prime Minister Yitzhak Shamir was prepared to talk. Dennis Ross advocated firmly for US engagement based on the recent *intifada*, which had proved to the leadership of both Israel and Palestine that military victory was unachievable. Political negotiation was the only option.

In pursuit of a political outcome and with incoming President Bush's full approval, George Shultz in December 1988 had opened a "substantive dialogue" with the PLO in the Tunis meeting. This engagement irritated Prime Minister Shamir, but Shultz had recognized that Yasser Arafat had met American criteria by accepting "the right of all parties concerned in the Middle East conflict to exist in peace and security." Arafat was also ready to call Israel by name, thus ending years in which refusal to name the nation indicated a refusal to recognize its existence.[16] The Tunis meeting presented Baker with an opportunity to pursue dialogue with the PLO and determine if a basis for peace was possible. In Ross' opinion, "there was a need to push something, to launch something that could take advantage of ... a new dynamic."[17] In 1989, however, Baker would not get involved beyond making phone calls and attending meetings in Washington and New York. He would not travel to the region. "Baker was convinced," said Ross in a 2001 interview, "that the Middle East was a loser as an issue... It would suck him in and suck him dry and he'd have nothing to show for it."[18]

On April 6 1989, Prime Minister Yitzhak Shamir called on the new President Bush. They enjoyed a tête-a-tête in the Oval Office with only the Israeli Ambassador, Moshe Arad, and NSC official Richard Haass present. Bush raised his concern about settlements in the disputed territories, "Look, you know, Prime Minister, the questions of settlements really is important to me, it matters..." Shamir waved him off, saying, "Not a problem, no problem, don't worry about it."[19] It took several conversations with Ambassador Arad for the two leaders to realize that they had talked past each other. Shamir was saying that Bush was exaggerating the settlements' significance. Bush understood that he had Shamir's pledge not to do anything that would give *him* a problem. He thus took it as bad faith when the Israeli government announced two new settlements within ten days of the White House meeting. Afterward, Bush never fully trusted Shamir. He passed the task of creating a working relationship with the Israeli Prime Minister to his Secretary of State. Baker accepted the responsibility and developed the habit of saying to Shamir, "if you think what I'm saying is tough, Mr. Prime Minister, you ought to hear what my good friend of thirty years, President George Bush, is saying."[20]

DEBATE OVER AN INTERNATIONAL CONFERENCE ON THE MIDDLE EAST

However, during his first visit to Moscow, on May 10, 1989, Baker asked Shevardnadze to support an Israeli four-point plan to elect Palestinian delegates who would negotiate self-rule. The Palestinians were refusing to cooperate because they thought the Israeli plan would prejudice their claim to an independent state. Most of the Arab world supported them, including Syria, a Soviet client state. Unexpectedly, Shevardnadze agreed both to support the Israeli plan and to use his influence with Syrian President Hafez al-Assad. However, Soviet support had a price. The US should endorse a "parallel" process that would lead to an international conference on the Middle East, chaired by both the United States and the Soviet Union.[21] This was an old idea that dated back to Soviet Foreign Minister Andrei Gromyko and his co-chairmanship of the International Conference on the Middle East back in 1973.[22] He had sought joint chairmanship in order to ensure that the Kremlin had a hand in any settlement of the Israeli-Arab dispute.

Neither Jerusalem nor Washington had shown any interest in helping Moscow achieve this goal. Baker therefore declined Shevardnadze's offer on the grounds that an international conference would distract from the proposed elections in the West Bank. Washington believed these elections were the only viable way to launch a peace process. To his aides after the meeting, Baker said: "No reason to encourage this conference business. Sooner or later it'll go away. I doubt Shevardnadze has his heart in it."[23] The truth was that Baker had other priorities, namely improved relations with the Soviet Union. Thus, in the first eighteen months of the administration, there was no consistent US policy toward the Middle East.

BAKER'S SPEECH BEFORE AIPAC

Among the new administration's Middle East experts, discussions focused on support for the Israeli proposal to hold elections in the West Bank and Gaza, and how the representative Palestinians would be chosen. Baker paid little attention, being absorbed by the tumultuous events in the Soviet Union and Eastern Europe. Ross, his deputy Bill Burns, and John Kelly, the Assistant Secretary of State for Near Eastern Affairs, maintained the relationship with Israel as well as the dialogue with the PLO. At the NSC, Haass was responsible for Middle East policy. A forthcoming project was the drafting of the speech that Baker should deliver that spring to AIPAC's annual meeting. Ross and Haass advised Baker that the speech should propose a shift in policy, from unconditional support for Israel to a more nuanced backing. Dan Kurtzer, on the Policy Planning staff, drafted it, and it drew no dissent from any adviser at either the State Department or the NSC.[24] Baker could rightfully rely on their combined opinion; they knew more about the shoals of Jewish politics than he did.

On May 21, following a longstanding tradition, the Secretary of State addressed AIPAC's annual gathering. His speech clearly departed from Reagan's unquestioning commitment to Israel: "For Israel, now is the time to lay aside, once and for all, the unrealistic vision of a greater Israel.[25] ...For Palestinians, now is the time to speak with one voice for peace." Israel should abandon all ideas of annexing the West Bank and Gaza, reopen closed Palestinian schools in the occupied territories, halt all Jewish settlement activity, and move toward negotiations "whose successful outcome will, in all probability, involve territorial withdrawal."[26]

The Palestinians should amend the PLO charter, which called for the elimination of Israel, renounce the concept of a phased takeover of Israel, "practice constructive diplomacy, not attempt to distort international organizations, such as the World Health Organization and ...translate the dialogue of violence [the *intifada*] into a dialogue of politics and diplomacy." He endorsed the Israeli proposal to allow Palestinians in the West Bank and Gaza to elect leaders to negotiate peace with Israel. This "has given us something to work with." Israel, he added, "has taken a stand on some important issues, and this deserves a constructive Palestinian and broader Arab response."[27]

Although Baker's remarks were consistent with longstanding American policy on the Middle East, they nevertheless departed from the Reagan administration's tone. The speech lacked the laudatory emotional references to Israel as a beleaguered and strategic American ally that had been standard when officials of the Reagan administration addressed AIPAC. Many of the 1,200 people in the audience were stunned and dismayed. In structure, the speech was almost clinically balanced between what it called on Israel to do and what it called on the Palestinians and Arabs to do. Later, some AIPAC members and Israeli government officials complained about this evenhandedness, which in their view reflected the President and Baker's lack of a gut-level pro-Israel affinity.[28] In retrospect, it was a mistake for Baker to have delivered this speech so early in his tenure at State.

LOAN GUARANTEES

In September 1989, Israeli finance minister Shimon Peres requested $400 million in loan guarantees to enable his government to raise funds from commercial banks for the construction of housing to resettle one hundred thousand Soviet Jews. The entire plan was expected to cost $3 billion. Recent US restrictions had made Soviet Jewish immigration into the United States more difficult, and Israel was the second most sought-for destination.[29] The President responded coolly to the request, and Baker justified the denial on grounds that the US opposed additional Israeli settlements in the West Bank because they violated UN Security Council Resolution 242.[30] On March 1, 1990, Baker testified before the House that US support for the loan guarantees was contingent on satisfactory assurances from Israel that it would not use the funds in occupied territories. At a minimum, the administration needed advance notice of plans for new settlements and a strict accounting of how the $400 million was disbursed.[31]

Two months later, overriding the administration's objection, Congress approved the housing loan guarantees to move and settle Soviet Jews in Israel. The legislation expressed Congress's sense that the guarantees should not apply to settlements outside Israel's pre-1967 boundaries – the Green Line. Over the next several months, Baker would repeat this provision to Israeli leaders both privately and in public statements. Meanwhile, the president did not issue the guarantees. Shamir angrily charged that for the very first time, the US government was putting conditions on its support for Israel. This was not 100 percent true: Shamir chose to ignore the fact that the $3 billion transferred annually to Israel as part of the Camp David Agreement of 1978 was still unconditional. Baker knew that a portion of US funds were being used for new settlements on the West Bank, but he did not want to see more American taxpayer dollars facilitating settlement expansion.[32]

Bush, speaking in a press conference with the Japanese Prime Minister on March 3, 1990, lit a firestorm when he said, "My position is that the foreign policy of the United States says we do not believe there should be new settlements in the West Bank or in East Jerusalem. And I will conduct that policy as if it's firm, *which it is*, and I will be shaped in whatever decisions we make to see whether people can comply with that policy. And that's our strongly held view."[33] Bush not only expressed his anger privately but was ready to erupt publicly against the expansion of settlements. The following month a new settlement was constructed in the Christian quarter of East Jerusalem, provoking the State Department's spokeswoman to call it "an insensitive and provocative action." The Israeli Foreign Ministry responded, "It is the right of Jews to live everywhere… and especially in Jerusalem."[34] The Israeli relationship with Washington devolved into verbal spats.

Until then, settlements in East Jerusalem had not been mentioned suggesting tacit US acceptance. Bush's reference to East Jerusalem as a prohibited area for new settlements thus created an uproar among Israeli hardliners and members of the American Jewish community. Baker, irritated that Bush had publicly included East Jerusalem, told the President he had "fucked up" if his goal was to improve relations with Shamir.[35] Only their long friendship allowed the Secretary of State to scold his boss this way.

With much else on his mind in the fall of 1990, Baker gave less time to Israeli-Palestinian issues.[36] His energy and time went to the reunification of Germany in NATO, the growing opposition to *perestroika* and *glasnost* from apparatchiks in Moscow, and from August onwards diplomatic pressure on Saddam Hussein to withdraw from Kuwait. Nevertheless, Baker understood the political sensitivity of American Jewish support for the President's overall agenda. He therefore combined telephone calls, letters and meetings in New York and Washington to gain Arab, Palestinian, and Israeli agreement on key points necessary to begin any Israeli-Palestinian dialogue. Baker also met with the new Israeli Foreign Minister, David Levy, when he came to Washington in September 1990, one month after the Iraqi invasion of Kuwait.

Levy had a reputation as a hardliner on settlement issues. The purpose of the meeting was threefold: seek Israeli restraint in the face of Iraqi aggression; propose confidence-building measures with Syria; and establish conditions for the disbursement of the loan guarantee. Baker was prepared to work with Levy and achieve an understanding on both prior notification of settlement construction and itemized budgetary expenditures for these settlements. Levy sought to show that Israel would be a responsible partner. He asked Baker to convey to the Syrian leaders Israel's proposed confidence building measures, such as allowing Palestinians to return to Israel from the Gulf, reduced army patrols in the West Bank, and the opening of universities to Palestinian students. He also promised that Jewish immigrants would not settle beyond the Green Line.[37] He could not, however, keep these commitments, and on October 18 he formally retracted his pledge not to settle Soviet émigrés in East Jerusalem. Baker was bitterly disappointed, not only by Levy's retraction but by the news that Shamir's government was taking Soviet émigrés on bus tours of settlements beyond the Green Line and offering them financial incentives to settle there. Shamir and Levy's actions smacked of bad faith. The White House refused to release the $400 million loan guarantee.

FOUR POINT, TEN POINT, AND FIVE POINT PLANS

Just before his first meeting with President Bush in April 1989, Shamir had presented to Baker his four-point plan for the selection of Palestinian delegates. Ross advised Baker that the four points were weak and unacceptable to Arab governments because there was no commitment to discuss a permanent Palestinian state. The day before the meeting with Shamir, President Mubarak of Egypt had presented a ten-point plan that called for negotiations with the PLO, not with a pre-selected group of Palestinian delegates as envisioned by the U.S.-Soviet plan.[38] This was impossible for Shamir, who considered the PLO a terrorist organization. Seeking to bridge the difference, on November 1, 1989, Baker proposed a five-point plan. Based on Israel's four points, it should act as a framework under which Egypt would facilitate bringing Palestinian Arabs, minus the PLO, into discussions about elections with the goal of establishing proper representation for the Palestinians. Shamir's skepticism of the Bush administration, filled with Texan oilmen who did business with Arabs, made him highly suspicious of Baker's five points.[39] For the next eleven months, the players in Washington and Jerusalem shuffled their feet, avoiding commitments and back pedaling on proposals. Baker found this process frustrating.[40] He sought to establish a working relationship with Shamir to compensate for the lack of trust between the prime minister and President Bush, but the slightest comment sent the Israelis flying off the handle.

Bush's public reference to East Jerusalem in March 1990 gave Shamir an excuse to back out of negotiations with the Palestinians. He polled his cabinet, forced a vote of confidence in the Knesset, and on March 15, 1990, allowed his coalition government to fall. The narrow issue was whether one member of the Palestinian delegation could have two residencies, one of which was in East Jerusalem. Shamir's new and more hardline cabinet ended efforts to begin a US-mediated dialogue with the Palestinians. Baker felt battered and betrayed. He had given Shamir the benefit of the doubt but discovered that the prime minister was not serious about peace.[41] Baker told himself that he should have listened to his instincts and stayed away from the Middle East cauldron.

ISRAEL AND THE GULF WAR

In the months following Saddam Hussein's invasion of Kuwait, US officials feared that Israel would pursue its traditional strategic doctrine of reprisal for any attack against its people. It might also take preemptive action against Iraq. The conventional wisdom in the White House was that any direct Israeli action or indirect participation with US-led forces would likely fray the anti-Saddam coalition. Baker was therefore unwavering in efforts to ensure that Israel stayed out of the conflict. Throughout the autumn of 1990 and early months of 1991, Baker was determined to restrain Israel from any preemptive action. According to *US News and World Report*, the Israelis were "the unpredictable factor in the ever complicated diplomatic arithmetic."[42] A senior Israeli military official told his US counterparts that two factors would affect Israel's response to the Iraqi threat: how the United States responded, and the extent of the threat to Israel.[43] Although he kept his plans ambiguous, Shamir pledged to Bush in December 1990 that Israel would not act on its own.[44]

Washington's restraint toward Israel entered a second phase in early 1991, as the January 15 deadline for military action approached and war looked increasingly likely. When asked if US military action would lead Saddam to attack Israel, Iraqi Foreign Minister Tariq Aziz replied, "Yes, absolutely yes."[45] Bush decided that in the event of hostilities, Israel must not become a co-belligerent even if Iraq attacked it. Therefore, Bush tasked Baker to forestall Israeli action through a strategy of coercive diplomacy, combining positive and negative inducements.[46]

Baker had received "feelers" from Arab capitals to the effect that Arab military forces could not be perceived as allied with Israel. Even though Israel had decided against preemptive action, senior officials in Jerusalem remained acutely aware of the Iraqi threat. Defense Minister Moshe Arens pressured Defense Secretary Cheney for operational coordination and real-time satellite intelligence of Iraqi deployments, but both the NSC and State Department refused to allow the Pentagon to share the full range of US intelligence with Israel.[47] As part of the positive inducement, Cheney in September 1990 sought to ship Patriot antimissile batteries to Israel, and Baker resisted the move. He was concerned about any appearance of US-Israeli cooperation, but he gave way when Cheney reminded him of the political costs. Should Israel be attacked, both Baker and Cheney would have to explain to an angry Congress why they had not done more to protect Israel.[48]

After Baker's January 9 meeting with Aziz in Geneva, restraining Israel became even more important. Three days later, Deputy Secretary Eagleburger, Assistant Secretary of Defense Paul Wolfowitz, and senior NSC staffer Merrill Ruck met with Shamir in Jerusalem in an effort to secure a pledge of Israeli restraint. Shamir and Arens viewed the prominence of the US delegation as a positive sign: finally, Washington was taking them seriously. Furthermore, Eagleburger's mission brought a full package of positive incentives. The Americans assured Israeli leaders that the US could eliminate Saddam's Scud missile capability within the first twenty-four hours of hostilities and offered to station Patriot anti-missile batteries in Israel. They offered these batteries unconditionally, not contingent on an Israeli pledge of restraint.[49]

What Eagleburger did not offer was the full range of intelligence data, including real-time reconnaissance information on western Iraq. Neither did he offer IFF by which the Israeli air force could distinguish between "friend or foe" aircraft. Among other things, Eagleburger's mission was intent on getting an Israeli commitment to consult with Washington before taking military action. Shamir remained ambiguous on whether Israel would retaliate against enemy fire, but he repeated his earlier promise to consult with the Bush administration before any use of force.[50]

Once the war started and Scud missiles began to fall, the Israeli leaders came under increasing pressure from their own citizens and military officials to retaliate. Some Israeli cabinet members, as well as the Air Force chief of staff, lobbied Shamir to take military action. Shamir was also under the pressure of precedent: Israel had never stood idle while under attack. Several times during the first days of the war, Defense Minister Arens demanded that Cheney either provide IFF codes or order US forces to stand down while Israel acted against targets in western Iraq. Each time, Cheney advised him that only President Bush could make such a decision. Shamir would have to call him.[51] After one Scud attack, Bush asked Shamir to contact him personally if Israel sustained substantial casualties or suffered a non-conventional attack.[52] Arens was in the White House on January 17, 1991, when Scud missiles fell near his home. He left the Oval Office to take a call from his wife, but when he returned to the meeting, no one asked after his family. He was offended: how could Israel's closest ally not understand the nature of this threat?

HOUSING LOAN GUARANTEES – PART II

Only days after the US and its allies launched the air offensive against Saddam, Israeli Finance Minister Yitzhak Moda'i announced that he would ask the US government for $13 billion in additional aid - $10 billion in loan guarantees for resettling Soviet émigrés and $3 billion in compensation for the damage inflicted by Iraqi Scud missiles on Israeli cities. The quid pro quo was clear: finance us, and we will stay out of the Gulf War. The announcement sent Baker scrambling. Eagleburger, then in Israel, immediately protested to Shamir about the timing of the request. Washington had either to approve the loan guarantees and financial aid or take the risk that Israel might respond militarily against Iraq and fracture the Gulf coalition. Either option was a serious problem for the administration, but paying off Israel would be less damaging internationally.

Domestically, it was a costly option. Baker had emphasized throughout 1989 and 1990 that the United States would not accept continued settlement construction in disputed territories. The denial of the $400 million loan guarantees, despite Congressional approval, had set down a marker. Paying off Shamir with $10 billion for settling Soviet émigrés would mean Washington was reneging on its principled stand to hold Israel accountable for settlement building in the occupied territories. For Shamir, the issue was no longer about necessary funding for construction, it was a point of principle. He wanted to prove that the Bush administration supported absorption of Soviet Jewish migrants. When Baker told Shamir that the administration would have to oppose his request for loan guarantees, he recalls Shamir saying, "I am told we can get them anyway."[53]

On February 14, 1991 the Israeli Ambassador to the U.S., Zalman Shoval, told Reuters news agency, "We sometimes feel we are being given the runaround" by the United States. "We have not received one cent of aid in spite of the fact that we have had immense direct military costs… not to mention even the indirect economic costs, such as the loss of tourism."[54] Baker exerted his prerogative as Secretary of State and called in the ambassador for a formal dressing down. He was livid that the Shoval had chosen to complain to Reuters instead of following diplomatic procedure and raising his criticism with Assistant Secretary for Near Eastern Affairs John Kelly, or with Baker himself. He considered declaring him *persona non grata*.[55] The President followed up the meeting with a cable to Shamir, calling the ambassador's public statements "outrageous and outside the bounds of acceptable behavior by the ambassador of any friendly country."[56] The encounter left Shoval chastened, and he apologized publicly soon afterwards. In his autobiography, Baker is keen to point out that he and Shoval later worked closely together to persuade Shamir to participate in the Madrid conference.[57]

Six days later, Baker instructed the US Agency for International Development to release the $400 million loan guarantees despite the fact that he had just read in the Washington Post that Shamir proposed to build twelve thousand new housing units in the West Bank and Gaza.[58] He also gave Israel a further $650 million for reconstruction.[59] Baker was a realist and he had a more pressing need for Israeli cooperation.

The swift victory in the Gulf War changed the dynamic and permitted more positive exchanges between US and Israeli leaders. In the extraordinarily difficult moments when Iraq directed Scud missile attacks at Israel, both Shamir and Baker found a way to work together. Shamir understood the importance of non-intervention in a war among Arab nations, and Baker came to admire his restraint. In meetings, Shamir was taciturn, slow moving and given to procrastination, leaving it to his aides to argue with Dennis Ross and US Ambassador William Andreas Brown.[60] Years later, Baker remembered that "Shamir kept his word and never leaked."[61] In the context of the Iraq war and its aftermath, Baker valued a man's word and his refusal to leak to the press. He too kept his word, but unlike Shamir he saw the advantage of communicating selectively with journalists.

AFTERMATH OF WAR

The victory over Saddam's military gave the Bush Administration a new opportunity to try to restart an Israeli-Palestinian dialogue. For short-term tactical reasons, Syrian President Assad had joined the US-led coalition against Saddam Hussein. In its aftermath, King Hussein of Jordan sought to make amends for his earlier refusal to join the US coalition against Saddam Hussein. The king was not a major player, but he accepted the proposal for a joint Jordanian-Palestinian delegation to any peace talks, and he supported Baker where he could.[62] Shamir, however, remained adamantly opposed to an international conference with the PLO. He sought to leverage his restraint in the face of the Scud missile attacks, but knew it did not amount to much.

President Bush had repeatedly rejected any suggestion that Iraqi withdrawal from Kuwait be linked to Israeli withdrawal from the West Bank and Gaza. However, in the spring of 1991, following Iraqi withdrawal, Bush made it clear to Aaron David Miller that Arab-Israeli peace "was a priority worth devoting some serious time to."[63] The stars had shifted in the Middle East. The collapse of the Soviet Union had reduced Assad and Arafat's influence, but they still had the capacity to act as spoilers and block dialogue. The Saudis and Egyptians expected a US peace initiative in the wake of America's success in driving Saddam out of Kuwait, but they came to realize that more was expected of them. They would have to play a larger role and contribute both military and financial resources to any regional security plan for the region.

The Middle East team at State, Dennis Ross, Dan Kurtzer, Bill Burns, and Aaron David Miller, developed policies and Baker adapted these plans as he went along. All four were Jewish, and they began calling themselves "Baker's Jew Boys." Baker did not care about their religious identity. His inherent fairness and determination to find a balance between Israeli and Arab needs was the driving force. If anything, he had a tendency to be less sensitive to Jewish concerns and the "Jew Boys" may have given him a better perspective on Israeli concerns.[64] At the NSC, Richard Haass also led a group concentrating on Middle East policy. Together, the teams proposed a two-track diplomatic approach to the Israeli-Palestinian problem. On one track, the U.S. would seek to facilitate bilateral negotiations between the Arab states and Israel. On the second track, it would encourage a dialogue between the Israelis and the Palestinians, which would address Palestinian issues including their political aspirations. Baker pursued both tracks tenaciously, calibrating pressure on Assad, Shamir, and the Palestinians. For nine months, he hunted down one leader after another, maneuvering each to a position where they could not say no.

Though he felt little enthusiasm for the task, Baker had found his purpose in the post-Gulf war period: he would create the conditions to start an Israeli-Palestinian peace process. However, negotiating with the Israelis was maddening. They often put forward arcane arguments and drew out negotiations to excruciating length to extract maximum advantage over as broad a spectrum as they could.[65] Kissinger and others had warned Baker of this negotiating style, and he developed his own form of riposte. He began saying, "Look, I will try to accommodate your concerns here but I've got other concerns with the Syrians. If you give me what is necessary to work with, I will accommodate you by a separate side letter." The Israelis would respond, "What are you promising the Syrians?" Baker would not reveal the details, but he knew that the Israelis had their own means to find them out.[66]

Baker drove the diplomacy toward a peace conference that met the Arab world's need for an international symbol but calmed Israel's fear of confronting serious international pressure. The Arab nations, particularly Syria, had to participate, and getting Palestinian buy-in was a prerequisite to Arab presence. Also, getting Assad to the table was essential to hooking Shamir. Finally, to help the Israelis, they had to discuss water, refugees, economic development, and regional security. These less stressful conversations could help build a degree of trust between the parties.

THE MADRID CONFERENCE

Organizing the conference, scheduled for the end of October 1991, required all of Baker's energy, talent and persistence. Having entered the State Department determined not to get embroiled in Arab-Israeli problems, he ended up logging more miles and hours on this problem than on any other issue. Throughout the spring and early summer of 1991, he sought to create an entanglement that would oblige the Israelis and Palestinians to continue talking long after the conference ended. He met constantly with key players, cajoling and humoring them, although some of his Texan talk bewildered interpreters. He would say, "don't let a dead cat lie on your doorstep," which roughly means make sure the other guy takes the blame. This confounded interpreters, but Baker sought constantly to threaten to dump the cat on Assad's or Shamir's doorstep.

In his encounters with Assad who loved to debate and go off on a lengthy tangent, disconnected from the issue at hand, Baker sought to get him back on track, "You know, Mr. President, if a bullfrog had wings, it wouldn't scrape its balls on the ground." US Ambassador Ed Djerejian, who spoke both English and Arabic, was stunned. The interpreter said he could not even translate the phrase into English, let alone Arabic. Forlornly, Baker had to come up with a tamer explanation about the dog that would have caught the rabbit if he had not stopped running. Assad did not understood this phrase: nor did Baker.[67] Assad took his revenge by prolonging the meeting. He had developed a tactic for exhausting his interlocutors: he would keep meetings going for several hours, serving plentiful sweet tea, and never allow time for a bathroom break.[68] Baker called these encounters 'bladder diplomacy.'

POST-GULF WAR HOPES FOR ARAB-ISRAELI DIPLOMACY

Shortly before the commencement of ground operations against Iraq, Baker outlined before the House Foreign Affairs Committee the administration's conception of the "New World Order" and identified resolution of the Arab-Israeli conflict as one of its cornerstones.[69] The Administration's success in holding together the Soviet, Arab, and Western partnership raised hopes in Washington that the Soviets were moving in the direction of Western principles and values: freedom, democracy, and individual rights. The underlying truth was that the Soviet Union was crumbling, and its ability to support its allies in the Arab world had melted away. No longer could Moscow help Assad counter Israel as part of the Cold War struggle. In the Soviets' weakness and accepting Moscow's indications of shared values, the time was propitious to engage the Israelis and Palestinians in a dialogue for peace.

Baker's plan for an international conference had three elements: first, Shamir had to face a position where he could not back out; second, the conference needed sufficient symbolism for the Arabs and not too much substance for the Israelis; and third, it was necessary to get non-PLO Palestinians to sit down with Israelis. To achieve this, Baker used all the tools in his negotiating box: coercion, rewards, and embarrassment.

He made his first official trip to Israel on March 12, 1991, well over two years after taking office. In a private dinner, Shamir gave the impression that he was ready to accept Baker's proposed conference, and he welcomed the idea of a US security guarantee on the Golan Heights should Syria and Israel reach agreement. Baker also met in Jerusalem with Palestinian leaders, something no previous secretary of state had done in that city. He used the same negotiating style with the Palestinians that he used with the Israelis. He criticized them for PLO conduct in the war against Saddam Hussein and told them flat-out that the PLO could not control the Palestinian delegation to the forthcoming conference. "If you play along with me," he told them, "if you'll go through the right motions and so forth, maybe we can get you more of what you want…"[70] Baker came as close as he could to talking with the PLO itself. This broke with Washington's refusal to have personal contacts since the PLO had declared its support for Saddam Hussein in 1990, causing Washington to suspend its dialogue. Ten months later, after their meeting, the Palestinian delegation expressed guarded satisfaction, telling the international press that the US "was concerned about their plight."[71] Baker had begun to woo the Palestinians by talking tough in public about Israeli intransigence. While he met with the Palestinians, he coordinated closely with the Israelis on substance.

In the following weeks, Baker worked hard to gain Shamir's confidence on a proposed conference and on Palestinian representation, but he remained unyielding on Shamir's demand that citizens in the West Bank and Gaza publicly distance themselves from the PLO. At times, Baker exploded in fury when confronted by what he considered frivolous Israeli demands. He knew how to put on a show of frustration while retaining his focus on the matter at hand. Shamir came to respect Baker's honesty and his toughness. After its military success in Iraq, America was pre-eminent in the region persuading Shamir to go along with the proposed conference, but never enthusiastically.

Between March and October, Baker shuttled back and forth between Middle East capitals. He argued that the time was ripe for bilateral peace treaties between Israel and its neighbors Lebanon, Syria, and Jordan. Secondly, he argued for an interim self-government arrangement for the Palestinians, followed by permanent status negotiations. Third, they could achieve confidence-building measures through multilateral discussions on water, environment, refugees, arms control, and economic development. The Soviet Union should co-chair the multilateral deliberations. In the course of these meetings, Baker succeeded in getting Arab leaders and Palestinian representatives from the occupied territories to drop their demands that PLO officials, as well as Palestinians from East Jerusalem, participate in the bilateral discussion on interim self-governance. Instead, the Syrians and Jordanians agreed that only delegates from the occupied territories would represent the Palestinians, as part of a joint Palestinian-Jordanian delegation. This was clearly a façade, as everyone knew that the PLO in Tunis called the shots, but it was an essential cover for the Israelis, who would never agree to negotiate directly with Yasser Arafat's PLO.

Shamir insisted on knowing who would be on the Palestinian delegation, but the Palestinians withheld their list of delegates. When Baker met with the Palestinian delegation on the eve of the Madrid conference, he still did not have their delegate list. Without it, Prime Minister Shamir might not appear, so Baker needed the names. When the Palestinians again refused to provide the list, Baker slammed his fist on the table in fury. Papers and coffee cups shuddered. He then walked out shouting "the souk is closed." Hanan Ashrawi, the Palestinian with perhaps the closest relationship to Baker, was stunned and frightened. Turning to Ross, she asked, "What's next?" Ross had seen Baker's explosions before and knew that he would eventually calm down. But in the moment, he replied, "give him the list."[72] Baker got what he wanted. Theatrics combined with the short fuse of tiredness, worked. When he returned to the room, he gathered the Palestinians around him as a coach would gather his team halfway through a ball game.[73]

The conference was originally meant to take place in the Netherlands, but with just nine days to go before it opened, President Assad recalled a Dutch vote at the United Nations against Syria and refused to meet there. With only a week to go, Baker's team had to scramble to find another host. From their hotel rooms in Jerusalem, adviser Dan Kurtzer proposed Spain. They called Prime Minister Felipe González, who accepted on King Juan Carlos I's behalf the opportunity to host such a prestigious event. However, there was a problem. Prominently hung in the royal palace was a magnificent seventeenth-century tapestry depicting the Lady of Justice: she was naked! Removing her from the palace required the king's approval and time was short. Just in time, royal consent arrived and the offending beauty was removed and replaced with another, less sensitive tapestry from the royal collection.[74]

None of these frantic preparations was observable when Gorbachev and Bush arrived in Madrid on October 29 to host the conference and dine privately with the king. Under the auspices of Spanish royalty, both leaders were prepared to make a considerable effort to start the dialogue and end the state of war in the Middle East.[75] When the conference opened on October 30, there was a visible sigh of relief among Baker's delegation: Shamir had shown up. Syria's foreign minister, Farouk al-Sharaa, was there. The Palestinian-Jordanian delegates, headed by Haidar Abdel Shafi, were in their seats. Baker's advisers were relieved to note that there were no representatives from East Jerusalem, no diaspora Palestinians, and no one with direct PLO association, despite the general awareness that the absent figure of Yasser Arafat overshadowed the proceedings. Baker would later admit that the gathering was a charade and Shamir knew it.[76] The conference did nothing to change life under Israeli occupation, but it gave the Palestinians a forum to tell their story.

This was Baker's conference. Presidents Bush and Gorbachev sat in the presidential chairs, but Baker had cajoled the parties to attend and developed intricate formulas to make the Israeli government, in the words of one Baker aide, "say yes, in spite of itself."[77] The two-day gathering was not intended to reach formal agreements, but to begin a series of face-to-face meetings that Israelis and Palestinians had avoided since the 1980s. For a decade thereafter, there would be no overt conflict between them. Cynics described the Madrid conference as empty symbolism, and there were plenty of symbols of post-Cold War collaboration, but substantive outcomes existed too. Madrid began the dialogue among diplomats, known as "track two negotiations" that resulted in the Oslo Accords, after Norwegian mediators brought Shamir's successor Prime Minister Rabin and Arafat's advisors into secret negotiations. Frustrated by the Palestinian delegation's inability to move forward without Arafat's approval, the Israelis decided to negotiate secretly with the PLO, leading to the "Declaration of Principles" on interim self-governance. The Madrid conference, shrouded in symbolism, set the course for the series of bilateral and multilateral meetings that culminated in the handshake between Prime Minister Yitzhak Rabin and PLO leader Yasser Arafat on the White House lawn on September 13, 1993. By then, Bush was out of office and the two men were guests of Bush's successor, President Bill Clinton.

The following year, Israel made peace with Jordan, and discussions with Syria avoided war between these neighbors. Baker had assessed correctly that Syria would ultimately leave the radical anti-Israel camp and that Palestinians would seek to negotiate directly with Israel. On the domestic front, Baker kept the support of the American Jewish community by linking a freeze in Israeli settlement activity to approval of US aid for the resettlement of Soviet Jews. Russia did not gain a foothold in the Middle East, but it played an important role in co-chairing the multilateral meetings.

President Bush and Baker had broken the taboo of direct talks and legitimized Arab-Israeli negotiations. The master negotiator got neighboring Arab states to the table, making it difficult for Shamir to stay away. Russian support for multilateral discussions went a long way toward enabling the parties to discuss problems of mutual concern. Domestic support from the American Jewish community was strengthened. At Washington's request, the Saudi king had played a quiet role behind the scenes, strongly urging Syria to attend and demonstrating respect for the only nation that could maintain global stability. Baker could rightly claim that US power and his prestige and brought the parties face to face. Thereafter, it was up to the Israeli and Palestinian leadership, but he had started the process. With all the warnings from Nixon, Kissinger and Shultz, he had waded into the quagmire of Middle East peace and extracted a significant achievement. Now Baker had to return his attention to the meat and potato of US/Soviet relations, arms control.

EIGHT

ARMS CONTROL

A rms control was the meat and potatoes of US-Soviet relations throughout the Cold War. For a quarter-century, strategic nuclear arms control negotiations had concentrated on managing nuclear competition. Indeed, during the height of the Cold War, there was little else to talk about. US and Soviet officials steeped in the intricacies of throw weights and trigger mechanisms had created a specialty profession akin to tax lawyers. Both were necessary, but their business was too esoteric for public appreciation.

As President Reagan's chief of staff, Baker had become familiar with the broad outlines of arms control and with Reagan's commitment to diminish if not abolish nuclear weapons. He knew that conservatives in both the Republican and Democratic parties closely monitored arms control negotiations to ensure that the US negotiators were not weakening the national defense posture. Republicans recalled that during the 1970s, détente with the Soviet Union had contributed to President Ford's bitter fight with then California Governor, Ronald Reagan. The governor believed that Ford and his Secretary of State, Henry Kissinger, had underestimated the Soviet threat and were too eager to make deals with the Soviets rather than confront them from a position of strength. President Ford's National Security Advisor, Brent Scowcroft, now held the same post under Bush. He remembered those fights well and sought to move carefully on strategic arms control. Baker was less cautious, but he joined Scowcroft in his skepticism of Reagan's Strategic Defense Initiative (SDI), a controversial program to build a national missile defense system.

As Vice President, Bush had not criticized Reagan on SDI, but after the November 1988 election he called for a review of arms control policy. In choosing Scowcroft as his national security advisor, he selected a man who had led Reagan's commission on US strategic nuclear forces while remaining formally outside the administration. Scowcroft believed in the importance of strategic balance between the Soviets and Americans and did not think SDI could create an effective shield: "The goal of strategic arms control ought to be to improve the stability of the balance and to reduce the chances that a crisis would produce an impetus toward the use of nuclear weapons."[1] He also saw SDI as a major obstacle to a strategic arms accord. Soviet negotiators constantly demanded that the US drop its plans for a space-based missile defense. Preparing to enter office in January 1989, Scowcroft recommended that the president focus on conventional forces and seek to reduce Soviet and American troop levels in Europe.

Outgoing members of Reagan's national security team had bragged about eliminating whole weapons systems. They proudly pointed to the Intermediate Nuclear Force (INF) agreement of 1987 and Gorbachev's pledge to reduce conventional forces. Scowcroft was unimpressed. In his mind, arms control should have nothing to do with the number of weapons. Instead, the US commitment to defending Western Europe should be demonstrated in the *type* of nuclear weapons that could act as a counterweight to the preponderance of Warsaw Pact men and machines stationed in Eastern Europe.[2] US troop levels in Europe would never equal those of the Soviet Union, so the deterrent against an invasion by the Warsaw Pact countries had to come from NATO's short-range nuclear weapons. However, both the placement of these weapons and their modernization created deep political unrest in West Germany. Ever since Chancellor Helmut Schmidt had agreed to allow Pershing II missiles on West German soil, a large swath of the German electorate felt they were nothing but a target for a Soviet pre-emptive strike. Schmidt's successor, Chancellor Helmut Kohl, and other political leaders repeated the mantra, "the shorter the range, the deader the German." Negotiations over the modernization of short-range nuclear forces (SNF) were thus a source of friction between the British and American proponents and Kohl, who was keenly aware of the deep animosity among the German people. As chief of staff to Ronald Reagan, Baker had met Kohl and come to admire his political skills. Kohl was conservative, cautious, and well aware of his country's need for NATO protection against a hostile Soviet Union. Gorbachev's appointment as General Secretary of the Communist Party in March 1985 brought younger leadership that was changing old Soviet ways. Recognizing that a reformist Soviet leader could move in unpredictable directions, Kohl and his foreign policy advisor, Horst Teltschik, kept close to the American president.

Unlike Scowcroft, Baker came to the State Department with a general knowledge, but without an immersion in the intricacies of arms control; he therefore relied upon both Scowcroft and the president to guide him. At State, he appointed smart Foreign Service officers, known for their pragmatism, to lead his arms control efforts. Reginald ("Reggie") Bartholomew was the Under Secretary for Arms Control and International Security, and Richard Burt, the former ambassador to West Germany, became the negotiator for the Strategic Arms Reduction Treaty, known as START. Reflecting Baker's recognition that arms control would be a constant issue in negotiations with the Soviets, both men were included, occasionally, in Baker's "lunch bunch."

In the first months of the new administration, when the entire range of U.S. foreign policy was under strategic review, Baker did not make any moves to change the military balance between the superpowers. START negotiations dragged on, as did the longstanding negotiations for the Mutual and Balanced Force Reductions (MBFR) and Conventional Armed Forces in Europe (CFE). Washington and Moscow sought to reduce the balance, but new ideas in arms control were hard to find. Instead, Gorbachev publicly called for major bilateral cuts in troop levels and tanks. To those seeking to reduce armament levels, these calls were appealing, but to the hawks in the Republican Party, the Soviet leader's winning smile concealed an underlying evil intent. Gorbachev gained the prize for improving public relations while American conservatives awaited the outcome of Bush's strategic review. Baker was aware of this domestic anxiety, and of European frustration at the slow pace of the foreign policy appraisal. But in the early weeks of 1989, neither Bush nor he were ready to propose changes.

DEVELOPING A NEW ARMS CONTROL POLICY

On March 6, Baker led the delegation to the next round of CFE negotiations in Vienna. The US position called for greater reductions from the Warsaw Pact than from NATO in order to equalize the forces in Eastern and Western Europe at a level approximately 5-10 percent below existing NATO totals. America's European allies roundly criticized Baker's proposal as insufficient and unimaginative because it required the Warsaw Pact to make reductions of over 50 percent in each category while NATO made little reductions.[3] Congressman Les Aspin, chairman of the House Armed Services Committee, accused NATO of lacking vision on a new security arrangement. Others claimed that the Bush administration was stuck in a Cold War mentality and deaf to the opportunities Gorbachev was offering. For a man sensitive to congressional criticism and determined to create a bipartisan foreign policy, these criticisms stung. Aspin's remarks especially goaded Baker to finish the strategic review and develop more creative ideas. However to his right, conservatives were determined that a more realistic Republican administration should counter Gorbachev's charm offensive. In the midst of this domestic tension, Shevardnadze accepted the US proposal and even advocated for deeper cuts on both sides.

Scowcroft, meanwhile, was changing his arms control philosophy. From advocating a reduced nuclear balance in Europe, he moved to urging the removal of Soviet conventional forces—troops, tanks and artillery—from the Warsaw Pact countries "to the degree that the Europeans could breathe and expand and liberalize."[4] In his view, it was troops and tanks, not nukes that had held Eastern Europeans fearful that the repression of the Hungarians in 1956 and the Czechoslovaks in 1968 might recur. Scowcroft recommended that the President shift his focus from missile systems and strategic nuclear forces to conventional forces. Baker concurred.

The NATO summit, coming at the end of May 1989, invigorated Bush's national security team to think creatively about arms control. Scowcroft and the NSC took the lead in devising a "dramatic" US strategy that "would commit the Soviets to some really irrevocable steps."[5] He sought "deep slashes" in conventional forces and proposed a reduction of 25 percent in the approximately 320,000 US troops stationed in NATO countries, with the Soviet Union making an equal reduction. Baker, thinking about the traditional military balance in Europe, proposed a reduction in tanks, but Scowcroft dismissed his proposal because they were not the central issue: "Soviet troops did not need tanks to repress movements towards liberalization in Eastern Europe."[6] Also, a reduction in tanks was overly complex given the variety of armored vehicles that the Defense Department would want to exclude from the agreement. Bush, Scowcroft and Baker rightly anticipated that Defense Secretary Cheney and the Chairman of the Joint Chiefs of Staff, Admiral William Crowe, would object to a 25 percent cut in conventional forces and would propose instead a cut of 30,000 troops, or 10 percent. Cheney argued, "Look, we're winning. Why do we want to mess with any of this? We've found a winning formula. The Soviets are on the defensive. Let's just stay where we are."[7]

Nevertheless, Cheney and Crowe confronted a formidable trio who were determined to take dramatic action and show the Soviets and Western allies that President Bush was not Reagan warmed over. When pressed to distinguish combat forces from support troops – the latter comprising half the total troop strength – Cheney and Crowe found ways to reduce support troops without harming the overall US defense posture. Baker leaned toward a greater reduction in conventional forces, but he recognized the need to maintain unity within Bush's national security team. He therefore accepted the compromise of a 20 percent cut.

To prevent NATO leaders from learning about the new US proposal through the press, Baker sent his deputy, Eagleburger, and Scowcroft's deputy, Gates, on a confidential mission to London, Paris, Bonn, and Rome to quietly explain the US proposal to European leaders. On the continent, they found European leaders eager to reduce their defense costs and willing to see a reduction in US force presence. Both US diplomats rightly concluded that the terrain was hospitable to Bush's announcement of a unilateral reduction in US forces. Finally, Washington was ready to act with boldness.

In London, however, Prime Minister Thatcher received both men with suspicion, commenting on Eagleburger's size and purpose. She dubbed them Tweedle Dee and Tweedle Dum, two fictional characters from English nursery rhymes. It was not meant as a compliment. The Prime Minister remained convinced that modernization of short-range nuclear forces (SNF), in particular the Lance II missile, had to continue. In her mind, only nuclear weapons could deter Soviet troops from pouring westward over the borders of Eastern Europe. Sitting beside Bush a few weeks later in May at the NATO heads of government dinner, she lectured him: "We must not give in on this [SNF] modernization… You're not going to give in, are you?"[8] Bush demurred. He knew that Baker was attending the Foreign Minister's dinner and he had no assurance that Baker could reach a deal with his fellow ministers that Thatcher would accept. Long after dinner, around midnight, Baker called Bush with his solution. He proposed that when implementation of the CFE was well underway, the US enter into negotiations on a partial reduction, but not elimination, of SNF. Bush listened carefully, but was unsure whether Thatcher would accept this. He sent Baker back to the NATO Council that same night to gain British approval.

Baker sat beside Geoffrey Howe, listened to the British foreign secretary's arguments, and did not object. At 2 a.m., the American had gained the NATO Council's agreement to proceed with negotiations on CFE and postpone those on SNF to a later date. The night had been filled with patient listening, tough negotiations and final consensus. The Germans had succeeded in putting off negotiations on cruise missiles, and the Americans had found a solution that kept NATO together.

The next morning, Thatcher enthusiastically endorsed the agreement, determined to maintain Britain's special transatlantic relationship. She had lost the argument over SNF, but never displayed her soreness.

Baker was wary of Soviet commitments to reduce SNF. He had been caught off guard at his first meeting with Gorbachev earlier that May, when the Soviet leader revealed that he was about to announce a unilateral 500-missile reduction in short-range nuclear forces. He had asked Baker to keep this confidential while he discussed it within the Politburo, where the offer was controversial. But as Baker and his team boarded their plane for home, Gorbachev blindsided the Americans by announcing his proposal publicly. The Secretary of State had kept the confidentiality only for Gorbachev to surprise him with his public announcement before Baker could prepare an official response. With this incident fresh in his mind, Baker realized that Gorbachev was a cunning operator. He would not be caught out again.

MGM-34 MIDGETMAN – A TEST FOR START

Baker entered the START negotiations, in Geneva that June, with clear instructions to keep a new and smaller inter-continental ballistic missile (ICBM) out of the agreement. Only a month before, Martin Marietta had produced this ICBM, with a range of 6,000 miles and known, appropriately for its size as MGM-134 Midgetman. This small ICBM was a guided missile that flew with constant speed to deliver a warhead at a specified target with a high degree of accuracy. It was designed for deployment on a hardened road vehicle or rail car; its mobility making it much harder to locate than the stationary missile silos of standard ICBMs.[9] Easily concealed and thus not readily verifiable, as required under START, the US had a distinct technological advantage. Given its ability to avoid satellite detection, the Defense Department was determined that Midgetman not be included in the START negotiations. The Soviets, on the other hand, insisted that ICBMS – both large and small - be included and verified. Baker leaned on his new START negotiator, Richard Burt to reach a compromise with the

Soviets. Burt had found a compromise and his negotiating strategy won him an admirer in Baker, but a critic in Cheney, who complained of his "over eagerness." Burt habitually sidestepped the tiresome routine of daily speeches in arms control formal sessions and instead would have his morning coffee at a nearby patisserie with Victor Karpov, his Soviet counterpart. Over espressos and without aides, the two identified areas of common agreement. They would then return to their respective experts to determine how to implement potential accords. Burt knew that Karpov had a deputy negotiator from the KGB with close personal ties to a member of the Politburo. He thus calculated that any potential compromise would be checked for orthodoxy before it became an official Soviet position.[10]

Together, Karpov and Burt were able to give the stalemated START talks some momentum. Burt earned Baker's respect for his ability to accelerate the talks, but back in Washington, Cheney complained to Scowcroft that Burt was sidestepping the traditional arms control process. Scowcroft passed the complaint onto Baker, who had to make Burt sit through the formal meetings. It reminded Baker of the time Cheney, then President Ford's chief of staff, had scolded him for speaking ill of Henry Kissinger at an off the record meeting in Oklahoma. The upshot was that little progress was made on START that summer of 1989. Baker would have another chance when he and Shevardnadze had their ministerial meeting that September.

THE WYOMING MEETING OF FOREIGN MINISTERS

Arms control was a paramount topic for Baker's meeting with Shevardnadze Jackson Lake Lodge in Wyoming's Grand Teton National Park. Surrounded by mountains and fish streams, Baker and Shevardnadze held a one-on-one meeting lasting three hours and emerged with a significant advancement in arms control.[11] For the first time, Shevardnadze dropped the Soviet demand that the US abandon its plans for SDI. The drop was conditional: the Soviets retained the right to abrogate the Strategic Arms Limitation Treaty (SALT) if the US moved to deploy SDI in violation of the 1972 Antiballistic Missile Treaty (ABM). With or without that condition, the removal of the Soviet blockage on further strategic weapons negotiations unless plans for SDI were constrained was a major breakthrough. Work on completing the START negotiations could now move forward.

Shevardnadze also agreed to demolish the Krasnoyarsk radar installation, which the US had always claimed violated the ABM treaty. In the past, Soviet negotiators had refused to admit that Krasnoyarsk's giant sonar transmitter, situated in the center of Siberia rather than Russia's coastal zone, violated the ABM.[12] Surrounded by the magnificence of the Grand Tetons, Baker and Shevardnadze agreed to dismantle the complex, thus ending a symbol of the Soviet military threat. Later, joined by their experts, Baker and Shevardnadze continued their dialogue focusing on inspections, verification and data exchange. These were important confidence-building measures that had caused intense disagreement in the past. Now both men were determined to build mutual trust. An important part of their talks focused on monitoring stocks of chemical weapons and on notifying each other of strategic military exercises. By the second day, they had reached agreement on chemical weapons, an issue critical to congressional approval of an arms control agreement. Baker and Shevardnadze agreed to exchange "general data" on each country's chemical weapons capabilities before the end of the year and to send inspectors to each other's chemical weapons plants and storage sites. Baker proposed a variety of verification measures that should apply to any future strategic arms treaty. Details on intrusive inspections and which verification measures to employ were left to experts to work out. Shevardnadze also made a new proposal on conventional arms by agreeing to include certain fighter aircraft and bombers that had previously been off limits to US negotiators. Baker could boast that he and Shevardnadze had made more progress on arms control at the Wyoming meeting than Reagan and Gorbachev had achieved at their last summit in Moscow.[13]

BAKER COMMUNICATES A NEW STRATEGY

One month later, Baker gave two policy speeches, one to the Foreign Policy Association in New York and one to the Commonwealth Club in San Francisco. The New York speech, on October 17, focused on Soviet foreign and defense policies, as well as the implications of *perestroika* for Soviet economic, political, and legal systems.[14] Baker told his audience that in defense policy and arms control, the Soviets had shown a better understanding of the need for mutual security. They had shifted their positions in both conventional and strategic nuclear arms control to "correspond more closely with long-held Western assumptions about preventing war and producing greater stability." In the last few months, Gorbachev had promised to cut the defense budget and "promised to turn swords into plowshares by transforming tanks into tractors."[15] Now, he said, Washington was looking for results.

The San Francisco speech, on arms control, was scheduled for October 23. But one week earlier, a devastating earthquake had shaken the San Francisco area, leaving 63 people dead and 3,757 injured. Baker asked if he should cancel his appearance, but decided that "the truly American character of facing up to disaster, takings its measure, and then getting on with the work" was more important.[16] In the talk, he emphasized that Gorbachev's program of change presented the "clearest opportunity to reduce the risk of war since the dawn of the nuclear age." But, he added that an enduring and strategically significant arms control regime required four principles to "guide our search for a stable, predictable strategic relationship." They were:

1. Reductions in first strike, or surprise attack capabilities;
2. Predictability through openness – the Soviets' military activities should be more transparent;
3. A broadened arms control agenda beyond the traditional East-West nuclear forces, notably to North Korea; and
4. Institutionalization of a safer world through the destruction of weapons and extending the duration of agreements.[17]

Together, the New York and San Francisco speeches set out the US strategy for engaging the Soviet Union on military matters. Democrats had criticized the Bush administration for lacking a coherent policy response to Gorbachev. Now the two speeches provided that coherence. Furthermore, Baker clearly showed himself as an activist who wanted to engage Gorbachev despite the Soviet leader's uncertain future.[18] American and European critics had complained that the new Bush strategy was too long in coming, but the delay had allowed his national security team to take account of the cascading events in Eastern Europe in the momentous year of 1989. More tumult was still to come.

THE MALTA SUMMIT

When President Bush, at Ambassador Matlock's recommendation, sought to meet with Gorbachev before the end of the year, he asked to keep the meeting as informal as possible to encourage a free flow of ideas and build trust between the two men. Unlike previous summit meetings which had focused on arms control, Bush sought to engage in a broader discussion and test Gorbachev's 'new thinking.'

In the weeks before the Malta summit, Under Secretary Bartholomew assembled the proposals of experts. General Edward Rowny, the special advisor for arms control, recommended to Baker that the President avoid making the meeting an "arms control summit."[19] There were risks, and few gains, in discussing a new strategic arms treaty because complex and divisive issues remained that allowed little room for compromise. Rowny wrote that should Gorbachev raise the ABM treaty and START, it would be a loser for the US because any discussion was bound to jeopardize SDI. Bush should therefore focus on process, not substance. Also, the Defense Department sought to avoid naval arms control entirely. "The US navy is not on the table."[20] The arms control experts feared that Bush might agree to disarm without the Soviets' doing anything fundamental to its military structure. In the briefing book prepared for the President's meeting at Malta, arms control was relegated to chapter 6.

Arms control and Eastern Europe, however, topped the Soviets' list of issues to discuss. At Malta, Gorbachev raised the need to work toward a reduction of strategic offensive weapons, including sea-launched cruise missiles, in which the US had a significant advantage.[21] Bush had read Rowny's memorandum and avoided entering into specifics. Instead, he sought to keep the discussion to a more general level, emphasizing that he welcomed *perestroika* and hoped for its success. This was not Baker's meeting and he understood that his role was to listen and prepare to follow up outstanding issues with his Soviet counterpart.

As they left storm-wracked Malta, Baker and Shevardnadze received their marching orders. They should prepare for a full-scale "watershed" summit in 1990 and seek a comprehensive program of arms control with the goal of "creating a fundamentally new model of security."[22] In addition to quickening progress on START and the "radical reduction of Soviet and US stationed forces in Europe", the Soviet draft called for discussion of "Open Skies, Open Seas, Open Land and Open Space" proposals. The intent was to offer each side the opportunity to inspect the other's arms reduction efforts from the air, at sea and by visits to silos on land. Verification through inspection should lead to stronger bilateral trust while allowing Washington the opportunity to pursue an ambitious arms control agenda before the 1990 summit. From the hesitant position Bush had brought to Malta, an invigorated arms control work program lay ahead. Baker was ready to go to work. He would do two things: travel to Moscow, and discuss arms control with congressional leaders. Both were indispensable parties to future treaties on START, CFE, and chemical weapons.

ARMS CONTROL RESUMES ITS PLACE IN BILATERAL RELATIONS

Returning to Moscow in February 1990 to follow up on the Malta Summit, Baker had two purposes: persuade Gorbachev that a united Germany would be more stable if anchored inside NATO than outside it, and advance the CFE and START negotiations. He found Gorbachev reticent about the reduction of conventional forces. During his meeting at St. Catherine's Hall on February 9 and in the company of retired Marshal Akhromeyev, now a special advisor to the Soviet President, Gorbachev rejected the US request to keep an additional 30,000 thousand US troops on the periphery of Europe beyond the agreed maximum of 195,000 each. He then proceeded to deliver a speech on START, focusing on the minutia of counting rules for air-launched cruise missiles (ALCM). It was evident that the monologue was intended for Marshal Akhromeyev and his Soviet colleagues.[23] Baker was concerned. The budget savings that Gorbachev so desperately needed would not come from the reduced strategic weapons but from reduced troop and conventional armaments in Europe. Gorbachev, who had just emerged from a meeting with the Central Committee, must have come under considerable pressure. The Soviet leader clearly needed to demonstrate that he could stand up to the Americans.

Despite Gorbachev's turgid monologue in St. Catherine's Hall, Gorbachev proposed that his senior military aide, Akhromeyev negotiate one-on-one with Richard Burt. At his command, the two men slipped off to the Soviet guesthouse to begin a nightlong session with only interpreters. Akhromeyev announced to Burt that he was a committed communist having survived the German siege of Leningrad for close to 900 days on coffee and cigarettes. However, he doubted whether Gorbachev was as committed to communism as he was. With this preliminary out of the way and without colleagues to prompt him, Akhromeyev began an unexpected retreat from the longstanding Soviet positions. He agreed to the US positions on limiting the number of bomber aircraft on which ALCMs would be loaded. He also agreed to undercount actual ALCM loads for each class of bomber and to exclude bombers that did not carry ALCMs, so long as each bomber was limited to one bomb per aircraft. On sea-launch cruise missiles (SLCM), Akhromeyev accepted the long-standing American insistence on not limiting such weapons in the START treaty itself, but making unverifiable declarations each year on the number of SLCMs each side intended to deploy. This was an extraordinary Soviet capitulation to the American insistence on keeping its ALCMs and SLCMs beyond the constraints of an international treaty.

Early the next morning, Burt reported the good news to Baker and the American team who were startled by Akhromeyev's willingness to compromise on previously very difficult issues, such as limits on ALCMs and SLCMs. There was nothing to suggest that Akhromeyev was flying solo, but rather that he was under instructions to make unilateral concessions.[24] Each American began to ask why the Soviets had relented and why they had made this move in a nightlong one-on-one session. Baker hypothesized that Gorbachev and Shevardnadze urgently needed an agreement, one that could only be reached in an intimate session without the presence of Soviet military officials. The next day, their theories were turned on their head. Nearing the end of a lengthy negotiating session, Shevardnadze raised his hand, "Oh! I nearly forgot. We shall revisit the agreement on ALCM loading. Ambassador Burt did not understand our position."[25] Baker groaned. Here was another ploy to deceive the American delegation. Burt had been used, but why?

As military advisor to Gorbachev, Akhromeyev might make the concessions to Burt, but he was no longer the first deputy minister of defense and chief to the General Staff. Consequently, he did not speak for the Soviet military. Once informed of his concessions, the military had objected vigorously. Gorbachev should have given the General Staff a direct voice in deciding such matters and allowed it to participate in the negotiations.[26] When Shevardnadze came to Washington two months later, the Soviet position on arms control incorporated new conditions and a partial retreat from February's ICBM agreements. The result was deadlock. Nor did they make headway two weeks later, when US negotiators met in Moscow with Viktor Karpov, and General Bronislav Omelichev from the General Staff.

At this point, Baker sought permission to make modest compromises to meet some of the Soviet military objections. He passed them confidentially to Shevardnadze when they met to discuss German unification in Bonn on May 5, and on May 18 he raised them with Gorbachev in Moscow. This time, members of the General Staff as well as the new foreign policy advisor, Yevgeny Primakov, were in the room with Gorbachev and Shevardnadze. The situation was near to impossible for Gorbachev. If they were to achieve agreement on a START treaty, the Soviets had to make nearly all the compromises. Baker's team recognized that they could not resolve the impasses before the forthcoming end of May summit.

It was increasingly evident to Baker that German unification had become the critical issue in the bilateral relationship. Throughout the next eight months, the means of achieving German unification, the number of Bundeswehr troops to be stationed in East Germany, the housing of Soviet troops back home, and East Germany's inclusion in NATO sucked up all the oxygen in bilateral negotiations. Arms control lost its prominence as the leitmotif of bilateral relations, becoming symbolic of old antagonisms. The trust created between Shevardnadze and Baker in the Grand Tetons endured despite heavy pressure from Central Committee members, who hurled criticism at Shevardnadze because of his acquiescence on Germany. Gorbachev was too powerful to attack directly on the movement toward German unification, but Shevardnadze was a softer target, even though his personal animosity toward Germans made him more hardline than Gorbachev on German unification.

BALTIC CHALLENGES

Events in the Baltics sank any hope for progress on long-range nuclear weapons and reduction in conventional forces. Parliamentary elections in early 1990 had resulted in a victory for the Reform Movement, Sąjūdis, and on March 11 the Lithuanians declared the re-establishment of the state of Lithuania with Vytautas Landsbergis as head of state and Kazimira Prunskienė as leader of the Cabinet of Ministers. In Moscow, conservative forces pressed Gorbachev to reject Lithuania's declaration. They understood that if Lithuania left the Soviet Union, the other two Baltic States would follow. To survive, Gorbachev listened to his generals, as well as Politburo hardliners. It was evident that progress on arms control would be difficult. Shevardnadze might use the excuse that Baker had to submit any arms control treaty to the Senate for ratification, but the truth was that the Lithuanian American community and human rights groups in the United States adamantly opposed any agreement with Moscow that might be seen as legitimizing Soviet repression.

CNN and other networks closely followed events in Vilnius, Lithuania's capital, creating public pressure on President Bush to concede nothing to the Soviets so long as their economic sanctions and oil embargo against Lithuania continued. With Gorbachev constrained by conservative forces at home, both super powers had little room to maneuver. Baker knew that any violent Soviet crackdown, in the Baltic States or elsewhere, could put the entire US-Soviet relationship at risk. He therefore prepared for little progress on arms control.[27] Even discussions on the exodus of Soviet Jews, human rights, and regional issues were relegated to a back burner. Relations between Moscow and Washington fell under a late winter chill. No amount of public assurances could hide the concern that Kremlin apparatchiks were forcing Gorbachev's hand, and both Bush and Baker felt considerable pressure from Congress and the national press to defend the independence movement in Lithuania.

When Baker and Shevardnadze met again on May 5, 1990 in Bonn they made no progress. Instead, Baker claimed that the Soviets took back some concessions already agreed to on arms control. Baker's staff thought that Shevardnadze seemed paralyzed.[28] It was clear that he was wrestling with a number of issues, all of which involved the reduction of Soviet power in Europe. On a confidential basis, Baker gave Shevardnadze some US military compromises designed to meet Soviet military objections. But the critical sticking points were more than strategic long-range weapons in the START negotiations. They concerned the inclusion of a united Germany in NATO, self-determination for the Baltic States, force strength in the CFE negotiations, and the withdrawal of 380,000 Soviet troops from Eastern Europe. In the spring of 1990, START had taken a back seat to bargaining over Europe's future.

SOVIET BACKSLIDING

Preparatory to the summit meeting planned for Washington early that summer, Baker flew to Moscow to meet with Gorbachev on May 18. Arms control now played third fiddle to Lithuania and the challenges of German unification within NATO. Baker's private meetings with Gorbachev and Shevardnadze ended when their respective delegations entered the Great Hall to discuss arms control. After unrelenting demands upon Gorbachev and his team, Baker believed he had an agreement on ALCMs. He had made some reductions, but the Soviet leaders had made the larger concessions. On ALCMs, the US walked back its previous demand for a 900-1,000 kilometer (560-621 mile) range, which had existed since Reagan's last Defense Secretary Frank Carlucci had sought the option of developing a medium-range nuclear missile on tactical aircraft. Now, in 1990, Baker agreed to the Soviet position that START should cover aircraft capable of flying 600 kilometers (373 miles) or more. This placed more US aircraft under the treaty's constraints. In exchange, the Soviets agreed to exclude from the range limit a new American conventional cruise missile then undergoing tests and known as Tacit Rainbow.[29]

Baker also believed he had an agreement on a numerical limit of 880 sea launched cruise missiles (SLCMs). He was satisfied that on ALCMs and SLCMs, as well the remaining START issues, both sides were "on the verge of closing out." He had been eager to score gains with his tough bargaining skills, but he paid less heed to the broader consequences of imposing one-sided compromises on Gorbachev and Shevardnadze. Shevardnadze believed that he could resolve all the major issues in the START negotiations by the time the Washington summit in late May.

The next day Baker and Shevardnadze met for three and a half hours. The agenda was broad: arms control, Germany, Lithuania, internal developments in the Soviet Union, Africa, Afghanistan, and proposed dates for a summit meeting in Washington. In that meeting, Baker reminded Shevardnadze that he had agreed to the ALCM range of 600 kilometers only on the condition that Tacit Rainbow was grandfathered (exempted).[30] Gorbachev had not raised conditions during their meeting the previous day, and the subsequent introduction of new conditions meant that "now the Soviets were jeopardizing the whole package if they let the military impose certain technical conditions after the agreement had already been reached."[31]

On SLCMs, Baker was under pressure from the Pentagon not to agree to a maximum limit on cruise missiles launched from surface ships and submarines. He also knew that inspection and verification of sea-based missiles was a no-go for Secretary Cheney and the Pentagon. On the other side, the Soviets sought a limit of zero cruise missiles. Earlier in the February 1990 negotiations, the US delegation had somewhat arbitrarily called for a maximum limit of 1,000 SLCMs even though congressional budgetary restrictions had reduced the limit to 637 missiles and only 399 missiles had been built.[32] Despite the lower production, in early 1990 Richard Burt had negotiated tenaciously for the 1,000-missile ceiling.

On ALCMs, the two sides had resolved the disagreement over the flying range. But a second problem existed, namely the "counting rule" for the number of ALCMs to be attributed to each type of heavy bomber. Baker continued to bargain hard on the counting rule, offering a number way below that which Shevardnadze had proposed. Shevardnadze looked across at his friend of fifteen months and winced. "How could you ask for such a low number! You know that I cannot accept that figure."

Baker remained steely faced, ignoring the memory of fishing expeditions and dinner in Eduard's apartment. "I know that you can get that number."

"No, I can't," responded Shevardnadze, baffled by the hardness of his friend's demand.

"Well then, I offer 100!"

"That's not much better."

"It's as good as you get," Baker retorted.

Shevardnadze sighed, knowing that he still had to pass the agreement by Gorbachev. As they left the meeting and got into the Secretary's limousine, Baker turned to his START negotiator, Richard Burt, and grinned with pride.[33] He had won. Or had he?

An hour later, as Baker and his advisers reached the state guesthouse, a senior Soviet official approached to inform them that new conditions were to be imposed upon the grandfathering of Tacit Rainbow. The generals wanted limits on the missile's future modernization and guarantees that it would not be transformed at a later date into a nuclear weapon. That night, tired and frustrated, Baker shared with the president that this was "another example of walking back after the fact – in this case after Gorbachev had explicitly agreed." In his Night Notes to Bush, Baker went on, "It was a long and at times difficult day… We got another reminder of the [Soviet] military's role in the process and what it's like to do business now." He concluded that "Gorbachev is clearly feeling squeezed and is going to react strongly to any step that causes him potential problems."[34]

As they approached the May 1990 summit, Soviet negotiators were under instructions to settle the matter, and in an effort to accommodate the United States they accepted a limit of 760 SLCMs. Despite this concession, Baker continued to bargain, demanding a number closer to the original US ceiling of 1,000 cruise missiles. Gorbachev, in an effort to resolve the issue, proposed that they split the difference. Baker stood up and shook hands with him across the table: "You've got a deal."[35] They reached a limit of 880 missiles, and the Soviet negotiators could do nothing but capitulate. Hard bargaining had brought a meaningless victory for Baker and his START negotiator as the US had no plans to build that many missiles, but it left deep resentment among the Soviet leadership and especially the Soviet generals.[36]

Despite hard feelings on both sides, both Baker and Gorbachev sought a successful May summit and therefore declared to the press that they had "resolved all major obstacles to a strategic arms reduction treaty."[37] The treaty would cut their nuclear missile arsenals by approximately 30 percent but permit both sides to deploy new generations of sea-, air- and land-based strategic weapons. To their respective citizens, it appeared that Baker and Shevardnadze had agreed upon limits to ALCMs and SLCMs, but in reality they needed to do more work. Emerging from the May meetings in Moscow, Baker admitted to journalist Tom Friedman that the negotiations had been very tough, with neither side willing to concede: "These have been some of the most intensive discussions we have had with our Soviet counterparts during this Administration."[38]

A significant development had come out of the meetings. The two sides had reached a compromise on chemical weapons in which both would immediately cease production of all poison gas and reduce their respective stockpiles to 5,000 tons, and then after eight years to 500 tons each.[39] Baker had agreed to abandon longstanding US plans to build new types of poison-gas weapons because he knew that these plans had strong opposition in Congress.[40] The reduced chemical stockpile level of 500 tons should continue until every nation capable of making chemical weapons had signed the worldwide ban.[41] Flying home, Baker carried the chemical weapons reduction as good news of immediate interest to Congress and American citizens. He had also kept the plans for the May 30 summit in Washington on track.

Stark divisions remained over German unification within NATO and Lithuanian independence, as well as several complex strategic arms reduction issues. How should they prevent circumvention of the START treaty, place limits on the Soviet Backfire bomber, constrain the testing of heavy missiles, monitor each side's missile production facilities, and verify limits on missiles loaded on trucks? Nevertheless, when they met on May 30, they agreed on enough critical issues for both presidents to announce progress and state that US-Soviet relations had essentially returned to normal. The Chemical Weapons Treaty showed that they had developed new areas of cooperation, as well as agreements on maritime boundaries and student exchanges. In short, both leaders could claim that bilateral relations in 1990 were back to where they had been at the high point of détente in 1972-73.[42] Furthermore, there were good prospects that relations would remain more cooperative and maybe permanent. President Bush was pleased to attribute much of this to the State Department and tell the press "Baker's talks in Moscow had provided a breakthrough."[43]

THREE FINAL HURDLES TO A START TREATY

Saddam Hussein's invasion of Kuwait and the mobilization of an international coalition to repel the Iraqi army consumed Baker's time from August 2, 1990 through the withdrawal of US and coalition forces in February 1991. Meanwhile, Burt and the START negotiators continued to seek approximately a one-third reduction in long-range weapons overall and a fifty percent reduction in ballistic missile warheads. By mid-January 1991, 98 percent of the treaty was completed.

However, the White House was clear that it still had "some real differences" with the Soviets on arms control issues, and Baker's spokeswoman Margaret Tutwiler pointed out that "work remains."[44] Stories that the Soviets were circumventing the treaty by transferring large numbers of tanks and other weapons into Soviet Central Asia – a region not covered by the START treaty – had to be verified. If they were true, chances of the US Senate ratifying START were low. Furthermore, despite Baker's ability to overcome high hurdles on ALCMs and SLCMs, three issues remained unresolved: downloading of warheads, data denial, and the definition of a "new missile." Negotiators on both sides indicated that they were unable to settle these differences. Bush therefore asked Gorbachev to send his new Foreign Minister, Alexandr Bessmertnykh, to Washington to resolve these questions at the highest level.

With Eduard Shevardnadze having resigned in December 1990, Baker no longer had a good friend as his negotiating partner. He knew Bessmertnykh as a man with a reputation for independence, keen intelligence, and knowledge of the ways of Washington from his time as Soviet Ambassador to the United States. Baker acknowledged that he was a serious interlocutor who became a dependable counterpart until mid-August 1991.

With Bessmertnykh Baker played tough cop, insisting that there would be no summit meeting unless problems in the Baltics, as well as remaining issues within START, were resolved satisfactorily. His familiar posture as hard bargainer was all the more necessary in Washington as both Scowcroft and conservatives in the Republican Party were watching closely to prevent any overt concessions. On Monday, January 29, Baker and Bessmertnykh emerged from a meeting with the president at the White House to announce that the summit meeting scheduled for February 11-13 would be delayed until later in the year. Putting a best face on the increasingly visible new tensions between Washington and Moscow, the two foreign ministers attributed the postponement to the Persian Gulf War and the stalled START negotiations rather than US displeasure over Soviet actions in the Baltic States.[45] There was another pressing item on Baker's agenda: ongoing Soviet support for the war against Saddam Hussein. He could be tough against Soviet actions in the Baltics, and negotiate hard on the remaining START issues, but he could not undermine Gorbachev's position at home or lose Soviet support for the ground assault on Iraq. The balance was delicate.

DOWNLOADING OF WARHEADS AND DATA DENIAL

The process of reducing the number of warheads placed on a missile, known as downloading, was a highly debatable process which created a rift among Bush's national security team.[46] Scowcroft, knowing the Soviet military leadership's increasing dissatisfaction with Gorbachev, had become increasingly cautious about a possible Soviet breakthrough in any arms control agreement. He therefore sought strict terms on the conversion of multiple warheads placed on powerful intercontinental strategic missiles and known by the acronym "MIRVed ICBM."[47] Arnie Kantor, the NSC's arms control expert, was surprised at his boss's insistence on strict terms and wondered whether the success of the Gulf War had made Scowcroft think he would win all his battles.[48] Baker, however, was anxious to continue collaborating with Gorbachev and complete the START treaty. His policy bumped up against Scowcroft, who feared that Baker cared more about achieving a START agreement than about its substance.[49]

The Soviet military had engaged in its own form of downloading, leaving the Pentagon suspicious that the Soviets were developing two new missiles – one land-based and the other submarine-based – both capable of carrying an increased number of warheads. To conservative civil servants within the Defense Department, this created a risk that the Soviets could break out of the START treaty's restraints. Furthermore, Scowcroft worried that a weakened Gorbachev might have to become more militaristic to avoid being ousted. He therefore insisted that START negotiators remain tough on this issue. He would have preferred to ban downloading altogether, but under pressure from the Pentagon, he accepted the idea of permitting each side to download only one type of missile.[50] Baker, on the other hand, was prepared to accept at face value the Soviet agreement to reduce their warheads and was "more flexible, looking at the broader political perspective" of taking another step forward in U.S.-Soviet relations.[51] This division among the national security leaders remained hidden from the public, but it hindered efforts to complete the treaty. Burt feared that caution in Washington and Gorbachev's weakness would doom signature of START.[52]

THE LAST HEAVE FOR CFE

The CFE treaty had been signed the previous year, but in the spring of 1991, hardliners in Moscow sought to wiggle out of specific articles. They saw the treaty as Shevardnadze's "overall surrender to the West" and now, with him out of the way, it was time to rebalance the agreement in the Soviets' favor by exempting three thousand pieces of equipment. As they asserted control, these hardliners argued that these instruments were assigned to newly created "coastal defense" units or to "naval infantry regiments" and thus beyond the reach of the CFE treaty. However, Bush, Scowcroft and Baker considered the treaty already endorsed, with twenty-two countries signing onto the agreement. Baker therefore made it clear to Bessmertnykh: "This issue here is not whether you can have forces that you call coastal defense or naval infantry. This issue is that our presidents have signed a treaty that mandates certain numbers. The integrity of the treaty depends on maintaining the integrity of those numbers."[53]

Baker was getting increasingly irritated with the Soviet negotiators because he recognized that the generals were calling the shots from behind the scenes. In his Nightly Report to the president, he wrote, "I really hit him over the head....We've got to keep Gorbachev himself involved."[54] Bush understood that only the Soviet president could control his generals and prevent the unravelling of the treaty. On April 25, Baker flew to Kislovodsk, in southern Russia, to meet with Bessmertnykh. It was a mountain resort and represented the Soviet minister's effort to offer a Wyoming-type getaway for a bilateral meeting. The two continued to bargain over who should negotiate the latest exemptions on coastal defense or naval infantry. Should it be their respective presidents? Or General Moiseyev, the Soviet Chief of the General Staff, and James Woolsey, the chief US negotiator on CFE? Bessmertnykh lacked Shevardnadze's political clout with Gorbachev, and he sought to pass this task to a military man, who would then discover just how tough and disagreeable negotiations with the Americans could be. Gorbachev agreed to put Moiseyev in the hot seat across from the US negotiators. "Let him experience American adamancy firsthand and then explain to his president why he could not force the Soviet position down the Americans' throats."[55]

Six weeks later, after Moiseyev failed to get General Colin Powell, his counterpart as General Chief of Staff, to agree to the exemptions for "coastal defense" and "naval infantry," the Soviets blinked. Bessmertnykh brought a letter with new ideas to Baker at the American Embassy in Lisbon. Baker sent Woolsey back to Moscow to draw up agreements on CFE and all other outstanding matters, including the number of ICBMs and SLBMs each side could have. On Friday, June 14, the CFE treaty was formally ratified at an extraordinary conference of ambassadors in Vienna. It was now time for the US Senate to ratify the treaty.

On July 11, with Bessmertnykh in Washington to discuss final issues before Bush would agree to a summit in Moscow at the end of the month, Senators Joe Biden and Richard Lugar announced their full support of CFE. Lugar was a dependable Republican ally of the president and Biden, now in his fourth term and Chair of the Senate Judiciary committee had a reputation as a political moderate who sought the approval of both political parties. Baker appealed to both sides of the aisle to ratify the CFE treaty. Biden stated,

> This treaty will eliminate a fundamental cause of tension in Europe since the end of World War II, which has been the huge numerical advantage of Soviet conventional forces. This superiority threatened the security and prosperity of the West for many years. This superiority also fueled a nuclear arms race. In every strategic doctrine adopted by NATO for forty years, from massive retaliation to flexible response, nuclear weapons were intended to compensate for the Soviet edge in conventional arms.[56]

Baker cherished the bi-partisan approach to his management of US foreign policy.

Only Senator Jesse Helms objected to the treaty, on the ground that it had become irrelevant with the collapse of the Warsaw Pact, the reunification of Germany and the fall of communist regimes in Eastern Europe. Furthermore, the "great cracks that are appearing in the surface of the Soviet empire ... have already established the withdrawal of Soviet troops at rates exceeding the provisions of this treaty."[57] He criticized the US negotiators for having "come up with, not a mouse, but with a goose egg. It is so meaningless that there is no point in opposing it."[58] Despite Helms's criticism of Baker's team, he was alone in dismissing the treaty. When it came time to vote, he joined Senator Lugar, who argued that the CFE treaty was so tilted to the benefit of NATO that "I predict it must pass the Senate by a large margin."[59] On November 25, 1991, the Senate ratified CFE by 94-0.[60] The Soviet Union would survive for exactly one more month.

A HANDSHAKE ON START

For Mikhail Gorbachev, the most important issue in July 1991 was not START but conclusion of a trade agreement with the United States and the grant of Most Favored Nation (MFN) status, which would lower tariffs on Soviet exports. He was prepared to make concessions on arms control to ensure that the postponed summit, now planned for late July in Moscow, went ahead. To that end he instructed Bessmertnykh to make whatever compromises were necessary to finish the treaty.[61]

Baker, though buoyed by the Senators' support for CFE, was bogged down on difficult technical issues over START. Negotiators on both sides struggled to resolve the remaining obstacles and finally came down to one final hurdle: throw-weights on new missiles.[62] After nine years of negotiation, they had yet to agree on what constitutes a nuclear missile's throw-weight, which is all parts of the missile other than the booster rocket that sends it into space.[63] Because the Soviets generally had the larger missiles (including new ones they were currently developing), they were anxious to establish a narrow definition of "throw-weight." The Americans wanted a broader definition that would more heavily restrict the Soviet arsenal.[64]

On July 17, 1991, President Bush attended the G-7 meeting of heads of state in London. Gorbachev was not invited to the G-7 meetings, but due to his urgent need to gain the seven leaders support for his economic reform plans, he had begged for an invitation. After first rejecting the request, Baker persuaded the President to accept Gorbachev's attendance at the end of the meeting. Bush agreed to host him for a one-on-one luncheon at Winfield House, the US Ambassador's residence.

As the day started, negotiators had not reached agreement on throw-weights on new missiles. At 9:30 that morning, Bessmertnykh telephoned Baker who was staying at the Churchill Hotel, asking to meet with him for fifteen minutes that morning to share "a new position" that the Soviet had come up with for resolving the issue.[65] At 11:10, Bush gathered his senior foreign policy team, including Baker and Scowcroft, at Winfield House. Together, they examined their bottom line position on throw-weights and tried to guess what Bessmertnykh might offer. Bessmertnykh arrived at 11:40 and privately laid out to Baker the Soviets' new formula, which was close to what the Americans were seeking. Baker told Bessmertnykh that he thought the Soviet proposal could "form the basis for a mutually satisfactory" solution. He surmised that the reason for Bessmertnykh's secretiveness was to avoid the appearance that Gorbachev was trading the START treaty for economic aid.[66] Not only Republican right-wingers but also Soviet military were determined to avoid such a tradeoff. Fifteen minutes later, Baker walked into the dining room where the luncheon with Gorbachev would take place. He shared Bessmertnykh's position with the president and Scowcroft while Bessmertnykh waited outside in the hall. Receiving the news, Bush and Scowcroft got up and went out to confirm with the Soviet Foreign Minister that as far as they were concerned the deal was done, pending final discussions with Gorbachev and review by US arms control experts back home.

The Pentagon experts combed through the Soviet proposal and telephoned Baker to tell him that it addressed their concerns. Baker knew that this information was important enough to interrupt the quiet luncheon between Bush and Gorbachev in the Winfield House dining room. With only their respective interpreters, the two leaders finished eating and retired to a small drawing room alone. There, they confirmed the START agreement, and the prolonged negotiations ended with a simple handshake. The relief on both sides was enormous. The summit was scheduled, and Baker made plans to arrive in Moscow on July 29.

There were several issues that Baker needed to discuss with Bessmertnykh before Bush arrived in Moscow. Flying in from Mongolia, where he fulfilled a promise made a year earlier after Saddam's invasion of Kuwait had forced him to cancel a visit, Baker was tired and irritable, refusing the Soviet request to make a joint Soviet-US trip to the Middle East. Nor would he commit to a Middle East conference by the end of the year. US support for Gorbachev's economic reforms did not go beyond a commitment to sign a bilateral trade agreement and submit it to Congress for approval. While regional issues should be discussed, the ceremonial high point of the summit was the signing of the START treaty and the commitment by the two powers to scale back their fleets of long range-nuclear missiles and bombers in the longest and most complicated nuclear arms-control agreement yet agreed to.

Underlying the mood of the summit were US concerns about Gorbachev's ability to implement his economic reforms and about Moscow's relationship to the twelve Soviet republics and the Baltic States.

While Bush supported Gorbachev's efforts to hold the union together, he and Baker understood that Gorbachev's power was waning and that of the Russian, Byelorussian, Kazakh, and Ukrainian presidents was rising. Bush therefore held a private session with Gorbachev's nemesis, Russian president Boris Yeltsin. He also met with Nursultan Nazarbayev, the leader of Kazakhstan. Combined with his subsequent visit to Ukraine's capital Kyiv, these meetings made it clearer than ever before that Bush took the republics and their aspirations seriously. He also recognized that Yeltsin and Leonid M. Kravchuk, the Ukrainian leader, had developed significant independent power bases.[67]

Meanwhile, back in Washington, the Senate voted to begin deploying an anti-missile defense system by 1996, with one hundred missiles to defend against a limited missile attack fired by a rogue Soviet commander. The vote imperiled the 1972 ABM Treaty with the Soviet Union, which banned space-based weapons and national anti-missile systems, but Gorbachev was no longer strong enough to protest. The Senate could not find the funds to support Gorbachev's economic reforms, but it found an additional $10-15 billion to develop the anti-missile defense system, which Senator Sam Nunn called "a valuable investment against the possible damage of a nuclear attack on an American city."[68] The president and Baker were focused on a new global order, but the Senate was still fighting the Cold War.

On July 31, 1991, Presidents Bush and Gorbachev signed START, which limited the US and Russia to 6,000 nuclear warheads and 1,600 nuclear delivery vehicles each, and called for drastic reductions in each nation's nuclear stockpile. The result was a 25-35 percent cut in strategic warheads. Problems with verification continued, however, and the Senate waited more than a year before it finally ratified the treaty, by a vote of 93-6, on October 1, 1992.[69] By that time Baker had left the State Department to become Bush's Chief of Staff and campaign manager at the White House. Gorbachev and Bessmertnykh were no longer in their jobs, the Soviet Union having disintegrated. In its place, Russian President, Boris Yeltsin assumed the international responsibilities of the former USSR, including START.

Meeting with Brian Mulroney and Douglas Hurd at NATO summit, 1991. *US government photograph, courtesy of the Baker Institute for Public Policy.*

President and Baker confer with Chancellor Helmut Kohl, Camp David. *NARA, courtesy of the George H.W. Bush Presidential Library.*

Baker meets with U.S. troops in Ta'if, Saudi Arabia. *US government photograph, courtesy of the Baker Institute.*

Meeting the travelling press corps on Baker's plane, September 1990. *US government photograph, courtesy of the Baker Institute.*

Baker's press conference. *US government photograph, courtesy of the Baker Institute.*

Baker negotiates with Iraqi Foreign Minister, Tariq Aziz, Geneva, January 9, 1991. *US government photograph, courtesy of the Baker Institute.*

Briefing Bob Strauss following the failed coup against Gorbachev, August 1991. *NARA, Courtesy of the George H.W. Bush Library.*

Madrid Conference, October 1991. *US government photograph, courtesy of the Baker Institute.*

Barbara Bush congratulates Baker upon receiving the Medal of Freedom, July 1991. *US government photograph, courtesy of the Baker Institute.*

NINE

HORROR MIRROR - THE BREAKUP OF YUGOSLAVIA

The citizens of two significant federations, the Union of Soviet Socialist Republics (USSR) and the Socialist Federation of Yugoslavia (Yugoslavia) raised expectations for freedom as East European nations became independent. If Poland, Hungary, Czechoslovakia, Romania, and Bulgaria could achieve independence, why not the republics under the central rule of Moscow and Belgrade? The liberalizing achievements of 1989 and 1990 aroused ordinary Yugoslav and Soviet citizens to hope that they too could live within their own national boundaries. Maybe, their own ethnic and religious groups might be subsumed within a broader national identity. These deep nationalist stirrings – suppressed during decades of authoritarian rule – rose to the fore as the Cold War gradually ended. By 1991, the impetus to separate from the center gained strength. Mikhail Gorbachev recognized the symptoms and dreaded the ethnic fractiousness of Yugoslavia as a "horror mirror" of what might occur in the Soviet Union.[1]

Baker had heard and touched these stirrings for freedom and self-determination, but he preferred the stable relations of known governments and leaders with whom he could anticipate predictable behavior. He had developed a high level of trust with Shevardnadze and would seek to develop trust with his successor, Bessmertnykh. Reliable leadership in Moscow and central control over nuclear weapons and material was essential to US national security. Yugoslavia, without nuclear assets, was less important, but no reader of history forgot that World War I had started in the Bosnian town of Sarajevo. Therefore, Bush's national security team sought to hold both federations together and to postpone quarrelsome self-determination which could descend into violent conflict, undermining regional stability. Gorbachev dreaded "suicidal nationalism" and spent hours developing a Union Treaty to hold the vast Soviet empire together.

Baker gave priority to helping Gorbachev and supported his Union Treaty. Consequently, he passed to his deputy Larry Eagleburger the task of holding Yugoslavia together. In the midst of preparing for military action in Iraq, avoiding a Soviet clamp down in the Baltic States, and seeking a Middle East peace process, Baker did not have the bandwidth to maintain unity in both federations. He focused on the Soviet Union and left to others the challenge of either holding Yugoslavia together or allowing it to fragment without undue violence. The challenge in the Balkans probably was impossible to resolve without foreign military intervention, but neither the United States nor Western Europe were prepared to go to war over the Balkans. Short of military action, could Baker muster the resources to hold the six republics and two autonomous provinces together? In the autumn of 1990 and focused on repelling Saddam Hussein from Kuwait, the Balkans was a sideshow.

The Socialist Federation of Yugoslavia had begun to splinter after the death of Josip Broz Tito in 1980, and a decade later the new Serbian President, Slobodan Milošević filled the vacuum left by Tito's death. He prevented the rotation of the Yugoslav presidency among the federal states, turned a blind eye toward Bosnian persecution of Kosovar Muslims and used Serbian nationalist sentiments to stoke ethnic conflicts within the other republics. Furthermore, Milošević ensured that Serbian military officers held senior positions in the Yugoslav National Army (JNA), effectively creating a Serbian military force.

YUGOSLAVIA

On October 18, 1990, the National Intelligence Estimate (NIE) was presented to the president. It warned that

> Yugoslavia will cease to function as a federal state within a year, and will probably dissolve within two. Economic reform will not stave off the breakup... A full-scale inter-republic war is unlikely, but serious intercommunal conflict will accompany the breakup and will continue afterward. The violence will be intractable and bitter. There is little the United States and its European allies can do to preserve Yugoslav unity.[2]

Guided by Brent Scowcroft, Baker decided that the US should devote less effort to holding Yugoslavia together. Instead, they should rely on European allies who had indicated a willingness to manage the problems in the Balkans. Geographically in their backyard, the offer of the European Economic Community (EEC) to assume responsibility for Yugoslavia's future seemed logical. It was also a significant relief to a US national security team focused on creating and holding together the international coalition against Saddam Hussein.

Despite the focus on Iraq, a so-called "Balkan mafia" emerged in Washington led by two senior officials: Scowcroft, who had served as assistant air attaché in the US Embassy Belgrade from 1962-1963 and Eagleburger, a pragmatic Foreign Service officer who spoke his mind and cared little for the niceties of diplomatic life. He had spent seven years in Yugoslavia, including his time as President Carter's ambassador. Both Scowcroft and he had experienced the frictions between distinct ethnic groups, but saw no advantage in splintering the country. Ethnic divisions did not coincide with religious differences and the patchwork of communities was too complicated to please all citizens.

After reading the NIE and listening to his national security colleagues, Baker chose the cautious policy of maintaining the unity of the Yugoslav federation. In the winter of 1990, Poland, Hungary,

Czechoslovakia, Romania, and Bulgaria were struggling to introduce democratic institutions and practices, as well as convert to free market economies with the aid of both European and US governments. Baker was determined to avoid, at all costs, national independence through violent means. He therefore urged dialogue between Lithuanian Prime Minister Landsberger and Moscow as well as between Milošević and leaders of the five other republics in the Balkans. Only through diplomatic negotiations would these two regions contain incipient violence.

The Balkans were distinct from the problems in the Baltics. In South Eastern Europe, the perceived Soviet weakness served to erode the cultural glue that had held Yugoslavia together. During the Cold War, European governments and the United States had provided extensive economic and financial support to bolster Tito's independence from Moscow, but with the end of the global conflict in sight, creditors were demanding payment of interest on Yugoslavia's debts. Without the productive capacity to generate sufficient revenue to pay for public services, each of the six Yugoslav republics and two autonomous provinces sought to keep their tax revenues at home and avoid transferring them to the federal capital in Belgrade. Low productivity and growing indebtedness warned West European bankers that Yugoslavia was approaching economic collapse. Meantime, with a lessening of Cold War tensions and threats in the Gulf, both the Bush administration and West European allies were focused on mobilizing the coalition to force Saddam Hussein to withdraw from Iraq. They gave less attention to propping up the Yugoslav Federation.[3]

Beginning in April 1990, a series of elections in both Croatia and Slovenia led each to hold a referendum that gave overwhelmingly support to those favoring independence.[4] The minority Serbian population in Croatia, who had felt safe under the former communist system, now felt vulnerable and turned for support to Milošević's brand of Serb nationalism.[5] In Kosovo, Milošević had spoken out in favor of the Serbian population and ignored the violence enacted against the minority Albanian Muslim population. Similar to the Soviet Union, geographic borders did not reflect differences between people and cultures.

US congressional interest in Yugoslavia also complicated the crisscross of ethnic and religious tensions throughout the Yugoslavia federation. Senator Bob Dole led a delegation to Kosovo in August 1990 to witness and report on the state of Kosovo's Albanian population. His delegation witnessed the misery of many Albanians and returned determined to raise US awareness of their plight. In November that year, Republican Senator Don Nickles introduced a bill to prohibit $5 million in economic assistance to Yugoslavia unless the Serbs ceased their human rights violations in Kosovo.[6] The Nickles Amendment became law the following year, but Baker invoked his discretionary authority to prevent it taking effect.[7] He talked with Nickles and argued that the sanction was aimed at the wrong target. Nickles intended to hurt Serbia, but the sanctions attacked Yugoslavia leaving Milošević free to rant that the US was bullying "brave little Serbia." Were the sanctions to go into effect Milošević would rally his supporters more firmly around him.[8]

With clear notice of cracks both in Yugoslav unity and in the American approach to the Balkans, Baker sent an experienced Foreign Service officer, Warren Zimmerman, as ambassador to Belgrade with instructions to maintain the integrity of Yugoslavia. Zimmerman spoke Serbian and had served as a junior Foreign Service officer in Belgrade some twenty-one years earlier. He was Baker's choice and appeared to be the ideal ambassador to stand up to Slobodan Milošević. The Serbian leader's response was to reject any request to meet with Zimmerman. The ban lasted ten months until Milošević relented. Meantime, Moscow with its own Serbian majority in Russia supported Milošević while warning him against pursuing a violent breakup. For Gorbachev leading a federation with twelve distinct republics, territorial integrity overrode demands for self-determination.

EAGLEBURGER VISITS YUGOSLAVIA

In February 1991, Baker asked Eagleburger to extend his February tour of Eastern European capitals to visit Yugoslavia. He was well aware that Eagleburger had spent seven years of his foreign service in Yugoslavia, earning him the nickname "Lawrence of Macedonia" for his humanitarian response to the 1962 earthquake in Skopje.

Eagleburger was reluctant, reminding Baker that Senator Helms, the ranking member of the Senate Foreign Relations Committee, had criticized him for a so-called "financial stake" in Yugoslavia. (When working for Kissinger Associates, Eagleburger had been on the board of one Serbian and one Slovenian company, both of which sought to introduce best Western business practices.) As a result of his promise to Helms, Eagleburger had committed to refrain from involvement in Yugoslavia. He was also reluctant to return to the Balkans, telling Baker that Yugoslavia was lurching toward nationalism, separatism and major violations of human rights.[9] Baker responded that Eagleburger had won the respect of Yugoslav's leaders for his clear love of the country and pragmatism. If anyone had influence with the leaders of the republics, it was him. Flattered, Eagleburger agreed to go, but he warned Baker that he should not expect him to halt the rapid disintegration of the Yugoslav Federation.

From a friendship with Milošević earned during his early days in Belgrade, Eagleburger now confronted a pugilistic Milošević. He listened to his old drinking partner and told him bluntly that Serbian strong-arm tactics against the Albanian people were hurting relations with the United States. Human rights were taken into account when the US government decides where to "use our taxpayer's money or which countries to advise our businesses to invest in."[10] Milošević had visited the United States in the late 1970s and early '80s as the head of Beobanka, one of the major state-run banks in Yugoslavia. The purpose of his frequent visits to the United States was to raise investment funds for Serbia and he had mastered the mechanisms for gaining foreign loans and credit guarantees. Now, in response to Eagleburger's threats, he bristled, arguing that the Serbs had to defend themselves against "Islamic fundamentalism" and the rape of Serbian women in Kosovo. Before the meeting broke up, he made one more comment. This time in perfect English, he said "Serbs live all over Yugoslavia. The unity of Yugoslavia is the only way they can live in one country."[11] It was an ominous sign of Serbian expansion to follow.

Eagleburger returned to Washington to warn Baker "Yugoslavia was heading in a downward spiral where the leverage of the United States was likely to be minimal."[12] With Milošević's hostility in favor of Serbian nationalism and the combative response from the other republics, Yugoslavia continued to unravel and Baker stayed away, unwilling to get involved in a losing cause. The State Department observed developments, but the integrity of Yugoslavia was not a priority until the spring of 1991 when America's closest allies in Europe began to argue among themselves over the value of self-determination versus the integrity of traditional borders.

GERMAN POLICY CONFRONTS EUROPEAN PARTNERS

In the aftermath of Germany unification, Chancellor Kohl sought territorial integrity and the avoidance of self-determination that might unravel Europe's boundaries. He needed good relations with Moscow, recognizing that movements toward self-determination which undermined territorial integrity could destabilize the Soviet Union. Kohl knew that Yugoslavia was a tinderbox, with six republics and two autonomous provinces vying with each other for greater autonomy following the death of Tito. Tito had held the Yugoslav republics together with iron will, but his death released deep historical and cultural divisions among the disparate peoples gathered together in a Yugoslav federation. Previous West German governments under Willy Brandt and Helmut Schmidt had been Yugoslavia's best friend during the 1970s and 1980s, recognizing the need to have a unified Slavic majority as a bulwark against the Soviet Union. In support of this, German bankers, backed by the government, had invested heavily in Yugoslav infrastructure.

During the 1980s Hans-Dietrich Genscher, the leader of the West German Free Democratic Party (FDP), was considered Yugoslavia's best diplomatic friend, arguing for continued economic and technical support. In early 1991, Genscher stressed the importance of the territorial integrity of Yugoslavia and the rejection of violence, but parliamentarians from all German political parties returned from visits to Zagreb and Ljubljana with tales of Serbian abuse, rape and assault.[13] These politicians became increasingly outspoken in their support for Slovene and Croatian independence, and were less sanguine about the ability or desirability of holding together the Yugoslav federation. Furthermore, German media, reflecting the opinion of the parliamentarians, constantly reminded the German public of the plight of Croatian citizens. They lived under Milošević's threats to send in the Serbian-led Yugoslav National Army (JNA) to protect Croatia's Serbian minority who suffered discrimination in employment and assaults on their property. Some said that Genscher's commitment to Yugoslav unity led him to underestimate the separatist voices in Slovenia and Croatia. Nevertheless, by May 1991 and in the face of parliamentary pressure, Genscher shifted his position. Now he argued for a negotiated settlement with the Croatian leader, Franjo Tudjman. When that pressure broadened to include the German media and members of his own FDP party, Genscher concluded that self-determination for both Croatia and Slovenia was the preferred outcome.[14]

Despite growing objections from his French and British colleagues, Genscher decided to get ahead of his German critics and declared that Slovenia and Croatia should be recognized as sovereign states.[15] Under his leadership as foreign minister, German diplomacy now demonstrated new political muscle to lead a European initiative to recognize the new states. After all, the Croatian people had supported Germany during World War II, and public pressure to remember their contribution was growing among the German electorate. Genscher found allies in the Austrian and Italian governments, but he failed to persuade the French and British foreign ministries of the wisdom of supporting independent Slovenia and Croatia. He also confronted Washington, where the "Balkan mafia" persuaded Bush and Baker to maintain the territorial integrity of the Yugoslavia Federation.

Balkan experts in the United States warned that Slovenian and Croatian independence would weaken an already fragile central government, giving greater space to Serbian leader Milošević. Should both republics become independent, violent conflict throughout the other republics was inevitable. Slovenian and Croatian self-determination would result in the loss of self-determination for other republics.[16] For Baker, the real problem lay not with Croatia and Slovenia, but with Bosnia-Herzegovina, where religious and ethnic conflicts failed to coincide with geographic distributions. Here there was no possible solution based on "self-determination." However, tensions between European capitals over Yugoslavia goaded Baker to intervene. European foreign ministers urged him to become more involved. He should seek to influence Genscher and to postpone, if not reject, Slovenian and Croatian moves for independence. Genscher was steeped in the controversy and both Paris and London argued that the newly united Germany was asserting itself in ways that were unacceptable to a stable European balance of power. Baker's interjection, they claimed, could help restrain Genscher. The US Secretary of State could guide his German colleague to see the consequences of his action and refrain from following the German popular clamor for Croatian independence.[17]

As Baker prepared to leave for the Commission on Security and Cooperation in Europe (CSCE) conference in Berlin that June 1991, Scowcroft warned him that conflict among the republics would be bloody and long. He should therefore give his best effort to holding the federation together and warn the Yugoslav leaders of the consequences should they decide to pursue their personal ambitions. He should seek to persuade each Yugoslavian leader that accommodation among them was still possible.[18]

Genscher's cure lay in reliance upon the CSCE conference. With the Soviet Union among its members, Genscher relied upon this multilateral body to find a solution to Serbia's explicit nationalism and the need to protect other ethnic groups in the Balkans. In his mind, CSCE and the Helsinki process with its baskets to address key social, economic and human rights issues provided a golden bridge between the European Community (EEC) and the long-sought European peace between its Western and Eastern halves, as well as the Soviet Union.[19] Baker was not enthusiastic about the CSCE, considering it unwieldy, cumbersome and sometimes threatening to US leadership of NATO. However, the reluctance of his own colleagues to place Washington out in front over Yugoslavia and Baker's reliance upon the EEC to take the lead resulted in his acceptance of a role for the CSCE and his attendance at the June 19 meeting in Berlin. At meetings on the side of the conference, Baker used the gathering to discuss arms control and START with his Soviet counterpart… Arms control remained the central issue in US-Soviet relations and Baker had acquired a mastery of the minutia debated in these sessions. A bilateral meeting with Bessmertnykh compensated for the tedium of lengthy speeches required at annual CSCE gatherings.

Around the CSCE meeting, both the Secretary and his wife Susan Baker had spent two days in Berlin as guests of the Genschers with visits to cultural sites, including a beer house. Rarely did James Baker spend time visiting cultural places. He had done so, somewhat reluctantly, with Shevardnadze to visit a monastery outside Moscow in 1990, but his preference was to focus on the substance of his meetings.[20] Nevertheless, this early summer and seeking to please his German host, Susan Baker urged him to accept the Genschers' invitation to listen for a twenty minute Bach fugue performed on Johann Sebastian Bach's original organ. It was not too long. He might catch a quick nap and Baker obliged. Once it was over and on the ride back to the hotel, Baker shared with Genscher his reluctance to get involved in the quagmire of Yugoslavia. Genscher advised his Texan friend with whom he had worked closely to achieve German unification, "Listen to Tudjman, Marković and Milošević. Then determine whether there is anything you can do to postpone the announcement of independence. I'm not asking you to threaten military action. This is not Saddam's invasion of Kuwait, but I ask you to listen to the Yugoslav leaders and make up your mind."[21]

He went on to stress that this was a European problem that presented a test of European political will to defend democracy and human rights. With Genscher's indication that this was a problem best solved by the Europeans, Baker left for Belgrade with a mission to recommend holding the federation together through dialogue. He avoided committing any US assets to glue Tito's republics together. Flying out of Berlin the morning of June 21, Baker's mind was on the problems he faced in

Belgrade. He knew that he confronted one of the toughest negotiating sessions of his career. Six bull headed national leaders each sought their own sandpit and the toughest of all, Milošević, was determined to lead *all* Serb people in a new union whether they resided in Serbia or beyond in the other republics. However, armed with the commitment of all thirty-five CSCE members to unity, reform, human rights, and a peaceful solution of the crisis, Baker knew he was not alone. Landing in Belgrade, he drove to Zimmerman's official residence to meet with the leaders of the Yugoslav federation, as well as the leaders of six Yugoslav republics. He would urge them to seek a negotiated outcome, not war.[22]

BAKER'S FIVE PRINCIPLES

Back in March that year, President Bush had declared that the United States "will not encourage those who would break the country [Yugoslavia] apart."[23] Two months later, a State Department statement made it clear that "the United States will not encourage or reward secession," and reiterated US support for the territorial integrity of Yugoslavia within its present borders. In support of this position, the State Department's office of Policy Planning had worked with Baker's staff to develop a set of principles that he would use often in his remaining seventeen months as Secretary of State. Any secession plan for Yugoslavia and later for the Soviet Union and the newly independent states should respect the following five principles:

- Peaceful self-determination consistent with democratic values;
- Respect for existing borders with changes only through consensual and peaceful dialogue;
- Respect for democracy and the rule of law;
- Human rights and particularly minority rights; and,
- Respect for international law and obligations.[24]

They remained the US guideposts for the emerging post-Cold War political structures whose purpose was to minimize the risks of turbulence. In Belgrade that June, Baker handed out a laminated sheet with these principles to the leaders of the six republics, including Slobodan Milošević. In December that year and again in February 1992, he distributed the same principles to the leaders of the newly independent states of the former Soviet Union.

MEETINGS IN BELGRADE WITH YUGOSLAV LEADERS

In Belgrade that June, Margaret Tutwiler was determined that Baker should have downtime on his own before and between nine consecutive meetings: seven with the leaders of Serbia, Croatia, Slovenia, Bosnia-Herzegovina, Macedonia, Montenegro, and Kosovo, as well as two meetings with the Prime Minister of Yugoslavia, Ante Marković. Each meeting was grueling and Baker prepared his arguments with particularity for each leader. His roughest meeting was with Milošević. Baker began the meeting gently saying that the US had enjoyed friendly relations with Serbia: "We don't challenge the unity or integrity of Serbia; there's not an economic blockade." He then swung into action. According to Ambassador Zimmerman who accompanied him, Baker branded the Serbian leader as the principal source of the crisis and accused him of propelling his people, his republic and Yugoslavia toward civil war. Baker said he had come from Berlin with the proxies of all thirty-five CSCE member governments: "We reject any claims by Serbia to territory beyond its borders. If you persist, Serbia will be made an outcast, a pariah." Baker also slammed Milošević for stirring up ethnic tensions, repressing Albanian rights in Kosovo, and undermining the Yugoslav President.[25] In his response, Milošević was combative, conceding nothing.

In his meeting with Franjo Tudjman of Croatia, Baker told him that unity was the best way to preserve human rights and achieve democracy: "If Yugoslavia fragments, who will preserve the rights of minorities? The United States will not recognize unilateral secession, which can only trigger violence and bloodshed. Those who fail to negotiate will be responsible if violence breaks out."[26] Baker then asked if the Croatian independence declaration could be limited to rhetorical statements and allow negotiations with the Yugoslav Federation to take place. His appeal struck a stonewall. Tudjman responded that the Croatians had already made the decision to leave and they refused to change. He assured Baker that the JNA, would not act against Croatia. Baker shook his head in disbelief over Tudjman's claim that the JNA – Milošević's Serbian military force – would not attack him. Afterwards, a member of Tudjman's team curled his lip as he complained that the "owner of the biggest ranch in Wyoming [couldn't escape] the American tradition of demonizing secession."[27]

Meeting with Milan Kučan of Slovenia, Baker told him that Yugoslavia was a powder keg that only needed one match to set it off. "If Slovenia walks away (from the Yugoslav Federation) you will change the balance of forces in favor of Milošević."[28] Kučan was prepared to negotiate a relationship with the Yugoslav federal institutions after declaring independence and he talked about institutional arrangements similar to those existing among the members of the EEC. It was evident to Baker that Kučan was preparing for an independent Slovene state, but he failed to anticipate that Milošević and the JNA would attack him in Slovenia, despite the fact that very few Serbians inhabited that republic.

Baker never gave a green light to Milošević to invade any of the breakaway republics, but his answers to the Serbian leader had an unintended purpose. His deliberate imprecision on whether US military action could result from incursions against Slovenia and Croatia allowed Milošević to conclude that Washington did not intend to stop him by force.[29] Furthermore, Baker's focus on the importance of democracy left room for Milošević to read between the lines. He understood that the Americans might isolate the JNA and make him a pariah, but they would not take military action. Milošević concluded that it was worth incurring that risk.[30] Four days after Baker's visit, Slovenia and Croatia declared their independence and on June 27, the JNA invaded Slovenia. Fighting occurred for only ten days,[31] but the absence of military rebuttal reflected the unwillingness of the United States and the Europeans to prevent conflict. From that time onwards, Yugoslavia descended into violent conflict.

Amidst the threat of war, both James and Susan Baker attended a grand banquet that night in Belgrade with crystal chandeliers and fine porcelain that bombs would shatter the following year. The hosts raised toasts to friendship, but the hypocrisy was blatant. The leaders of the strongest Yugoslav republic were bent on war and they needed to clear out the Americans and European Commission officials before they settled their own scores. Perhaps if Baker had arrived six months earlier, he could have persuaded the Croatian and Slovenian leaders to pursue negotiation, but back in the winter of 1990, Baker had concentrated on the deadline for US led coalition forces to attack Saddam Hussein.[32] Even then, there was no assurance that Milošević would have ceased his scheme of a greater Serbia. Only military action might have caused him to reflect. After Iraq, neither US nor the European leaders had any appetite for another military excursion. In the summer of 1991, the Balkans found themselves on their own.

A DAY IN TIRANA

The next day, Baker flew on to Albania's capital, which had not seen a high-ranking American official in fifty-two years. The contrast with Belgrade was breathtaking. As his limousine sped away from the airfield toward Tirana, people ran across lush green fields carrying homemade American flags. Colored with crayons, the flags were stapled to wooden sticks, many of them upside down. They did not know James A. Baker, III: he might have been President Bush, but they knew that years of isolation from the Western world were about to end. When Baker reached the central square where a rickety wooden platform was constructed, hundreds of thousands of people awaited this important American visitor. The crowds were wild and Secret Service ushered both Bakers quickly into a "kinda church."[33]

His security estimated that three hundred thousand people were in the square and the platform was worse than rickety. Baker grinned. As a politician, he had never shied away from crowds. At Republican conventions, he had watched Ronald Reagan's receive an electric jolt from adoring supporters. Now Baker had his own crowd clamoring for "Mr. Becker", "Mr. Beaker" and "Welcome Mr. Baker, Albania has been waiting for you for 50 years."[34] With Susan Baker beside him, wearing a red, white and blue frock, Baker turned to the crowd with a mixture of pride at the outpouring of fervor for America and the realism that his words would probably not carry over the crackling Albanian loudspeaker system.

> On behalf of President Bush and the American people, I come here today to say to you: Freedom works. At last, you are free to think your own thoughts ... At last, you are free to choose your own leaders. Albanians have chosen to join the company of free men and women everywhere.[35]

A token aid package of $6 million in powdered milk, medical equipment and medicine accompanied his words. This was the first assistance that the United States had ever donated to Albania, a state suffering from hunger and malnutrition because of poor harvests and the upheavals incurred with its struggle to transition to free markets.

Baker went on to address the Albanian parliament and stress that the nature of American-Albanian relations would depend upon whether government went ahead with its promised constitutional, free market, and free election reforms. The day had been heady, but memories of the previous bargaining in Belgrade grounded Baker to the reality that he and the Bush administration could not shoulder these problems. Instead, European offers to accept responsibility for conflict in their "backyard" had to be accepted.

Two days later, as Baker walked into the White House to report upon his meetings in Yugoslavia and Albania with Bush and Scowcroft, the JNA marched into Slovenia. In the Oval Office, Baker was pleased to see NATO's Secretary General Manfred Woerner, who saw no role for NATO - and thus the United States - in the crisis. President Bush said, "We're not doing contingency planning. We're not thinking of intervening."[36]

Baker cautioned, "Once the shooting starts, and I think it will, it'll be a mess... the equal danger of various gangs starting to shoot at each other. The Yugoslavs will use their army. NATO will not get involved. The emergency mechanism of CSCE will likely be used."

"And do what?" asked Scowcroft.

"Nothing," replied Baker. Even though he had been the messenger of a strong commitment from all thirty-five members of CSCE to the leaders of the six republics, Baker feared that "the political demands in Yugoslavia are so great that we may be unable to stop the crisis."[37]

No member of the President's national security team advocated intervention. Baker and the "Balkan mafia" saw no US national security interest and relied upon the European Council, the governing body of the EEC, and the bold words of its incoming chairman, the Dutch Prime Minister Ruud Lubbers.[38] On September 7 after the European traditional summer break, Dutch Foreign Minister Hans Van den Brock convened a meeting of the European Council in The Hague to discuss ways to end the violence in Yugoslavia, but the meeting achieved little.[39] As Serbian violence against the Muslim population of Bosnia and Herzegovina rose, the UN Security Council passed a resolution to use "all necessary means" to protect lives.[40] The phrase, created to legitimize the use of military force against Saddam Hussein, was raised again to protect the Muslim communities in the Balkans. France and Britain committed the bulk of the ten thousand troops to protect food convoys delivering humanitarian aid and the Dutch added four hundred troops. But none were prepared to militarily confront Milošević and Tudjman's forces. In 1991 and 1992, the United States and West European leaders shut their eyes to "the systemic use of brutality" and "inhuman treatment" of civilians.[41]

THE CHICKEN KIEV SPEECH

Gorbachev's fear of "suicidal nationalism" in Yugoslavia extended to Ukraine. He had noted the centrifugal behavior in Yugoslavia, the Baltic States, Moldova and Ukraine, the latter being critical to every branch of Soviet industries and its capital Kiev, known as 'the mother of Russian cities.' He would make every effort to keep these divisive regions in one federation.[42] Gorbachev's new Union treaty would divest economic authority to the Soviet republics, but keep a firm hold on monetary, foreign affairs and defense policy under his presidency at the center. He hoped that this would satisfy those Ukrainians seeking greater freedoms. Gorbachev, however, badly underestimated the strength of the independence movement in Ukraine.

US policy toward Ukraine's movement toward independence divided Secretary of State Baker from Defense Secretary Cheney. Baker was determined that the Soviet Union should dismantle peacefully "and that meant, above all, preventing a Russian-Ukrainian crisis."[43] He understood how important Ukraine was to the Soviet economy and culture. Therefore, he recommended that Washington not provoke or exacerbate a dispute that could be avoided. Cheney, on the other hand, failed to understand the integral relationship between Russia and Ukraine. He had two reasons for supporting Ukraine's move for independence: Warsaw Pact troops would have to withdraw eastward for one thousand miles thus removing a strategic threat to NATO.[44] Second, it would animate the Ukrainian-American community who tended to vote Republican. The division between the two agencies was real, but divergent opinions remained discrete between the two cabinet members.

Two years earlier on the side of the Cambodia Conference, Baker had relayed his concerns over East European nations pursing independence from the Soviet Union to Shevardnadze. In Paris that July 1989, Baker had shared his view that "freedom is not the same as independence." President Bush he reported would not support independence movements that replaced a far-off tyrant with a local despot. Baker's caution pleased Shevardnadze who reluctantly had accepted the overwhelming victory of *Solidarność* and the likely declaration of Polish sovereignty. In Hungary, similar rejection of Soviet control was also evident. Baker's prudent words indicated that the US would move cautiously and not seek to create divisions between Moscow and the Soviet Socialist republics. It suggested that Washington accepted the status quo.

Now in late July 1991, the Moscow summit had achieved the signing of the START treaty with Bush and Gorbachev confident in their personal relationship. From Moscow, the Soviet leader had a warning for Bush: do not encourage "suicidal nationalism" in Ukraine. He suggested that it might be preferable for the president to cancel that visit. [45] In response, Bush sought to calm his friend and shared with him the text of the speech he would deliver to the Verkhovna Rada (legislatures) on August 1. He would not cancel the visit, but he would amend the speech in order to ensure balance and not incite those who sought independence. He therefore accepted language that Baker had used two years earlier with Shevardnadze, "freedom is not the same as independence." To ensure balance, Bush retained the words

> Some people have urged the United States to choose between supporting President Gorbachev and supporting independence-minded leaders throughout the U.S.S.R. I consider this a false choice… We will maintain the strongest possible relationship with the Soviet Government of President Gorbachev, but we also appreciate the new realities of life in the U.S.S.R and therefore, as a federation ourselves, we want good relations, improved relations with the republics. [46]

But after talking with Gorbachev, the speechwriter added

> And yet freedom is not the same as independence. Americans will not support those who seek freedom in order to replace a far-off tyranny with a local despotism. They will not aid those who promote a suicidal nationalism based upon ethnic hatred.[47]

Twelve dates later, those last three sentence inserted only the prior day provoked an outcry from William Safire of the New York Times who charged that America had forgotten its own roots. If Bush was ready to carry out Gorbachev's propaganda on the Union Treaty, "Why didn't he call on Kuwait to sign a union treaty with Iraq?"[48] Safire gave Bush's speech the ignominious title of "Chicken Kiev." Like Chicken Licken in the European folk tale, Bush feared that the sky would fall if

Ukraine gained independence. Beyond the media, Bush and Baker had to face criticism from Senators on both side of the aisle as well as a bipartisan resolution from House members. The House resolution called fellow members to support the people of Ukraine "in their struggle to take their place among the family of free and democratic nations." [49] Bush's speech to the Ukrainian legislature had endorsed the American values of freedom and democracy, but those words were forgotten in the public wrangle over the three sentences inserted in Moscow to please Gorbachev. The Ukrainian-American community reacted negatively to the speech and they lobbied Congress energetically. Republicans in Congress remembered the impact of the Polish-American community that had protested President Ford's remarks accepting Soviet dominance over Poland. Their response had been to vote for Democratic Governor Jimmy Carter and contribute to Ford's defeat in the presidential elections of 1976. Republicans were determined to avoid a repeat of this shift by Ukrainian Americans in the 1992 elections. They therefore favored early recognition of Ukraine's independence.

The speech fired debate in the administration with Cheney arguing for immediate recognition of Ukrainian independence and Baker arguing for withholding recognition until the republic's elected leaders had taken steps to fulfill arms treaty obligations. In order to persuade President Bush, officials from both State and Defense set discretion aside and publicly criticized each other. A Defense official taunted the State Department for finding "the breakup of the Soviet Union a worrisome prospect because of 'nostalgia' for dealing with a strong, central Soviet government that no longer exists."[50] Baker was furious. Disagreement with the Defense Department was acceptable, but publishing their disagreement was deplorable. Baker had kept his disagreements with Cheney over the size of the unilateral cut in ground forces within the NSC, and his disagreement with Treasury Secretary Brady over financial support to the Soviet Union within their bi-weekly breakfasts. Now, only 15 months before the presidential election, Baker firmly rejected the internecine battle that had characterized the Reagan administration. Meantime, blood had spilled onto the public floor.

Bush had not talked about how he would resolve the conflicting points of view. He waited to meet the Ukrainian American delegation which arrived at the White House on November 27. Cheney did not attend that meeting, but he had met with the president, Baker and Scowcroft beforehand to convince the President of the wisdom of early recognition.[51] They emerged from that meeting agreeing that the president would support "delayed recognition" with the understanding that this would be a matter of weeks not months.[52] To Baker's dismay, the delegation of 15 Ukrainian American leaders leaked the content of their meeting to the press, spinning the president's words to support early independence. They related that the United States would "salute Ukrainian independence" next week and "move forward" on formal diplomatic recognition.[53] The nuance of Baker's 'delayed recognition' was lost and when Gorbachev learned of the meeting's outcome in the American press, he was reportedly furious. Bush calmed him in a Saturday telephone call. He also called Yeltsin. Baker called Shevardnadze who had been called back into service as Foreign Minister, probably to appease Washington. He too was mightily displeased. On December 1, over ninety percent of Ukrainians voted for independence and the White House announced "The United States looks forward to the kind of normal relations with Ukraine that one would expect to have with a democratizing country." The president's speech in Kiev lay in the past and the dispute between Baker and Cheney was now moot.

By March 1992, the Presidential election campaign had begun, and no candidate would take up the war banner to keep Yugoslavia whole. Baker, as a seasoned political operative, knew that talk of US military action would doom Bush's chances for re-election. He therefore demurred from further US action in the Balkans and recognized that Ukrainian-American support for the Republican ticket might decline as a result of the president's speech, as indeed it did.[54] He had enough on his plate with reshaping relations with Yeltsin's Russia. He could not prevent Yugoslavia's ruthless ethnic competition from turning violent, but joined with Gorbachev to prevent the Soviet Union's disintegration from erupting into suicidal conflict.

TEN

THE END GAME

The fourth year of his presidency presented George H.W. Bush with two serious domestic challenges. First, the fiscal deficit was significantly larger than anticipated, requiring belt tightening and reduced government expenditures.[1] Second, a growing isolationism was turning American voters sour on foreign obligations. Overseas, the President and his Secretary of State called for a "New World Order" in which the US would be the linchpin of a global system based on liberal democracy and free markets. Voters, however, were not interested in grand philosophical ideas, preferring attention to pocketbook issues. A disconnect existed between calls to resolve domestic problems and the consequences of a much weakened Soviet Union. The latter was a strategic problem of global proportions. Should Gorbachev's "horror mirror" occur and the Soviet empire break apart along ethnic and religious lines in a manner similar to Yugoslavia, the world would be a very unstable place. Baker recognized that.

> The dangers of protracted anarchy and chaos are obvious. Great empires rarely go quietly into extinction. No one can dismiss the possibility that darker political forces lurk in the wings, representing the remnants of Stalinism or the birth of nationalist extremism or even fascism, ready to exploit the frustrations of a proud but exhausted people in their hour of despair.[2]

How might US government policy reduce the consequences of a fracturing Soviet Union? What could it do to prevent the spread of nuclear weapons material? What measures should it take to support the economic reforms in the Soviet Union and later, the newly independent states? With an election only fourteen months away, President Bush and his advisors devoted most of their time to addressing domestic problems. Baker, Scowcroft and Cheney continued to devise and implement US foreign policy.

Having read the National Intelligence Estimate for 'Soviet policy and politics in the 1990s,'[3] Bush, Scowcroft, and Baker knew that the Soviet president and their good friend Mikhail Gorbachev was vulnerable to a putsch from members of his own Politburo. When Soviet intransigence hardened in arms control negotiations and the Soviet troops cracked down on the citizens of Vilnius in January 1991, all three recognized that Gorbachev's authority was waning. To retain his power, he had bent to the Kremlin apparatchiks who reviled his reforms. In the early months of 1991, Baker decided to try "getting as much as we could out of the Soviets before there was an even greater turn to the right or shift into disintegration."[4] He would stick with Gorbachev until he had accomplished three goals: force Saddam out of Kuwait, complete the Strategic Arms Reduction Treaty (START) agreement, and ensure Senate ratification of the Conventional Forces Europe (CFE) treaty.[5]

By the summer of 1991, US relations with the Soviet Union were in a delicate mode, reminiscent of 1979 and the period leading to the end of détente. Baker and the national security team now pursued hardheaded US security interests in order to keep US-Soviet dealings as stable as possible. The Secretary was aware that Gorbachev's key aide and the intellectual father of *perestroika,* Alexandr Iakovlev, had resigned from the Communist party in mid-August warning of a coup d'état.[6] The hardliners in the Politburo had mobilized and Baker was concerned that a coup against Gorbachev would affect his good friend, Eduard Shevardnadze, who as a perceived liberal might face arrest. He was also conscious of pending signatures to Gorbachev's favored project, the new Union Treaty of Sovereign States. It should distribute Soviet power on internal matters to the twelve republics and the three Baltic States in a loose confederation, but keep Moscow's control over defense, international relations, and monetary policy. For Bush and Baker, the Union Treaty represented a consistent and stable epicenter from which Gorbachev could delegate powers to the several states while retaining those authorities that mattered most to the United States: defense, foreign policy and the value of the ruble. Gorbachev was due to sign that treaty on Tuesday, August 20. Baker was aware that hardliners in the Politburo adamantly opposed the treaty on grounds that devolution of economic and social policy to the republics presented a grave threat to the central authority of the Soviet Union.[7] He surmised that opponents might pre-empt the formal signing of this treaty. He was correct.

THE AUGUST DAYS

Both Baker and Bush were on vacation on Monday, August 19 when the news came across the wires that President Gorbachev had resigned the previous day for health reasons and would remain at Foros, his summer dacha on the Black Sea. Bush doubted the veracity of the report and asked the White House to connect him with Gorbachev, but the coup plotters had cut the telephone line to Foros. Like his efforts to reach Deng Xiaoping after the repression in Tiananmen Square in June 1989, Bush could not reach the Soviet president. Two days later, Gorbachev regained his telephone line. The first person he spoke to was his political rival, Russian President Boris Yeltsin. From listening to the radio on the small Sony that Raisa Gorbachev kept in her possession, Gorbachev knew that the coup plotters were also bent on removing Yeltsin. Now both rivals recognized that they needed each other if they were to defeat the eight-man putschists, and the only way for Gorbachev to return to Moscow was to rely on Yeltsin's help and his aircraft. Two days later, he received a call from President Bush. On both sides of the call, there was considerable relief. "There is a God," exclaimed Gorbachev through his interpreter, "I have been here four days in a fortress."[8] The rumor in Moscow was that Gorbachev had engineered the coup to emerge stronger in his fight for the Union Treaty, but one look at Raisa Gorbachev as they liberated the family from Foros revealed a sick woman who had suffered a stroke. The stress of house arrest and terror that the plotters would strike down Gorbachev had over powered her.

During the height of the coup, Baker had called foreign ministers Hans Dietrich Genscher and Douglas Hurd who recommended calling a meeting of the NATO Council. Late in the evening of August 20 and before knowing the outcome of the coup, Baker flew to Brussels for a meeting of NATO foreign ministers to discuss the consequences of events in the Soviet Union. He also sought a meeting of the Commission on Security and Cooperation in Europe (CSCE) because the Soviets were members of that institution. At the same time, massive protests against the coup plotters were taking place in Moscow, Leningrad, and several other major Soviet cities. When Defense Minister Marshal Dmitry Yazov brought in the military to squash the protestors, both the officer corps and enlisted men rebelled, refusing to fire on their fellow countrymen. After three days of massive popular protest, the eight Kremlin coup plotters, including Yazov, surrendered. They knew that without the cooperation of the military, they lacked the power to overcome the popular uproar against their actions.

In his telephone call on August 21, Bush found an upbeat Gorbachev, who despite his isolation retained the vigor to reject the plotter's demand for his resignation and insisted on returning to Moscow.[9] On the third day of his captivity, Russian Vice President Rutskoi arrived at Foros to liberate the Gorbachevs. It was wiser, he claimed for Gorbachev to fly back to Moscow in his plane as the plotters might try to shoot down Gorbachev's presidential aircraft. As Gorbachev landed in Moscow, he said to his aides, "we are flying to a new country."[10] He had no clear idea what that newness might be, except for the probable rise to power of Boris Yeltsin and the new power of ordinary men and women who turned out in thousands to welcome him back to the capital. They became a force in their own right and a tool that Yeltsin would use to achieve supreme power.[11] Gorbachev's own future was unpredictable.

Yeltsin saved Gorbachev, allowing him to resume the presidency, but he tore up Gorbachev's Union Treaty by which the Soviet Union might hold together. He obliged Gorbachev to confront and sack the plotters from their prominent government positions. Then Yeltsin appointed their successors, forcing Gorbachev to accept his choices without a murmur. Furthermore, to emphasize his one-upmanship, he humiliated Gorbachev before the Russian parliament, lashing out at the failure of his economic reforms. It was clear that all power had passed to Yeltsin. Gorbachev was president of the Soviet Union in name only. Baker raised the question "For how long?"

Bush and Baker recognized immediately that the political leadership of the Soviet Union had changed forever. Until Gorbachev returned to Moscow, the outcome of the plot was uncertain. Even when the putsch shriveled and the plotters arrested, Soviet experts in the US warned that similar attempts to prevent the distribution of power to the republics could follow. There were significant implications for US policy that had banked upon Gorbachev's ability to pass the Union Treaty. Now that Yeltsin had gained the greater influence, it was doubtful that Gorbachev's efforts to retain the republics would succeed despite his watering down of the original Union Treaty to a mere confederation. How should the US government respond? Baker urged caution: events could unfold in unexpected ways.

Gorbachev was now beholden to Yeltsin and US strategy needed serious rethinking. Who would control nuclear weapons in a disintegrating Soviet Union? Who would implement the START agreement, signed only three weeks before, and the CFE Treaty awaiting ratification in the US Senate? Would the Russian ruble remain the currency or would each nation seek its own currency? Who should inherit the Soviet seat at the United Nations? Who would assume responsibility for the international treaties signed by the Soviet Union? These were uncertain days requiring clear thinking and a new approach. Baker spoke to his advisers and thought ahead, preparing for changes in both economic support and arms control. Throughout the autumn of 1991, he called Yeltsin who assured him that he and Gorbachev talked constantly on the telephone. For his part, in his calls with Baker, Gorbachev praised Yeltsin for his courage. Both Soviet leaders had an interest in assuring the Americans that they could work together.[12]

As Baker flew out of Andrews Air Force Base the night of August 20, he called Andrei Kozyrev, Yeltsin's foreign minister who had flown to Paris to set up a government in exile should the plotters expel Yeltsin from Moscow. Landing in Brussels the next morning it became evident that the coup had failed. Still, Kozyrev needed a meeting with Baker and jumped on the express train to Brussels. Baker knew Kozyrev slightly from Boris Yeltsin's first visit to Washington in September 1989. Then, Baker and Scowcroft were taking stock of the Russian politician to determine whether he was a serious leader or an irresponsible politician. Now both foreign ministers needed to sum each other up. Foreign Minister Bessmertnykh had gone AWOL during the coup, suggesting that he was not fully on Gorbachev's team. Yeltsin's team was in the ascendancy and it was necessary for Baker to consider Kozyrev his new Russian colleague.

During his hour and a half with Baker, Kozyrev responded to questions, among other things, about Gorbachev's health.[13] President Bush was eager to know how his friend had fared from his detention and Kozyrev realized that the personal mattered to these American leaders. Then he listened to the US government's core objectives: central control over nuclear assets was essential, and recognition of Estonia and Latvia's independence would indicate acceptance of the principle of self-determination. Finally, only the determined pursuit of economic reforms toward free markets could assure Western economic support. In August 1991, it was clear to Kozyrev that Baker would have preferred a continuation of Gorbachev's Union Treaty for its stability.

ENGAGING WITH YELTSIN

Three weeks later, Baker flew to Moscow for the CSCE's third conference on human rights. He found the experience "surreal." Next to the Russian White House (the official workplace of the Supreme Soviet of Russia, and later the seat of Russian parliament), he saw barricades and flowers placed in memory of the three men who had died in defending this emblematic Russian building. This was a different Moscow, one inclined to listen to ordinary citizens and reject the totalitarian authority of the Soviet state. Baker was hard headed, knowing that he had to work with the successor government. He met with Ivan Silayev, Yeltsin's prime minister and de-facto head of the new government. Silayev greeted him in the Kremlin's palatial St. Catherine's Hall where he had met with Gorbachev on so many previous occasions. Then he drove to meet the new head of the KGB, Vadim Bakatin, in the grey, cement building that few Americans had ever entered. Bakatin stood at the front door to welcome his guest.[14] It was crystal clear to Baker that the Soviets had changed, but how much? He and Bush should acknowledge Gorbachev and his efforts to hold the union together, but recognize that Boris Yeltsin was now clearly in control. That autumn all White House calls were addressed to both Yeltsin and Gorbachev.[15] Washington understood the new Soviet reality. Yeltsin held the greater power and his chief economist Yegor Gaidar's called for the privatization of state owned enterprises, the end of subsidies and the freeing up of prices to be carried out within five hundred days. Gorbachev remained president in name with responsibility for international relations, primarily with the United States and Western Europe. Baker understood the organizational chart, but he was anxious.

He also had other issues on his mind. Baker knew that the independence of the Baltic States was important for domestic reasons with vibrant US communities demanding self-determination for their country of origin, particularly Lithuania. He was also concerned about the other twelve Soviet republics. Should they seek to break away, there was a real possibility that territorial, economic and military disputes between the republics could ensue.[16] What if warlords took over some of the regional capitals in Central Asia or in the Ukraine? What if the KGB or someone in the Red Army decided to fight a civil war?[17]

Back in June, Baker had been unable to prevent the breakup of Yugoslavia and he was troubled that similar ethnic and religious divisions could lead to violent conflict in the crumbling Soviet Union. Gorbachev's 'horror mirror' became increasingly likely. Back in June 1991, when Sergei Tarasenko, Shevardnadze's former aide, met with Baker on the edge of the CSCE conference in Berlin, he warned of potential conflict and recommended that President Bush reiterate the importance of the ten principles set out in the Helsinki Accords. Baker preferred his own five principles, which he had delivered to the Yugoslav leaders during his visit to Belgrade in June 1991. Now, Baker reiterated those principles that should guide the emerging Soviet states:

- Peaceful self-determination consistent with democratic values;
- Respect for existing borders with changes only through consensual and peaceful dialogue;
- Respect for democracy and the rule of law;
- Human rights and particularly minority rights; and,
- Respect for international law and obligations.[18]

In addition to applying his five principles to the Soviet republics, Baker also developed new policies to take into account the transitional leadership in Moscow. He requested that the new Soviet Economic Commission, formed after the failed August coup, develop a comprehensive economic reform plan in collaboration with the World Bank and the IMF. This would lend credibility, enable foreign aid to go to priority projects and not be squandered. Second, he offered technical assistance targeted at food transportation and distribution, energy production, and the conversion of the many Soviet military installations to civilian use. Finally, he sought a humanitarian aid package to help Soviet citizens live through another harsh Russian winter. Baker had heard that in Vladivostok, the most eastern city of the Soviet Union human suffering had reached intolerable levels requiring an immediate response. He related that President Bush and his administration cared about the elderly and children exposed to malnutrition and violence.

Baker understood the enormity of the problem and proposed a comprehensive plan, but he could not commit monies. Treasury Secretary Nicholas Brady made it clear to Baker that he would not approve the appropriation of new funds for the Soviet Union. He would not spend taxpayer's money to support a system that was in chaos. In his view, those funds would end up in a vast black hole.[19] In his gentlemanly manner, Brady asserted the dominance of the Treasury Department over financial affairs. It should assume the lead over financial support for the Soviets and the forthcoming newly independent states. Brady's point man was David Mulford, the Undersecretary of Treasury for International Affairs and a man known for his stubbornness. Baker acquiesced. As the former Treasury Secretary, he was mindful of the legal and technical aspects that guided that department. Meantime, he focused on the geopolitical challenge of stabilizing the newly emerging states. Both cabinet members approached the problem from distinct corners, but over breakfast meetings they wrapped their disagreements in courtesies.[20]

SEPTEMBER 1991 – PRESIDENT'S NUCLEAR INITIATIVES

With the prospect of the Soviet President losing control over strategic and tactical nuclear weapons located throughout the Soviet Union, Bush and his national security team devised a new strategy. First, the administration would seek to bolster Gorbachev and his efforts to retain power through the Union Treaty. Second, should Gorbachev fail, they would have to strengthen relations with Russian President Yeltsin. Would he inherit the security and economic powers currently held by the president of the Soviet Union? This was a time for serious strategic planning carried out by only a few people and fast. On September 4, Baker held a press conference at the State Department in which he said that the United States would prefer that the Soviet Union's arsenal of twenty-eight thousand nuclear weapons remain under a central command authority rather than falling under the control of the republics. "We do not want to see the transformation that's taking place in the Soviet Union either create or add to the problems of nuclear weapons proliferation. And I think that it would be probably on balance best, if not necessarily they ended up all . . . in one republic, but that they ended up under one central command authority." [21] Baker's message sought to avoid doing anything that might hasten an uncontrolled breakup of the Soviet Union. However, his remarks suggested that both the substance and rhetoric of US policy toward the Soviet Union were changing. Without mentioning Gorbachev or Yeltsin, Baker referred to "Soviet leaders" and "the Soviet peoples" as the interlocutors with whom Washington would have to deal.[22] Given the uncertainty over the heirs to the Soviet Union, it was wiser not to mention leaders' names.

Civil strife in Georgia, Armenia, Azerbaijan, Moldova, and Tajikistan underscored the problem of uncontrollable republics seeking greater autonomy and control over their security and economy. Might they use the tactical nuclear weapons located on their territory as bargaining chips in negotiations with Moscow? The dangers of nuclear arms in unstable regions had become all too clear. The Chief of the Soviet General Staff, General Vladimir N. Lobov, raised these risks with Baker in Moscow on September 13. A week later, in a newspaper interview with *Rabochaya Tribuna*, Lobov urged negotiations to reduce tactical weapons.[23] Gennadi E. Burbulis, a senior aide to Yeltsin reiterated his recommendations. "Yes, we understand perfectly well that one of the most urgent problems associated with the collapse of the totalitarian Soviet system, one that alarms the entire international community, is the problem of control over nuclear arms on the territory of the union." Burbulis added that the Russian Republic had a "greater responsibility" over nuclear weapons in the entire territory of the Soviet Union.[24]

In Washington, Bush gathered his senior national security team to draft a radical disarmament plan. Secretly and at remarkable speed, George Bush worked to change the terms of reference with the Soviet Union. In a primetime TV address on September 27, 1991, the President announced major changes to US nuclear forces and practices. The address entitled "Reducing United States and Soviet Nuclear Weapons," became known as Presidential Nuclear Initiatives (PNI).[25] Bush was changing the US nuclear posture and he encouraged the Soviet leaders to do the same with a view to "effectively discourage the spread of nuclear weapons… We can enhance stability and actually reduce the risk of nuclear war."[26] He therefore directed the elimination of an entire worldwide inventory of ground-launched short-range nuclear weapons. Nuclear artillery shells and short-range ballistic missile warheads should come home while preserving an effective air-delivered nuclear capability in Europe. The United States:

> will withdraw all tactical nuclear weapons from its surface ships and attack submarines as well as those nuclear weapons associated with our land-based naval aircraft…The bottom line is that under normal circumstances, our ships will not carry tactical nuclear weapons… Many of these land and sea-based warheads will be dismantled and destroyed. Those remaining will be secured in central areas where they would be available if necessary in a future crisis.[27]

The President was unilaterally undertaking the deepest reductions in arms reduction on a wide range of nuclear weapons systems. The following morning, the crews for the B-1 strategic bomber climbed into their cockpits, started their engines and taxied away from the alert aircraft parking area. By the end of that day, there were no US bombers on alert for the first time in over thirty years.[28]

Gorbachev's response was positive. The PNI had enhanced Gorbachev's status as a major international figure and Moscow's primary link with the outside world. Furthermore, arms control was the yardstick of relations with Washington. He was therefore inclined to meet the US nuclear initiative, if not better it. On October 5, he announced the elimination of all nuclear artillery shells and nuclear warheads on tactical missiles. He withdrew from service and stored at central bases nuclear warheads on anti-aircraft missiles. He removed all tactical nuclear weapons from surface ships and multipurpose submarines and stored all nuclear weapons of ground-based naval aviation assets in centralized sites. Furthermore, the Soviets would reduce the size of their armed forces by seven hundred thousand men. Together, both leaders were determined to "resolutely advancing the process of disarmament… thereby moving close to the goal… of a non-nuclear world, a safer and more stable world."[29] However, the call to eliminate all intercontinental ballistic missiles (ICBMs) with multiple warheads (MIRVs) was still problematic for Gorbachev. Moscow considered them the mainstay of its deterrence system, while Washington considered them the most destabilizing of all Soviet weapons. It was clear in Washington that further negotiations on MIRVed ICBMs (Intercontinental ballistic missiles outfitted with several warheads contained in multiple independently targeted reentry vehicles, enabled one missile to hit a number of different targets) was needed. In addition, political control over these and other strategic nuclear weapons had begun to look uncertain, if not uncontrolled.

CONGRESSIONAL ACTION TO CONTAIN THE SOVIET NUCLEAR ARSENAL

Senator Sam Nunn (D-GA) had long focused on issues of nuclear safety. Back in the 1970s, he had discovered serious deficiencies in the security of US tactical nuclear weapons placed in Western Europe. Shaken by what he found, Nunn remained committed to observing the safeguards that had, or had not, been put in place to reduce the risks of deploying thousands of nuclear weapons. After the August coup d'état, Nunn flew to Moscow to meet with Gorbachev. Did the Soviet leader have total control over Soviet nuclear weapons? Nunn recollected that Gorbachev's answers "did not have the same ring of conviction as his statements during our earlier meetings. It seemed to me that either he was not himself clear about the status of command and control of nuclear weapons during that crucial period, or he was not comfortable discussing the matter candidly with me."[30] There was good reason to be concerned. Power was slipping from Gorbachev's grasp and with that a growing risk of nuclear weapons and material falling into unreliable hands.

Upon his return, Nunn was convinced that Washington had to make every effort to help the Soviet leadership maintain control over its nuclear weapons. In the Senate, he sought the authorization for funds to assist the Soviet Union in converting its defense establishment. He also called for confidence-building measures and military exchanges to shore up stability in the Soviet military. These measures should convey Washington's goodwill and support a safe transition to a post-Soviet world.[31] Nunn found an ally in Les Aspin, the Democrat chair of the House Armed Services Committee. Aspin proposed redirecting $1 billion in fiscal year 1992 defense funds to provide food, medicine and other types of humanitarian assistance to Moscow, and tied this assistance directly to nuclear security: "During the Cold War, the threat was a deliberate Soviet attack. Now, the bigger threat seems to be chaos in a nation with 30,000 nuclear weapons."[32] Aspin believed that investing less than one-half of one percent of the defense budget to stabilizing a highly dangerous situation was a sensible, if not compelling, means to advance US national security. Working together, Nunn and Aspin combined their proposals into a single new initiative. Their amendment would authorize the expenditure of defense funds to provide Moscow with humanitarian aid, technical assistance to safely transport, store and dismantle nuclear and chemical weapons, assist in defense conversion, and perform environmental cleanup of defense sites. Finally, it should train and house decommissioned officers of the Strategic Rocket Forces.[33]

However, the amendment met serious opposition from the national security team. Defense Secretary Cheney described Aspin's proposal as "foolish" and Bush stated, "I'm not going to cut into the muscle of defense of this country in a kind of an instant sense of budgetary gratification so that we can go over and help somebody when the needs aren't clear and when we have requirements that transcend historic concerns about the Soviet Union."[34] The president was concerned that reprogramming the Defense Department budget at a time of belt tightening was a mistake. Baker also opposed the Nunn-Aspin amendment, aware of the deteriorating domestic budget and the need to introduce austerity measures, including cuts to the Defense budget.[35]

He also recognized that reducing US defense expenditures risked weakening US military capabilities at a time when the end of a forty-five-year Cold War with the Soviet Union was not assured. Furthermore, he supported Bush's reasoning that reprogramming defense funds for non-defense purposes was setting a dangerous precedent. Proposals to reprogram appropriated funds was a prerogative of the executive branch, not the House Armed Services Committee. Baker therefore joined in opposing the Nunn-Aspin initiative while recognizing that loss of control over Soviet nuclear material, weapons and scientists was a real and serious danger.

Key leaders in Congress, as well as experts in the policy and academic communities began to assess the nature of the threat and consider approaches to reducing the danger posed to US and global security. The White House was not enthusiastic about the Nunn-Aspin initiative, but chose not to oppose it publically so long as the disbursement of funds remained discretionary. However, Republicans in both the House and Senate remained adamantly opposed to re-programming funds for Soviet humanitarian aid, and shortly before the vote both Nunn and Aspin withdrew their amendment. They had succeeded in raising public awareness of the nuclear security issue. Now advocates emerged within the State Department and Congress to consider a more systematic and robust approach to the challenge of assisting the Soviet Union.[36] Nunn, alert to the urgency of finding support, turned to Richard Lugar, a widely respected senior Republican on the Senate Foreign Relations Committee. Lugar recognized the challenges and joined Nunn to champion nuclear security assistance to Russia. Like Nunn, Senator Lugar was deeply engaged in international security and nonproliferation issues. He was also concerned about the evolving loss of central control in the Soviet Union.

THE HARVARD REPORT

On November 19 and only six days after the withdrawal of the Nunn-Aspin amendment, a team of Harvard analysts led by Ashton Carter briefed a select group of senators, including Nunn and Lugar. The briefing coincided with the publication of their report on the Soviet nuclear arsenal titled *Soviet Nuclear Fusion: Control of the Nuclear Arsenal in a Disintegrating Soviet Union*. It provided a systematic examination of the problem that Nunn, Aspin, and now Lugar had been worrying about. It gave background information on the entire Soviet nuclear weapons enterprise, including the nuclear command and control system. The authors noted, "The dangers of illicit diversion of key weapon-related technology should not end with the non-strategic and strategic deployments alone but extend to fissionable materials, components, delivery systems and command control systems."[37] The proliferation risks from a disintegrating Soviet state were multidimensional and complex and "loose nukes" had become the shorthand for this challenge. The authors argued that the US had a significant stake in ensuring that any political settlement that might emerge from the dissolution of the Soviet Union not result in several new nuclear weapons states in the region. Not only would such states lack the knowledge or capability to exercise responsible control, but also their possession of nuclear weapons could become a destabilizing factor in the Eurasian region.[38]

NUNN-LUGAR INITIATIVE

The response to the Harvard report was instantaneous. Nunn and Lugar began to draft new legislation, given the cumbersome name of "The US-Russian Cooperative Threat Reduction Program" and known colloquially as Nunn-Lugar. They gathered the support of sixteen senators for a $500 million proposal to provide assistance for the safe transport, storage, destruction, and nonproliferation of Soviet weapons of mass destruction. Then they turned to building domestic support for the initiative. Their terse and urgent language called for a program of assistance that was not a handout to a longtime adversary but an act of enlightened self-interest and an investment in America's own national security. In a *Washington Post* op-ed piece, they wrote, "We believe that Congress must act now to authorize a program of cooperation with the Soviet Union and its republics on the destruction of these weapons, including such related tasks as transporting, storing and safeguarding them prior to destruction."[39]

Baker remained apprised of congressional developments, but chose not to get involved. He remained skeptical of the legislative process, but he supported the underlying need to transport, store, destroy and avoid proliferation of Soviet nuclear weapons. His closest advisers had read the Harvard report and sided with its conclusions, but timing was important and they were unwilling to undermine Gorbachev' authority prematurely. A policy of wait and see evolved.

In the bill before the House and Senate, Senators Nunn and Lugar reduced their original $500 million appropriation. Instead, they proposed a new amendment: $400 million to be appropriated each fiscal year to carry out the deactivation of nuclear warheads, destruction of ICBMs, their silos and missile launchers, eliminate bombers, destroy nuclear air-to-surface missiles, sea-launched cruise missiles (SLCM)s, strategic nuclear submarines and to seal nuclear test tunnels.[40]

US focus on nuclear deactivation should be in Ukraine, Belarus, and Kazakhstan, the third, fourth, and eighth largest nuclear weapons states, whose independence seemed imminent in November 1991. Senators agreed and on November 25 adopted the amendment by a vote of 86-8. Two days later, the House adopted the measure by acclamation. It remained for the President to sign the amendment into law. Both Bush and Baker knew that it was the responsibility of the Secretary of State to design policies and programs to implement the intent of Nunn-Lugar. Beyond leading the US government effort to persuade those governments to turn over their nuclear material and warheads to Russia, Baker now sought to develop relationships with emerging leaders of the former Soviet republics. There was no US embassy or consulate in those twelve states from whom to seek advice. The State Department would have to carve out relationships from the stone-faced Communist bosses who had ruled those republics as personal fiefdoms with an iron fist.

YELTSIN'S ASCENDENCY

Early in December 1991, Baker stated publicly "the Soviet Union, as we know it, is finished."[41] Cheney joined in with a matter-of-fact statement on *Meet the Press*: "The center is dead, the old Soviet Union is dead and now we've got to get on with a new organization... Reality is now being shaped primarily by Boris Yeltsin and other leaders."[42] This was a clear break from President Bush's conciliatory stance. His support of the status quo was becoming untenable with both the secretaries of State and Defense nudging Gorbachev off the dais. With the Union Treaty in tatters, Yeltsin sought the independence of the Russian republic. His control over political events was at its zenith giving him the audacity to choose Yegor Gaidar's radical "shock therapy."

Gaidar's plan had gone into effect two months earlier and by December the impact was explosive. Inflation rose, buyers hoarded household goods, state enterprises were privatized, releasing hundreds of workers with no onward employment prospects. The value of the ruble collapsed and pensioners had barely enough to eat, let alone heat their small apartments through a Russian winter. Particularly hard hit were people who travelled to work in Siberia, the Far East and the Russian Arctic. Their anticipated hardship pay of triple-wages collapsed and they found themselves with no saving and not enough food to feed themselves and their families. There were even reports of unpaid workers collapsing in streets from hunger and people freezing to death because they could not afford to heat their homes.[43] Yeltsin relented, but not before Russian citizens began to mock his reforms. A Moscow teacher told National Geographic: "The rich get richer and the rest of us tread water or drown. I work much harder than I did in the old days, and sometimes that makes it hard to remember what we've gained. Freedom is sweet, but it's also a heavy, heavy load."[44] "The situation in this country and its capital is very much like that of seventy-four years ago" wrote the Moscow newspaper *Nezavisimaya Gazeta*. "People queue for bread, the empire is falling apart, the number of small sovereign republics is mushrooming and armed citizens in exotic uniforms are marching through the streets and squares of former district centers under the multicolored banners of new independent states."[45]

Despite President Bush's effort to postpone the granting of independence, Ukrainian politician Leonid Kravchuk declared independence on December 1. One week later the leaders of Belarus and

Ukraine, as well as Boris Yeltsin for Russia gathered at a hunting lodge in the forest of Belavezha, near Minsk. On December 8, they asserted their independence and declared that the Soviet Union no longer existed. However, without Soviet President Gorbachev present, they questioned their legal right to terminate the Soviet Union. Yeltsin's legal adviser, Sergei Shakhrai came up with the answer. He reminded the leaders that their three nations, together with the now-defunct Transcaucasian Democratic Federative Republic, had formed the Union of Soviet Socialist Republics back in 1922. Together, they had legally created the Soviet Union and together they had the legal authority to end "the Soviet totalitarian empire."[46] It only remained for nine other Soviet republics, led by Kazakhstan, to join them on December 12. Twelve former Soviet republics created a Commonwealth of Independent States (CIS) with Russia assuming the debts of the Soviet Union and its defense policy. These decisions required urgent decisions and actions on the US part.

Baker thought ahead. Mentally "he lined up the need for Russia to keep the UN Security Council seat and the bulk of Soviet era nuclear weapons. It should keep the gold reserves, but reach agreements with the other republics on their distribution. Baker should persuade the Kazakhs, the Ukrainians and the others to allow Russia to emerge as the big power."[47] To carry out these plans, he made time to work with Yeltsin's ministers to ensure coordination as he pursued a new relationship with each member of the CIS. He also needed Kozyrev's agreement on the two critical issues facing the CIS: control over nuclear warheads and monetary policy. Baker wanted to ensure payment of debts to international creditors and the preservation of financial stability. The IMF and World Bank were best placed to undertake this financial work, and with these institutions in the foreground, Washington could stay informed of developments and influence events from behind.[48] All the while, in Washington concern over control of nuclear weapons and material grew.

In the early winter of 1991 and with the Secretary of State's responsibility for implementing the Nunn Lugar Act, Baker became immersed in the breakup of the Soviet Union and its consequences for nuclear weapons, political stability, economic support and humanitarian needs. Three years earlier, he had begun his leadership of the State Department focused on the Soviet Union and he had never let Soviet challenges slip far from his mind. Now he had a new purpose that would take him to the furthest reaches of the Eurasian continent. He may not have been an enthusiast for the Nunn-Aspin amendment, but he came around to recognize its need and shifted his stance to support two friends, senators with whom he had spent peaceful hours: hunting with Nunn and spending time with Lugar.[49]

With announcement of the Belavezha Accord that December, a new urgency broke out in the White House. Declarations of independence and the forthcoming burial of the Soviet Union implied the need to interact with twelve new nations, four of whom held strategic nuclear weapons. What ethnic and religious divisions might erupt among them? How should the former Soviet army based in Ukraine respond to events, and under whose command? There were more men under arms in Ukraine than the combined forces of Germany and France. How stable were the new states and how solid was this CIS? The White House now dropped its previous cautious and "go-slow" policy and revved up its support for Yeltsin to build an effective and credible Russian government. All the while, Bush ever loyal to his good friend Mikhail Gorbachev, understood the need to work with Boris Yeltsin.

BAKER'S PLAN TO SUPPORT A PEACEFUL DISSOLUTION OF THE SOVIET UNION

In his speech delivered at his alma mater, Princeton University, on December 12, Baker, laid out a comprehensive, whole of government plan. It should advise the US Congress, Republican supporters and the Soviet government of a new policy of support for Russia and the newly emerging states. The administration would help dismantle Soviet nuclear weapons, stabilize the economy, establish democratic institutions, and overcome food and medical shortages. Baker's speechwriter Andrew Carpendale created a new allegory for Baker:

> If, during the cold war we faced each other as two scorpions in a bottle, now the Western nations and the former Soviet republics stand as awkward climbers on a steep mountain, held together by a common rope. A fall towards fascism or anarchy in the former Soviet Union will pull the West down, too. Yet, equally as important, a strong and steady pull by the West now can help them to gain their footing.[50]

The allegory was compelling, but the reality was less convincing. There were no new US funds for aid to the Soviet Union. A year before the 1992 presidential election and with the US economy slowing down, there were no new monies. Bush might propose to reprogram previously appropriated funds, and the Defense Department could transport the humanitarian aid to distant parts of Russia out of its Operation and Maintenance budget, but no new grants, loans or credit would arise. Instead, brave pilots would fly C-130s and C-5s into Soviet cities where no American aircraft had ever landed, let alone in the frigid winter. Baker had a comprehensive plan, but little money to implement it. Only a magician could turn threadbare cloth into a major new government initiative.

Two days after the Princeton speech Baker left for Moscow to meet with both Gorbachev and Yeltsin. Gorbachev was spitting fury that both Baker and Cheney had talked publicly of the end of the Soviet Union. He believed that his American friends had betrayed him. Only Bush remained quiet, waiting until Gorbachev himself acquiesced to Yeltsin's drumbeat to oust him from the Kremlin. Baker knew well the reality of Gorbachev's finality in office, but he was a southern gentleman. He might be frank in an interview with Strobe Talbott of Time Magazine, but he would never insult a man to his face.[51] On December 15, Baker returned to Moscow. After meeting with Yeltsin once again in St. Catherine's Great Hall, he met with Gorbachev. Whereas Yeltsin had "swaggered" Gorbachev was "subdued." Pathetically he asked Baker, "What do you plan to discuss with me today?" His face was flushed, suggesting liquor or high blood pressure. To ease his plight, Baker handed him a Velamint, a small gesture of friendship as well as a light remedy for dry throats. He hoped that history would be "kind" to Gorbachev, especially if he stepped aside quickly and gracefully.[52] However, a real fear existed that criminal proceedings could begin against Gorbachev, and Baker knew the advice he must give to Yeltsin, "magnanimity in victory was praiseworthy, vindictive behavior was shameful." He advised Yeltsin not to humiliate a good friend of President Bush.[53]

After the one-on-one meeting with Gorbachev, Baker gathered his whole team for the next day's meeting with Yeltsin's foreign minister, Andrei Kozyrev. They had critical questions to ask:

James A. Baker, III (JAB III): How will the new Commonwealth of Independent States (CIS) function? Will it be similar to the political and economic union that the European Economic Commission seeks to achieve, or a looser gathering like the British Commonwealth? Who will speak for the CIS and with whom should the US government deal? Will it have a common defense policy? We need answers before our meetings in Byelorussia and Ukraine.

Kozyrev: The CIS is an umbrella organization, made up of completely independent states. President [Leonid] Kravchuk of Ukraine said on December 14 that it was purely a consultative body.

JAB III: Thinking aloud and without interfering in internal affairs, might the five principles, which we have guided democratic governments around the world be used as criteria for admission to CIS? We are loathe to see authoritarian leaders cloak their policies in democratic rhetoric. How will Ministers of Defense relate to the CIS agreement reached at [Belavezha]?

Kozyrev: Regarding strategic dimensions, nuclear weapons of strategic importance will remain under the joint command of the CIS. Thus, membership of Kazakhstan takes on particular importance.

JAB III: Will this apply to tactical weapons as well?

Kozyrev: Yes [clearly confused about anti-aircraft defense and ABM systems].

JAB III: What about ground, air and sea forces?

Kozyrev: Central control will be under Marshal [Yevgeny] Shaposhnikov who will be present at the meeting with Yeltsin [December 17].

JAB III: How do you plan to coordinate foreign policy?

Kozyrev: We shall only consult, not coordinate.

Dennis Ross (Director of State Department's Policy Planning Staff): For ten months, the US worked with the Soviet Union on Middle East Peace process. What is our partnership now?

Kozyrev had no response.

Reginald Bartholomew [Undersecretary of State for Arms Control]: What is our partnership on conventional arms transfers? Who will chair the delegations to our meetings?

Andrei Kolosovskiy (Russian chargé d'affaires in Washington): Russia will be the partner. On nuclear issues, there will be a representative of the single command. On conventional forces, each republic will participate as appropriate.

Kozyrev: Major ministries will remain in Moscow and many problems will be solved here.

Kolosovskiy: Many of the republics do not have cadres for independent foreign ministries. This is not a problem for Russia, which will take over the Soviet Ministry of Foreign Affairs.

Bartholomew: The US hopes to move ahead quickly on START, CFE and questions of nuclear command and control. We shall need to meet with representatives of several republics. Who will chair the meetings on your side?

JAB III: With whom should we deal at the republic and oblast [province] level on humanitarian issues? We need to demonstrate to the American people that resources will be used properly. There should be no diversions and the distribution system will work well. How should we proceed?

[Robert] Strauss [US Ambassador to Soviet Union, and subsequently Russia]: Could we use US military and army trucks to deliver humanitarian aid?

Kozyrev: We are open to that possibility. There is a body in the Russian government with responsibility for coordinating the humanitarian assistance.

Kolosovskiy: Interjected: It is hard to say how it works.

[Ed] Hewitt [NSC senior advisor for the Soviet Union]: Grain under Commodity Credit guarantees [CCC] cannot be un-loaded due the non-payment of shipping fees. With whom should we raise this issue?

JAB III: The continuation of credit flows and credit guarantees requires payment of previous obligations

Kozyrev: I am less optimistic on our payment of previous debts. Our payment on previous debts becomes more and more difficult. Russia would like to continue with the G-7 agreement, but there is no money.

JAB III: I assume this means a deferral of payment on the principal. Repayment of these debts is an integral part of our humanitarian aid.

Strauss: Under the G-7 agreement, the provision for a $1 billion loan is collateralized by gold. Is gold available?

Kozyrev: The disarray is so great. We are very nervous. This is why we seek to dissolve central organs of government. Russian Prime Minister [Ivan] Silayev's commission has no answers and we do not know the size of our gold reserves nor any data.

JAB III: How much is owed to the shipping companies?

[James] Collins [deputy chief of mission at US Embassy Moscow]: $60 million.

Hewitt: Repayment on the CCC guarantees should begin in January 1992.

JAB III: If Russia and the other republics lose access to commercial credit markets, this will make humanitarian assistance all the more important. We need answers.

[Thomas] Niles [US assistant secretary of state for European and Canadian Affairs]: What is happening to revenue flows from oil and gas?

Kozyrev: These funds go to the Russian government, but they do not account for much.[54]

Baker and his team left the meeting dejected. The lack of clear answers on the future shape of the CIS, command of strategic and tactical nuclear weapons and willingness to pay Soviet debts caused deep unease. The stability of the future government appeared unlikely.

There was no greater encouragement in their meeting the next day with Russian President Yeltsin.[55]

JAB III: The transformations sweeping the area are of obvious concern to the United States while we reiterate our intention to keep out of Russia's internal affairs.

Yeltsin: Russia accepts all the international obligations of the former union, except for foreign assistance which will be phased out rapidly. Our relations with Ukraine are difficult and we stand on opposite sides of the barricades. That is why we have invited Byelorussia to join as a counterpart and to avoid clear divisions.

JAB III: I have six points to make which I hope you will support and mention in our subsequent press conference:

Baker went on to stress the importance of disabling and dismantling nuclear weapons covered by START and to stress the importance of non-proliferation of nuclear technology. He finished by seeking the names of cities and officials with whom the US could work on delivering humanitarian aid. The Russian leader responded,

I told President Bush in my telephone call of December 8 that Russia could not survive without US aid. We prefer US commercial ships for delivery of this aid, but we can accept US military ships. I am aware of the rumor that 50 percent of German shipments sent in 1990 ended up in North Korea.

JAB III: That is why we have to have our people on the ground.[56]

The State Department, working with the Defense Department, could deliver humanitarian aid, but Baker was unable to initiate financial support. Treasury Secretary Nick Brady, held the leadership on financial matters with the Soviet Union and the Russian Federation. Brady, an investment banker, was more concerned about debt and a country's credit worthiness. Interest had to be paid and a major installment on the debt was due on January 1, 1992. Failure to pay would demonstrate credit unworthiness with repercussions throughout the international financial system. Baker, on the other hand focused more on the geopolitical future with the need to support a stabilization program through international economic support. Both men respected each other as they breakfasted together with only an aide in tow, but their appreciation of the challenges confronting the disintegrating Soviet Union and the emerging CIS differed significantly.[57]

Despite their civility, their disagreements and Baker's inability to take charge of financial matters led to a prolonged examination of Russian economic weaknesses and delays in delivering much needed credit. The Treasury Department was not part of the National Security Council structure and thus a distinct channel of communication brought conflicting positions before Bush and his Chief of Staff John Sununu.[58] Sununu kept the discord within a small circle around the President and avoided a media leak. Baker might not have Treasury's financial tools, but he would use his considerable diplomatic tools to persuade and cajole. Meantime, the future of the Soviet system looked unpredictable and he sought to visit the former Soviet republics to assess the situation and determine needs.

BAKER'S WINTER TRAVELS TO CENTRAL ASIA, UKRAINE AND BELARUS

After meeting with Yeltsin and his national security team, Baker flew to Kyrgyzstan to meet with President Askar Akayev, who sought diplomatic recognition. Baker turned the request, which would be repeated eleven more times in different capital cities, into a duet in which the request for diplomatic recognition and economic aid was met by an offer of humanitarian and technical aid on condition that the nation abided by Baker's five principles, plus a commitment to denuclearization. The principles, drafted six months earlier for the Yugoslav republics, remained applicable to the newly independent states and were reproduced as handouts on laminated cards. Baker with his advisors and selected press corps visited Kyrgyzstan, Kazakhstan, Belarus, and Ukraine in the depth of winter. Their food was horsemeat and hotel rooms were shabby, but warm.

The memorable moment came in Alma Ata where after dinner with plentiful vodka, President Nursultan Nazarbayev invited Baker and Ambassador Robert Strauss to drink more, sweat, and soak bare naked in his personal *banya*. A Kazakh variation of the Finnish and Russian sauna, the Kazakh banya required that Nazarbayev whack Baker on the back with bark twigs before plunging into the steam bath. Much to the fellow Texan's delight, Ambassador Strauss joked to the accompanying security detail, "Get me the President of the United States on the phone! His Secretary of State is buck naked and he's being beaten by the President of Kazakhstan."[59] As the evening wore on, it emerged that Baker and his team were seriously worried over the possibility that an independent Kazakhstan could turn into a rogue state, exercising its own military control over the former Soviet Union's nuclear weapons. Nazarbayev poured cold water over these fears while he performed the same task over the hot stones in the *banya*.[60] However, he made it clear to his two American guests that while he had no aspiration to join the nuclear club, he would not relinquish nuclear weapons and material without getting something in exchange. He was after security guarantees, but Baker knew that the US could not become a security guarantor for the former Soviet republic with a 3,500-mile border with Russia.

Baker turned tough, sternly warning Nazarbayev that three American missiles were targeted at each one of the ICBMs stationed in Kazakhstan. The Kazakh leader expressed no fear, but he needed to know what benefit his country could receive in exchange for nuclear disarmament. He had received attractive offers which he played off against the American delegates: Libyan leader Muammar Gaddafi was pleading with Nazarbayev to keep the nuclear arsenal in place "for the good of Islam." Another envoy from the Middle East offered $6 billion to Kazakhstan to defray the maintenance costs of its nuclear forces.[61] Instead of funds, Baker offered a meeting with President Bush and the opportunity in Washington to discuss economic assistance. That meeting took place five months later. Meantime, the Kazakh leader remained "the nuclear holdout" and "a temporary nuclear power."[62] The danger was all too clear and Baker accelerated his meetings with the Russians and the Ukrainians.

The visit to Kiev and meeting with Ukrainian President Leonid Kravchuk was perhaps the most delicate. Kravchuk was not prepared to transfer nuclear weapons stationed on his soil to Russia. They were his primary leverage in any negotiations with Yeltsin, and Russian officials were behaving in a high-handed, arrogant manner with Ukrainian colleagues. Kravchuk repeated that the Ukrainian people would not be treated as a colony. Baker took this message to Brussels and meetings with NATO and European Community ministers. The outlook at the end of 1991 was bleak. He informed the alliance and the Europeans of the dangers that lay ahead. On Christmas Day 1991, the Soviet flag would come down from the Kremlin, but the Russian flag which arose in its place presented an unpredictable future.[63]

NEW STATES AND NEW EMBASSIES

That winter, discussions at the State Department heated up on how to advance US goals in Russia and the newly independent states. Who would oversee the distribution of humanitarian aid, who would report on economic and political developments in far-flung corners of the former Soviet empire? With a squeeze on the US federal budget to meet the austerity needs of the time, the Under Secretary of State for Management proposed that US Embassy Moscow be the central point for these tasks. The ambassador could send out teams on temporary duty to oversee the distribution of US goods and report on developments.

Baker convened a meeting in his conference room on the seventh floor at State Department and declared, "We're gonna open up embassies in all twelve of the new independent states."

Somebody replied, "Well Mr. Secretary, we'll probably just expand our Moscow embassy and run it out of there."

Baker responded: "No, we're gonna have twelve new states."

"Well it will be a lot easy if we do it [from Moscow] than in Moldova."

According to Richard Armitage, who was about to head up delivery of foreign aid to the former Soviet republics, "Baker went nuts." Armitage was astonished: "I'm thinking this was a promotion opportunity, twelve new embassies, twelve new ambassadors, twelve new deputy chiefs of mission, everyone gets something."

Finally, Baker got his point across and those around the table fell silent. It took a while. Then he said, "Now we're gonna have twelve different USAID [US Agency for International Development] posts."

"No, no," was the response, "we'll run aid out of Moscow."

Baker lit off again: "Look, these people broke away and you're talking about putting them back together in the Russian Federation. NO, okay?"

Armitage knew that an uphill battle lay ahead.[64] When they all left the room, Baker turned to Armitage: "Look, this is unpopular. Giving aid to our former enemies is going to be very unpopular. It's an election year and you're going to have to do it all yourself."

Armitage said, "What are you talking about?"

"Well, the President and I don't think there's much in it for us politically. So you do as much as you can."

Armitage got $481 million dollars, but no political help. The Defense Department gave Armitage C-130s and C-5s. They filled them with medicines, hospital equipment, food, clothing and Meals Ready to Eat. Armitage undertook the logistics of flying the humanitarian aid into distant cities and delivering the aid to hospitals, old-age homes, and orphanages. Intrepid members of the State Department's On-Site Inspection Agency (OSIA) traveled ahead of the flights to determine where the aid should go. When the C-130s landed on unlit runways previously unknown to American pilots, they mobilized ground transportation. In response to the impossible task of determining the final destination of humanitarian aid - be it hospitals, orphanages, or the warehouses of enterprising government officials - Armitage wrote a letter to each OSIA member. He accepted responsibility for final delivery and would take the blame if the goods ended up in North Korea. He protected Baker. That winter, his prize was the offer to become Secretary of the Army in the second Bush administration. Secretary Cheney was adamant: "It's not if, but *when* we win."[65] Armitage demurred. He was less assured.

Within the White House, there was considerable debate over whether the president should speak to the nation about the end of the Soviet Union and what it meant for the United States. President Bush, in keeping with his refusal to dance on the Berlin Wall in November 1989 was reluctant to speak to the nation so as not to irritate Gorbachev. Internally, Baker and the NSC staff argued, 'You need to make a speech because you need to explain to the American people what it all means. Gorbachev is no longer going to be leader and we need to work with the new people.'[66] On Christmas Eve, Bush accepted his advisers' strong recommendation recognizing that the end of the Soviet empire was a momentous occasion for the United States and presented opportunities. He instructed the NSC to draft a speech to deliver on Christmas Day. It should state that the American values of freedom and liberty were in the ascendency. "This is a day of great hope for all Americans. Our enemies have become our partners, committed to building democratic and civil societies. They ask for our support, and we will give it to them."[67] Bush also recognized that Americans faced challenges at home. For many, 1991 was a difficult year and he committed to attacking domestic economic problems "with the same determination we brought winning the Cold War." With a presidential election only eleven months away, Bush's advisers were telling him to focus on domestic issues, but the demise of the Soviet Union was revolutionary in its impact and Bush's national security team could rightly claim some credit.

BAKER'S COORDINATING CONFERENCE, JANUARY 1992

Baker's challenge was to raise international grants and credits, humanitarian aid, and technical advice. Following the model of raising monies and troops for the Gulf war, Baker convened a conference to coordinate the international aid, avoid duplication of effort, and ensure that no former Soviet republic was left out. Relying on the influence that the United States had acquired during that war and Moscow's participation in that effort, forty-seven nations sent their foreign ministers to Washington. Baker was at the zenith of his influence on the international stage and knew personally most of the ministers gathered under his roof. His problem was the inability to back up his convening power with serious US financial commitments. French Foreign Minister Roland Dumas proclaimed that the Washington conference was worth doing, but that "France regrets the United States of America, which has only contributed 20 percent of urgent food aid, is in charge of coordination."[68] Fortunately, Dumas' prickly relationship with Baker did not undermine the genuine trust and friendship between Bush and French President Mitterrand.

Other European leaders, who claimed that they had not been consulted ahead of the conference, reminded Baker that in 1947 at the end of World War II the US did not simply coordinate the Marshall Plan for European recovery, but fully financed it. Baker could afford to shrug off this European sniping. He had other things on his mind beyond cantankerous Europeans who could not contain the unraveling chaos in the Balkans, despite their offer to take charge of a problem in their own backyard.

Beyond the $10.6 billion committed to support Russia and the twelve newly independent states, Baker gained a joint statement from the international community to support the economic and political reforms in the former Soviet Union and the newly independent states.[69] Backed by some funds and a willingness to meet again in May 1992, Baker focused the world's attention on the consequences of a disintegrating empire. Then he was off to Moscow to attend the Russian conference on Middle East peace. His life seemed to rotate around Moscow, but domestic politics were never far from his frontal lobe.

Early in February, State Department spokesperson Margaret Tutwiler persuaded Baker to attend the launch of Armitage's fleet of C-130 and C-5's transporting humanitarian aid to far-flung corners of the former Soviet republics. Together with his colleague and friend, Hans-Dietrich Genscher, Baker took a front seat at Frankfurt's Rhine-Main Air Base to witness the launch. Together, the Germans and Americans would make the point of sending 62 flights to distinct cities. Baker had another purpose and he called Armitage up to the front. "After my remarks, can you do something?"

"What's that?" Armitage asked.

Baker asked again, "Are you the telling these planes when to take off?"

"Well yes sir," replied Armitage.

"Uh," Baker said, "you know I'm gonna make my remarks and then Hans [Dieter Genscher] is gonna make his..."

Armitage grinned, understanding what his boss wanted. "I can do that, Mr. Secretary."

Thus, when Genscher got up to speak, Armitage ordered the planes to take off. Few watching the TV that day heard the German minister's remarks above the engine roar.[70] For American watchers on the evening news broadcast, Baker was the principal player.

CHELYABINSK-70

Perhaps the most significant visit that February 1992 was to the All-Union Scientific Research Institute for Technical Physics at Chelyabinsk-70, some two-hour drive from Ekaterinburg. There, Soviet nuclear scientists had designed nuclear bombs throughout the Cold War. No American official had ever visited this industrial site, which was not even marked on Soviet maps. As Baker's cavalcade approached, the institute staff crowded around windows to watch the arrival of the US Secretary of State, his advisers, and accompanying press corps. Viktor Mikhailov, Russia's Deputy Minister for Atomic Energy, and Yevgeny Avrorin, the chief scientist at Chelyabinsk-70, sat Baker in the front row of a classroom before a white board. There, they showed off the sophisticated products now in development for civilian purposes. They included various applications of nuclear medicine and nuclear magnetic resonance, synthetic microscopic diamonds, fiber-optical equipment, and computer software. The scientists sought joint mathematical research with the American nuclear weapons laboratory at Los Alamos and suggested that private investors might have an interest in working with them. Baker was impressed. "This is every bit as remarkable for us as is it for you ... We know that right now your options at home are limited and outlaw regimes and terrorists may try to exploit your situation and influence you to build new weapons of war. We want to help you find new projects that will allow you to remain in your country and earn a decent living, applying your skills to the cause of science and peace, rather than forging weapons of war." [71] Baker toured laboratories and was shown various experiments involving plutonium, tritium and uranium-235, material designed to obliterate US cities in a nuclear confrontation. Now, in the new age and knowing the power of American television, Baker asked the director and accompanying Minister for Energy if they would allow him to be filmed by an American network crew as he visited a memorial on the grounds of Chelyabinsk to one of the founders of the Soviet nuclear program. Horrified at the prospect of losing their anonymity and claiming that it had never been done, the minister denied the request until the scientists shouted out, "Let him do it, let him do it." Under pressure, the director relented and the scientists applauded. A revolution was taking place and unimaginable change was underway. Said Baker: "See, it is a new day."[72]

BACK HOME - PRIMARY SEASON

Flying back from Russia on the eve of the New Hampshire primary, Baker saw the polls that gave Pat Buchanan "a lot of votes."[73] Quietly he mused, "I may be looking at going back to the campaign."[74] He had resisted several calls to help nudge the president to visit one or another key state. He was too busy, "You know being Secretary of State is a humongous job. It's a big job, a difficult job, you're gone a lot. And I really didn't do much politics." When the calls for help came, Baker answered, "Look, I've got all I could say grace over here. I can't."[75] He meant it.

He still had to raise international funds to support Yeltsin's economic reforms. He still insisted on his five-point democratic principles. He still had to ensure that the Israeli-Palestinian dialogue stayed on track, and that the Central American peace agreements held. The North American trade talks were stuck and his close adviser Bob Zoellick needed to kick start those negotiations. There were calls to counter the violence in Bosnia and Herzegovina. Throughout, Baker stayed focused. He would not get distracted from his main purpose of assuring that Russia and the newly independent states were stable and moving towards democratic and economic reform. To achieve this he set up Enterprise Funds for the Eastern Europe, Russia, Ukraine, and the Baltic States where the US government provided seed funding and appointed boards of financial experts to help kick-start free-market economies and encourage investment in new businesses.[76] He would not only help Yeltsin, but also nations with a sizeable immigrant population in the United States, such as Lithuania and the Ukraine. However, Baker resisted all calls for significant US intervention. This was an election year and he knew that Bush had to focus on domestic issues, US cities, the budget, and an electorate that was fed up with international engagements, no matter how successful they might be.

Meantime, calls to save a presidential campaign that lacked both focus and energy rose in number so that Baker recognized he had to help. He groaned to the members of his inner circle and warned them that he expected them to follow him to the campaign. By July 1992 and the summit meeting with Yeltsin in Washington, Baker had raised a total of $24 billion from the international community for Russia and the newly independent states. El Salvador was implementing its peace agreement and Nicaragua's new democratic leadership was in place. Talks between the Palestinians and Israelis sputtered on and the North American trade talks proceeded slowly. The Europeans were due to hold votes on further economic and political integration, a process that Baker and Bush supported. By the summer of 1992, Baker's foreign policy was on track and steady. He could look back to extraordinary accomplishments in arms control and radical change in the relationship with the Soviets and their successor republics. There was always more to do, but his close friend was calling him back to domestic politics. Baker did not want to leave the State Department and his command over the key international issues of the day, but loyalty to George Bush called.

That August and with the Republican Convention approaching, Baker knew he had to run the campaign from his old job as White House chief of staff. Together with his closest advisers, they closed their international files and drove half a mile eastward to 1600 Pennsylvania Avenue to lead the presidential campaign. Over the next few months, Baker never got involved in foreign policy, but left that to his deputy and successor, Larry Eagleburger. None among Baker's team was enthusiastic about the move. They acted out of duty and loyalty to men whom they admired, and whom they hoped might have another chance at guiding world events after the November 1992 elections.

EPILOGUE

In his 1993 State of the Union address, George H.W. Bush declared victory when he announced "By the grace of God, America won the cold war." [1] In the same speech he was less assertive, acknowledging that his administration "help[ed] to manage progress and help[ed] to lead change…" that ended the cold war. [2] He recognized that the end was achieved through the combined efforts of Mikhail Gorbachev, Helmut Kohl, Polish heroes and American leaders. Imbued with the modesty of gentlemen who sought power not to aggrandize themselves but to serve a nation, Bush did not puff his own achievements. Instead, he recognized the US government's helpful role in managing the process. The guiding principle of his national security team was the stable management of the international system and the avoidance of risk. How critical was James A. Baker III to this process? Would it have happened without him?

Baker was the man who implemented the Bush administration's foreign policy. He was the master negotiator who confronted allies and foes with his mixture of southern charm, gentlemanly qualities and steel nerves. Baker, who had worked assiduously in the Reagan administration, moved away from the Reagan foreign policy of supporting militarily anti-communist governments. Under President Bush he sought diplomatic solutions, allowing the UN to mediate a peace agreement in El Salvador and encourage democratic elections in Nicaragua. He confronted Reagan's fulsome support for Israel when he cajoled both the Israeli Prime Minister and the leaders of the West Bank Palestinians to meet face to face in Madrid and commit to an ongoing dialogue, later known as the Oslo process. He overcame his initial reluctance to a regional trading agreement and lent his weight to overcoming the toughest problems that stood in the way of reaching a North American Free Trade Agreement, known as NAFTA. Thanks in large part to his efforts, the Bush administration's achievements in foreign policy were significant.

The failures were not insignificant, namely the inability to hold the Yugoslav Federation together and prevent the Serbian leader, Slobodan Milosevic from aggressively invading Croatia, Slovenia and Bosnia Herzegovina. Baker had lived the dilemma when he visited Belgrade in June 1991 to meet each of the six federated leaders. There, he smelled the Serbian President Milosevic's ambition to dominate the region. But Baker was a domestic politician who knew that there was no appetite in America for yet another war to resist Milosevic and hold Yugoslavia together. Despite the assurances of the Dutch Prime Minister to send peacekeepers to Yugoslavia, Baker and Scowcroft knew that the Europeans had no stomach for that task. They had no political will and without US leadership, the problem would eventually go 'to hell in a handbasket.' The responsibility of leadership required the determination of which wars to fight and which wars to avoid. Yugoslavia was one of them.

More pressing for Baker was the quandary of how enable the Soviet Union to disintegrate without the violence of Yugoslavia, but without using US financial resources. He was fully aware that his ability to gain be-partisan support on Capitol Hill would end if he sought credit or loans for Moscow. The politician with a good grasp of America's mood and needs would not stand before the House and Senate to beg for money. He had cajoled the UN Security Council members to approve "all necessary means" to repel Saddam Hussein from Iraq and thus goaded US Senators to support a war in Iraq, but there was no further efforts to persuade. Baker was a realist who knew the limits of persuasion. He would fail if he sought to raise economic and technical support necessary to shepherd Russia and the newly independent states from central command economies to democratic socialism and free market economies. Instead, Baker recreated his global coalition that had successfully routed Saddam Hussein the year earlier and raised $24 billion in pledges for the economic transformation of Russia and the newly independent states. He had greater sway internationally than he had domestically: he understood his limits.

Some have claimed that Baker was unethical in his pursuit of certain causes and not others. I retort that Baker was fundamentally an ethical, patriotic political leader. However, he did not let his patriotism lead him into ideological battles. He believed in freedoms, but not chaos. He was principled, but not rigid. He was a pragmatist with a keen eye for the possible. His time as Secretary of State is remarkable for the control that he exercised with Bush and Scowcroft over the implementation of US foreign policy.

The character and personal decisions of key men made a significant difference. In Washington, the caution with which Bush and his team reacted to the cascade of freedom movements in Eastern Europe in 1989 lowered the risk that Kremlin apparatchiks might force Gorbachev to abandon his reform program. Bush, Baker and Scowcroft deliberated carefully between support for democratic and freedom movements and ensuring that the Soviet reformer retained power. As events moved toward the breakup of the Warsaw bloc, Bush and his national security team trod carefully. They did not rush. They resisted pressures to announce a new foreign policy because they were unsure on which side of the scale they should place the preponderance of American power. Only when the clamor from European leaders and Gorbachev approached screaming point did they announce support for the Open Skies treaty. Their support sent the signal that confidence-building measures with the Soviet Union should be deepened. To many this was inadequate, but to Gorbachev and the reformers it sent a clear message. Bush and his team would work to solidify trust between the two antagonists. Nine months later, was this trust broken when Baker met with Gorbachev in the Kremlin?

The question of whether Baker gave a broad commitment to Gorbachev in February 1990 not to expand NATO one inch further east has to be taken in the context of a discussion focused on the unification of the two Germanys and the incorporation of East Germany in NATO. The

Soviets were adamantly opposed to placing their industrial powerhouse in the western alliance. For the Soviet military, this presented a red line. Thus, both Gorbachev and Baker were laser focused on whether and how East Germany might be placed within the western alliance. Any indication of NATO's encroachment eastward beyond East Germany would have wrecked US persistence in unifying the two Germanys. For the Russians subsequently to claim that Baker's promise not to expand NATO further east is to take his words out of context.

Weeks before the Chinese government sent in military units from distant regions to kill the workers and students gathered in Tiananmen Square, Bush and his national security team should have known of the risks. Days earlier, Gorbachev had visited Beijing and noted the ferment of people seeking freedoms. Yet the Bush administration sent no warning of the consequences should Premiere Li Peng send in the tanks. Inexperience with China or naiveté toward flourishing freedom movements does not explain Washington's silence. They should not have been surprised when Li Peng acted and violent repression followed not only in Beijing's sacred square, but throughout China. The uproar from Congress and defenders of human rights was strident. There is no explanation for the prior silence. Baker should have anticipated these events and taken action to deter them. Instead, he recognized that the president had the greater knowledge of Chinese leaders and passed management of 'the middle kingdom' events to the White House and his deputy, Larry Eagleburger.[3] This was not a shirking of responsibility, but a recognition of the president's desire to manage the problem. A challenge that Baker accepted readily was the creation of a global coalition to uphold the principle of inviolable sovereign borders in the Persian Gulf.

In the first post-Cold War conflict, Baker helped Bush gather the largest military alliance since World War II to persuade Saddam Hussein to withdraw from Kuwait. It was an extraordinary feat of persuasion and purchase. Only in defense of Crimea have we witnessed an international coalition mobilized to defend a sovereign people. US leadership was at its zenith and the Soviets too weak to defend Saddam Hussein, their long-standing ally. This was the generals' war, but Baker understood that after Saddam's defeat the Gulf remained a volatile region with Islamists ready to take advantage of geo-political weakness and Saddam still strong enough to seek revenge. The US military won the war and Baker did not press Defense Secretary Cheney for 'no fly zones' or a stepped-up US presence in the Gulf. Instead, Baker urged action upon the Gulf States, but offered minimum US support. Had there existed a robust Gulf security cooperation agreement, events leading to the US invasion of Iraq in 2003, might not have occurred. A greater reliance on regional diplomacy might have succeeded in curtailing Saddam's search for weapons of mass destruction.

Instead, Baker took the confidence of victory and applied it to another related problem: peace between the Israelis and Palestinians. Back in September 1990, he had witnessed the agreement between the Soviet and US presidents to co-chair a Middle East peace effort. Now his advisers urged him to use the unique standing of the United States to bring together two parties whose animosity dated back to 1949 and the creation of the state of Israel. Baker employed the same means he had used to coral the coalition to repel Saddam from Iraq. Now he cajoled Egypt, Gulf and European allies to support a face-to-face summit around the Spanish king's table. He gave international leadership to Gorbachev to work with Washington and begin an Israeli/Palestinian dialogue on shared regional problems, such as water and the environment. This dialogue became known as the Oslo process and culminated in a handshake between Prime Minister Yitzhak Rabin and PLO leader Yasser Arafat on the White House lawn in the presence of Bush's successor, President Clinton. With Baker's grit and determination, a process that seemed impossible in early 1991 became a reality.

In an effort to support his new friend, Foreign Minister Genscher, Baker agreed to meet with the six leaders of the Yugoslav Federation. But he had no illusion that he could prevent the Serbian leader, Milosevic from enlarging his influence. His one day visit to Belgrade may have raised expectations, but no one expected US troops to be sent to contain Milosevic. As President Bush enunciated, 'We have no dog in this fight.'[4] Relieved by the European offer to assume responsibility for restoring peace in the Balkans, Baker and Bush knew that Europeans had no political will for serious peace making. Also, as good politicians, both appreciated that voters would not tolerate the dispatch of American forces to fight again so far from home. They therefore accepted the European offer and questioned no further. However, the disintegration of Yugoslavia was a different matter from the collapse of the Soviet Union: the Soviets had nuclear weapons.

Baker understood the necessity of enabling the Soviet empire to disintegrate peacefully. He knew that loss of the republics and global influence was compounded by intense personal deprivations. Ordinary citizens were cold and hungry in the winters of 1990, 1991 and 1992. He had lectured the Russian and CIS leaders on the importance of the rule of law, private property and a currency valued at market rates, but their capacity to turn a centralized economy into a liberal free market economy was minimal. The World Bank and IMF might send technical advisers, but they could not change a culture of autocracy. Serious doubts remained that Baker's effort to raise $24 billion in international pledges would result in infrastructure and manufacturing projects in Russia and the newly independent states. Instead, enterprising individuals with good Kremlin connections manipulated the reforms to enrich themselves, and broad citizen involvement to share in the benefits from the sale of state owned enterprises proved illusory. The underlying problem was that comprehensive reform was politically difficult to implement because many in the Soviet leadership remained ideologically resistant to change. The size of the problem was greater than anyone nation could undertake.

In 1989, Baker had initiated Enterprise Funds for all the countries of Eastern Europe and later for Ukraine and the Baltic States. American financial experts were appointed to oversee the use of seed funds to kick-start those economies and invest in new businesses. However, two years later, the United States faced a mild recession and the prospect of funding Russia, an enemy of 45 years was unacceptable politically. Thus when Graham Allison and Grigory Yavlinsky presented their 'Grand Bargain,' Baker conceded that White House support was not there. His advisers were sympathetic, recognizing that their bargain was not a handout, but an incentive for Russian leaders to adapt to free market principles. The carrot was the offer of significant grants, technical assistance from the World Bank, IMF and European Development Bank as well as national loans and credits. It was a step-by-step process, strictly contingent on Russia delivering on the recommended economic reforms. But both Scowcroft and Treasury Secretary Brady were adamantly opposed to any extension of loans or credit, beyond agricultural commodity credits. Baker conceded. He had doubted whether Russia was capable of making the necessary reforms, and in Brady's mind, no program should affect the US economy. Within weeks of its publication in June 1991, Baker had rejected the 'Grand Bargain.' By the end of the year Gorbachev had gone.

As the spring of 1992 approached, Europeans focused on consolidating their integration process. The new Russian President, Boris Yeltsin asserted free market principles, but struggled to make those radical changes without impoverishing Russian citizens. The newly independent states talked of democracy and human rights, but failed to find leaders who knew how to sustain such principles. Election year in the United States revealed tiredness with foreign interventions and a focus on domestic challenges. Bush raised taxes despite his earlier commitment not to raise them, race riots in Los Angeles revealed the depth of racial discrimination and the faces of starving Somali children goaded Bush to do "God's work." In the month after losing the presidential election, Bush lost his 'pragmatic idealist' Secretary of State, Jimmy Baker. Now he responded emotionally and on December 9 the president dispatched 28,000 US troops to create a protected environment for conducting humanitarian operations in Somalia. Without Baker to remind him of the impracticality of doing "God's work" in the midst of two warring factions, military operation ultimately failed and President Clinton withdrew the reduced US presence in March 1994. Baker, the pragmatist would have warned his boss and close friend of many years that intervening in Somalia's tribal wars was a fool's errand. They would have talked at length and Bush would have recognized, once again, the thoughtfulness of a man who chose carefully which battle to fight and focused every sinew to win. He remained a master negotiator.

AUTHOR'S INTERVIEWS

(Positions are those occupied in the period 1989-1992)

Cresencio S. Arcos	Deputy Assistant Secretary, Department of State
Richard Armitage	Special Envoy for Newly Independent States
James A. Baker, III	Secretary of State
Susan Baker	Wife of Secretary of State
Raymond Burghardt	Deputy Chief of Mission, US Embassy Beijing
William J. Burns	Deputy Director, State Department Policy Planning
R. Nicholas Burns	National Security Advisor and Director for Soviet Affairs
James Cunningham	Chief of Staff to NATO Secretary General Manfred Woerner
Edward Djerejian	US Ambassador to Syria
Tom Friedman	Diplomatic Correspondent, The New York Times
Robert Hutchings	National Security Advisor for Eastern European affairs
Wolfgang Ischinger	Foreign Policy advisor to Chancellor Helmut Kohl
James D. Jameson	YPO leader and member of US Trade Delegation to Moscow
Andrei Kozyrev	Foreign Minister to President Boris Yeltsin

Robert M. Kimmitt	Under Secretary for Political Affairs & Ambassador to Germany
Daniel C. Kurtzer	Policy Planning staff responsible for Middle East
Jack F. Matlock Jr.	US Ambassador to Soviet Union
Aaron David Miller	Policy Planning staff responsible for the Middle East
Janet Mullins	Assistant Secretary for Legislative Affairs
Pavel Palazhchenko	Interpreter for Mikhail Gorbachev
Thomas R. Pickering	US Permanent Representative to the United Nations
Charles D. Powell	Advisor to Prime Minister Margaret Thatcher
Dennis Ross	Director, State Department Policy Planning & special advisor to Secretary Baker on the Soviet Union and the Middle East
Stapleton Roy	State Department Executive Secretary
John H. Sununu	Chief of Staff to President George H.W. Bush
Horst Teltschik	Foreign Policy advisor to Chancellor Helmut Kohl
Jeffrey Trimble	Moscow correspondent for US News & World Report
Margaret D. Tutwiler	Assistant Secretary for Public Affairs
William H. Webster	Director, Central Intelligence Agency
Philip Zelikow	European Affairs at National Security Council
Robert Zoellick	Counsellor to the Secretary and later Under Secretary for Economic Affairs
Olin Wethington	Assistant Secretary for International Affairs, US Treasury Department

BIBLIOGRAPHY

Books, Journals and Other Resources

Aitken, Jonathen. *Nazarbayev and the Making of Kazakhstan: From Communism to Capitalism* (London: Continuum, 2009), 139.

Adamishin, Anatoly and Schifter, Richard, *Human Rights, Perestroika, and the End of the Cold War,* Washington D.C.: U. S. Institute of Peace Press, 2009.

Arbatova, Nadia Alexandrova. "Horror Mirror: Russian Perception of the Yugoslav Conflict" Paper presented at the Consensus Building Institute Conference on *Russian and American Perspectives: Ethnic Conflict in the former Soviet Union,* Harvard University, October 25-26, 1994.

Allison, Graham and Yavlinsky, Igor. *Window of Opportunity: the Grand Bargain for Democracy in the Soviet Union.* New York: Pantheon Books, 1991.

American Presidency Project. "Statement by Press Secretary Fitzwater on the Restoration of Lithuanian Independence," March 11, 1990. http://www.presidency.ucsb.edu/ws/index.php?pid=18240.

Aronson, Bernard. "Preliminary Thoughts on Central America" (unpublished manuscript, February 2, 1989), Aronson Personal Papers.

Aslund, Anders. *Russia's Capitalist Revolution: Why Market Reform Succeeded and Democracy Failed,* Peter Institute for International Economics 20007.

Brands, Hal. *Making the Unipolar Moment: U.S. Foreign Policy and the Rise of the Post-Cold War Order.* Ithaca: Cornell University Press, 2016.

Brooks, Stephen and Wohlforth, William G. "Power, Globalization, and the End of the Cold War: Reevaluating a Landmark Case for Ideas," *International Security* 25, no. 3.Winter 2000/01.

Brown, Archie. *The Rise and Fall of Communism.* London: Bodley Head, 2009.

Roberts, Adam. 'An 'incredibly swift transition': reflections on the end of the Cold War,' *The Cambridge History of The Cold War,* Volume III, eds. Melvyn P. Leffler and Odd Arne Westad. Cambridge: Cambridge University Press, 2011.

Baker III, James A. *The Politics of Diplomacy: Revolution, War & Peace, 1989-1992,* with Thomas M. DeFrank (New York: Putnam's & Sons, 1995).

———. Speech to the Center for Strategic and International Studies, May 4, 1989, *Washington Post,* May 5, 1989.

———. "Points of Mutual Advantage: Perestroika and American Foreign Policy," Speech, *Foreign Policy Association,* New York, NY, October 16, 1989. The Department of State Bulletin, December 1989.

———. 'A New Europe, A New Atlanticism: Architecture for a New Era" Speech to the Berlin Press Club, December 12, 1989. US Department of State, Bureau of Public Affairs. http://digitalcollections.library.cmu.edu/awweb/awarchive?type=file&item=690688

———. *Work Hard, Study... and Keep out of Politics!* with Steve Fiffer. Evanston: Northwestern University Press, 2008.

———. Interview with Russell Riley, James S. Young, and Robert Strong, George H. W. Bush Oral History Project. March 17, 2011, Houston, TX. https://millercenter.org/the-presidency/presidential-oral-histories/james-baker-iii-oral-history-2011-white-house-chief.

———. "Points of Mutual Advantage: Perestroika and American Foreign Policy" Foreign Policy Association, New York, NY, October 16,

1989. https://babel.hathitrust.org/cgi/pt?id=osu.32437010892640;view=1up;seq=490

_____. Secret Night Notes to President George H.W. Bush, "My Meeting with Gorbachev," May 19, 1990. State Department Cable 190830Z, declassified May 29, 1997.

_____. *"A New Europe, A New Atlanticism; Architecture for a New Era*, Berlin Press Club, Berlin, December 12, 1988. http://digitalcollections.library.cmu.edu/awweb/ awarchive?type=file&item=690688

_____."U.S. Position on the Reunification of Germany," November 29, 1989. *American Foreign Policy: Current Documents 1989.* Washington DC: Department of State Bureau of Public Affairs, Office of the Historian, 1990. https://babel.hathitrust.org/cgi/pt?id=mdp.39015024825450;view=1up;seq=398.

_____. "Challenges at the End of the Cold War." Foreign Policy Association. New York, November 2015.

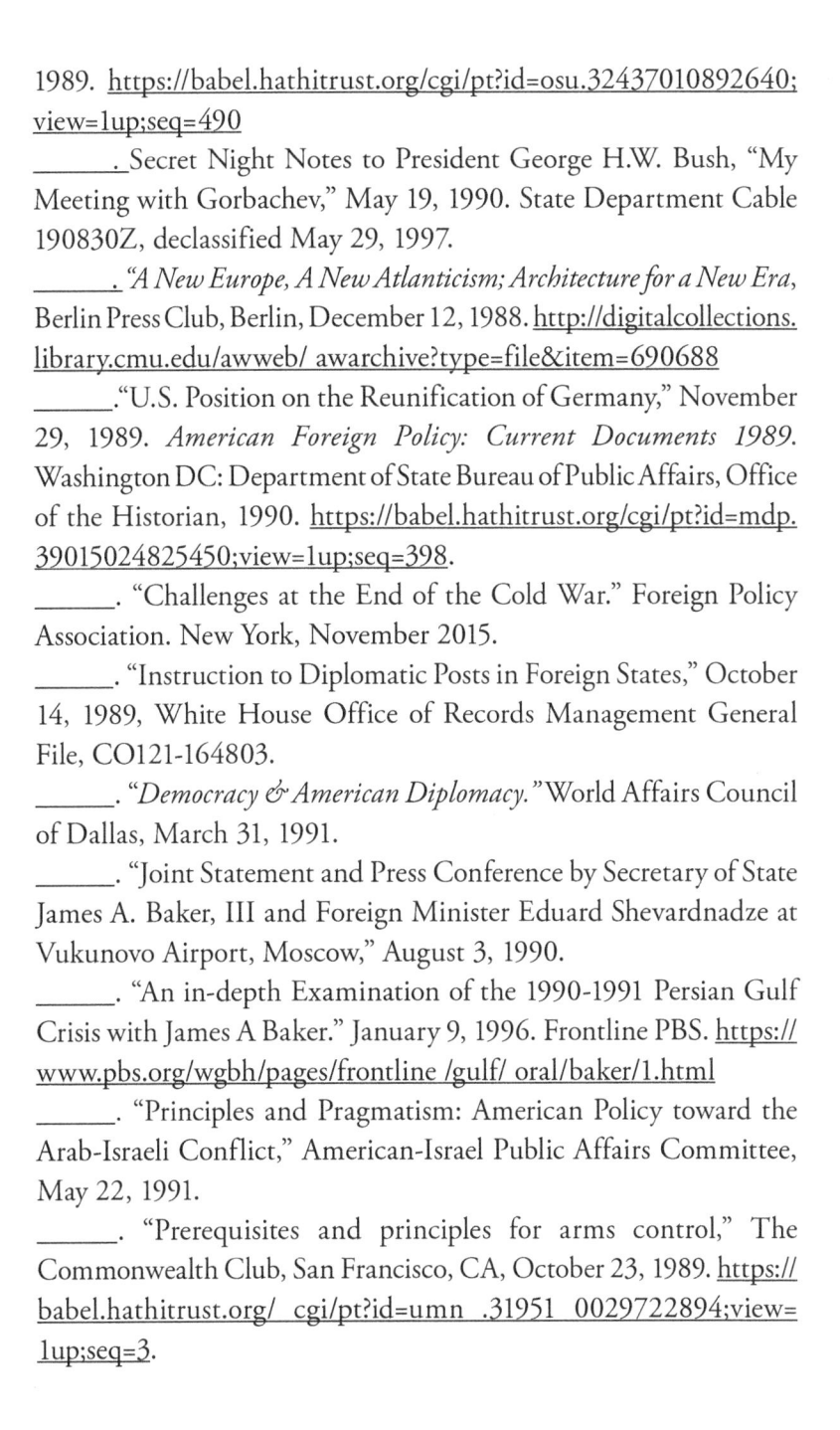

_____. "Instruction to Diplomatic Posts in Foreign States," October 14, 1989, White House Office of Records Management General File, CO121-164803.

_____. *"Democracy & American Diplomacy."* World Affairs Council of Dallas, March 31, 1991.

_____. "Joint Statement and Press Conference by Secretary of State James A. Baker, III and Foreign Minister Eduard Shevardnadze at Vukunovo Airport, Moscow," August 3, 1990.

_____. "An in-depth Examination of the 1990-1991 Persian Gulf Crisis with James A Baker." January 9, 1996. Frontline PBS. https://www.pbs.org/wgbh/pages/frontline /gulf/ oral/baker/1.html

_____. "Principles and Pragmatism: American Policy toward the Arab-Israeli Conflict," American-Israel Public Affairs Committee, May 22, 1991.

_____. "Prerequisites and principles for arms control," The Commonwealth Club, San Francisco, CA, October 23, 1989. https://babel.hathitrust.org/ cgi/pt?id=umn .31951 0029722894;view=1up;seq=3.

_____."America and the Post-Coup Soviet Union." Princeton University, December 12, 1991, CSPAN, https://www.c-span.org/video/?23366-1/post-coup-soviet-union.

_____. Interview with Robert Riley 2011. https://www.bing.com/videos/search?q=James+a+Baker+III+interview+with+Robert+Riley&view=detail&mid=FD6C32D3F34D20B3E378FD6C32D3F34D20B3E378&FORM=VIRE

Baker, Susan G. *Passing it On: An Autobiography with Spirit.* Houston: Radiant Star Books, 2013.

Bernstein Paul I. and Wood, Jason D. *The Origins of Nunn-Lugar and Cooperative Threat Reduction,* Center for the Study of Weapons of Mass Destruction at National Defense University Press, Case Study Series No. 3, April 2010. http://ndupress.ndu.edu/Portals/68/Documents/case studies/CSWMD_CaseStudy-3.pdf.

Beschloss, Michael R. and Talbott, Strobe. *At the Highest Levels: the Inside Story of the End of the Cold War.* London: Little Brown & Co., 1993.

Bozo, Frederic, Rey, Marie-Pierre, Nuti, Leopoldo, Ludlow N. Piers. eds., *Europe and the End of the Cold War: a Reappraisal.* Abingdon, UK: Routledge, 2008.

Bozo, Frederic, Nuti Leopoldo, Rey, Marie-Pierre, Rother, Berno eds. *The Euromissile Crisis and the End of the Cold War.* Washington: Woodrow Wilson Center Press, 2015.

Brown, William Andreas. "The Road to Madrid – James Baker and the Middle East Peace Talks." Association for Diplomatic Studies and Training, https://adst.org/2015/06/the-road-to-madrid-james-baker-and-the-middle-east-peace-talks/.

Burns, William. *The Back Channel: A Memoir of American Diplomacy and the Case for Its Renewal,* New York, Random House, 2019

Bush, George H.W.to Mikhail Gorbachev, January 17, 1989, Wilson Center Digital Archive. https://digitalarchive.wilsoncenter.org/document/134824.pdf?v=db6b0e029da02d17ca326d764946cc60

_____. *All the Best, George Bush: My Life in Letters and Other Writings.* New York: Scribner, 2013.

_____. "Remarks Delivered to the Texas A&M University Commencement Ceremony," College Station, Texas, May 12, 1989). The American Presidency Project, https://www.presidency.ucsb.edu/documents/remarks-the-texas-am-university-commencement-ceremony-college-station

_____. Speech to the citizens of Mainz, May 31, 1989. https://usa.usembassy.de/etexts/ ga6- 890531.htm

_____. "Address to the Nation on Panama," Washington, D.C. December 20, 1989. https://millercenter.org/the-presidency/presidential-speeches/december-20-1989-address-nation-panama.

_____. Letter to Chancellor Kohl, George Bush Presidential Library and Museum. See also, transcript of telephone conversation that followed the letter at https://digitalarchive.wilsoncenter.org/document/116233.pdf?v=2f57a8d6362a28058115bc202e0a6d21.

_____. "Remarks on Soviet Military Intervention in Lithuania," January 13, 1991. http://www.presidency.ucsb.edu/ws/index.php?pid=19216.

_____. "National Security Directive 26: U.S. Policy Toward the Persian Gulf," October 2, 1989, http://fas.org/irp/offdocs/nsd/nsd26.pdf.

_____. "Remarks and an Exchange with Reporters on the Iraqi Invasion of Kuwait," August 5 1990. https://www.presidency.ucsb.edu/ documents/ remarks-and-exchange-with-reporters-the-iraqi-invasion-kuwait-0.

_____."Remarks to the Military Airlift Command in Dhahran," Dhahran, Saudi Arabia, 22 November 1990. https://www.presidency.ucsb.edu/documents/remarks-the-military-airlift-command-dhahran-saudi-arabia

_____. "Bush Announces End to Gulf War," February 27, 1991, audio. https://www.history.com/topics/us-presidents/bush-announces-end-to-gulf-war-video.

_____. "The President's News Conference Following Discussions with Prime Minister Toshiki Kaifu of Japan in Palm Springs, California," statement, March 3, 1990.

_____. "Remarks at the Opening Session of the Middle East Peace Conference in Madrid, Spain," October 30, 1991.

_____. "Address to the Nation on Reducing United States and Soviet Nuclear Weapons," September 27, 1991. https://www.presidency.ucsb.edu/documents/address-the-nation-reducing-united-states-and-soviet-nuclear-weapons.

_____. "End of the Soviet Union: Address to the Nation on Gorbachev's Resignation," December 26, 1991, https://www.nytimes.com/1991/12/26/world/end-soviet-union-text-bush-s-address-nation-gorbachev-s-resignation.html.

_____. Remarks on awarding James A Baker, III the Congressional Medal of Freedom. https://www.youtube.com/watch?v=yXG91-SztE0

Bush, George H.W. and Scowcroft, Brent. *A World Transformed*. New York: Vintage Books, Random House 1996.

Bush, George W. *41: A portrait of my Father*, New York: Penguin Random House, 2014.

British Foreign Office Material III. Washington telegram No. 240, January 29, 1990.

Campbell, Kurt M. Carter, Ashton B. Miller, Steven E. and Zraket, Charles A. *Soviet Nuclear Fission: Control of the Nuclear Arsenal in a Disintegrating Soviet Union*. Cambridge, MA: Belfer Center for Science and International Affairs at the Harvard Kennedy School, November 1991), https://www.worldcat.org/title/soviet-nuclear-fission-control-of-the-nuclear-arsenal-in-a-disintegrating-soviet-union/oclc/25107115

Caraley, James Demetrios. *The New American Interventionism: Lessons from Successes and Failures*. Essays from *Political Science Quarterly*. New York: Columbia University Press, 1999.

Chamberlain, Neville. "Peace for Our Time" 10 Downing Street, London, September 30, 1938. Euro Docs archive, Harold B. Lee Library, Brigham Young University. https://www.history.com/news/chamberlain-declares-peace-for-our-time-75-years-ago

Chernyaev, Anatoly S. *My Six Years with Gorbachev*, trans. Robert D. English & Elizabeth Tucker. University Park, Pennsylvania: Pennsylvania State University Press, 2000.

_____. The Diary of Anatoly Chernyaev, 6th Installment, Final Year of the Soviet Union, 1991. National Security Archive, https://nsarchive2.gwu.edu//NSAEBB/ NSAEBB 345/index.htm

Chollet, Derek H. and Goldgeier, James M. "Once Burned, Twice Shy? The Pause of 1989," in Wohlforth, ed., *Cold War Endgame*.

Cohen, Leonard J. *Broken Bonds: Yugoslavia's Disintegration and Balkan Politics in Transition*. 2nd ed. Boulder, CO: Westview Press, 1999.

Crocker, Chester A., Hampson, Osler Fen, Aall, Pamela, eds., *Leashing the Dogs of War: Conflict Management in a Divided World*, Washington D.C.: US Institute of Peace Press 2007.

Dannreuther, Roland. "The Gulf Conflict: a Political and Strategic Analysis," *Adelphi Papers* 32. Director of Central Intelligence, "Whither Gorbachev: Soviet Policy and Politics in the 1990s," *National Intelligence Estimate*. November 1987. https://www.cia.gov/library/ readingroom/docs/CIA-RDP89M00699R002201790013-5.pdf.

Dobbins, James. *Foreign Service: Five Decades on the Frontlines of American Diplomacy*. Washington, DC: The Rand Corporation and Brookings Institution Press, 2017.

Engel, Jeffrey A. *The China Diary of George H.W. Bush: the Making of a Global President*. Princeton: Princeton University Press, 20008.

_____. *When the World Seemed New: George H.W. Bush and the End of the Cold War*. Boston: Houghton Mifflin Harcourt, 2017.

Ericson, Richard E. "The Classical Soviet-Type Economy: Nature of the System and Implications for Reform" *The Journal of Economic Perspectives*, Https://www.jstor.org/ stable/1942862

Fink, Susan D. "From 'Chicken Kiev' to Ukrainian Recognition: Domestic Politics in U.S. Foreign Policy Toward Ukraine," *Harvard Ukrainian Studies* 21, No. 1 /2 .June 1997. https://www.jstor.org/stable/pdf/41036641.pdf

Frankel, Glenn. *Beyond the Promised Land: Jews and Arabs on the Hard Road to a New Israel.* New York: Touchstone, 1994.

Gaddis, John Lewis, *The Cold War: A New History*, New York: The Penguin Press, 2005.

_____, *Surprise, Security, and the American Experience.* Joanna Jackson Memorial Lecture, Boston: Harvard University Press, 2004.

_____, *We Now Know: Rethinking Cold War History.* Oxford, UK: Oxford University Press, 1997.

_____, *The United States and the End of the Cold War: Implications, Reconsideration, Provocations,* Oxford, UK: Oxford University Press, 1992.

Gaidar, Yegor. *Collapse of an Empire.* Washington, DC: Brookings Institution Press, 2007.

Galkin Aleksandr and Anatolij Tschernjajew, Anatolij eds., Rose Blanchard, trans. "Transcript of February 9, 1990 conversation between Gorbachev, Baker, and Shevardnadze," *Michail Gorbatschow und die deutsche Frage.*

Garthoff, Raymond L. *The Great Transition: American Soviet Relations and the End of the Cold War.* Washington, DC: The Brookings Institution, 1994.

Garton, Ash. Timothy. *The Magic Lantern.* Grant Books, Penguin Group, 1990.

_____. *The File.* New York: Vintage Books, Random House. 1997

_____. In Europe's Name," in *American Diplomacy and the End of the Cold War,* Hutchings, Robert L.

_____."The Crisis of Europe: How the Union Came Together and Why It's Falling Apart," *Foreign Affairs,* September/October 2012.

_____, *In Europe's Name: Germany and the Divided Continent.* New York: Random House, 1993.

_____. Poland, Europe, Freedom. Speech delivered to Old Divinity School, St. Johnson College, Cambridge. https://www.youtube.com/watch?v=fdlBjhgBjCQ&t=1018

Gates, Robert M. "Soviet Sinology: An Untapped Source for Kremlin Views and Disputes Relating to Contemporary Events in China." PhD dissertation, Georgetown University, 1974.

_____. *From the Shadows: The Ultimate Insider's Story of Five Presidents and How They Won the Cold War*. New York, Simon Schuster, 2007.

Genscher, Hans-Dietrich. "German Unity within a European Framework," Speech delivered at Tutzing Protestant Academy, Tutzing, Germany, January 31, 1990.

_____. *Rebuilding a House Divided*. trans. Thomas Thornton. New York: Broadway Books, 1998.

_____. "Recognizing Slovenia, Croatia Brought Peace, Genscher Says," June 25, 2011. *Deutsche Welle*. https://www.dw.com/en/recognizing-slovenia-croatia-brought-peace-genscher-says/a-15182463 .

Gerges, Fawaz A. "Regional Security after the Gulf Crisis: the American Role," *Journal of Palestine Studies*, 20:4 (Summer 1991). http://www.jstor.com/stable/2537435

Goldgeier, James and Shifrinson, Center for New American Security. Podcast. December 2, 2019. https://www.cnas.org/publications/podcast/josh-shifrinson-and-jim-goldgeier discuss-nato-expansion

Gorbachev, Mikhail. "Address by Mikhail Gorbachev at the UN General Assembly Session (Excerpts)," December 07, 1988, CWIHP Archive.

_____. CSPAN, https://www.c-span.org/video/?5292-1/gorbachev-united-nations.

_____. *Perestroika: New Thinking for Our Country and the World*. New York: Harper & Row. 1987

Gorbachev, Mikhail, *Perestroika: New Thinking for Our Country and the World*. New York: Harper & Row, 1987

Gordon, Michael R. and Trainor, General Bernard E. *The General's War: The Inside Story of the Conflict in the Gulf*. Boston: Little Brown & Co., 1995.

Gow, James. *Triumph of the Lack of Will: International Diplomacy and the Yugoslav War,* New York: Columbia University Press, 1997.

Gunderson, Jon. Recollections of the Consul General in Kiev, *Association for Diplomatic Studies and Training Association*. https://adst.org/2014/03/ukraines-push-for-independence/

Haass, Richard. *War of Necessity, War of Choice: A Memoir of Two Iraq Wars*. New York: Simon & Schuster, 2009.

_____. Interview with Stephen Knott and Bob Strong, May 27, 2004, New York, NY.

_____. Presidential Oral Histories. George H.W. Bush Presidency. Miller Center, University of Virginia, Oral History, May 27, 20004. https://millercenter.org/the-presidency/presidential-oral-histories/richard-haass-oral-history

Halberstam, David. *War in a Time of Peace: Bush, Clinton and the Generals*. New York: Simon & Schuster, 2001.

Harrison, Hope M. *After the Berlin Wall: Memory and the Making of the New Germany, 1989 to the Present*, Cambridge UK: Cambridge University Press ((2019)

Hays, Jeffrey. "Shock Therapy and Economic Policy under Yeltsin," Facts and Details, http://factsanddetails.com/russia/Economics_Business_Agriculture/sub9_7b/entry-5168.html.

Hutchings, Robert L. *American Diplomacy and the End of the Cold War: An Insider's Account of U.S. Policy in Europe, 1989-1992*. Washington D.C.: The Woodrow Wilson Center Press, 1997.

—— "American Diplomacy and the End of Cold War in Europe," in *Foreign Policy Breakthroughs: Cases in Successful Diplomacy*, eds. Robert Hutchings and Suri, Jeremy. New York: Oxford University Press, 2015.

Jamieson, James D. "Personal Recollections of his visit to the Soviet Union September 1990" GPS, University of California, San Diego. Private papers.

Jentleson, Bruce W. *The Peace Makers: Leadership Lessons from Twentieth Century Statesmanship*. New York: W.W. Norton Co. 2018.

Journal of Palestine Studies. "Chronology: 16 February-15 May 1991," Vol. 20, 1991.

Kaufman, Richard F. and Hardt. John Pearce. *The Former Soviet Union in Transition*. Armonk, NY: M.E. Sharpe, 1993.

Kramer, Mark. "The Myth of a No-NATO-Enlargement Pledge to Russia," *The Washington Quarterly* 32, no.2 April 2009.

Kengor, Paul. *The Crusader: Ronald Reagan and the Fall of Communism*. New York: Regan Books, 2006.

Koch, Susan J. "The Presidential Nuclear Initiatives of 1991-1992," Center for the Study of Weapons of Mass Destruction at National Defense University, Case Study Series No. 5, September 2012, https://wmdcenter.ndu.edu/Publications/Publication-View/Article/627149/the-presidential-nuclear-initiatives-of-1991-1992/

Kohl, Helmut and Gorbachev, Mikhail. "Joint Declaration of the Federal Republic of Germany and the Soviet Union," *WEU Press Review*, June 13, 1989, https://www.tandfonline.com/doi/abs/10.1080/00396338908442489?needAccess=true&journalCode=tsur20.

_____. Record of Conversation between M.S. Gorbachev and Chancellor of FRG H. Kohl, June 13, 1989
Wilson Center Digital Archive, https://digitalarchive.wilsoncenter.org/document/120808.

_____. "Ten-Point Plan for German Unity," Speech to the Bundestag. Bonn, November 28, 1989. http://germanhistorydocs.ghi-dc.org/sub_document.cfm?document_id=223.

Kynaston, David. *Family Britain 1951-57: Tales of a New Jerusalem*. London: Bloomsbury, 2009.

Kučinskas, Linas. "Lithuania's Independence: the Litmus Test for Democracy in the USSR." *Lituanus: Lithuanian Quarterly Journal of Arts and Sciences* 37, no.3. Fall 1991. http://www.lituanus.org/1991_3/91_3_01.htm

Laruelle, Marlene and Radvanyi, Jean, *Understanding Russia: the Challenges of Transformation*, London: Rowman & Littlefield, 2019.

Lasensky, Scott B. "Friendly Restraint: U.S.-Israeli Relations during the Gulf Crisis of 1990-1991," *The Middle East Review of International Affairs Journal*, 3:2. Summer 1999. http://www.rubincenter.org/1999/06/lasensky-1999-06-03/.

Leffler, Melvyn P. "Ronald Reagan and the Cold War: What Mattered Most," *Texas National Security Review:* Vol 1, Issue 3, May 2018.

Leffler, Melvyn P. and Westad, Odd Arne, eds., *The Cold War, Volume III – Endings*, The Cambridge History of the Cold War, Cambridge UK: Cambridge University Press, 2010.

Leffler, Melvyn P. and Legro Jeffrey W. eds. *In Uncertain Times: American Foreign Policy after the Berlin Wall and 9/11*. Ithaca: Cornell University Press (2011)

LeoGrande William M. and Kornbluh, Peter. *Back Channel to Cuba: The Hidden History of Negotiations between Washington and Havana*. Chapel Hill: UNC Press Books, 2014.

Libal, Michael. *Limits of Persuasion: Germany and the Yugoslav Crisis, 1991-1992*. Westport, CT: Praeger, 1997.

Lilley, James and Lilley, Jeffrey. *China Hands: Nine Decades of Adventure, Espionage and Diplomacy in Asia*. New York: Public Affairs, 2004.

Mahnken, Thomas G. "The Reagan Administration's Strategy Toward the Soviet Union," in Williamson Murray and Richard Hart Sinnreich eds., *Successful Strategies: Triumphing War and Peace from Antiquity to the Present*. Cambridge: Cambridge University Press 2014.

Mann, James. "Did President George H.W. Bush Mishandle China?" *A China File Conversation*, December 4, 2018. http://www.chinafile.com/conversation/did-president-george-hw-bush-mishandle-china.

_____.*The Great Rift: Dick Cheney, Colin Powell and the Broken Friendship that Defined an Era*. New York: Henry Holt and Company, 2019.

Marlo, Francis H. *Planning Reagan's War: Conservative Strategists and America's Cold War Victory*. Washington, D.C.: Potomac Books, 2012.

Marsh, Gerald, "The Ups and Downs of Downloading," *Bulletin of the Atomic Scientists*, Vol. 47, No. 9, November 1991.

Matlock Jr., Jack F. *Autopsy on an Empire: The American Ambassador's Account of the Collapse of the Soviet Union*. New York: Random House, 1995.

_____. *Hearing on US Policy toward NATO Enlargement.* Testimony before the House Comm. on International Relations, 104th Cong. 31 (1996).

_____. *Super–power Illusions: How Myths and False Ideologies Led America Astray – and How to Return to Reality*, New Haven: Yale University Press, 2010

McNees, Stephen K. "The 1990-91 Recession in Historical Perspective," *New England Economic Review*, January/February 1992.

McCulloch, Rachel. "The United States-Canada Free Trade Agreement," *Proceedings of the Academy of Political Science* 37, no. 4, 1990.

Meacham, Jon. *Destiny and Power: The American Odyssey of George Herbert Walker Bush.* New York: Random House, 2015.

Miller, Aaron David. *The Much Too Promised Land: America's Elusive Search for Arab-Israeli Peace.* New York: Random House Inc. 2008.

Morris, Edmund. *Dutch: A Memoir of Ronald Reagan.* New York: Random House, 1999.

National Security Strategy of the United States. (Washington, DC: The White House, August 1991) http://nssarchive.us/NSSR/1991.pdf

Newsweek Magazine, "Interview with Boris Yeltsin," *The Year of Yeltsin, Decade of Democracy*: International Edition, January 6, 1992.

Nicolson, Harold. *Diplomacy*, Washington, D.C.: Institute for the Study of Diplomacy 1988.

Noren, James and Kurtzweg, Laurie. "The Soviet Economy Unravels: 1985-1991" in *The Former Soviet Union in Transition*, Study Papers Submitted to the Joint Economic Committee, Congress of the United States (1993).

Nunn, Sam and Lugar, Richard G. "The Nunn-Lugar Initiative: Cooperative Demilitarization in the Former Soviet Union." in *The Diplomatic Record 1992–1993*. Boulder, CO: Westview Press, 1995.

Nunn-Lugar Cooperative Threat Reduction Act of 2007, S. 198, 110th Cong. 2007. https://www.congress.gov/bill/110th-congress/senate-bill/198 This bill outlines the achievements in decommissioning of Russian arms since the inception of the Act in 1991 (Soviet

Nuclear Threat Reduction Act of 1991, H.R. 3807, 102nd Cong. (1991) https://www.govtrack.us/congress/bills/102/hr3807

Oberdorfer, Don. *The Turn: From the Cold War to a New Era, the United States and the Soviet Union, 1983-1990.* New York: Poseidon Press, 1991.

Palazchenko, Pavel. *My Years with Gorbachev and Shevardnadze: The Memoir of a Soviet Interpreter.* University Park: The Pennsylvania State University Press, 1997.

Pavlov, Yuri. *Soviet-Cuban Alliances, 1959-1991*, 2nd ed. University of Miami: North-South Center Press, 1996.

Plokhy, Serhii. *The Last Empire: The Final Days of the Soviet Union.* New York: Basic Books, 2014.

Pond, Elizabeth. *Beyond the Wall: Germany's Road to Unification.* Washington D.C.: Brookings Institution 1993.

Reddaway, Peter and Glinski, Dmitri. *The Tragedy of Russia's Reforms: Market Bolshevism Against Democracy.* Washington D.C.: U.S. Institute of Peace Press, 2001.

Rodder, Andreas, Bozo, Federic, and Sarotte, Marie Elise eds., "German Reunification: A Multinational History," *Cold War History.* New York: Routledge, 2017.

Rodman, Peter W. *Presidential Command: Power, Leadership and the Making of Foreign Policy from Richard Nixon to George W. Bush.* New York: Alfred A Knopf, 2009.

Rose, Charlie. "A conversation with Sergei Lavrov, Russian Foreign Minister," PBS, Charlie Rose Show. September 25, 2008. https://smallwarsjournal.com/blog/a-conversation-with-sergei-lavrov

Rosenbaum, David. "The Houston Summit: Three Key Economic Issues Undecided as Meeting Ends," *New York Times,* July 12, 1990, http://www.nytimes.com/1990/07/12/business/the-houston-summit-three-key-economic-issues-undecided-as-meeting-ends.html.

Ross, Dennis. *The Missing Peace: The Inside Story of the Fight for Middle East Peace.* New York: Farrar, Straus and Giroux, 2004.

_____. *Doomed to Succeed the U.S. – Relations from Truman to Obama* . New York: Farrar, Straus and Giroux, 2016.

_____. Interview with Bill Quandt and Philip Zelikow. http://millercenter.org/president/bush/oralhistory/dennis-ross

Ross, Dennis with Makovsky, David. *Myths, Illusions and Peace: Finding a New Direction in the Middle East.* 2009

Rothkopf, David. *Running the World: The Inside Story of the National Security Council and the Architects of American Power.* New York: Public Affairs, 2005.

Salmon, Patrick, Hamilton, Keith, Twigge, Stephen Robert eds., *German Unification 1989-1990,* Documents on British Policy Overseas, series 3, vol. 7, no. 47. Abingdon, UK: Routledge 2009.

Sarotte, Mary Elise. *1989: The Struggle to Create Post-Cold War Europe.* Princeton: Princeton University Press, 2009.

_____. *The Collapse: the Accidental Opening of the Berlin Wall*, Basic Books, Perseus Book Group (2014)

Savranskaya, Svetlana, Blanton, Thomas and Zubok, Vladislav. eds. *Masterpieces of History: The Peaceful End of the Cold War in Europe, 1989.* New York: National Security Archive Fund, 2010, 342,

_____. "Document No. 36: Record of Conversation between Aleksandr Yakovlev and Henry Kissinger, January 16, 1989."

_____. *Masterpieces of History,* 345, "Document No. 37: Record of Conversation between Mikhail Gorbachev and Henry Kissinger, January 17, 1989."

_____. *Masterpieces of History,* 619, "Document No. 110, Soviet Transcript of the Malta Summit, December 2-3, 1989" in "Bush and Gorbachev at Malta: Previously Secret Documents from Soviet and U.S. Files on the 1989 Meeting, 20 Years Later." National Security Archive, https://nsarchive2.gwu.edu//NSAEBB/NSAEBB298/Document%2010.pdf.

Schweizer, Peter. *Reagan's War: The Epic Story of His Forty-Year Struggle and Final triumph Over Communism.* New York: Anchor Books, 2002.

Scowcroft, Retired General, Brent, interview with Philip Zelikow, Ernest May, James McCall, and Fareed Zakaria, Presidential Oral Histories. George H.W. Bush Presidency. Miller Center, University of Virginia, Oral History, November 12 and 13, 1999. Part II. https://millercenter.org/the-presidency/presidential-oral-histories/brent-scowcroft-oral-history-part-i

Scowcroft, Brent and Bush, George H.W. *A World Transformed.* New York: Vintage Books, Random House, 1996.

Sell, Louis. *From Washington to Moscow: US Soviet Relations and the Collapse of the USSR.* Durham: Duke University Press, 2016.

Shamir, Yitzhak. *Summing Up: The Memoirs of Yitzhak Shamir.* London: Weidenfeld & Nicholson, 1994.

Sheehy, Gail. *The Man Who Changed the World; the Lives of Mikhail S. Gorbachev.* New York: HarperCollins Publishers, 1990.

Shevardnadze, Eduard. *The Future Belongs to Freedom*, trans. Catherine A. Fitzpatrick. New York: The Free Press, 1991.

Shields, John M. and Potter, William C. eds. Senator Sam Nunn, foreword to *Dismantling the Cold War: U.S. and NIS Perspectives on the Nunn-Lugar Cooperative Threat Reduction Program*, (Cambridge, MA: The MIT Press, 1997).

Solomon, Richard H. and Quinney, Nigel, *American Negotiating Behavior: Wheeler-Dealers, Legal Eagles, Bullies and Preachers.* Washington, D.C.: US Institute of Peace Press, 2010.

Sparrow, Bartholomew. *The Strategist: Brent Scowcroft and the Call of National Security.* New York, Public Affairs, 2015.

Spohr, Kristina. "Precluded or Precedent Setting?: The 'NATO Enlargement Question' in the Triangular Bonn-Washington-Moscow Diplomacy of 1990-91" *Journal of Cold War Studies* 14, no. 4. Fall 2012.

Spohr, Kristina and Hamilton, Daniel S. eds. *Exiting the Cold War, Entering a New World.* Washington D.C. John Hopkins University SAIS, 2019.

U.S. Department of State, "Country Reports for Human Rights Practices for 1990," Joint Committee Report submitted to the Committee on Foreign Relations, US Senate, and the Foreign Affairs Committee, US House of Representatives. 1990.

_____. Department of State cable 384861, December 2, 1989. Declassified 2004.

_____. "The Breakup of Yugoslavia, 1990-1992," Department of State Office of the Historian, https://history.state.gov/milestones/1989-1992/breakup-yugoslavia

_____. "US Policy toward Yugoslavia," US Department of State Dispatch. June 3, 1991.

_____. Memorandum of Meeting with Manfred Woerner, Oval Office, June 25, 1991.

Stent, Angela. *Russia and Germany Reborn,* Princeton: Princeton University Press, 2000.

_____, *The Limits of Partnership: U.S. Russian Relations in the Twenty-First Century.* Princeton: Princeton University Press, 2014.

St. Louis Fed's historical USD-DM exchange rate tool https://fred.stlouisfed.org/series/EXGEUS

Taubman, William. *Gorbachev: His Life and Times.* New York: W. W .Norton & Co. 2017.

Thatcher, Margaret. *Margaret Thatcher: The Downing Street Years.* London: HarperCollins, 1993.

_____."Shaping a New Global Community" (speech to the Aspen Institute, August 5, 1990). Margaret Thatcher Foundation, https://www.margaretthatcher.org/document/108174

Teltschik, Horst. "Gorbachev's reform Policy and the Outlook for East-West Relations, 'Aussempolitik,'" 3 (1989) in *American Diplomacy and the End of the Cold War*, Hutchings.

_____. *329 Tage: Innenansichten der Einigung.* Berlin: Siedler Verlag, 1991.

Treaty on the Final Settlement with Respect to Germany, Federal Republic of Germany-German Democratic Republic-France-U.S.S.R.-U.K.-U.S., September 12, 1990.

Treaty on Conventional Armed Forces in Europe (CFE). Resolution of Advice and Consent to Ratification, 102nd Congress, November 25, 1991, https://www.congress.gov/treaty-document/102nd-congress/8/

Treaty between the United States of America and the Union of Soviet Socialist Republics on Strategic Offensive Reductions (START I)," Nuclear Threat Initiative. http://www.nti.org/learn/ treaties-and-regimes/treaties-between-united-states-america-and-union-soviet-socialist-republics-strategic-offensive-reductions-start-i-start-ii/.

United Nations Document. "The Need for Convening a Middle East Peace Conference," New York 1989, https://www.un.org/unispal/document/auto-insert-206430/

_____. UN Security Council Resolution 242. November 22, 1967. http://unispal.un.org/UNISPALNSF/0/7D35E1F729DF491C85256EE700686136.

_____. UN Security Council Resolution 781 (S/RES/781 (1992)), October 9, 1992, http://unscr.com/en/resolutions/doc/781.

Unger, Craig. *House of Bush, House of Saud: the Secret Relationship between the World's Most Powerful Dynasties*, New York: Simon & Schuster, 2004.

US News & World Report staff. *Triumph Without Victory: The Unreported History of the Persian Gulf War*. New York: Random House, 1992.

Villiers Negroponte, Diana. *Seeking Peace in El Salvador: the Struggle to Reconstruct a Nation at the End of the Cold War*, New York: Palgrave Macmillan, 2012.

Wachtel, Andrew and Bennett, Christopher, "The Dissolution of Yugoslavia," in *Confronting the Yugoslav Controversies: A Scholar's Initiative*. 2nd ed, edited by Ingrao, Charles et al. West Lafayette, IN: Purdue University Press, 2012.

Walters, Alex. "Kazakhstan, US Complete Secret Nuclear Transfer Mission," *Edge*, September 2011, https://www.edgekz.com/kazakhstan-u-s-complete-secret-nuclear-transfer-mission.

Wells, Samuel F. Jr. ed. et al. *The Strategic Triangle: France, Germany, and the United States in the Shaping of the New Europe*, Washington D.C.: Woodrow Wilson Center Press, 20006.

Westad, Odd Arne. *The Cold War: a World History*. New York: Basic Books, 2017.

Wohlforth, William C. ed., "Part I: Oral History: The Princeton Conference" in *Cold War Endgame: Oral History, Analysis, Debates*. University Park, Pennsylvania: Pennsylvania State University Press, 2003.

Yankelovich, David. *Polling the Nation*, PBS, November 1990. http://www.pbs.org/fmc/interviews/yankelovich.htm

Yavlinsky, Grigory and Allison, Graham. *Window of Opportunity: The Grand Bargain for Democracy in the Soviet Union*. New York: Pantheon Books, 1991. https://www.abebooks.com/servlet/BookDetailsPL?bi=5537433139&searchurl=sortby%253D17%2526an%253DGRAHAM%252BALLISON%252B%252526%252BGRIGORY%252BYAVLINSKY&cm_sp=snippet-_-srp1-_-title1

Yongqing Douglas Yang, "The Panamanian Paradox: A President's Struggle to Remove Manuel Noriega" (bachelor's thesis, University of Wisconsin-Madison, 2010) \https://liberalarts.temple.edu/sites/liberalarts/files/YangPanamanianParadox.pdf.

Zimmerman, Warren. *Origins of a Catastrophe: Yugoslavia and its Destroyers – America's Last Ambassador Tells What Happened and Why*. New York: Times Books, 1996.

Zelikow, Philip and Rice, Condoleezza. *Germany Unified and Europe Transformed: A Study in Statecraft*. Cambridge: Harvard University Press, 1995.

_____, *To Build a Better World: Choices to end the Cold War and Create a Global Commonwealth*. New York: Hachette Book Group Inc. 2019.

Zubok, Vlad. *A Failed Empire: The Soviet Union in the Cold War from Stalin to Gorbachev*. Chapel Hill: University of North Carolina Press, 2007.

ARCHIVES:

George H.W. Bush Presidential Library and Museum, College Station, TX
Nicholas Burns files, George H.W. Bush Presidential Library and Museum

David Pacelli Files, George H.W. Bush Presidential Library and Museum.
William Pryce files, George H.W. Bush Presidential Library and Museum
Nicholas Rostow files, George H.W. Bush Presidential Library and Museum
James A. Baker III papers. Mudd Library, Princeton University.
Don Oberdorfer papers. Mudd Library, Princeton University.
Daniel Kurtzer papers. Mudd Library, Princeton University.
Cold War International History Project, Woodrow Wilson Center for Scholars, Digital Archive.
American Presidency Project, University of California at Santa Barbara.
George H.W. Bush Oral history. Miller Center, University of Virginia
Public Papers of the Presidents of the United States. George H.W. Bush
Miller Center, University of Virginia, George H.W. Bush Oral History Project.
National Security Archive at George Washington University, Washington, DC
British Foreign Office Archive, Kew Gardens, London, United Kingdom

NEWSPAPER ARTICLES AND TV SHOWS:

Associated Press (AP)
ABC Primetime Live
CBS Evening News
Charlie Rose Show PBS
Chicago Tribune
Christian Science Monitor
CSPAN
Deutsche Welle
Die Zeit
Der Spiegel
Federal News Service
Frontline, PBS
Le Monde
Los Angeles Times
Moscow Times

NBC – Meet the Press
New York Newsday
Rice News, Rice University
Tass Agency
Time
The Atlantic
The Nation
The New York Times
UPI news service
Washington Post

Congressional Hearings

Hearing on the Nomination of James A. Baker III: Hearing before the Committee on Foreign Relations, 101st Cong. 17 (1989).

Hearing on U.S.-U.S.S.R. Economic Relations, before the Senate Committee on Finance, 101st Congress, 4 and 25 (1989)

Hearing on US Policy Toward China, before the Senate Committee on Foreign Relations, 101st Congress, 2 (1990).

Hearing on United States Policy Toward China, before the House of Representatives Committee on Foreign Affairs, 101st Congress, 2 (1990).

Hearing on the Imperatives of Economic Reform: Change in Soviet and East European Economics, before the House Ways and Means Committee, 101st Congress, 14 (1990).

Hearing on Soviet Trade Opportunities before the Senate Committee on Commerce, Science and Transportation, 102nd Congress, 1st Session (1991)

Hearing on American Strategy in the Persian Gulf, before the Senate Foreign Relations Committee, 101st Congress (1990)

Hearing on Foreign Operations, Export Financing, and Related Programs Appropriations for Fiscal Year 1991 before the Senate Subcommittee of the Committee on Appropriations, 101st Congress (1990).

Hearing on 1991 Foreign Policy and 1992 Budget Request before the Senate Committee on Foreign Relations, 102nd Congress, 1st session (1991).

Hearing on Opportunities to Build a New World Order before the House Foreign Affairs Committee, 102nd Congress. (1991).

Hearing on the CFE Treaty, before the Senate Committee on Foreign Relations, 102nd Congress (1991).

Hearing on Foreign Financial Assistance Programs, before the House Foreign Affairs Committee, (1992).

Hearing on Examining America's Role in the World, James A. Baker testimony before the Senate Committee on Foreign Relations, 114th Congress, (2016).

ENDNOTES

End Notes for Introduction

1 Peter Schweizer, *Reagan's War: The Epic Story of his Forty-Year Struggle and Final Triumph over Communism*, (New York: Anchor Books, 2002). Paul Kengor, *The Crusader: Ronald Reagan and the Fall of Communism*, (New York: Regan Books, 2006). Francis H. Marlo, *Planning Reagan's War: Conservative Strategists and America's Cold War Victory*, (Washington, D.C.: Potomac Books, 2012). Thomas G. Mahnken, "The Reagan Administration's Strategy Toward the Soviet Union," in Williamson Murray and Richard Hart Sinnreich eds., *Successful Strategies: Triumphing War and Peace from Antiquity to the Present*, (Cambridge: Cambridge University Press 2014). Also Reagan's recognition of Gorbachev's contributions in Edmund Morris, *Dutch: A Memoir of Ronald Reagan*, (New York: Random House, 1999).

2 Melvyn P. Leffler, "Ronald Reagan and the Cold War: What Mattered Most," *Texas National Security Review:* Vol 1, Issue 3 (May 2018)

3 Odd Arne Westad, *The Cold War: a World History*, (New York: Basic Books, 2017)

4 Adam Roberts, 'An 'incredibly swift transition': reflections on the end of the Cold War,' *The Cambridge History of The Cold War,* Volume III, eds. Melvyn P. Leffle30and Odd Arne Westad, (Cambridge University Press, 2011).

5 Robert Gates, *From the Shadows: The Ultimate Insider's Story of Five President and How they Won the Cold War* (New York: Simon & Schuster, 1996) 456. Bartholomew Sparrow, *The Strategist: Brent Scowcroft and the Call of National Security* (Philadelphia, Pennsylvania, Public Affairs. 2015) 267.

6 Mary Elise Sarotte, *1989: The Struggle to Create Post-Cold War Europe*, (Princeton: Princeton University Press, 2009). Elizabeth Pond, *Beyond the Wall: Germany's Road to Unification*, (Washington D.C.: Brookings Institution 1993).

7   Robert L. Hutchings, *American Diplomacy and the End of the Cold War: An Insider's Account of U.S. Policy in Europe, 1989-1992* (Washington D.C.: The Woodrow Wilson Center Press, 1997)
8   Mark Kramer, "The Myth of a No-NATO-Enlargement Pledge to Russia," *The Washington Quarterly* 32, no. 2 (April 2009). James Goldgeier, Joshua Shifrinson,
9   Susan D. Fink, "From 'Chicken Kiev' to Ukrainian Recognition: Domestic Politics in U.S. Foreign Policy Toward Ukraine," *Harvard Ukrainian Studies* 21, No. 1 /2 June 1997)
10 "Did President George H.W. Bush Mishandle China?" *A China File Conversation*, December 4, 2018, http://www.chinafile.com/conversation/did-president-george-hw-bush-mishandle-china
11 Hal Brands, Making *The Unipolar Moment: U.S. Foreign Policy and the Rise of the Post-Cold War Order* (Ithaca: Cornell University Press, 2016).

End Notes for Chapter 1

1   Rowland Evans and Robert Novak, "Gorbachev Rolls Baker," *Washington Post*, May 12, 1989, https://www.washingtonpost.com/archive/opinions/1989/05/12/gorbachev-rolls-baker/82822621-8c6b-4bfc-9219-49a8b233674d/?utm_term=.68f140980c19
2   James A. Baker III, *The Politics of Diplomacy: Revolution, War & Peace, 1989-1992*, with Thomas M. DeFrank (New York: Putnam's & Sons, 1995), 30-31.
3   Robert Kimmitt interview with the author, August 4, 2016.
4   Mikhail Gorbachev's speech to the 43rd UN General Assembly, New York, December 7, 1988, https://astro.temple.edu/~rimmerma/gorbachev_speech_to_UN.htm
5   Savranskaya, Svetlana, Thomas Blanton, and Vladislav Zubok, eds. *Masterpieces of History: The Peaceful End of the Cold War in Europe, 1989* (New York: National Security Archive Fund, 2010), 342, "Document No. 36: Record of Conversation between Aleksandr Yakovlev and Henry Kissinger, January 16, 1989."
6   Savranskaya, Blanton, and Zubok, *Masterpieces of History*, 345, "Document No. 37: Record of Conversation between Mikhail Gorbachev and Henry Kissinger, January 17, 1989."
7   Philip Zelikow, interview with the author, October 5, 2018, Charlottesville, VA. Zelikow and NSC colleagues were adamantly opposed to Kissinger's proposal, seeing it as a way for Kissinger to exercise undue influence over the George H.W. Bush administration.

8   Ibid.
9   Ibid.
10 When at Treasury in 1985, Margaret Tutwiler called herself a messenger. She was Baker's No. 1 link to Washington lobbyists, to business, to the press, to political players within the Government and to the Republican Party faithful beyond the Capital Beltway. Peter T.Kilborn, "Working Profile: Margaret D. Tutwiler," The New York Times, December 6, 1985 https://www.nytimes.com/1985/12/06/us/working-profile-margaret-d-tutwiler-the-political-key-to-the-treasury.html
11 "Address by Mikhail Gorbachev at the UN General Assembly Session (Excerpts)," December 07, 1988, History and Public Policy Program Digital Archive, CWIHP Archive. http://digitalarchive.wilsoncenter.org/document/116224
12 James A. Baker III quoted in William C. Wohlforth, ed., "Part I: Oral History: The Princeton Conference" in *Cold War Endgame: Oral History, Analysis, Debates* (University Park, Pennsylvania: Pennsylvania State University Press, 2003), 25.
13 Alexandr Bessmertnykh quoted in Wohlforth, ed. *Cold War Endgame,* 26-27.
14 Vice President George H.W. Bush letter to Secretary General Mikhail Gorbachev, January 17, 1989, MC#197, Box 108, Folder 1. James A. Baker III Papers. Mudd Library, Princeton University.
15 Zelikow interview.
16 James Baker's handwritten notes on meeting with Mulroney, February 10, 1989, MC#197, Box 108, Folder 2. Baker Papers.
17 Ibid.
18 Thomas Friedman, "Baker, Outlining World View, Assesses Plan for Soviet Bloc," *New York Times*, March 28, 1989, http://www.nytimes.com/1989/03/28/world/baker-outlining-world-view-assesses-plan-for-soviet-bloc.html.
19 Ibid.
20 SNF was intended to provide the European allies with a nuclear defense against the preponderant Soviet conventional forces – troops, artillery, tanks and armored personnel carriers. See Chapter 8, Arms Control.
21 Jack F. Matlock Jr., *Autopsy on an Empire: The American Ambassador's Account of the Collapse of the Soviet Union* (New York: Random House, 1995), 186-189.
22 Ibid., 188-189
23 Ibid., 189
24 Jack F. Matlock quoted in Wohlforth, ed., *Cold War Endgame.*
25 Matlock, *Autopsy on an Empire*, 195.
26 Jack Matlock, interview with the author, January 16, 2019, Durham, NC.
27 Ibid.
28 Dennis Ross memorandum to Baker, March 7, 1989. Baker Papers.

29 Bartholomew Sparrow, *The Strategist: Brent Scowcroft and the Call of National Security*, (New York, Public Affairs, 2015), 287.
30 Derek H. Chollet and James M. Goldgeier, "Once Burned, Twice Shy? The Pause of 1989," in Wohlforth, ed., *Cold War Endgame*, 150.
31 Philip Zelikow, interview with the author, October 5, 2018, Charlottesville, VA.
32 Richard "Dick" Cheney joined the more conservative faction following his confirmation as Secretary of Defense on March 21, 1989.
33 Aleksandr Bessmertnykh quoted in Wohlforth, ed., *Cold War Endgame*, 26-27.
34 Anatoly Chernyaev quoted in Wohlforth, ed., *Cold War Endgame*, 21.
35 Peter Reddaway & Dmitri Glinski, *The Tragedy of Russia's Reforms: Market Bolshevism Against Democracy*, (Washington D.C. US Institute of Peace Press, 2001), 119-123.
36 Secretary of State James A. Baker III address delivered to the Center for Strategic and International Studies, May 4, 1989; quoted in Don Oberdorfer, "Baker, in Moscow Talks, to Ask Conciliatory Action." *Washington Post*, May 5, 1989.
37 Thomas Friedman, "Baker Plans Test of New Thinking," *New York Times*, May 9, 1989, http://www.nytimes.com/1989/05/09/world/baker-plans-test-of-new-thinking-while-in-moscow.html.
38 Ibid.
39 Michael R. Beschloss and Strobe Talbott, *At the Highest Levels: the Inside Story of the End of the Cold War* (London: Little Brown & Co., 1993), 60.
40 Pavel Palazchenko, *My Years with Gorbachev and Shevardnadze: The Memoir of a Soviet Interpreter* (University Park: The Pennsylvania State University Press, 1997), 134.
41 Susan G. Baker, *Passing it On: An Autobiography with Spirit* (Houston: Radiant Star Books, 2013), 67.
42 Ibid.
43 Eduard Shevardnadze, *The Future Belongs to Freedom*, trans. Catherine A. Fitzpatrick (New York: The Free Press, 1991), 72.
44 James Baker advised them that a currency that responded to market forces and a pricing system that was based on supply and demand were both necessary if they were to move from a centrally controlled economy to a free market economy.
45 Beschloss and Talbott, *At the Highest Levels*, 65.
46 Ibid.
47 Lance II was a short range, road mobile and liquid propelled ballistic missile aimed at the Soviet Union with the purpose of deterring the preponderant Soviet army from marching westward into Europe.

48 James Baker quoted in Wohlforth, ed., *Cold War Endgame*, 32.
49 Ibid.
50 Ibid., 33.
51 Dennis Ross, US note taker at the 1989 Moscow meetings, interviewed by Don Oberdorfer, MC#162, Box 2, Folder 31. Don Oberdorfer Papers. Mudd Library, Princeton University.
52 Don Oberdorfer quoted in Wohlforth, ed., *Cold War Endgame*, 33.
53 James A. Baker III, *Work Hard, Study… and Keep out of Politics!* with Steve Fiffer (Evanston: Northwestern University Press, 2008), 205.
54 Bernard Aronson, "Preliminary Thoughts on Central America" (unpublished manuscript, February 2, 1989), Aronson Personal Papers.
55 Baker quoted in Wohlforth, ed., "Part I: Oral History: The Princeton Conference" in *Cold War Endgame: Oral History, Analysis, Debates*, 25.
56 Robert Gates, "Soviet Sinology: An Untapped Source for Kremlin Views and Disputes Relating to Contemporary Events in China" (PhD dissertation, Georgetown University, 1974).
57 Reference to George Shultz's breakfast meeting with Soviet experts shortly after Gorbachev's appointment as general secretary of the Soviet Communist Party in March 1985. See Robert M. Gates, *From the Shadows: The Ultimate Insider's Story of Five Presidents and How They Won the Cold War*, (New York, Simon Schuster, 2007)
58 Robert M. Gates, "Sovietology: The Uneven Cycles of Kremlin Reform [adaptation of speech delivered on April 1, 1989]," *Washington Post*, April 30, 1989.
59 Molly Moore, "Cheney Predicts Gorbachev Will Fail, Be Replaced: Soviet Union's Next Leader Likely Will Be Far More Hostile to the West, Secretary of Defense Says," *Washington Post*, April 29, 1989.
60 General Brent Scowcroft, interview with Philip Zelikow, Ernest May, James McCall, and Fareed Zakaria, George H.W. Bush Oral History Project, University of Virginia Miller Center, November 12-13, 1999, Washington, DC, https://millercenter.org/the-presidency/presidential-oral-histories/brent-scowcroft-oral-history-national-security-advisor.
61 Don Oberdorfer, "Gorbachev Vows Halt to Arms to Managua," *Washington Post*, May 16, 1989. https://www.washingtonpost.com/archive/politics/1989/05/16/gorbachev-vows-halt-of-arms-to-managua/25fb37ff-44ce-4f7b-ae37-36d82807878c/?utm_term=.37e886b3028c
62 Michael R. Gordon, "East Bloc is said to Cut Managua Aid," *New York Times*, October 4, 1989, www.nytimes.com/1989/10/05/world/east-bloc-is-said-to-cut-managua-aid.html.

63 Yuri Pavlov, Soviet-Cuban Alliances, 1959-1991, 2nd ed. (University of Miami: North-South Center Press, 1990).
64 Letter from George H.W Bush to Mikhail Gorbachev, January 17, 1989, Wilson Center Digital Archive. https://digitalarchive.wilsoncenter.org/document/ 134824.pdf?v =db6b0e029da02d17ca326d764946cc60
65 "At times, this pause did cause problems." Sergei Tarasenko, quoted in Wohlforth, ed., *Cold War Endgame*, 31.
66 Baker quoted in Wohlforth, ed., *Cold War Endgame*, 25.
67 President George H.W. Bush. "Remarks Delivered to the Texas A&M University Commencement Ceremony," (speech, College Station, Texas, May 12, 1989). The American Presidency Project, www.presidency.ucsb.edu/ws/?pid=17022.
68 David Hoffman, "Bush Message to Gorbachev Was Deliberately Vague; Caution, Tests and Gradual Change Appear Key to President's Soviet Strategy," *Washington Post*, May 13, 1989.
69 Zoellick quoted in Wohlforth, ed., *Cold War Endgame*, 28-29.
70 Margaret Thatcher, *Margaret Thatcher: The Downing Street Years* (London: HarperCollins, 1993), 782-783.
71 Prime Minister Thatcher thought the Plaza and Louvre Accords, both of which Baker had concluded as Treasury Secretary to bring about a depreciation of the US dollar, had been "ill-judged." It served the interests of US exports, but manipulated the stability of other currencies.
72 James Markham, "NATO Chiefs Agree to a Compromise in Missile Dispute," *New York Times*, May 31, 1989, www.nytimes.com/1989/05/31/world/nato-chiefs-agree-to-a-compromise-in-missile-dispute.html.
73 George H.W. Bush and Brent Scowcroft, *A World Transformed* (New York: Alfred A. Knopf, 1998), 81.
74 Baker with DeFrank, *The Politics of Diplomacy*, 95.
75 Thatcher, *The Downing Street Years*, 788-789.
76 James Baker with DeFrank, *The Politics of Diplomacy*, 96.
77 "Le sommet des chefs d'Etat et de gouvernement de l'OTAN à Bruxelles, [Summit of NATO Heads of State and Government in Brussels]" *Le Monde*, May 31, 1989. https://www.lemonde.fr/archives/article/1989/05/31/le-sommet-des-chefs-d-etat-et-de-gouvernement-de-l-otan-a-bruxelles.
78 Dennis Ross interview with Don Oberdorfer, October 30, 1990, MC#162, Box 2, Folder 31. Oberdorfer Papers.
79 Ibid.
80 James Baker note to Tom Brokaw, September 1989, MC#197, Box 109, Folder 1. Baker Papers.

81 Susan G. Baker, *Passing It On: an Autobiography with Spirit*, (Houston: Bright Sky Press, 2010) 68.
82 Dennis Ross' interview with the author, Washington Institute for Near East Policy, Washington, D.C. 2015.
83 Baker with DeFrank, *The Politics of Diplomacy*, 158.
84 James A Baker, III interview with the author, September 30, 2015, Houston, TX.
85 Bartholomew Sparrow, *The Strategist: Brent Scowcroft and the Call of National Security* (New York: Public Affairs, 2015), 272.
86 Philip Zelikow, interview with the author, October 5, 2018, Charlottesville, VA.
87 James A. Baker III, interview with Russell Riley, James S. Young, and Robert Strong, George H. W. Bush Oral History Project, University of Virginia Miller Center, March 17, 2011, Houston, TX, https://millercenter.org/the-presidency/presidential-oral-histories/james-baker-iii-oral-history-2011-white-house-chief.
88 Baker with DeFrank, *The Politics of Diplomacy*, 156.
89 James A. Baker III, "Points of Mutual Advantage: Perestroika and American Foreign Policy" (speech, Foreign Policy Association, New York, NY, October 16, 1989). *The Department of State Bulletin*, December 1989, 10-14. https://babel.hathitrust.org/cgi/pt?id=osu.32437010892640;view=1up;seq=490
90 Ibid.
91 Mary Elise Sarotte, *1989: the Struggle to Create Post-Cold War Europe* (Princeton: Princeton University Press, 2009), 36-37.
92 Eduard Shevardnadze *The Future Belongs to Freedom* (Vintage Publishing, 1991)
93 104
94 Jack Matlock, interview with the author, January 16, 2019, Durham, NC.
95 Savranskaya, Blanton, and Zubok, *Masterpieces of History*, 619, "Document No. 110, Soviet Transcript of the Malta Summit, December 2-3, 1989"; Chernyaev quoted in Wohlforth, ed., *Cold War Endgame*, 22.
96 Savranskaya, Blanton, and Zubok, *Masterpieces of History*, 645.
97 Anatoly S. Chernyaev, *My Six Years with Gorbachev*, trans. Robert D. English & Elizabeth Tucker (University Park, Pennsylvania: Pennsylvania State University Press, 2000), 234.
98 Ibid.
99 James A. Baker, III, *"A New Europe, A New Atlanticism; Architecture for a New Era,* Prepared address before the Berlin Press Club, Berlin, December 12, 1988. http://digitalcollections.library.cmu.edu/awweb/awarchive?type=file&item=690688
100 Ibid.

End Notes for Chapter 2

1 Gates, "Soviet Sinology."
2 Boris Meissner, 'Dad neue Denken' Gorbatschows und die Wende in der sowjetischen Deutschlandpolitik,' cited in Daniel S. Hamilton 'Gorbachev and the GDR,' Daniel S. Hamilton & Kristina Spohr eds. *Exiting the Cold War, Entering a New World,* (Washington D.C. John Hopkins University SAIS, 2019), 155.
3 Célia Héron, "Les 20 Ans d'un pique-nique qui a fait basculer l'histoire [Twenty years since a picnic that made history]," *Le Monde,* 19 August 2009, https://www.lemonde.fr/europe/article/2009/08/19/les-20-ans-d-un-pique-nique-qui-a-fait-basculer-l-histoire_1230049_3214.html.
4 James Dobbins, *Foreign Service: Five Decades on the Frontlines of American Diplomacy* (Washington, DC: The Rand Corporation and Brookings Institution Press, 2017).
5 Ibid.
6 Philip Zelikow and Condoleeza Rice, *Germany Unified and Europe Transformed: A Study in Statecraft* (Cambridge: Harvard University Press, 1995), 63.
7 In a survey taken in April 1989, 56 percent of West Germans thought that reunification should remain a goal of FRG policy. This compared to 80 percent of West Germans who had backed reunification in 1987. Emnid Poll reported in *Der Spiegel,* April 10 1989, cited in Zelikow and Rice, *Germany Unified.*
8 Robert Hutchings, Woodrow Wilson Center Public Policy Fellow, interview with the author, March 30, 2016, Washington, DC.
9 Peter W. Rodman, *Presidential Command: Power, Leadership and the Making of Foreign Policy from Richard Nixon to George W. Bush* (New York: Alfred A Knopf, 2009), 182.
10 President George H.W. Bush speech to the citizens of Mainz, May 31, 1989.
11 Diane Sawyer and Sam Donaldson covered live events in Berlin. "ABC's Primetime Live November 9, 1989 Berlin Wall Falls," YouTube video, from ABC primetime news, November 9, 1989, posted by "gb13k," November 8, 2009, https://www.youtube.com/watch?v=BjZ2z0mNGvI.
12 Erich Honecker later complained that "those damn bananas were to blame for the end of the GDR." James A. Baker note to author.
13 Mary Elise Sarotte, *1989: The Struggle to Create Post-Cold War Europe* (Princeton: Princeton University Press, 2009).
14 Baker with Fiffer, *Work Hard,* 286.

15 Kohl was in Poland to commemorate the 50th Anniversary of the Nazi attack on Poland. His presence testified to the improving relations between Poland and West Germany.
16 *Pravda*, November 15, 1989, in *American Diplomacy and the End of the Cold War*, Hutchings, 95.
17 Horst Teltschik, "Gorbachev's reform Policy and the Outlook for East-West Relations, 'Aussempolitik,'" 3 (1989) in *American Diplomacy and the End of the Cold War*, Hutchings, 95.
18 Michael Dobbs, "Gorbachev to Press Arms Cut at Talks," *Washington Post*, November 30, 1989. The Four Powers – the Soviet Union, the United States, the United Kingdom, and France – agreed at the Potsdam Conference in August 1945 to administer Berlin.
19 Frederic Bozo, Marie-Pierre Rey, Leopoldo Nuti, N. Piers Ludlow, eds., *Europe and the End of the Cold War: a Reappraisal* (Abingdon, UK and Oxon, NY: Routledge, 2008) 125.
20 Thatcher, *Downing Street Years*, 794.
21 Three weeks earlier, at a White House gathering of selected journalists, Bush had stated clearly his determination to remain prudent in the face of liberalizing events in Eastern Europe. See New York Times, October 19, 1989.
22 Baker with Fiffer, *Work Hard,* 290.
23 Horst Teltschik conversation with author, March 20, 2015, Washington, DC.
24 James A. Baker notes, November 10, 1989, Folder 11, Box 108, Series 8c, James A. Baker III Papers. This theme was taken from the President's speech to the citizens of Mainz on May 31, 1989: George H.W. Bush, "A Europe Whole and Free" (remarks to the citizens in Mainz, Federal Republic of Germany, May 31, 1989). US Diplomatic Mission to Germany, https://usa.usembassy.de/etexts/ga6-890531.htm.
25 Chris Wallace, Chief Correspondent, ABC, Primetime Live, November 9, 1989, ABC- TV Series 1989, https://www.paleycenter.org/collection/item/?q=in+living+color&f=all&c=tv&advanced.
26 Franz Brotzen, "Baker Institute panel members recall fall of the Berlin Wall, German unification," *Rice News*, Rice University, November 6, 2009, http://news.rice.edu/2009/11/06/baker-institute-panel-members-recall-fall-of-the-berlin-wall-german-unification.
27 Sarotte, *1989,* 53; citing "Mundliche Botschaft des Generalsekretars Gorbatschow an Bundeskanzler Kohl [Oral Message of General Secretary Gorbachev to Federal Chancellor Kohl]," 10, November 1989, doc 80 DESE 505.
28 James Baker notes from meeting with Amb. Dubinin, November 12, 1989, Folder 11, Box 108, Series 8C, James A. Baker III Papers.

29 Robert L. Hutchings, *American Diplomacy and the End of the Cold War: an Insider's Account of U.S Policy in Europe, 1989-1992* (Washington, DC: Woodrow Wilson Center Press, 1997), 9.

30 Robert Hutchings, "American Diplomacy and the End of Cold War in Europe," in *Foreign Policy Breakthroughs: Cases in Successful Diplomacy*, ed. Robert Hutchings and Jeremy Suri (New York: Oxford University Press, 2015), 151.

31 Back benchers are elected members of Parliament who hold no government responsibilities. They are a political force within each party, exercising leverage through their ability to vote out their parliamentary leader, including a sitting prime minister. In November 1990, they voted to remove Thatcher, voting instead for John Major as prime minister.

32 Mikhail Gorbachev and Helmut Kohl, "Joint Declaration of the Federal Republic of Germany and the Soviet Union," *WEU Press Review*, June 13, 1989, https://www.tandfonline.com/doi/abs/10.1080/00396338908442489?needAccess=true&journalCode=tsur20.

33 Record of Conversation between M.S. Gorbachev and Chancellor of FRG H. Kohl, June 13, 1989, Wilson Center Digital Archive, https://digitalarchive.wilsoncenter.org/document/120808.

34 Richard von Weizsacker, "Only Cooperation Can Create Peace," *Die Zeit*, September 30, 1983.

35 Timothy Garton Ash, "In Europe's Name," in *American Diplomacy and the End of the Cold War,* Hutchings.

36 Kristina Spohr, "Precluded or Precedent-Setting?: The 'NATO Enlargement Question' in the Triangular Bonn-Washington-Moscow Diplomacy of 1990-1991," *Journal of Cold War Studies* 14, no.4 (Fall 2012), 10.

37 In June 1945, the Soviets, British, United States, and later the French under the Allied Control Council, agreed to occupy and militarily govern four distinct sectors of Berlin.

38 Chancellor Helmut Kohl, "Ten-Point Plan for German Unity," (speech to the Bundestag (West German legislature) Bonn, West Germany, November 28, 1989), http://germanhistorydocs.ghi-dc.org/sub_document.cfm?document_id=223.

39 Horst Teltschik conversations with the author at the "Conference on German Unification," November 12, 2014, George H.W. Presidential Library and Museum, College Station, TX.

40 James A. Baker III, interview with the author, September 30, 2015, Houston, TX.

41 Statement by Secretary of State Baker, "U.S. Position on the Reunification of Germany," November 29, 1989, in Nancy L. Golden and Sherrill

Brown Wells, eds., *American Foreign Policy: Current Documents 1989* (Washington DC: Department of State Bureau of Public Affairs, Office of the Historian, 1990), 346-347, https://babel.hathitrust.org/cgi/pt?id=mdp.39015024825450;view=1up;seq=398.

42 Horst Teltschik conversation with the author, November 12, 2014.

43 General Secretary Mikhail Gorbachev's speech to the Central Committee, December 9, 1989, in *American Diplomacy and the End of the Cold War*, Hutchings, 104.

44 Don Oberdorfer "Soviets Vowed Not to Suppress Changes in Europe, Baker Says," *Washington Post*, December 8, 1989.

45 Hutchings, *American Diplomacy and the End of the Cold War*, 97.

46 Brent Scowcroft interview with Philip Zelikow et al., November 12 and 13, 1999, Washington, DC.

47 Hutchings, *American Diplomacy at the End of the Cold War*, 98.

48 Jon Meacham, *Destiny and Power: The American Odyssey of George Herbert Walker Bush* (New York: Random House, 2015), 623.

49 Dobbins, *Foreign Service*, 72.

50 Barry Schweid, "Baker, in Bold Visit to Potsdam, Offers Aid to East Germany," Associated Press, December 12, 1989.

51 St. Louis Fed's historical USD-DM exchange rate tool: https://fred.stlouisfed.org/series/EXGEUS. The exchange rates for DM:USD for September 1990, when the Treaty on the Final Settlement was signed, were 1.5701DM to 1USD; and November 1989 when the wall was breached were 1.8300DM to 1USD. The range of financial aid is perplexing until one understands that much of the financial support came in credit guarantees to FRG banks, as well as donations of coal and potatoes that do not show up as financial aid.

52 Bush and Scowcroft, *A World Transformed*, 77-78.

53 Ibid.

54 This was the Treaty on European Union, also known as the Maastricht Treaty. It was signed by the heads of government in Maastricht, the Netherlands in December 1991.

55 Robert Hutchings, interview with the author, March 30, 2016, Washington, DC.

56 Notes written by James A. Baker for the First Cabinet meeting, January 23, 1989, Box 108, James A. Baker III Papers.

57 Timothy Garton Ash, "The Crisis of Europe: How the Union Came Together and Why It's Falling Apart," *Foreign Affairs*, September/October 2012.

58 Dobbins, *Life in the Foreign Service*.

59 Patrick Salmon, Keith Hamilton, Stephen Robert Twigge, eds., *German Unification 1989-1990,* Documents on British Policy Overseas, series 3, vol. 7, no. 47 (Abingdon, UK: Routledge 2009), 22 and 262.
60 Washington telegram No. 240, January 29, 1990. British Foreign Office Material III, Georgetown University 1989/90.
61 Zelikow and Rice, *Germany Unified and Europe Transformed,* 173.
62 Referring to West Germany. Salmon et al., *German Unification 1989-1990,* xxii.
63 Mark Kramer, "The Myth of a No-NATO-Enlargement Pledge to Russia," *The Washington Quarterly* 32, no. 2 (April 2009), 45.
64 Hans-Dietrich Genscher, "German Unity within a European Framework," (speech, Tutzing Protestant Academy, Tutzing, Germany, January 31, 1990).
65 Spohr, "Precluded or Precedent-Setting," 13.
66 Zelikow and Rice, *Germany Unified and Europe Transformed,* 176.
67 Zelikow and Rice, *Germany Unified and Europe Transformed,* 183.
68 Horst Teltschik, *329 Tage: Innenansichten der Einigung* [329 Days: Internal Views of the Agreement] (Berlin: Siedler Verlag, 1991), 110.
69 James A. Baker III, "Notes from February 2, 1990 Press briefing following meeting with FRG Foreign Minister Genscher," February 2, 1990. Series 12, Subseries 8c, Folder 14. James A. Baker III Papers.
70 Kramer citing Genscher bei Baker in Washington: Gesprache uber NATO-Mitgliedschaft bisher zu statisch," *Frankfurter Allgemeine Zeitung,* February 3, 1990. Cited in Zelikow and Rice, *Germany Unified and Europe Transformed,* 176.
71 Spohr, "Precluded or Precedent-Setting?" 18.
72 Thomas A. Friedman, "Upheaval in the East: the Germanys; Baker and West German Envoy Discuss Reunification Issues," *New York Times,* February 3, 1990, http://www.nytimes.com/1990/02/03/world/upheaval-east-germanys-baker-west-german-envoy-discuss-reunification-issues.html.
73 Beschloss and Talbott, *At the Highest Levels,* 182. Dennis Ross spoke freely with Beschloss after the meetings in order to create a contemporaneous report of the meeting.
74 Ibid.
75 Ibid.
76 James A. Baker III, "Notes from 2/7-9/90 Ministerial Meeting with Foreign Minister Shevardnadze," Moscow. MC197#, Series 12, Folder 13, James A. Baker III Papers.
77 Zelikow and Rice, *Germany Unified and Europe Transformed,* 180. As members of the NSC, both authors therefore had access to Robert Zoellick's notes taken during the meeting with Shevardnadze.

78 Ibid.
79 Dennis Ross, "Report of James A Baker, III meeting with Shevardnadze, February 8, 1990," Mudd Library, MC 197#, Series 12, Folder 13, James A. Baker III Papers.
80 Ibid.
81 Zelikow and Rice, *Germany Unified and Europe Transformed*, 182.
82 Salmon et al., eds., *German Unification 1989-1990*, 262.
83 "Mutzelburg an Ministerburo; Betr: Gesprach BM mit dem britischen AM Hurd am 6. Februar 1990," [Mutzelburg to Ministry Bureau; Betr: Talked BM with British FM Hurd on February 6, 1990] February 7, 1990, in "Aktenfreigabe aus Anlass des 20. Jahrestages von Mauerfall und Wiedervereinigung," [File Release on the Occasion of the Twentieth Anniversary of the Fall of the Berlin Wall and Reunification] in the Politisches Archiv, Auswärtiges Amt, Berlin 178.927E, 3; cited in Spohr, "Precluded or Precedent-Setting," 20.
84 Aleksandr Galkin and Anatolij Tschernjajew, eds., *Michail Gorbatschow und die deutsche Frage; Sowjetische Dokument 1986-1991* [Mikhail Gorbachev and the German question: Soviet Documents 1986-1991] (Munich: Oldenbourg 2011), Doc. 71, 312; cited in Spohr, "Precluded or Precedent-Setting," 22. The editors have collected documents from the Gorbachev Foundation. These records reveal more of Soviet leaders or their note takers believed was said, in contrast to the Western records, which reflect what was actually said.
85 Ibid.
86 Hanns Jürgen Küsters and Daniel Hofmann, eds., *Dokumente zur Deutschlandpolitik: Deutsche Einheit – Sonderedition aus den Akten des Bunkeskanzleramtes 1989/90* (Munich: R. Oldenbourg Verlag, 1998), Doc. 173, 794; cited in Spohr, "Precluded or Precedent-Setting," 23.
87 Philip Zelikow, then NSC Deputy Director for Europe, interview with the author, October 5, 2018, Charlottesville, VA.
88 Ibid.
89 *Hearing on US Policy toward NATO Enlargement, Before the House Comm. on International Relations*, 104th Cong. 31 (1996) (testimony of former US Ambassador to the Soviet Union Jack Matlock).
90 "Did the West Break Its Promise to Moscow?" *Der Spiegel*, November 26, 2009, http://www.spiegel.de/international/world/nato-s-eastward-expansion-did-the-west-break-its-promise-to-moscow-a-663315.html.
91 Russian President Dmitry Medvedev interview with *Der Spiegel*, "Oil and Gas is Our Drug," *Der Spiegel*, November 9, 2009, http://www.spiegel.de/international/world/spiegel-interview-with-russian-president-dmitry-medvedev-oil-and-gas-is-our-drug-a-660114-3.html.
92 Ambassador Jack Matlock's telephone interview with the author.

93 Aleksandr Galkin and Anatolij Tschernjajew, eds., Rose Blanchard, trans., "Transcript of February 9, 1990 conversation between Gorbachev, Baker, and Shevardnadze," *Michail Gorbatschow und die deutsche Frage [Mikhail Gorbachev and the German question]*, 338.
94 James A. Baker III, meeting with the author, February 11, 2015, Houston, TX.
95 "A conversation with Sergei Lavrov, Russian Foreign Minister," *Charlie Rose Show*, PBS, September 25, 2008. Cited in Mark Kramer, "The Myth of a No-NATO-Enlargement Pledge to Russia," 40.
96 Letter from President Bush to Chancellor Kohl, George Bush Presidential Library and Museum, College Station, TX. See also, transcript of telephone conversation that followed the letter at https://digitalarchive.wilsoncenter.org/document/116233.pdf?v=2f57a8d6362a28058115bc202e0a6d21.
97 Horst Teltschik, interview with the author, November 10, 2014, College Station, TX.
98 Spohr, *Precluded or Precedent-Setting*, 38.
99 Horst Teltschik, *329 Tage*.
100 Andreas Rodder, Federic Bozo, and Marie Elise Sarotte, eds., *German Reunification: A Multinational History*, Cold War History (New York: Routledge, 2017).
101 Treaty on the Final Settlement with Respect to Germany, Federal Republic of Germany-German Democratic Republic-France-U.S.S.R.-U.K.-U.S., September 12, 1990, 1696 U.N.T.S. 115, at 124 https://treaties.un.org/doc/Publication/UNTS/Volume%201696/v1696.pdf.

END NOTES FOR CHAPTER 3

1 David Kynaston, *Family Britain 1951-57: Tales of a New Jerusalem* (London: Bloomsbury, 2009), 81.
2 Baker with Fiffer, *Work Hard*, 10.
3 James A. Baker III remarks to the Foreign Policy Association of New York, November 2015 (check date) Author's notes from the meeting.
4 William Safire, "Free the Baltics," *New York Times*, May 25, 1989, www.nytimes.com/1989/05/25/opinion/essay-free-the-baltics.html.
5 Meacham, *Destiny & Power*, 600.
6 Ambassador James Lilley with Jeffrey Lilley, *China Hands: Nine Decades of Adventure, Espionage and Diplomacy in Asia*, (New York: Public Affairs, 2004), 308.
7 Ibid., 310.

8   Stapleton Roy, the Executive Secretary of the Department of State (1989-1991) saw the cables from Beijing and walked them across to Secretary Baker's office.
9   George H.W. Bush, *All the Best, George Bush: My Life in Letters and Other Writings* (New York: Scribner, 2013), 300.
10 Ezra F. Vogel, *Den Xiaoping and the Transformation of China*, (Cambridge, Massachusetts: TheBelknap Press of Harvard University Press, 2011) 224, 267-268
11 Jeffrey A. Engel, ed., *The China Diary of George H.W. Baker: The Making of a Global President* (Princeton, NJ: Princeton University Press, 2008), 457.
12 Stapleton Roy, US Ambassador to China 1991-1995, interview with the author, November 17, 2016, Woodrow Wilson Center, Washington DC.
13 Lilley and Lilley, *China Hands*, 302.
14 Margaret Tutwiler interview with the author, September 9, 2015, CIT Offices, Washington, DC.
15 Ibid., 328.
16 Meacham, *Destiny & Power*, 577-78.
17 The United States proposed to grant Most Favored Nation status to China with a view to increasing trade. MFN would give China trade advantages such as reduced tariffs on imported goods.
18 George H.W. Bush's personal diary, quoted in *The China Diary*, 457.
19 Meacham, *Destiny & Power*, 579.
20 Bush, *All the Best*, 430.
21 Lilley and Lilley, *China Hands*, 338.
22 Meacham, *Destiny & Power*, 580.
23 Fang was known as China's Andrei Sakharov.
24 Raymond Burghardt conversation with the author, April 27, 2016, Washington, DC.
25 Lilley and Lilley, *China Hands*, 334.
26 Raymond Burghardt conversation with the author, April 27, 2016, Washington, DC.
27 *Hearing on US Policy Toward China*, before the Senate Committee on Foreign Relations, 101st Congress, 2 (1990) (statement of Claiborne Pell, D-RI).
28 *Hearing on United States Policy Toward China*, before the House of Representatives Committee on Foreign Affairs, 101st Congress, 2 (1990) (statement of William S. Broomfield, R-MI).
29 Neville Chamberlain, "Peace for Our Time" (speech, 10 Downing Street, London, September 30, 1938). Euro Docs archive, Harold B. Lee Library, Brigham Young University. https://eudocs.lib.byu.edu/index.php/Neville_Chamberlain%27s_%22Peace_For_Our_Time%22_speech.

30 *Hearing on United States Policy Toward China*, before the House of Representatives Committee on Foreign Affairs, 2, statement of William S. Broomfield.
31 Ibid., 20 (statement of Deputy Secretary of State Lawrence Eagleburger).
32 *Hearing on US Policy Toward China*, before the Senate Committee on Foreign Relations, 8, statement of Lawrence Eagleburger.
33 Ibid., 24 (statement of Joseph Biden, D-DE). In 1989 and with Chinese agreement, the US had placed monitoring devices along China's northern border with the Soviet Union to detect the movement of Soviet troops.
34 Ibid., 25.
35 Ibid.
36 Don Oberdorfer, *The Turn: From the Cold War to a New Era, the United States and the Soviet Union, 1983-1990* (New York: Poseidon Press, 1991), 359-360.
37 Ibid., 360.
38 Ibid.
39 James Baker interview with Dan Rather of *CBS Evening News*, May 16, 1990, Moscow, Russia. MC#198, Box 163, Folder 7. James A. Baker III Papers.
40 Jack Matlock, *Autopsy on an Empire*, 231.
41 Ibid.
42 Matthew Fisher, "Moscow Condemns 'Hysteria in Baltics,'" *New York Times*, August 27, 1989, http://www.nytimes.com/1989/08/27/world/moscow-condemns-nationalist-virus-in-3-baltic-lands.
43 Beschloss and Talbott, *At the Highest Levels*, 175.
44 Alexsandr Yakovlev, the "godfather of glasnost." Quoted in Matlock, *Autopsy on an Empire*, 270.
45 Beschloss and Talbott, *At the Highest Levels*, 173.
46 Ibid., 173-174.
47 "Statement by Press Secretary Fitzwater on the Restoration of Lithuanian Independence," March 11, 1990. The American Presidency Project, http://www.presidency.ucsb.edu/ws/index.php?pid=18240.
48 According to the 1980 census there were 743,000 Americans of Lithuanian origin, 92,000 Latvians and 26,000 Estonians. See Robert Pear, "Baltic Americans Watch the Soviets with High Hope but Deep Skepticism," *New York Times*, October 27, 1988, http://www.nytimes.com/1988/10/27/us/washington-talk-ethnic-organizations-baltic-americans-watch-soviets-with-high.html.
49 Linas Kučinskas, "Lithuania's Independence: the Litmus Test for Democracy in the USSR." *Lituanus: Lithuanian Quarterly Journal of Arts and Sciences* 37, no.3 (Fall 1991). http://www.lituanus.org/1991_3/91_3_01.htm.
50 Beschloss and Talbott, *At the Highest Levels*, 197.

51 Ibid.
52 Susan Page, "Bush Warns the Soviets," *NY Newsday*, March 21, 1990.
53 http://www.presidency.ucsb.edu/ws/?pid=18269. See also Andrew Rosenthal, "U.S. in Sharper Tone, is Worried by Soviets' Pressure on Lithuania," *New York Times*, March 21, 1990. https://www.nytimes.com/1990/03/21/world/upheaval-east-us-sharper-tone-worried-soviets-pressure-lithuania.html.
54 Oberdorfer, *The Turn*, 402-403.
55 Under Gorbachev's leadership, the Soviet Communist party should no longer play a dominant role in the management of the Soviet Union. He therefore chose to become President of the Soviet state and relinquished his title as the General Secretary of the Communist party.
56 David Remnick, "Lithuanians Protest Soviet Use of Force: Landsbergis Blames Gorbachev and US," *Washington Post*, March 28, 1990.
57 Ibid., 404.
58 James Gerstenzang, "Bush Tells Gorbachev He's Not Trying to Make Trouble: Lithuania: A private message reiterates U.S. backing for a peaceful solution to the secession dilemma," *Los Angeles Times*, March 31, 1990. http://articles.latimes.com/1990-03-31/news/mn-195_1_soviet-union.
59 James A. Baker III, "Democracy & American Diplomacy," (speech to the World Affairs Council of Dallas, Dallas, TX, March 31, 1990).
60 Oberdorfer, *The Turn*, 403.
61 Margaret Thatcher, *The Downing Street Years*, 801.
62 Baker, *Politics of Diplomacy*, 240.
63 Ibid.
64 Oberdorfer, *The Turn*, 404.
65 David Hoffman and Ann Devroy, "White House Tones Down Its Comments," *Washington Post*, March 18, 1990.
66 William Safire, "World to Vilnius: Suffer," *New York Times*, April 23, 1990, http://www.nytimes.com/1990/04/23/opinion/essay-world-to-vilnius-suffer.html
67 William Safire, "The Grave Consequence" *New York Times*, April 2, 1990, https://www.nytimes.com/1990/04/02/opinion/essay-the-grave-consequence.html.
68 Richard Lacayo et al, "A Hurry-Up-Summit: Despite Lithuania and strategic-arms talks that have hit some snags, the Bush-Gorbachev meeting is pushed up to May 30," *Time*, April 16, 1990.
69 Richard L. Berke, "Evolution in Europe; 9 G.O.P. Senators Attack Bush on Lithuania," *New York Times*, April 28, 1990 http://www.nytimes.com/1990/04/28/world/evolution-in-europe-9-gop-senators-attack-bush-on-lithuania.html.

70 Ibid.
71 Beschloss and Talbott, *At the Highest Levels,* 211.
72 Assistant Secretary for Human Rights Richard Schifter's report of Baker's meeting, James A. Baker III Papers.
73 Beschloss and Talbott, *At the Highest Levels,* 212.
74 "The visiting prime minister of Lithuania criticized President Bush Friday for doing nothing more than calling for 'good faith.'" From Vincent Schodolski, "Latvia OK's Slow Break with USSR," *Chicago Tribune,* May 5, 1990. http://www.chicagotribune.com/news/ct-xpm-1990-05-05-9002060171-story.html.
75 George F. Will, "Bush: Read My Polls" *Newsweek,* May 7, 1990.
76 Leon Daniel, "Pressure increases for freedom in Baltics," UPI, August 22, 1991. https://www.upi.com/Archives/1991/08/22/Pressure-increases-for-freedom-in-Baltics/2446682833600/.
77 Susan Baker interview with the author, February 12, 2015, Houston, TX.
78 Maureen Dowd, "White House Sticks to its Subdued Reaction to Baltic Crackdown," *New York Times,* January 15, 1991. http://www.nytimes.com/1991/01/15/world/soviet-crackdown-washington-white-house-sticks-its-subdued-reaction-baltic.html.
79 In October 1956, Israel together with France and Great Britain had invaded Egypt to remove General Abdul Nasser and gain control over the Suez Canal. President Eisenhower did not support the French and British action and Nasser succeeded in nationalizing the canal. In the midst of this crisis, Khrushchev sent troops into Budapest where thousands of Hungarian protesters had taken to the streets demanding a more democratic political system and freedom from Soviet oppression.
80 Beschloss and Talbott, *At the Highest Levels,* 307.
81 George H. W. Bush. "Remarks on Soviet Military Intervention in Lithuania," (remarks and a question-and-answer session with reporters, January 13, 1991, South Lawn of the White House) http://www.presidency.ucsb.edu/ws/index.php?pid=19216.
82 Bessmertnykh quoted in quoted in William C., ed., "Part I: Oral History: The Princeton Conference" in *Cold War Endgame: Oral History, Analysis, Debates* (University Park, Pennsylvania: Pennsylvania State University Press, 2003), 25.
83 *Hearing on Examining America's Role in the World,* before the Senate Committee on Foreign Relations, 114th Congress, 5-6 (2016) (statement of James A. Baker III).
84 Ibid., 5.

END NOTES FOR CHAPTER 4

1. Richard E. Ericson, "The Classical Soviet-Type Economy: Nature of the System and Implications for Reform" The Journal of Economic Perspectives, Vol 5, No 4. Autumn 1991, 11. Https://www.jstor.org/stable/1942862
2. GOSPLAN was the state planning committee. Ibid., 15.
3. Gail Sheehy, *The Man Who Changed the World; the Lives of Mikhail S. Gorbachev*, (New York, HarperCollins Publishers, 1990), 108.
4. William Taubman, *Gorbachev: His Life and Times*, (New York: W.W. Norton & Co., 2017.
5. Richard Parker, "Inside the Collapsing Soviet Economy," *The Atlantic*, June 1990, https://www.theatlantic.com/magazine/archive/1990/06/inside-the-collapsing-soviet-economy/303870/
6. Ibid.,52
7. Anders Aslund, *Russia's Capitalist Revolution: Why Market Reform Succeeded and Democracy Failed*, Peter Institute for International Economics 20007, 55
8. Ibid., 61-62.
9. Taubman, *Gorbachev*, 450.
10. Ibid., 79.
11. "Interview with Boris Yeltsin," *The Year of Yeltsin, Decade of Democracy & other articles*, Newsweek Magazine: International Edition, January 6, 1992
12. Charles P. Wallace, "7 Firms Negotiate for Soviet Trade: Consortium Holds Exploratory Talks on Joint Ventures," *Los Angeles Times*, April 14 1988, http://articles.latimes.com/1988-04-14/business/fi-1834_1_joint-venture-agreements.
13. Francis X. Clines, "Soviets and 6 U.S. Concerns Sign Trade Pact," *The New York Times*, March 31, 1989, https://www.nytimes.com/1989/03/31/business/soviets-and-6-us-concerns-sign-trade-pact.html.
14. By December 1991, the American Trade Consortium would fold, and in January 1992, Chevron would fire James Giffen.
15. Parker, *The Atlantic,* 20.
16. The Central Intelligence Agency (CIA) estimated a growth rate, on average of 1.5 percent.
17. James A. Baker III, *The Politics of Diplomacy: Revolution, War and Peace, 1989-1992*, with Thomas M. DeFrank (New York: G. P. Putnam's Sons, 1995), 63.
18. According to Gosplan estimates, this "second economy" may have accounted for $150 billion a year, equivalent to 11 percent of Soviet gross domestic product. Parker, "Inside the Collapsing Soviet Economy," *The Atlantic*, June 1990.
19. Ibid.

20 Taubmann, *Gorbachev*, 450.
21 James Noren and Laurie Kurtzweg, "The Soviet Economy Unravels: 1985-1991" in *The Former Soviet Union in Transition*, Study Papers Submitted to the Joint Economic Committee, Congress of the United States (1993), 14.
22 *Hearing on The Imperatives of Economic Reform: Change in Soviet and East European Economics*, before the House Ways and Means Committee, 101st Congress, 14 (1990) (statement of Hon. James A. Baker III as prepared for delivery);
23 Ibid., 613.
24 Ibid., 625-626.
25 Ibid., 627.
26 Ibid., 632
27 Baker with DeFrank, *Politics of Diplomacy*, 248-249.
28 Ibid
29 David Hoffman, "Gorbachev's Appeals for Aid Show Increased Urgency," *Washington Post*, July 14, 1990. https://www.washingtonpost.com/archive/politics/1990/07/14/gorbachevs-appeals-for-aid-show-increased-urgency.
30 Bush and Scowcroft, *World Transformed*, 276-77, 286-87.
31 David Rosenbaum, "The Houston Summit: Three Key Economic Issues Undecided as Meeting Ends," *New York Times*, July 12, 1990, http://www.nytimes.com/1990/07/12/business/the-houston-summit-three-key-economic-issues-undecided-as-meeting-ends.html.
32 Ibid.
33 The Treaty on the Final Settlement with Respect to Germany was signed in Moscow on September 12, 1990.
34 Teltschik, *329 Tage* for May 15, 1990. Teltschik and the financiers met with "every significant politician in the Soviet Union." He came away convinced that Kohl was right to offer credit to the Soviet leadership at this time.
35 Mary Elise Sarotte, *1989*, 159-160.
36 Teltschik, *329 Tage*, 204.
37 Ibid., 221, 226-27.
38 Serge Schmemann," Evolution in Europe: Kohl Sees Soviets Amid Upbeat Mood," *New York Times*, July 16, 1990, http://www.nytimes.com/1990/07/16/world/evolution-in-europe-kohl-sees-soviets-amid-upbeat-mood.
39 Stent, *Russia and Germany Reborn,*138, citing Deutsche Bank President Alfred Herrhausen in *Der Spiegel*, November 20, 1989. See also *329 Tage*, Teltschik's recollections of May 8, 1990.
40 Stent, 139
41 Ibid.
42 Palazchenko, *My Years with Gorbachev and Shevardnadze*, 204.

43 In the meantime, Yeltsin was elected chairman of the Presidium of the Supreme Soviet and subsequently resigned six weeks later.
44 "Gorbachev introduces rescue plan for economy," Associated Press, October 17, 1990. http://journaltimes.com/news/national/gorbachev-introduces-rescue-plan-for-economy/article_e1090658-c708-5c5a-926c-d0195d472f4d.html
45 Ibid.
46 Young President Organizations is a global organization of young chief executives founded in 1950. Members must be under 45 years old and hold the top position in a qualifying company.
47 James D. Jamieson, Personal Recollections of his visit to the Soviet Union September 1990 (unpublished).
48 344 Ibid.
49 Ibid.
50 *Hearing on U.S.-U.S.S.R. Economic Relations*, before the Senate Committee on Finance, 101st Congress, 4 (1989) (statement of James A. Baker III), https://www.finance.senate.gov/imo/media/doc/hrg101-641.pdf.
51 Ibid., 8.
52 Most-favored-nation (MFN) treats other nations equally under World Trade Organization (WTO) agreements. It prevents countries from discriminating between their trading partners. Consequently, when MFN is granted, a lower customs duty rate on one product must be offered to all other WTO members. The Soviet Union was not a member of the WTO, but nonetheless sought MFN status.
53 *Hearing on U.S.-U.S.S.R. Economic Relations*, before the Senate Committee on Finance, 101st Congress, 25 (1989) (statement of Sen. Moynihan).
54 Caryle Murphy, "Saudis Rewarding Soviets with Loan of $1 billion," *Washington Post*, November 29, 1990, https://www.washingtonpost.com/archive/politics/1990/11/29/saudis-rewarding-soviets-with-loan-of-1-billion
55 Stephen K. McNees, "The 1990-91 Recession in Historical Perspective," *New England Economic Review*, January/February 1992, 15-18.
56 By 1992, the Soviet Union no longer existed and $700 million of this amount when to the newly independent state of Russia.
57 Richard F. Kaufman, John Pearce Hardt, *The Former Soviet Union in Transition* (Armonk, NY: M.E. Sharpe, 1993).
58 Graham Allison and Grigory Yavlinsky, *Window of Opportunity*: The Grand Bargain for Democracy in the Soviet Union, (New York, Pantheon Books, 1991), 23
59 Ibid., 28.
60 Ibid.

61 "Soviet Trade Opportunities," Hearing before the Committee on Commerce, Science and Transportation, United States Senate, 102nd Congress, 1st Session, July 31 1991, 17.
62 Ibid.,
63 Brent Scowcroft, interview with Philip Zelikow et al, November 12-13, 1999, Washington, DC.
64 Andrew Rosenthal, "US Seeks to Avoid Gorbachev Talks," *New York Times*, May 22, 1991, https://www.nytimes.com/1991/05/22/world/us-seeks-to-avoid-gorbachev-talks.html.
65 R.W. Apple, "Bailing Out Soviets: Bush Is Cautious," *New York Times*, June 12, 1991, https://www.nytimes.com/1991/06/12/world/bailing-out-soviets-bush-is-cautious.html.
66 Ibid.
67 Beschloss & Talbott, *At the Highest Levels*, 401.
68 R.W. Apple, "Summit in London; 7 nations voice support for Gorbachev," *New York Times*, July 17, 1991, http://www.nytimes.com/1991/07/17/world/summit-in-london-7-nations-voice-support-for-gorbachev.html.
69 Ibid.
70 Beschloss & Talbott, *At the Highest Levels*, 402.
71 Boris Yeltsin's remarks to Bush and Baker, Camp David, February 2, 1992. Nicholas Burns archive, George H.W. Bush Library, College Station, Texas.

End Notes for Chapter 5

1 General Secretary Mikhail Gorbachev, "Speech to the United Nations," (speech, New York City, December 7, 1988) C-SPAN, https://www.c-span.org/video/?5292-1/gorbachev-united-nations.
2 Five distinct guerilla groups joined under the umbrella of the FMLN in 1980: *Fuerzas Populares de Liberación Farabundo Martí* (FPL); *Ejército Revolucionario del Pueblo* (ERP); *Resistencia Nacional* (RN); *Partido Comunista Salvadoreño* (PCS); and *Partido Revolucionario de los Trabajadores Centroamericanos* (PRTC).
3 Yuri Pavlov, *Soviet-Cuban Alliances, 1959-1991*, 2nd ed. (Miami: North-South Center Press, 1996), 146
4 Beschloss and Talbott, *At the Highest Levels*, 57.
5 Ibid.
6 Bernard Aronson, "Preliminary Thoughts about Central America," (unpublished manuscript, February 2, 1989), Aronson Personal Papers, 4.
7 Ibid., 6.

8   William M. LeoGrande and Peter Kornbluh, *Back Channel to Cuba: The Hidden History of Negotiations between Washington and Havana* (Chapel Hill: UNC Press Books, 2014), 161.
9   Ibid., 227.
10 James A. Baker III, interview with the author, September 30, 2015, Houston, TX.
11 Pavlov, *Soviet-Cuban Alliances,* 120-121.
12 Baker with DeFrank, *The Politics of Diplomacy,* 49.
13 Cresencio Arcos, interview with the author, September 7, 2005, Washington, D.C.
14 Ibid.
15 The Senate did not block military aid to El Salvador.
16 H.R.1750 - 101st Congress (1989-1990): To Implement the Bipartisan Accord on Central America, https://www.congress.gov/bill/101st-congress/house-bill/1750/
17 Bernard Weinraub, "Bush and Congress Sign Policy Accord on Aid to Contras," *New York Times,* March 25, 1989, http://www.nytimes.com/1989/03/25/world/bush-and-congress-sign-policy-accord-on-aid-to-contras.html.
18 Pavlov, *Soviet-Cuban Alliances,* 133-134.
19 US State Department, cable 384861, December 2, 1989.
20 S.2954 - El Salvador Military Aid Reduction and Restrictions Act of 1990, 101st Congress (1989-1990) https://www.congress.gov/bill/101st-congress/senate-bill/2954/text
21 "Substitution Documents on Noriega Payments," National Security Council, William Pryce Files, CF00732-020. George H.W. Bush Presidential Library and Museum.
22 John D. Negroponte interview with author, January 20, 2019, Washington, D.C.
23 "Panama: Election Theft in Progress," February 11, 1989, Intelligence Analysis Report SC#12198-99, William Pryce Files. George H.W. Bush Presidential Library and Museum.
24 Yongqing Douglas Yang, "The Panamanian Paradox: A President's Struggle to Remove Manuel Noriega" (bachelor's thesis, University of Wisconsin-Madison, 2010) https://liberalarts.temple.edu/sites/liberalarts/files/YangPanamanianParadox.pdf.
25 Jill Smolowe, James Carney & Ricardo Chavira, "Panama Sparring (Again) With a Dictator," *Time,* May 8, 1989.
26 Baker with DeFrank, *The Politics of Diplomacy,* 184.
27 Lindsey Gruson, "Noriega Stealing Election, Carter Says," *New York Times,* May 9, 1989, https://www.nytimes.com/1989/05/09/world/noriega-stealing-election-carter-says.html.

28 "Points to be made re: Panama," National Security Council memorandum, May 11 1989, Nicholas Rostow Files, CF00741-020. George H.W. Bush Presidential Library and Museum.
29 Ibid.
30 "Draft Resolution from 21st meeting of Consultation of Ministers of Foreign Affairs [of the Organization of American States]," May 17, 1989, William Pryce Files, CF01577-016. George H.W. Bush Presidential Library and Museum.
31 Baker with DeFrank, *The Politics of Diplomacy*, 184.
32 Demetrios J. Caraley, *The New American Interventionism: Lessons from Successes and Failures*, (New York: Columbia University Press, 1999). 103
33 American Embassy Panama cable to Secretary of State James Baker, "Log of October 3, 1989 Coup Attempt," William Pryce Files, CF00732-008. George H.W. Bush Presidential Library and Museum.
34 Eloy Aguilar, "Noriega Dodges a Bullet, But the Gun May Still be Loaded," Associated Press, October 5, 1989.
35 James Baker, "Instruction to Diplomatic Posts in Foreign States," October 14, 1989, White House Office of Records Management General File, CO121-164803. George H.W. Bush Presidential Library and Museum.
36 Norman Kempster and Sara Fritz, "Mutiny not a U.S. Operation, Bush Asserts," *Los Angeles Times*, October 4, 1989, http://articles.latimes.com/1989-10-04/news/mn-481_1_united-states.
37 Timothy McNulty, "US Defends Inaction in Panama Uprising," *Chicago Tribune*, October 5, 1989, http://articles.chicagotribune.com/1989-10-05/news/8901190571_1_rebels-hands-rebel-leaders-gen-manuel-noriega.
38 Baker with DeFrank, *The Politics of Diplomacy*, 187.
39 "Excerpts from U.S. Account of Officer's Death in Panama," *New York Times*, December 18, 1989, http://www.nytimes.com/1989/12/18/world/excerpts-from-us-account-of-officer-s-death-in-panama.html.
40 Michael Gordon, "U.S. Troops Move in Panama in Effort to Seize Noriega; Gunfire is Heard in Capital," *New York Times*, December 20, 1989, https://www.nytimes.com/1989/12/20/world/us-troops-move-in-panama-in-effort-to-seize-noriega-gunfire-is-heard-in-capital.html.
41 President George H.W. Bush, "Address to the Nation on Panama," (speech, Washington, D.C. December 20, 1989) Miller Center of Public Affairs, https://millercenter.org/the-presidency/presidential-speeches/december-20-1989-address-nation-panama.
42 Mary Sheridan, "Holy See Urging Noriega to Leave Embassy Refuge," Associated Press, December 29, 1989.

43 James Baker, "Talking Points." December 25, 1989, David Pacelli Files, CF01576-006. George H.W. Bush Presidential Library and Museum.
44 John Sununu telephone interview with the author, June 18, 2018.
45 Estimated Panamanian casualties were 450, including 2-300 civilian casualties. 23 Americans were killed in action and 324 were wounded.
46 Andrew Rosenthal, "Noriega gives himself up to U.S. Military," *New York Times*, January 4, 1990, http://www.nytimes.com/1990/01/04/world/noriega-s-surrender-overview-noriega-gives-himself-up-us-military-flown-florida.html.
47 Greg Grandin, "How the 1989 War on Manuel Noriega's Panama Super-Charged US Militarism," *The Nation*, May 30, 2017, https://www.thenation.com/article/1989-war-panama-super-charged-us-militarism/.
48 Michael R Gordon, "Stealth's Panama Mission Reported Marred by Error, *New York Times*, April 4, 1990. https://www.nytimes.com/1990/04/04/us/stealth-s-panama-mission-reported-marred-by-error.html
49 Mark Uhlig, "Turnover in Nicaragua; Nicaraguan Opposition Routs Sandinistas; U.S. Pledges Aid, Tied to Orderly Turnover," New York Times, February 27, 1990, https://www.nytimes.com/1990/02/27/world/turnover-nicaragua-nicaraguan-opposition-routs-sandinistas-us-pledges-aid-tied.html.
50 Diana Villiers Negroponte, *Seeking Peace in El Salvador: the Struggle to Reconstruct a Nation at the End of the Cold War* (New York: Palgrave Macmillan, 2012).
51 John D. Negroponte interview with the author, August 7, 2018, Greenville, ME.
52 Rachel McCulloch, "The United States-Canada Free Trade Agreement," *Proceedings of the Academy of Political Science* 37, no. 4 (1990): 79-89.

END NOTES FOR CHAPTER 6

1 George H.W. Bush, "National Security Directive 26: U.S. Policy Toward the Persian Gulf," October 2, 1989, http://fas.org/irp/offdocs/nsd/nsd26.pdf.
2 Ibid.,
3 S. PRT 102-5, Department of State, "Country Reports for Human Rights Practices for 1990," Joint Committee Report submitted to the Committee on Foreign Relations, US Senate, and the Foreign Affairs Committee, US House of Representatives, at 1457 (1990). https://babel.hathitrust.org/cgi/pt?id=ien.35556020518650;view=1up;seq=1475.
4 William Safire, "Baltics to Baghdad," *New York Times,* March 30, 1990, https://www.nytimes.com/1990/03/30/opinion/essay-baltics-to-baghdad.html.

5 Richard Haass interview with Stephen Knott and Bob Strong, George H.W. Bush Oral History Project, University of Virginia Miller Center, May 27, 2004, New York, NY, http://millercenter.org/the-presidency/presidential-oral-histories/richard-haass-oral-history-special-assistant-president.

6 Don Oberdorfer, "Missed Signals in the Middle East," *Washington Post*, March 17, 1991, https://www.washingtonpost.com/archive/lifestyle/magazine/1991/03/17/missed-signals-in-the-middle-east/23132c7e-ba22-48dc-9533-84558f0d2cb5/?utm_term=.a8145199e06b.

7 Ibid.

8 Alan Cowell, "Iraq Chief Boasting of Poison Gas Warns of Disaster if Israel Strikes," *New York Times*, April 3, 1990, http://www.nytimes.com/1990/04/03/world/iraq-chief-boasting-of-poison-gas-warns-of-disaster-if-israelis-strike.html.

9 Ibid.

10 Craig Unger, *House of Bush, House of Saud: the Secret Relationship between the World's Most Powerful Dynasties* (New York: Simon & Schuster, 2004), 130.

11 Nora Boustany, "Doctrine, Dreams Drive Saddam Hussein," *Washington Post*, August 12, 1990, http://www.washingtonpost.com/wp-srv/inatl/longterm/iraq/stories/doctrine081290.htm.

12 Don Oberdorfer, *Washington Post*.

13 Boustany, *Washington Post*.

14 Ibid.

15 Oberdorfer, *Washington Post*.

16 Thomas Pickering interview with author, July 1, 2015, Washington, D.C.

17 State Department, "Text of Joint Statement and Press Conference by Secretary of State James A. Baker, III and Foreign Minister Eduard Shevardnadze at Vukunovo [sic] II Airport, Moscow," news release, Federal News Service, August 3, 1990.

18 Margaret G. Warner, "The Moscow Connection," *Newsweek*, September 17, 1990.

19 Ibid.

20 The Military Committee was reactivated, but not allowed to dilute the national command structure of the national fleets in the Gulf.

21 Warner, *Newsweek*.

22 Prime Minister Margaret Thatcher, "Shaping a New Global Community" (speech to the Aspen Institute, August 5, 1990). Margaret Thatcher Foundation, http://www.margaretthatcher.org/document/108174.

23 George H. W. Bush, "Remarks and an Exchange with Reporters on the Iraqi Invasion of Kuwait," (statement, August 5, 1990). The American Presidency Project, https://www.presidency.ucsb.edu/documents/remarks-and-exchange-with-reporters-the-iraqi-invasion-kuwait-0.

24 Baker, *The Politics of Diplomacy*, 286.
25 Beschloss and Talbott, *At the Highest Levels*, 254.
26 The term "all necessary force" was designed by the US government and became a euphemism for military action; see endnote 60 of this chapter.
27 David Hoffman, "Mubarak: Keep Pressure on Iraq: After Talks, Baker Stresses There Should Be No Deals with Saddam," *Washington Post*, September 9, 1990.
28 Ibid.
29 Norman Kempster, "Baker Asks NATO Nations to Bolster U.S. Forces in Gulf," *Los Angeles Times*, September 11, 1990.
30 David Hoffman, "Gulf Crisis Tests Baker as Diplomat, Politician," *Washington Post*, November 2, 1990.
31 Baker, *The Politics of Diplomacy*, 298.
32 George de Lama, "Baker praises Syria, seeks 'Arab solution'" *Chicago Tribune*, September 15, 1990.
33 Ibid.
34 Thomas L. Friedman, "Germany Pledges $1.87 Billion to Aid Gulf Effort" *New York Times*, September 16, 1990, https://www.nytimes.com/1990/09/16/world/confrontation-in-the-gulf-germany-pledges-1.87-billion-to-aid-gulf-effort.html.
35 Ibid.
36 Thomas Pickering interview with author, July 1, 2015, Washington, DC.
37 Emerging from the UN Security Council, the international press lay in wait to hurl questions at a Permanent Representative. Against the backdrop of the UN seal, Pickering and other ambassadors used this "stake out" to explain positions taken in Council meetings.
38 In May 1992, Baker replaced Pickering, sending him away as US ambassador to India.
39 Later John Bolton became a fierce critic of the UN which damaged his Senate confirmation as assistant secretary for International Organization Affairs, but his intellect was superb and President Donald Trump named him national security advisor in 2018, a position not requiring Senate confirmation. He resigned the post in 2019.
40 James A. Baker III interview for "The Gulf War: an In-Depth Examination of the 1990-1991 Persian Gulf Crisis," *Frontline,* PBS, 1996, https://www.pbs.org/wgbh/pages/frontline/gulf/oral/baker/1.html.
41 James A. Baker, quoted in "Part I: Oral History: The Persian Gulf War," in *Cold War Endgame,* ed. Wohlforth, 95.
42 Anatoly Chernyaev, quoted in "Part I: Oral History: The Persian Gulf War," in *Cold War Endgame,* ed. Wohlforth.

43 Ibid., 96.
44 Ibid.
45 49 percent of Americans did not find removal of Hussein from Kuwait reason enough to go to war; 45 percent did: "Here are some reasons that President Bush has given for our presence in the Middle East. For each, please tell me if it is something worth going to war over or not? To force Iraq to withdraw from Kuwait…" Yankelovich, Clancy, Shulman, November 1990. Archived in *Polling the Nations*.
46 Chuck Grassley (R-IA) and Mark Hatfield (R-OR) were the only GOP senators who voted against use of military force in January 91. The GOP representatives who voted against it were Silvio Conte (R-MA), Connie Morella (R-MD), Frank Riggs (R-CA).
47 "Closed Congressional Briefing on Gulf," October 24, 1990. MC #197, Box 109, Folder 7. James A. Baker III Papers.
48 Roland Dannreuther, "The Gulf Conflict: a Political and Strategic Analysis," *Adelphi Papers* 32, no. 264 (Winter 1991/92), 40.
49 Senator Claiborne Pell (D-RI), remarks in "Presidential meeting with Senate leadership," November 14, 1990, White House, Washington, DC. MC #197, Box 109, Folder 7. James A. Baker III Papers.
50 Speaker Tom Foley's remarks, ibid.
51 Thomas L. Friedman, "U.S. Jobs at Stake in Gulf, Baker Says," *New York Times*, November 14, 1990, https://www.nytimes.com/1990/11/14/world/mideast-tensions-us-jobs-at-stake-in-gulf-baker-says.html.
52 James A Baker, III interview with Russell Riley, James Sterling Young, and Robert Strong, George H.W. Bush Oral History Project, Miller Center, University of Virginia, March 17, 2011, Houston, TX, https://millercenter.org/the-presidency/presidential-oral-histories/james-baker-iii-oral-history-2011-white-house-chief.
53 George H.W. Bush, "Remarks to the Military Airlift Command in Dhahran," Dhahran, Saudi Arabia, 22 November 1990. George H. W. Bush Presidential Library and Museum, https://bush41library.tamu.edu/archives/public-papers/2482.
54 Margaret Thatcher, *The Downing Street Years*, PAGE.
55 Baker, *The Politics of Diplomacy*, 305.
56 Baker's handwritten notes, MSC #197, Box 109, Folder 7. James A. Baker III Papers.
57 Baker, *The Politics of Diplomacy*, 313.
58 Ibid., 309.
59 Baker's handwritten notes, MSC #197, Box 109, Folder 7. James A. Baker III Papers.

60 Under Secretary for Political Affairs Bob Kimmitt developed the phrase "all necessary means" and the State Department lawyers considered that it allowed for different interpretations, including further negotiations and sufficient international legal authority to wage war.
61 *Hearing on American Strategy in the Persian Gulf*, before the Senate Foreign Relations Committee, cited in the Federal News Service, December 5, 1990, statement of James A. Baker III.
62 Ibid.
63 James A. Baker III interview for *Frontline*.
64 Aleksandr Bessmertnykh, quoted in "Part I: Oral History: The Persian Gulf War," in *Cold War Endgame*, ed. Wohlforth.
65 James A. Baker III interview for *Frontline*.
66 Richard N. Haass, *War of Necessity, War of Choice: A Memoir of Two Iraq Wars* (New York: Simon & Schuster, 2009), 109.
67 James A. Baker III interview for *Frontline*.
68 Ibid. The transcript states "they," "they're," and "their" instead of "you" "you're" and "your."
69 Ibid.
70 Dennis B. Ross, interview with Bill Quandt and James McCall, George H.W. Bush Oral History, Miller Center, University of Virginia, August 2, 2001, Washington, DC, https://millercenter.org/the-presidency/presidential-oral-histories/dennis-b-ross-oral-history-state-departments-director .
71 James A. Baker III interview for *Frontline*.
72 George H. W. Bush, "Bush Announces End to Gulf War," February 27, 1991, audio, History.com, https://www.history.com/topics/us-presidents/bush-announces-end-to-gulf-war-video.
73 The Gulf Cooperation Council, formed in 1981, consists of Saudi Arabia, United Arab Emirates, Qatar, Bahrain, Oman, and Kuwait.
74 James A. Baker III interview for *Frontline*.
75 Doyle McManus, "Baker visits Kurdish Camp, Promises Help," *Los Angeles Times*, April 9, 1991.
76 Ibid.
77 James A. Baker III interview for *Frontline*.
78 Ibid.
79 Ibid.
80 President George H.W. Bush's remarks, https://www.presidency.ucsb.edu/documents/remarks-the-presentation-ceremony-for-the-presidential-medals-freedom-and-presidential
81 500 James A. Baker III interview for *Frontline*.

End Notes for Chapter 7

1. Dennis Ross, The Missing Peace: The Inside Story of the Fight for Middle East Peace (New York: Farrar, Straus, and Giroux, 2004).
2. James Baker testimony before the Senate Committee on Foreign Relations, 102nd Congress, 1st session. February 7, 1991. C-Span https://www.c-span.org/video/?16327-1/1991-foreign-policy-1992-budget-request
3. George H.W. Bush, *National Security Strategy of the United States*. (Washington, DC: The White House, August 1991) http://nssarchive.us/NSSR/1991.pdf
4. Fawaz A. Gerges, "Regional Security after the Gulf Crisis: the American Role," *Journal of Palestine Studies*, 20:4 (Summer 1991). https://www.jstor.org/stable/pdf/2537435.pdf?refreqid=excelsior%3A21756b5dad4a3cbe08b07dc4ba390ec1
5. Baker testimony before Senate Committee on Foreign Relations, p. 11.
6. Ibid.
7. Dennis B. Ross Interview with Bill Quandt and Philip Zelikow. George H.W. Bush Oral History, Miller Center, University of Virginia (August 2, 2001). http://millercenter.org/president/bush/oralhistory/dennis-ross
8. Ibid.
9. Baker with DeFrank, *The Politics of Diplomacy*, 116.
10. Steven R. Weisman, "War in the Gulf: Japan; Tokyo Leader, Facing a New Debate, Appeals for Support for War Aid, *New York Times,* January 26, 1991, http://www.nytimes.com/1991/01/26/world/war-gulf-japan-tokyo-leader-facing-new-debate-appeals-for-support-for-war-aid.html.
11. Dennis Ross, meeting with the author, July 28, 2015, Washington, DC.
12. *Nomination of James A. Baker III: Hearings before the Comm. on Foreign Relations*, 101st Cong. 17 (1989) (prepared statement of James A. Baker III), 208.
13. Ibid., 48.
14. Ibid., 87.
15. Ibid., 96.
16. Robert Pear, "The U.S. Agrees to Talks with the PLO, Saying Arafat Recognizes Israel and Renounces Terrorism," *New York Times*, December 15, 1988, http://www.nytimes.com/1988/12/15/world/us-agrees-talks-with-plo-saying-arafat-accepts-israel-renounces-all-terrorism.html.
17. Dennis Ross, interview George H.W. Bush Oral History, Miller Center. http://millercenter.org/president/bush/oralhistory/dennis-ross
18. Ibid.

19 Richard Haass, interview with Stephen Knott and Bob Strong, May 27, 2004, New York, NY.
20 Ambassador William Andreas Brown, "The Road to Madrid – James Baker and the Middle East Peace Talks." Moments in U.S. Diplomatic History, Association for Diplomatic Studies and Training, https://adst.org/2015/06/the-road-to-madrid-james-baker-and-the-middle-east-peace-talks/.
21 Beschloss and Talbott, *At the Highest Levels*, 62.
22 "The Need for Convening a Middle East Peace Conference," UN Document, New York 1989, https://unispal.un.org/DPA/DPR/unispal.nsf/0/1B0CEF605B8C99FC85256DC200688C37
23 Beschloss and Talbott, *At the Highest* Levels, 63.
24 Dan Kurtzer, telephone interview with the author, August 27, 2017.
25 Greater Israel is a term generally used by those in Israel who want the nation's final borders to include substantially more than pre-1967 Israel. It also includes East Jerusalem, the West Bank, the Gaza Strip and the Golan Heights.
26 James A. Baker III, "Principles and Pragmatism: American Policy toward the Arab-Israeli Conflict," (speech to the American-Israel Public Affairs Committee, May 22, 1991). *US Department of State Bulletin,* (July 1989), 24-27.
27 Ibid. See also Thomas L. Friedman, "Baker, in a Middle East Blueprint, Asks Israel to Reach Out to Arabs," *New York Times*, May 23, 1989, a http://www.nytimes.com/1989/05/23/world/baker-in-a-middle-east-blueprint-asks-israel-to-reach-out-to-arabs.html.
28 Aaron David Miller, *The Much Too Promised Land: America's Elusive Search for Arab-Israeli Peace* (New York: Random House Inc., 2008), 228.
29 Robert Pear, "Israel Asking U.S. for Aid on Housing for Soviet Émigrés," *New York Times*, October 2, 1989, https://www.nytimes.com/1989/10/02/world/israel-asking-us-for-aid-on-housing-for-soviet-emigres.html.
30 UN Security Council (UNSC) Resolution 242 called upon Israel to withdraw from territories gained in the 1967 war: United Nations Security Council (SC), Resolution 242, November 22, 1967, http://unispal.un.org/UNISPAL.NSF/0/7D35E1F729DF491C85256EE700686136.
31 *Foreign Operations, Export Financing, and Related Programs Appropriations for Fiscal Year 1991: Hearings on H.R. 5114, Day 5, Before a Subcommittee of the Committee on Appropriations*, United States Senate, 101st Cong. 191-193 (1990) (testimony of James A. Baker, Secretary of State of the United States).
32 Baker with DeFrank, *The Politics of Diplomacy*, 543.
33 George H.W. Bush, "The President's News Conference Following Discussions with Prime Minister Toshiki Kaifu of Japan in Palm Springs, California," (statement, March 3, 1990). The American Presidency Project, https://www.

presidency.ucsb.edu/documents/the-presidents-news-conference-following-discussions-with-prime-minister-toshiki-kaifu.

34 Anthony Lewis, "Abroad at Home: Israel against Itself," *New York Times*, April 27, 1990, http://www.nytimes.com/1990/04/27/opinion/abroad-at-home-israel-against-itself.html.
35 Miller, *The Much Too Promised Land*, 224.
36 Richard Haass interview with Stephen Knott and Bob Strong, May 27, 2004, New York, NY.
37 James A. Baker III notes following meeting with Foreign Minister David Levy, October 18, 1990, Folder 2, Box 109, James A. Baker III Papers.
38 The PLO claims to represent the interests of the people from the land of Palestine who lost their land upon Israeli Independence in 1948, and achieved prominence after the 1967 war. The US government had limited relations with the PLO, on grounds that factions within the PLO were considered to be terrorist organizations.
39 Miller, *The Much Too Promised Land*, 208-209.
40 Brown, "The Road to Madrid."
41 Baker with DeFrank, *The Politics of Diplomacy*, 128-129.
42 Scott B. Lasensky, "Friendly Restraint: U.S.-Israeli Relations during the Gulf Crisis of 1990-1991," The Middle East Review of International Affairs Journal, 3:2 (Summer 1999), http://www.rubincenter.org/1999/06/lasensky-1999-06-03/.
43 Michael R. Gordon and General Bernard E. Trainor, *The General's War: The Inside Story of the Conflict in the Gulf* (Boston: Little Brown & Co., 1995), 71.
44 Yitzhak Shamir, *Summing Up: The Memoirs of Yitzhak Shamir* (London: Weidenfeld & Nicholson, 1994).
45 George de Lama, "No progress from Baker, Aziz meeting," *Chicago Tribune*, January 10, 1991.
46 Lasenksy, "Friendly Restraint"
47 Staff of US News & World Report, *Triumph Without Victory: The Unreported History of the Persian Gulf War* (New York: Random House, 1992) 135. Abraham Ben-Zvi,
48 Gordon and Trainor, *The General's War*, 71-72.
49 Lasenksy, "Friendly Restraint."
50 Gordon and Trainor, *The General's War*, 195.
51 Ibid., 196.
52 The administration believed that Saddam Hussein possessed chemical and biological weapons. He was also near to developing a nuclear missile delivery system. See Brown, "The Road to Madrid."
53 Miller, *The Much Too Promised Land*, 199.

54 Daniel Williams, "US Offers Israel Little but Goodwill: Diplomacy: Euphoria over Warmer Relations Fades with a Growing List of Disappointments," Los Angeles Times, February 15, 1991, http://articles.latimes.com/1991-02-15/news/mn-1220_1_israel-alliance.
55 Baker with DeFrank, *The Politics of Diplomacy*, 545-546.
56 "Statement by Press Secretary Marlon Fitzwater on Statements Made by Ambassador Zalman Shoval of Israel," Public Papers of the Presidents of the United States: George H.W. Bush (1991, Book I), U.S. Government Publishing Office, February 15, 1991, http://www.gpo.gov/fdsys/pkg/PPP-1991-book1/html/PPP-1991-book1-doc-pg151.htm.
57 Baker with DeFrank, *The Politics of Diplomacy*, 547.
58 Thomas Friedman, "U.S. Approves $400 Million in Guarantees for Israeli Housing," *New York Times*, February 21, 1991, http://www.nytimes.com/1991/02/21/world/us-approves-400-million-in-guarantees-for-israeli-housing.html.
59 "Chronology: 16 February-15 May 1991," *Journal of Palestine Studies,* 20, no. 4 (1991), 197.
60 Brown, "The Road to Madrid."
61 James A. Baker III, discussion with the author, Foreign Policy Association meeting, New York, May 6, 2015.
62 Miller, *The Much Too Promised Land*, 199.
63 Ibid., 216.
64 Ibid., 207.
65 Brown, "The Road to Madrid."
66 Ibid.,
67 Miller, *The Much Too Promised Land, 197*
68 Edward P. Djerejian with William Martin, *Danger and Opportunity: An American Ambassador's Journey through the Middle East*, (Threshold Editions, Simon & Schuster, Inc., New York, 20008), 95.
69 James A. Baker III, "Opportunities to Build a New World Order" (statement before the House Foreign Affairs Committee, Washington, DC, February 6, 1991). *US Department of State Dispatch*, (February 11, 1991), 81.
70 Ibid.
71 Paul Adams, "Baker Visit a Spur to Israel, Palestinians," *The Christian Science Monitor,* March 14, 1991, https://www.csmonitor.com/1991/0314/otalk.html.
72 Dennis Ross, interview with the author, July 28, 2015, Washington, DC.
73 Aaron David Miller, interview with the author, August 28, 2017, Washington, DC.
74 Margaret Tutwiler, interview with the author, September 9, 2015, Washington, DC.

75 George H.W. Bush, "Remarks at the Opening Session of the Middle East Peace Conference in Madrid, Spain," (statement, October 30, 1991). The American Presidency Project, https://www.presidency.ucsb.edu/documents/remarks-the-opening-session-the-middle-east-peace-conference-madrid-spain.
76 Miller, *The Much Too Promised Land*, 222.
77 Richard B. Straus, "Israelis Won Peace Talks but don't Tell Them That," *Los Angeles Times*, November 10, 1991 http://articles.latimes.com/1991-11-10/opinion/op-2196_1_secretary-of-state-state-james-baker.

END NOTES FOR CHAPTER 8

1 Brent Scowcroft, interview with Philip Zelikow et al., November 12-13, 1999, Washington, DC.
2 Ibid.
3 Bush and Scowcroft, *A World Transformed*, 59.
4 Brent Scowcroft, interview with Philip Zelikow et al, November 12-13, 1999, Washington, DC.
5 Ibid.
6 Ibid.
7 Ibid.
8 Bush and Scowcroft, *A World Transformed*, 82.
9 Developed by the US Air Force in the 1980s, the Midgetman – MGM-134A was a small intercontinental ballistic missile, deployed on a mobile truck and thus easily moved around to avoid a first strike attempt by enemy forces. It would have also deterred a second strike.
10 Richard Burt interview with the author, December 16, 2015, Washington, DC.
11 Thomas Friedman, "U.S.-Soviet talks end with progress on arms control," *New York Times*, September 24, 1989, www.nytimes.com/1989/09/24/world/us-soviet-talks-end-with-progress-on-arms-control.html.
12 The ABM treaty required that large radars be placed only on the outer perimeter or coastal areas and not in the center of the continent where they might track and intercept warheads. Radars facing outward were acceptable under the ABM because they swept an area so distant from battlefields as to be useless in directing interceptors.
13 Friedman, "U.S.-Soviet talks end with progress on arms control," *New York Times*.
14 James A. Baker III, "Points of Mutual Advantage: Perestroika and American Foreign Policy" (prepared address, Foreign Policy Association,

New York City, NY, October 16, 1989), https://babel.hathitrust.org/cgi/pt?id=umn.31951002971980z.

15 Ibid.
16 James A. Baker III, "Prerequisites and principles for arms control," (prepared address, The Commonwealth Club, San Francisco, CA, October 23, 1989), https://babel.hathitrust.org/cgi/pt?id=umn.319510029722894;view=1up;seq=3.
17 Ibid.
18 Thomas Friedman, "Baker Sees in Gorbachev a new chance for peace," *New York Times*, October 24, 1989, http://www.nytimes.com/1989/10/24/world/baker-sees-in-gorbachev-a-new-chance-for-peace.html.
19 Gen. Edward L. Rowny, "Document 3: Department of State. Information Memorandum to Secretary Baker from Gen. Edward L. Rowny [Special Adviser for Arms Control]. November 17, 1989," 1, contained in "Bush and Gorbachev at Malta: Previously Secret Documents from Soviet and U.S. Files on the 1989 Meeting, 20 Years Later," National Security Archive Electronic Briefing Book No. 298, December 3, 2009, National Security Archive at George Washington University, Washington, DC, https://nsarchive2.gwu.edu//NSAEBB/NSAEBB298/Document%203.pdf.
20 Ibid.
21 Svetlana Savranskaya and Thomas Blanton, eds., "Document 10: Soviet Transcript of the Malta Summit, December 2-3 1989," contained in "Bush and Gorbachev at Malta: Previously Secret Documents from Soviet and U.S. Files on the 1989 Meeting, 20 Years Later," 13 and 24-25, National Security Archive, https://nsarchive2.gwu.edu//NSAEBB/NSAEBB298/Document%2010.pdf.
22 Soviet delegation at Malta, "Document 11: Directives for the Ministers of Foreign Affairs of the USSR and the United States. Draft by Soviet delegation at Malta. December 3, 1989. Source: George H.W. Bush Library, FOIA request," 2, contained in "Bush and Gorbachev at Malta: Previously Secret Documents from Soviet and U.S. Files on the 1989 Meeting, 20 Years Later," National Security Archive, http://nsarchive.gwu.edu/NSAEBB/NSAEBB298/Document%2011.pdf.
23 Belchoss and Talbott, *At the Highest Levels*, 183.
24 Raymond L. Garthoff, *The Great Transition: American Soviet Relations and the End of the Cold War* (Washington, DC: The Brookings Institution, 1994), 423.
25 Richard Burt interview with author, October 18, 2019, Washington D.C.
26 Garthoff, Great Transition.

27 Thomas Friedman, "Upheaval in the East: Moscow Reported to Yield on Neutrality of Germany; No Breakthrough on Arms," *New York Times*, April 7, 1990, http://www.nytimes.com/1990/04/07/world/upheaval-east-moscow-reported-yeild-neutrality-germany-no-breakthrough-arms.html.

28 Thomas Friedman, "Evolution in Europe; Soviets, Saluting U.S., Harden German Stand," *New York Times*, May 5, 1990, http://www.nytimes.com/1990/05/05/world/evolution-in-europe-soviets-saluting-us-harden-german-stand.html.

29 Tacit Rainbow was an American air-launch cruise missile designed to carry a conventional warhead, thus justifying the US Air Force argument that it be excluded from START.

30 Friedman, "Evolution in Europe," *New York Times*.

31 Ibid.

32 Garthoff, *The Great Transition*, 424.

33 Richard Burt, interview with the author, December 16, 2015, Washington, DC.

34 James A. Baker III, Secret Night Notes to President George H.W. Bush, "My Meeting with Gorbachev," May 19, 1990. Cable 190830Z, declassified May 29, 1997.

35 Thomas Friedman, "Evolution in Europe; How a U.S. missile nearly undid deal," *New York Times*, May 20, 1990, http://www.nytimes.com/1990/05/20/world/evolution-in-europe-how-a-us-missile-nearly-undid-deal.html.

36 Garthoff, *The Great Transition*, 423, n.24.

37 Thomas Friedman, "Evolution in Europe; U.S. and Soviets close to a pact on 30% cut in nuclear missiles; agree on chemical-arms curbs," *New York Times*, May 20, 1990, http://www.nytimes.com/1990/05/20/world/evolution-europe-us-soviets-close-pact-30-cut-nuclear-missiles-agree-chemical.html.

38 Ibid.

39 From the current US stockpile of 25,000 tons and Soviet stockpile of 50,000, ibid.

40 Michael R. Gordon, "Evolution in Europe; Arms Control Process: Back on Track," *New York Times*, May 20, 1990, http://www.nytimes.com/1990/05/20/world/evolution-in-europe-arms-control-process-back-on-track.html.

41 This bilateral treaty would spur the representatives of 40 nations gathered in Geneva to reach a worldwide chemical ban, the Chemical Weapons Convention, drafted in 1992 and signed in early 1993.

42 Garthoff, *The Great Transition*, 426.

43 Friedman, "U.S. and Soviets close to a pact on 30% cut in nuclear missiles; agree on chemical-arms curbs," *New York Times*.

44 Norman Kempster and James Gerstenzang, "Baker, Bessmertnykh to Talk; Summit Hangs in Balance," *Los Angeles Times*, January 25, 1991, http://articles.latimes.com/1991-01-25/news/mn-822_1_foreign-minister.
45 George de Lama and Timothy J. McNulty, "Baltics cast a shadow," *Chicago Tribune*, January 29, 1991, http://articles.chicagotribune.com/1991-01-29/news/9101090223_1_soviet-military-crackdown-vilnius-and-riga-soviet-actions.
46 Downloading was the process of reducing the amount of warheads on missiles. While some approved of this process as a means of spreading out nuclear material instead of concentrating it in areas that provided a more volatile target, others viewed it as additionally destabilizing as the preponderance of new targets would result in an increase in the possibility of preemptive strikes. From Marsh, Gerald, "The Ups and Downs of Downloading," *Bulletin of the Atomic Scientists*, Vol. 47, No. 9, November 1991.
47 MIRVed ICBMs were multiple independently targetable re-entry vehicles placed upon an intercontinental ballistic missile.
48 David Rothkopf, *Running the World: The Inside Story of the National Security Council and the Architects of American Power* (New York: Public Affairs, 2005), 283.
49 Sparrow, *The Strategist*, 437.
50 Beschloss & Talbott, *At the Highest Levels*, 371.
51 Robert C. Toth, "Bush, Advisers Clear up U.S. Position on START Pact: Arms control: Baker will present the new American position today. The goal is to complete the treaty in time for the summit in Moscow," *Los Angeles Times*, June 7, 1991, http://articles.latimes.com/1991-06-07/news/mn-129_1_strategic-arms-treaty.
52 Richard Burt, interview with author, December 16, 2015, Washington, DC.
53 Beschloss and Talbott, *At the Highest Levels*, 365.
54 Ibid.
55 Ibid., 367.
56 *Hearing on the CFE Treaty*, before the Senate Committee on Foreign Relations, 102nd Congress (1991) (statement of Joseph Biden, D-DE), https://fas.org/nuke/control/cfe/congress/22e.htm.
57 Ibid., statement of Jesse Helms (R-NC).
58 Ibid.
59 Ibid., statement of Richard Lugar (R-IN).
60 "The Treaty on Conventional Armed Forces in Europe (CFE)," Resolution of Advice and Consent to Ratification, 102nd Congress, November 25, 1991, https://www.congress.gov/treaty-document/102nd-congress/8/resolution-text.

61 Thomas L. Friedman, "U.S.-Soviet Talks Provide Few Gains" *New York Times*, July 12, 1991, http://www.nytimes.com/1991/07/12/world/us-soviet-talks-provide-few-gains.html.

62 Under the treaty, the Soviet Union committed to reduce the average throw-weight of all its missiles by 50 percent across the board. The US sought to define throw-weights as broadly as possible because that would require Moscow to shrink its missiles that much more. From Thomas L. Friedman, "Summit in London; Clearing the Final Hurdles to a Strategic Arms Accord," *New York Times*, July 18, 1991, http://www.nytimes.com/1991/07/18/world/summit-in-london-clearing-the-final-hurdles-to-a-strategic-arms-accord.html.

63 That is the missile nose cone, the guidance equipment, and the individual nuclear warhead or warheads.

64 Friedman, "Summit in London," *New York Times*.

65 Ibid.

66 Ibid.

67 R.W. Apple Jr., "Summit in Moscow; Bush in Moscow to Chart a New Course," *New York Times*, July 30, 1991, http://www.nytimes.com/1991/07/30/world/summit-in-moscow-bush-in-moscow-to-chart-a-new-course.html.

68 Eric Schmitt, "Summit in Moscow: Senate votes to deploy 'Star Wars,'" *New York Times*, August 1, 1991, http://www.nytimes.com/1991/08/01/world/summit-in-moscow-senate-votes-to-deploy-star-wars.html.

69 "Treaty between the United States of America and the Union of Soviet Socialist Republics on Strategic Offensive Reductions (START I)," Nuclear Threat Initiative, http://www.nti.org/learn/treaties-and-regimes/treaties-between-united-states-america-and-union-soviet-socialist-republics-strategic-offensive-reductions-start-i-start-ii/.

END NOTES FOR CHAPTER 9

1 The Diary of Anatoly Chernyaev, 1991. Sixth Installment of Former Top Soviet Adviser's Journal, National Security Archive, George Washington University, https://nsarchive2.gwu.edu//NSAEBB/NSAEBB345/index.htm and Nadia Alexandrova Arbatova, "Horror Mirror: Russian Perception of the Yugoslav Conflict" Paper presented at the Consensus Building Institute Conference on Russian and American Perspectives: Ethnic Conflict in the former Soviet Union, Harvard University, October 25-26, 1994

2 "The Breakup of Yugoslavia, 1990-1992," Department of State Office of the Historian, accessed December 20, 2018, https://history.state.gov/milestones/1989-1992/breakup-yugoslavia.

3   Ibid.
4   88.2 percent of voters in Slovenia's referendum voted for independence. See Andrew Wachtel and Christopher Bennett, "The Dissolution of Yugoslavia," in Confronting the Yugoslav Controversies: A Scholar's Initiative, 2nd ed, edited by Charles Ingrao and Thomas A. Emmert (West Lafayette, IN: Purdue University Press, 2012), 36-38.
5   In Croatia, the April 1990 election using first past the post rules resulted in a majority for the Croat Democratic Union which favored independence, but left the 12 percent Serbian population as losers. From Wachtel and Bennett, "The Dissolution of Yugoslavia," 36-37.
6   A.D. Horne, "Yugoslavs Unite Against Suspension of US Aid," Washington Post, May 23, 1991, https://www.washingtonpost.com/archive/politics/1991/05/23/yugoslavs-unite-against-suspension-of-us-aid/030a09ba-56b5-4ea7-993c-3bcf531b947c/
7   David Binder, "Bush Tells Belgrade that the U.S. May Consider Restoring Aid," New York Times, May 21, 1991. https://www.nytimes.com/1991/05/22/world/bush-tells-belgrade-that-us-may-consider-restoring-aid.html
8   Wachtel and Bennett, "The Dissolution of Yugoslavia," 131.
9   David Halberstam, War in a Time of Peace: Bush, Clinton and the Generals (New York: Simon & Schuster, 2001), 26.
10 Warren Zimmerman, Origins of a Catastrophe: Yugoslavia and its Destroyers – America's last Ambassador Tells what Happened and Why (New York: Times Books, 1996), 59–60.
11 Ibid., 60.
12 Halberstam, War in a Time of Peace, 26.
13 Michael Libal, Limits of Persuasion: Germany and the Yugoslav Crisis, 1991-1992 (Westport, CT: Praeger, 1997).
14 Timothy Garton Ash, In Europe's Name: Germany and the Divided Continent (New York: Random House, 1993), 395.
15 The German government recognized Croatia and Slovenia as independent states in the autumn of 1991.
16 Zimmerman, Origins of a Catastrophe, 136.
17 Hans Dietrich Genscher interview with Deutsche Welle, "Recognizing Slovenia, Croatia Brought Peace, Genscher Says," June 25, 2011. https://www.dw.com/en/recognizing-slovenia-croatia-brought-peace-genscher-says/a-15182463 .
18 Sparrow, The Strategist, 452.
19 The Conference on Security and Cooperation in Europe (CSCE) agreed to The Helsinki Final Act [Accords] in 1975. It established four "baskets" covering ten principles which included economic relations, political and

military issues, territorial integrity, the peaceful settlement of disputes, and respect for human rights. The Soviet Union, as well as the United States and Canada participated in the agreement, which was not a treaty. The thirty-five signatory nations agreed by consensus that the CSCE should implement the Accords that had a far-reaching effect in ending the Cold War.

20 Thomas Friedman, "Evolution in Europe: Russian Country Toured by Baker," The New York Times, May 18, 1990, https://www.nytimes.com/1990/05/18/world/evolution-in-europe-russian-country-toured-by-baker.html.

21 Hans-Dietrich Genscher, Rebuilding a House Divided, trans. Thomas Thornton (New York: Broadway Books, 1998), PAGE (IF KNOWN).

22 Zimmerman, Origins of a Catastrophe, 133.

23 "A Questionable Step on Yugoslavia," Chicago Tribune, May 25, 1991, https://www.chicagotribune.com/news/ct-xpm-1991-05-25-9102160709-story.html.

24 Margaret Tutwiler, "US Policy toward Yugoslavia," (statement released by Department Spokesman Margaret Tutwiler, May 24, 1991). US Department of State Dispatch (June 3, 1991), 395.

25 Zimmerman, Origins of a Catastrophe, 134.

26 Ibid., 135.

27 Lenard J. Cohen, Broken Bonds: Yugoslavia's Disintegration and Balkan Politics in Transition, 2nd ed. (Boulder, CO: Westview Press, 1999), 219.

28 Ibid., 136.

29 Warren Zimmermann, "Yugoslavia: 1989-1996," in Azrael, Jeremy R. and Emil A. Payin, eds., U.S. and Russian Policymaking with Respect to the Use of Force. Santa Monica, CA: RAND Corporation, 1996, http://www.rand.org/pubs/conf_proceedings/CF129/CF-129-chapter11.html.

30 Zimmerman, Origins of a Catastrophe, 137.

31 Fighting began June 27 and ended with a ceasefire negotiated July 7 (after eleven days); the JNA officially pulled out by July 18 (Libal, Limits of Persuasion, 21). Though it lasted eleven days, it is called the ten day war.

32 Zimmerman, Origins of a Catastrophe, 139.

33 Margaret Tutwiler interview with the author, September 9, 2015, Washington, DC.

34 Thomas Friedman, "300,000 Albanians pour into streets to welcome Baker," New York Times, June 22, 1991, http://www.nytimes.com/1991/06/23/world/300000-albanians-pour-into-streets-to-welcome-baker.html.

35 Ibid.

36 George H. W. Bush, James A. Baker III, Brent Scowcroft, and Manfred Woerner, "Memorandum of Conversation: Meeting with Manfred Woerner, Secretary General of NATO," Oval Office, Washington, DC, June 25, 1991. MemCons, George H. W. Bush Presidential Library and Museum.

37 Meeting with Manfred Woerner, Oval Office, June 25, 1991.
38 Chairmanship of the European Council rotates every six months among its member states. On July 1, 1991, it was the turn of the Netherlands and its Prime Minister Ruud Lubbers.
39 Paul L. Montgomery, "Europeans Pursue Talks on Yugoslavia," New York Times, September 7, 1991, https://www.nytimes.com/1991/09/07/world/europeans-pursue-talks-on-yugoslavia.html.
40 United Nations Security Council Resolution 781 (S/RES/781 (1992)), October 9, 1992, http://unscr.com/en/resolutions/doc/781.
41 Alan Riding, "Conflict in the Balkans," New York Times, August 14, 1992. http://www.nytimes.com/1992/08/14/world/conflict-balkans-mitterrand-will-send-troops-only-protect-bosnia-relief.html.
42 James Gow, Triumph of the Lack of Will: International Diplomacy and the Yugoslav War, New York, Columbia University Press, 1997
43 Baker, Politics of Diplomacy, 560.
44 Interview with Jon Gunderson, Consul General in Kiev, Association for Diplomatic Studies and Training Association. https://adst.org/2014/03/ukraines-push-for-independence/
45 Susan D. Fink, "From "Chicken Kiev" to Ukrainian Recognition: Domestic Politics in U.S. Foreign Policy toward Ukraine," Harvard Ukrainian Studies, Vol. 21.No. 1/2 June 1997. https://www.jstor.org/stable/pdf/41036641.pdf
46 "After the Summit: Excerpts from Bush's Ukraine Speech," The New York Times, August 2, 1991. https://www.nytimes.com/1991/08/02/world/after-summit-excerpts-bush-s-ukraine-speech-working-for-good-both-us.html
47 Ibid.
48 Rowland Evans and Robert Novak, "Bush's Kiev Backfire" The Washington Post, August 14, 1991, www.washingtonpost.com/archive/opinions/1991/08/14/bush-diev-backfire/
49 D. Ritter, and D. Hertel, 1991. Letter of 2 October 1991 to House of Representatives Ad Hoc Committee on the Baltic Nations and Ukraine.
50 D. Hoffman, "Rush to 'Welcome' Ukraine Vote, Skirting Immediate Recognition," The Washington Post, December 1, 1991.
51 Fink, "From "Chicken Kiev" to Ukrainian Recognition."
52 Baker, Politics of Diplomacy, 561.
53 John E. Yang, "Bush Decides to Accelerate U.S. Recognition of Ukraine," The Washington Post, November 28, 1991. https://www.washingtonpost.com/archive/politics/1991/11/28/bush-decides-to-accelerate-us-recognition-of-ukraine/246b3437-de2f-4f32-b4e7-66db3788a270/

54 Susan Fink estimates that only 55 percent of Ukrainian-Americans supported Bush in the 1992 election compared to 85 percent who supported him in 1988. See "From Chicken Kiev" to Ukrainian Recognition."

END NOTES FOR CHAPTER 10

1   On July 16 1990, OMB Director Richard Darman announced that the government faced a fiscal 1991 budget deficit of $166 billion, well above the $100.5 billion deficit forecast in January.
2   James A. Baker III, "America and the Post-Coup Soviet Union." delivered at Princeton University, December 12, 1991, CSPAN, https://www.c-span.org/video/?23366-1/post-coup-soviet-union. Excerpted in "Soviet Disarray: Baker Sees Opportunities and Disks as Soviet Republics Grope for Stability," *The New York Times*, December 13, 1991, https://www.nytimes.com/1991/12/13/world/soviet-disarry-baker-sees-opportunities-risks-soviet-republics-grope-for.html.
3   Director of Central Intelligence, "Whither Gorbachev: Soviet Policy and Politics in the 1990s," National Intelligence Estimate (November 1987), https://www.cia.gov/library/readingroom/docs/CIA-RDP89M00699R002201790013-5.pdf.
4   Baker with DeFrank, *The Politics of Diplomacy*, 475.
5   The Senate approved the CFE treaty nearly unanimously (ninety in favor, four against) on November 23, 1991.
6   Alexandr Yakovlev remained with Gorbachev personally until the flag of the Soviet Union came down and Gorbachev resigned.
7   William Taubman, *Gorbachev: His Life and Times* (New York: W.W. Norton & Company, Inc, 2017), 582.
8   Serhii Plokhy, *The Last Empire: The Final Days of the Soviet Union* (New York: Basic Books, 2014), 128.
9   Bush and Scowcroft, A World Transformed, 531-532; "Telecom with President Mikhail Gorbachev of the USSR," Bush Presidential Library, Memcons and Telecoms, http://bushlibrary.tamu.edu/research/pdfs/memcons_telcons/1991-08-21-Gorbachev/pdf.
10 Serhii Plokhy, *The Last Empire: the Final Days of the Soviet Union*, (New York: Basic Books, 2015), 134; and Taubman, *Gorbachev*, 614.
11 Ibid.
12 Taubman, *Gorbachev*, 624.
13 Ibid.
14 Plokhy, *The Last Empire*, 202.

15 Telephone interview with Nicholas Burns, November 5, 2018. Director for Soviet Affairs at the NSC.
16 Baker with DeFrank, *The Politics of Diplomacy*, 524.
17 Nicholas Burns interview.
18 "Special State Department Briefing with Secretary of State James Baker, State Department, Washington, DC," press conference, Federal News Service, September 4, 1991.
19 *Hearing on Foreign Financial Assistance Programs*, before the House Foreign Affairs Committee, cited in the Federal News Service, March 5, 1992, statements of Treasury Secretary Nicholas Brady. Also archived at CSPAN. org, https://www.c-span.org/video/?24809-1/us-foreign-financial-policy.
20 Olin Wethington, then assistant secretary of Treasury for International Affairs, interview with the author, September 14, 2018, Washington, DC.
21 "Special State Department Briefing with Secretary of State James Baker," September 4, 1991.
22 Thomas L. Friedman, "Soviet Turmoil; US hoping Moscow can retain control of Soviets' nuclear arms," *New York Times*, September 5, 1991, https://www.nytimes.com/1991/09/05/world/soviet-turmoil-us-hoping-moscow-can-retain-control-of-soviets-nuclear-arms.html.
23 Serge Schmemann, "Bush's Arms Plan; Soviets Hail US Arms Plan and Signal Their own Cuts: Britain and France Join in," *New York Times*, September 29, 1991, http://www.nytimes.com/1991/09/29/us/bush-s-arms-plan-soviets-hail-us-arms-plan-signal-their-own-cuts-britain-france.html.
24 Ibid.
25 George H.W. Bush, "Address to the Nation on Reducing United States and Soviet Nuclear Weapons," (statement, September 27, 1991). The American Presidency Project, https://www.presidency.ucsb.edu/documents/address-the-nation-reducing-united-states-and-soviet-nuclear-weapons.
26 Ibid.
27 Ibid.
28 Susan J. Koch, "The Presidential Nuclear Initiatives of 1991-1992," Center for the Study of Weapons of Mass Destruction at National Defense University, Case Study Series No. 5, September 2012, http://ndupress.ndu.edu/Portals/68/Documents/casestudies/CSWMD_CaseStudy-5.pdf, 1.
29 Mikhail S. Gorbachev statement of October 5, 1991, Tass Agency, translated by the *New York Times*: "Gorbachev's Remarks on Arms Cuts," *New York Times*, October 6, 1991, www.nytimes.com/1991/10/06/world/gorbachev-s-remarks-on-arms-cuts.html.
30 Senator Sam Nunn, foreword to *Dismantling the Cold War: U.S. and NIS Perspectives on the Nunn-Lugar Cooperative Threat Reduction Program*, eds.

John M. Shields and William C. Potter (Cambridge, MA: The MIT Press, 1997).
31 Paul I. Bernstein and Jason D. Wood, "The Origins of Nunn-Lugar and Cooperative Threat Reduction," Center for the Study of Weapons of Mass Destruction at National Defense University Press, Case Study Series No. 3, April 2010, http://ndupress.ndu.edu/Portals/68/Documents/casestudies/CSWMD_CaseStudy-3.pdf.
32 Senators Sam Nunn and Richard G. Lugar, "The Nunn-Lugar Initiative: Cooperative Demilitarization in the Former Soviet Union," in *The Diplomatic Record 1992–1993* (Boulder, CO: Westview Press, 1995).
33 Shields and Potter, eds, *Dismantling the Cold War*, 42.
34 Ibid., 142.
35 Philip Zelikow, then deputy director for Europe at the NSC, meeting with the author, October 5, 2018, Charlottesville, VA.
36 Ambassador Strauss and former Ambassador Jack Matlock supported the need for robust support for the Soviet Union.
37 Kurt M. Campbell, Ashton B. Carter, Steven E. Miller and Charles A. Zraket, *Soviet Nuclear Fission: Control of the Nuclear Arsenal in a Disintegrating Soviet Union* (Cambridge, MA: Belfer Center for Science and International Affairs at the Harvard Kennedy School, November 1991), https://www.belfercenter.org/publication/soviet-nuclear-fission-control-nuclear-arsenal-disintegrating-soviet-union.
38 Ibid.
39 Sam Nunn and Richard G. Lugar, "Dismantling the Soviet Arsenal: We've Got to Get Involved," *Washington Post*, November 22, 1991.
40 Nunn-Lugar Cooperative Threat Reduction Act of 2007, S. 198, 110th Cong. (2007). www.congress.gov/bill/110th-congress/senate-bill/198/text. This bill outlines the achievements in decommissioning of Russian arms since the inception of the Act in 1991 (Soviet Nuclear Threat Reduction Act of 1991, H.R. 3807, 102nd Cong. (1991) https://www.congress.gov/bill/102nd-congress/house-bill/3807/text).
41 Baker, "America and the Post-Coup Soviet Union." Princeton University, December 12, 1991. https://www.c-span.org/video/?23366-1/post-coup-soviet-union
42 NBC *Meet the Press*, December 15, 1991 https://search.alexanderstreet.com/preview/work/bibliographic_entity%7Cvideo_work%7C3230066 and cited in Thomas L. Friedman, "Soviet Disarray; Russia Asks Baker for a Recognition of Independence" *New York Times*, December 16, 1991, https://www.nytimes.com/1991/12/16/world/soviet-disarray-russia-asks-baker-for-a-recognition-of-independence.html.

41 Jeffrey Hays, "Shock Therapy and Economic Policy Under Yeltsin," Facts and Details, last updated May 2016, http://factsanddetails.com/russia/Economics_Business_Agriculture/sub9_7b/entry-5168.html.
42 Ibid.
43 "'Shock Therapy'--with Emphasis on Shock," *Newsweek*, January 12, 1992, https://www.newsweek.com/shock-therapy-emphasis-shock-197912
44 Jeffrey Hays, "Shock Therapy and Economic Policy Under Yeltsin,".
45 "'Shock Therapy'--with Emphasis on Shock," *Newsweek*, January 12, 1992.
46 "History in the Making: the Agreement that Ended the Soviet Union," *The Moscow Times*, December 7, 2016, https://themoscowtimes.com/articles/history-in-the-making-the-agreement-that-ended-the-soviet-union-56456.
47 Nicholas Burns interview.
48 Wethington interview with the author.
49 Baker interview with the author, February 11, 2015, Houston, TX.
50 Baker, "Post-Coup Soviet Union."
51 Strobe Talbott, "Gorbachev Says He'll Fight On, But He's Already: A Man without a Country," *Time*, December 23, 1991. Quoted in Beschloss and Talbott, *At the Highest Levels*, 452-454.
52 Taubman, *Gorbachev*, 637.
53 Ibid.
54 Notes taken at December 16 meeting with Foreign Minister Kozyrev, Moscow. USSR Chron File, December 16, 1991, OA/ID CFO 1407-016, George H.W. Bush Presidential Library and Museum.
55 Meeting with Russian President Boris Yeltsin, Moscow. USSR Chron File, December 18, 1991, OA/ID CFO 1407-016, George H.W. Bush Presidential Library and Museum. Yeltsin was accompanied by Deputy Prime Minister Gennady Burbulis, Defense Minister Yevgeny Shaposhnikov, Minister of Interior Victor Pavlovich Barannikov, incoming Defense Minister General Pavel Grachov, and Russian Deputy Foreign Minister Andrei Kolosovskiy.
56 Ibid.
57 Wethington, interview with the author.
58 John Sununu, then chief of staff to the president, telephone interview with the author, June 18, 2018.
59 Alex Walters, "Kazakhstan, US Complete Secret Nuclear Transfer Mission," *Edge*, September 2011, https://www.edgekz.com/kazakhstan-u-s-complete-secret-nuclear-transfer-mission.
60 Jonathan Aitken, *Nazarbayev and the Making of Kazakhstan: From Communism to Capitalism* (London: Continuum, 2009), 139.
61 Ibid.
62 Ibid.

63 Tom Friedman, The New York Times Diplomatic correspondent accompanied Baker on his December 1991 visit. He recalls the vivid image of seeing the Soviet flag lower above the Kremlin. Interview with the author, Washington D.C. September 6, 2018.
64 Richard Armitage, interview with the author, September 18, 2018, Arlington, VA.
65 Ibid.
66 Nicholas Burns interview.
67 "End of the Soviet Union: Text of Bush's Address to the Nation on Gorbachev's Resignation," *New York Times*, December 26, 1991, https://www.nytimes.com/1991/12/26/world/end-soviet-union-text-bush-s-address-nation-gorbachev-s-resignation.html.
68 Thomas L. Friedman, "U.S. is Criticized on Aid to Russia," *New York Times*, January 22, 1992, https://www.nytimes.com/1992/01/22/world/us-is-criticized-on-aid-to-russia.html.
69 The US commitment of $4 billion for food credit guarantees and technical assistance. The European Community committed $4 billion in food aid, much of which had already been donated, and Japan committed $2.6 billion. Ibid.
70 Armitage, interview with the author, September 18, 2018, Arlington, VA.
71 Thomas L. Friedman, "Ex-Soviet Atom Scientists Ask Baker for West's Help," *New York Times*, February 15, 1992, https://www.nytimes.com/1992/02/15/world/ex-soviet-atom-scientists-ask-baker-for-west-s-help.html.
72 Ibid.
73 On February 19, 1992, President Bush won 58 percent of the New Hampshire Republican primary vote to Pat Buchanan's 40 percent, a margin too close for comfort at the beginning of the primary season. From Robin Toner, "Bush Jarred in First Primary; Tsongas Wins Democratic Vote," *New York Times*, February 19, 1992, https://www.nytimes.com/1992/02/19/us/1992-campaign-new-hampshire-bush-jarred-first-primary-tsongas-wins-democratic.html.
74 Baker, interview with Russell Riley et al., March 17 2011, Houston, TX.
75 Ibid.
76 Nicholas Burns telephone interview.

End Notes for the Epilogue

1 Transcript of President George H.W. Bush's Address on the State of the Union, January 29, 1992, The New York Times www.nytimes.com/1992/01/29/us/state-union…
2 Ibid.
3 The 'middle kingdom' is the mandarin name for China.
4 Bush and Scowcroft, *A World Transformed*.

ABOUT THE AUTHOR

Diana Villiers Negroponte grew up in London and Europe during the Cold War and observed its ending from the London School of Economics with anticipation. An American trained lawyer with a Ph.D. from Georgetown University, she is also the author of Seeking Peace in El Salvador: the Struggle to Reconstruct a National at the End of the Cold War and edited The End of Nostalgia: Mexico Confronts the Challenges of Global Competition. She has written widely on Mexico, Central America, and the last years of the Cold War for The Brookings Institution, Woodrow Wilson Center, and Reviews of American History. She appears on CSPAN, CNN, and MSNBC and lives in Washington, D.C.

INDEX

A

Abdel Shafi, Haidar 209
Abrams, Elliot 136
AIPAC 194, 195, 196
 Baker's speech 31, 71, 91, 194
Akhromeyev, Sergei 19
Albania 51, 258, 259
 Tirana 258
Allison, Graham xxi, 123, 126, 304, 309, 327, 351
 Grand Bargain 68, 123, 124, 126, 304, 305, 309, 327, 351
Aquino, Corazon 43
Arab League 158, 159
Arafat, Yasser 192, 208, 210, 303
Arcos, Cresencio 139, 353
Armitage, Richard 291, 307, 376
Arms Control Treaties
 Anti-Ballistic Missile Treaty (ABM) 220
 Conventional Forces in Europe (CFE) 19, 61
 Intermediate Nuclear Forces (INF) 213
 Mutual & Blanced Force Reduction (MBFR) 214
 Short Range Nuclear Forces (SNF) 214, 217
 Strategic Arms Limitation Treat (SALT) 220
 Strategic Arms Reduction Treaty (START)> 30, 61, 266
 Strategic Defense Initiative (SDI) 213
Aronson, Barnard, Bernie
 Central America 19, 21, 22, 24, 32, 37, 127, 132, 133, 134, 135, 136, 139, 140, 141, 142, 144, 150, 151
 Cuba 22, 24, 61, 109, 111, 112, 119, 127, 133, 134, 135, 136, 137, 138, 141, 146, 150, 167, 320, 353
 Nicaraguan election 140, 151
Moscow xvi, xviii, xx, 4, 8, 11, 12, 13, 16, 17, 20, 22, 23, 24, 25, 27, 29, 32, 37, 38, 39, 43, 44, 45, 47, 48, 49, 50, 51, 54, 56, 58, 60, 61, 62, 64, 68, 80, 82, 83, 84, 85, 86, 87, 88, 89, 91, 92, 93, 94, 95, 103, 104, 105, 106, 108, 109, 110, 113, 114, 115, 116, 117,

121, 126, 127, 132, 133, 134, 136, 137, 138, 141, 158, 159, 161, 162, 163, 168, 174, 177, 179, 182, 193, 194, 197, 207, 214, 220, 223, 225, 226, 227, 228, 230, 231, 233, 234, 235, 237, 238, 245, 248, 249, 251, 254, 261, 263, 267, 268, 269, 270, 271, 272, 274, 275, 276, 277, 281, 284, 286, 287, 291, 292, 293, 294, 300, 307, 308, 311, 324, 328, 334, 335, 340, 342, 343, 346, 350, 356, 366, 367, 368, 373, 375

Ashrawi, Hanan 209
Aspin, Les 135, 215, 277
Assad, Hafez al- 125, 169, 194
Aziz, Tariq 97, 179, 183, 184, 200, 243

B

Bakatin, Vadim 271
Baker, James A. III
    arms control xv, xviii, 2, 11, 19, 20, 26, 32, 126, 159, 211, 212, 214, 219, 221, 223, 227, 228, 254, 266, 269, 297, 365
Brady, Nick 288
Bush G.H.W. xv, xvii, xviii, xx, xxi, xxii, 9, 10, 12, 13, 24, 41, 44, 46, 47, 48, 50, 51, 54, 61, 74, 82, 85, 89, 92, 97, 115, 125, 126, 140, 144, 150, 152, 173, 182,

192, 211, 227, 252, 263, 267, 269, 280, 352
Central America i, xvi, 12, 21, 22, 24, 127, 132, 134, 135, 136, 138, 139, 141, 144, 150, 151
Cheney xxii, 3, 11, 23, 26, 31, 38, 164, 176, 200, 219, 261, 264, 266, 284, 303
China xix, 2, 6, 23, 71, 72, 73, 74, 75, 76, 77, 78, 79, 80, 81, 82, 90, 93, 98, 161, 180, 302, 315, 317, 320, 329, 332, 335, 344, 345, 346, 377
CSCE xiii, 14, 36, 57, 58, 59, 63, 64, 95, 126, 253, 254, 255, 256, 260, 268, 270, 272, 369, 370
Finance committee 117
Five principles 255, 272, 285, 289
Four Points 198, 199
Gates xxii, 3, 14, 22, 23, 24, 27, 31, 38, 42, 96, 217, 317, 331, 335, 338
Iraq i, 7, 97, 121, 155, 156, 157, 158, 161, 162, 163, 164, 165, 166, 167, 168, 169, 171, 172, 173, 174, 175, 177, 178, 181, 182, 183, 184, 185, 187, 188, 190, 200, 201, 202, 203, 206, 208, 233, 246, 247, 248, 258, 262, 300, 303, 318, 356, 357, 358, 359
Israel settlements 196
NATO xviii, xix, 11, 28, 44, 49, 59, 65, 67, 168, 169, 214, 215, 217, 223, 236, 253,

259, 260, 261, 268, 291,
301, 302, 357, 370
Pragmatic idealism 98
Princeton speech 284
Human rights xix, 10, 11, 21,
32, 40, 71, 82, 92, 94, 98,
109, 119, 135, 138, 156,
157, 227, 249, 250, 253,
254, 255, 256, 270, 272,
302, 305, 309, 324, 348,
355, 370
Shevardnadze 13, 14, 15, 316,
343, 344
Soviet Union i, xiv, xviii, 2, 6, 9,
11, 12, 14, 18, 19, 22, 30,
41, 62, 84, 108, 109, 110,
114, 115, 120, 121, 123,
125, 126, 127, 141, 155,
157, 162, 164, 190, 194,
214, 228, 239, 256, 261,
269, 271, 272, 274, 283,
284, 290, 294, 300, 308
German unification ix, 15, 36,
40, 45, 46, 47, 48, 49,
50, 53, 55, 58, 61, 63, 65,
93, 171, 225, 226, 228,
231, 254, 323, 339, 340,
342, 343
Yeltsin xx, xxi, 102, 115, 239,
264, 267, 268, 269, 270,
271, 273, 274, 280, 281,
282, 283, 284, 285, 286,
288, 289, 291, 296, 297,
305, 307, 318, 321, 349,
351, 352, 375
Yugoslavia xx, 182, 245, 246,
247, 248, 249, 250, 251,
252, 253, 254, 255, 256,
257, 259, 260, 264, 265,
271, 300, 304, 315, 325,
326, 327, 368, 369,
370, 371
Baker, Susan 18, 106, 254, 258, 259,
307, 312, 348
William Winston 179
Barkley, Richard 51
Bartholomew, Reginald 286
Belavezha Accord 283
Bessmertnykh, Alexandr 232, 333
Bevan Aneurin 70, 71
Bevin, Ernest 70, 71, 98
Biden, Joe 81, 235
Bipartisan Accord on Central America
22, 140, 353
Bolton, John 172, 357
Boznia-Herzegovina 253, 256
Brady, Nicolas xxi, 76, 125, 167,
272, 373
Brezhnev Doctrine 3, 8, 38
Browning, Bish Edward 177
Brown, William Andreas 203,
312, 361
Brzezinski, Zbigniew 85
Buchanan, Pat 296, 376
Burbulis, Gennadi 274, 375
Burghardt, Raymond 78, 307, 345
Burns, William xxii, 312
Burt, Richard 6, 214, 218, 224, 229,
364, 365, 366, 367
Bush, George H.W. i, iv, ix, xiv, xxii,
1, 38, 102, 128, 129, 130,
154, 241, 243, 265, 299, 308,
311, 314, 315, 318, 320, 323,
324, 327, 328, 332, 333, 335,
336, 338, 339, 345, 352, 353,
354, 355, 356, 358, 359, 360,
361, 363, 364, 365, 366, 373,
375, 377
Berlin xvii, xviii, 33, 35, 37, 40,
42, 43, 45, 46, 47, 50, 51,

87, 126, 182, 253, 254,
256, 272, 293, 310, 311,
318, 320, 323, 325, 337,
338, 339, 340, 342, 343
Deng Xiaoping xix, 73, 74,
82, 267
Gorbachev xv, xx, xxi, 4, 5, 8, 9,
13, 14, 15, 16, 19, 22, 24,
35, 41, 44, 45, 49, 61, 88,
90, 112, 126, 127, 134,
135, 166, 168, 175, 188,
210, 232, 238, 239, 261,
268, 271, 283, 284, 293,
301, 302, 311, 312, 323,
333, 336, 347, 365
Gulf War xix, xxi, 155, 172, 185,
191, 199, 202, 203, 205,
206, 233, 293, 313, 326,
357, 359, 362
Lilley 72, 73, 74, 76, 78, 79, 320,
344, 345
Mainz 42, 313, 338, 339
Mitterand 54
Reagan ii, xiii, xiv, xv, xvii, xxi,
2, 5, 6, 8, 9, 10, 11, 17,
20, 21, 22, 24, 26, 30, 35,
37, 38, 43, 46, 71, 75, 87,
132, 133, 134, 136, 137,
138, 143, 152, 153, 156,
162, 192, 195, 212, 213,
214, 216, 220, 228, 258,
263, 299, 319, 320, 321,
323, 331
Scowcroft xiv, xv, xvii, xviii, xxi,
xxii, 3, 4, 5, 8, 9, 11, 13,
14, 23, 26, 27, 31, 34, 35,
41, 48, 50, 53, 65, 74, 78,
80, 81, 125, 128, 130, 147,
148, 166, 178, 182, 188,
212, 213, 214, 215, 216,
217, 219, 232, 233, 234,
237, 238, 247, 253, 259,
260, 264, 266, 270, 300,
301, 305, 314, 323, 324,
331, 334, 335, 336, 337,
341, 350, 352, 364, 370,
372, 377
Shamir 192, 193, 196, 197, 198,
199, 200, 201, 202, 203,
204, 205, 206, 207, 208,
209, 210, 211, 324, 362
Thatcher 26, 27, 28, 39, 44, 45,
46, 47, 48, 53, 55, 56, 91,
131, 165, 173, 178, 217,
218, 308, 325, 336, 339,
340, 347, 356, 358
Yeltsin xx, xxi, 102, 115, 239,
264, 267, 268, 269, 270,
271, 273, 274, 280, 281,
282, 283, 284, 285, 286,
288, 289, 291, 296, 297,
305, 307, 318, 321, 349,
351, 352, 375
Yugoslavia xx, 182, 245, 246,
247, 248, 249, 250, 251,
252, 253, 254, 255, 256,
257, 259, 260, 264, 265,
271, 300, 304, 315, 325,
326, 327, 368, 369,
370, 371

C

Carpendale, Andrew 283
Carter, Ashton 278, 314
    Harvard report 278, 279, 280
Castro, Fidel 19, 22, 24, 133,
135, 136

Glasnost 15, 16, 23, 30, 32, 38, 85, 100, 108, 134, 137, 138, 197, 346
  Gorbachev 24, 137, 138, 141
  Perestroika 15, 16, 18, 19, 23, 30, 35, 38, 83, 85, 93, 100, 105, 106, 108, 110, 115, 134, 137, 138, 197, 221, 223, 266, 309, 310, 317, 337, 364
  Secret meeting 137
  US relations xx, 14, 79, 134, 148, 173, 180, 266
Chamorro, Violeta 90, 151
Chelyabinsk-70 295
Chemical Weapons Treaty 231
Cheney, Dick 23, 38, 96, 320
  Gorbachev 38, 159, 335
  Iraq i, 7, 97, 121, 155, 156, 157, 158, 161, 162, 163, 164, 165, 166, 167, 168, 169, 171, 172, 173, 174, 175, 177, 178, 181, 182, 183, 184, 185, 187, 188, 190, 200, 201, 202, 203, 206, 208, 233, 246, 247, 248, 258, 262, 300, 303, 318, 356, 357, 358, 359
  Panama 143, 144, 145, 146, 147, 148, 149, 313, 353, 354, 355
  Soviet Union 263, 277, 280, 284, 335
Chernyaev, Anatoly 35, 66, 315, 334, 357, 368
Chicken Kiev speech 260
China xix, 2, 6, 23, 71, 72, 73, 74, 75, 76, 77, 78, 79, 80, 81, 82, 90, 93, 98, 161, 180, 302, 315, 317, 320, 329, 332, 335, 344, 345, 346, 377
  arms sales 162
Bush, G.H.W. i, iv, ix, xiv, xxii, 1, 38, 102, 128, 129, 130, 154, 241, 243, 265, 299, 308, 311, 315, 318, 320, 323, 327, 328, 332, 333, 335, 336, 338, 339, 345, 352, 353, 354, 355, 356, 358, 359, 360, 361, 363, 364, 365, 366, 373, 375, 377
  Gulf war xix, xxi, 155, 172, 185, 191, 199, 202, 203, 205, 206, 233, 293, 313, 326, 357, 359, 362
  Tiananmen xix, 71, 72, 73, 77, 78, 81, 84, 267, 302
  US Congress xviii, xix, 92, 96, 132, 133, 181, 189, 283
Commodity Credit Corporation 122
Commonwealth of Independent States (CIS) 282, 283, 285, 287, 289, 304
  Akayev, Askar 289
  Nazarbayev, Nursultan 239, 289
Conference on Security and Cooperation in Europe (CSCE) xiii, 14, 36, 57, 58, 59, 63, 64, 95, 126, 253, 254, 255, 256, 260, 268, 270, 272, 369, 370
Contras 20, 21, 133, 134, 135, 137, 138, 139, 140, 151, 353
Conventional Forces in Europe (CFE) xviii, 19, 55, 61, 69, 119, 214, 215, 217, 223, 227, 234, 235, 236, 237, 266, 269, 286, 325, 330, 367, 372

Croatia 248, 252, 253, 256, 257, 300, 317, 369
Crowe, William 216
Cruise missiles 184, 217, 223, 224, 228, 229, 230, 280
    ALCMs 224, 225, 228, 229, 230, 232
    SLCMs 224, 225, 228, 229, 230, 232, 280
Cuba 22, 24, 61, 109, 111, 112, 119, 127, 133, 134, 135, 136, 137, 138, 141, 146, 150, 167, 320, 353
    Glasnost 15, 16, 23, 30, 32, 38, 85, 100, 108, 134, 137, 138, 197, 346
    Mariel boatlift 137
    Perestroika 15, 16, 18, 19, 23, 30, 35, 38, 83, 85, 93, 100, 105, 106, 108, 110, 115, 134, 137, 138, 197, 221, 223, 266, 309, 310, 317, 337, 364
    Secret meetings 137

D

D'Aubuisson, Roberto 133
De Michelis, Gianni 170
Deng Xiaoping xix, 73, 74, 82, 267
Djerejian, Edward xi, 307
    Syria 165, 169, 170, 191, 194, 198, 205, 207, 208, 209, 210, 211, 307, 357
Dobbins, James 40, 55, 315, 338
    Mindszenty, Jozsef 40
    German unification ix, 15, 36, 40, 45, 46, 47, 48, 49, 50, 53, 55, 58, 61, 63, 65, 93, 171, 225, 226, 228, 231, 254, 323, 339, 340, 342, 343
Dobrynin, Anatoly 4, 105
Dubinin, Yuri 45
Dumas, Roland 43, 60, 294

E

Eagleburger, Larry 6, 27, 72, 78, 246, 298, 302
    China xix, 2, 6, 23, 71, 72, 73, 74, 75, 76, 77, 78, 79, 80, 81, 82, 90, 93, 98, 161, 180, 302, 315, 317, 320, 329, 332, 335, 344, 345, 346, 377
    Milosevic xx, 300, 303
    Senate ix, 5, 23, 39, 71, 76, 80, 81, 91, 92, 98, 111, 117, 118, 124, 135, 139, 140, 158, 160, 176, 177, 181, 184, 189, 191, 227, 232, 235, 236, 239, 250, 266, 269, 276, 278, 280, 300, 321, 324, 329, 330, 345, 346, 348, 351, 352, 353, 355, 357, 358, 359, 360, 361, 367, 368, 372, 374
    Yugoslavia xx, 182, 245, 246, 247, 248, 249, 250, 251, 252, 253, 254, 255, 256, 257, 259, 260, 264, 265, 271, 300, 304, 315, 325, 326, 327, 368, 369, 370, 371
El Salvador 16, 21, 22, 24, 127, 132, 133, 134, 135, 136, 138, 139, 141, 142, 143, 146, 151, 297, 299, 326, 353, 355, 379
Endara, Guillermo 144

European Bank for Regional Development (EBRD) 110
European Economic Community (EEC) 26, 43, 54, 56, 57, 60, 61, 247, 253, 254, 257, 260
Evans and Novak show 23, 31

F

Fang, Lizhi 78, 79, 98
Fitzwater, Marlin 79
Ford, Gerald xv, 2, 4, 23, 144
France i, 43, 51, 126, 165, 171, 184, 260, 283, 294, 325, 326, 339, 344, 348, 373
   Gulf war xix, xxi, 155, 172, 185, 191, 199, 202, 203, 205, 206, 233, 293, 313, 326, 357, 359, 362
   Soviet Union 51, 165
   German unification ix, 15, 36, 40, 45, 46, 47, 48, 49, 50, 53, 55, 58, 61, 63, 65, 93, 171, 225, 226, 228, 231, 254, 323, 339, 340, 342, 343
Frente Farabundo Marti, (FMLN) 134, 135, 136, 141, 142, 143, 151, 152, 352
Frente Sandinista, (FSLN) 135

G

G-7 Summit 125
Gaddis, John Lewis 316
Gates, Robert xxii, 3, 23, 27, 96, 317, 331, 335
   Baker 3, 14, 24, 31, 96
   Gorbachev 23, 24, 38
   NSC xvii, xviii, xxii, 1, 3, 9, 11, 14, 21, 24, 38, 40, 41, 46, 55, 56, 59, 60, 65, 78, 97, 134, 144, 145, 147, 150, 157, 159, 166, 193, 194, 195, 200, 201, 205, 216, 233, 263, 287, 293, 332, 342, 343, 373, 374
   Soviet Union 14, 23, 31
Genscher, Hans-Dietrich 26, 48, 57, 251, 294, 317, 342, 370
   Tutzing 57, 58, 59, 60, 62, 63, 317, 342
Germany i, ii, xv, xvi, xvii, xviii, xix, 2, 3, 6, 33, 37, 39, 40, 41, 42, 43, 46, 47, 48, 49, 51, 52, 53, 54, 55, 56, 57, 59, 60, 61, 62, 63, 64, 65, 66, 67, 68, 69, 71, 90, 98, 112, 113, 114, 126, 150, 155, 171, 175, 176, 182, 197, 213, 214, 223, 226, 227, 228, 236, 251, 252, 253, 283, 301, 302, 308, 311, 316, 317, 318, 319, 320, 322, 325, 326, 327, 331, 338, 339, 340, 341, 342, 343, 344, 350, 357, 366, 369
   Berlin xvii, xviii, 33, 35, 37, 40, 42, 43, 45, 46, 47, 50, 51, 87, 126, 182, 253, 254, 256, 272, 293, 310, 311, 318, 320, 323, 325, 337, 338, 339, 340, 342, 343
   Deutsche bank 113, 350
   Dresdner bank 113
   East, GDR 150
   Gorbachev meetings 347
   NATO xv, xviii, xix, 39, 42, 48, 49, 53, 57, 59, 60, 61, 62, 63, 64, 65, 66, 67, 69, 98, 112, 113, 155, 171, 197, 223, 226, 227, 301, 302

Unification i, ii, ix, xv, xviii, 15,
36, 40, 41, 43, 44, 45, 46,
47, 48, 49, 50, 52, 53, 55,
56, 58, 59, 61, 62, 63, 65,
68, 93, 113, 114, 171, 225,
226, 228, 231, 251, 254,
301, 322, 323, 331, 339,
340, 342, 343
West, FDR 6, 41, 42, 43, 47,
48, 52, 55, 57, 59, 64, 65,
66, 171, 213, 214, 339,
340, 342
Giffen, James 103, 349
American Trade Consortium
103, 349
Glasnost 15, 16, 23, 30, 32, 38,
85, 100, 108, 134, 137, 138,
197, 346
Glienicke Bridge 51
Gonzalez, Felipe 209
Gorbachev, Mikhail xiv, 3, 25, 37,
43, 54, 69, 73, 88, 99, 100,
129, 236, 245, 266, 283, 299,
308, 312, 317, 319, 323, 332,
333, 336, 340, 341, 343, 344,
352, 372
Berlin xvii, xviii, 33, 35, 37, 40,
42, 43, 45, 46, 47, 50, 51,
87, 126, 182, 253, 254,
256, 272, 293, 310, 311,
318, 320, 323, 325, 337,
338, 339, 340, 342, 343
Bush G.H.W. 34, 209
China xix, 2, 6, 23, 71, 72, 73,
74, 75, 76, 77, 78, 79, 80,
81, 82, 90, 93, 98, 161,
180, 302, 315, 317, 320,
329, 332, 335, 344, 345,
346, 377
coup d'etat 266, 276

economic reform 32, 35, 99, 100,
104, 107, 108, 111, 115,
118, 125, 237, 238, 239,
247, 266, 269, 270, 272,
296, 297, 305, 329, 350
German unification ix, 15, 36,
40, 45, 46, 47, 48, 49, 50,
53, 55, 58, 61, 63, 65, 93,
171, 225, 226, 228, 231,
254, 339
Iraq i, 7, 97, 121, 155, 156, 157,
158, 161, 162, 163, 164,
165, 166, 167, 168, 169,
171, 172, 173, 174, 175,
177, 178, 181, 182, 183,
184, 185, 187, 188, 190,
200, 201, 202, 203, 206,
208, 233, 246, 247, 248,
258, 262, 300, 303, 318,
356, 357, 358, 359
Lithuania 71, 82, 84, 85, 86, 87,
88, 89, 90, 91, 92, 93, 94,
96, 97, 98, 108, 226, 227,
228, 271, 297, 313, 319,
346, 347, 348
nuclear arms 212, 221, 236, 238,
274, 373
political reform 15, 47, 102, 115,
124, 294
Reagan ii, xiii, xiv, xv, xvii, xxi,
2, 5, 6, 8, 9, 10, 11, 17,
20, 21, 22, 24, 26, 30, 35,
37, 38, 43, 46, 71, 75, 87,
132, 133, 134, 136, 137,
138, 143, 152, 153, 156,
162, 192, 195, 212, 213,
214, 216, 220, 228, 258,
263, 299, 319, 320, 321,
323, 331

summit meeting xx, 12, 34, 49,
    57, 88, 127, 158, 175, 222,
    228, 232, 233, 297
Warsaw Pact xxi, 20, 39, 45,
    50, 52, 57, 59, 61, 63,
    64, 67, 68, 133, 213, 215,
    236, 261
Yeltsin xx, xxi, 102, 115, 239,
    264, 267, 268, 269, 270,
    271, 273, 274, 280, 281,
    282, 283, 284, 285, 286,
    288, 289, 291, 296, 297,
    305, 307, 318, 321, 349,
    351, 352, 375
Yugoslavia xx, 182, 245, 246,
    247, 248, 249, 250, 251,
    252, 253, 254, 255, 256,
    257, 259, 260, 264, 265,
    271, 300, 304, 315, 325,
    326, 327, 368, 369,
    370, 371
Gorbachev, Raisa 267, 268
Gromyko, Andrei 100, 194
Gulf Cooperation Council (GCC))
    185, 187, 190, 359
Gulf war xix, xxi, 155, 172, 185, 191,
    199, 202, 203, 205, 206, 233,
    293, 313, 326, 357, 359, 362

H

Han Xu 74, 78
Havel, Vaclav 61
Helsinki Final Act xiii, 49, 369
Hills, Carla 153, 154
Honecker, Erich 33, 39, 338
House of Representative:
    Archer, Bill 109
    Dornan, Robert 139
    Foley, Thomas 177, 358
    Hamilton, Lee 139
    Hoyer, Steny 95
    Hunter, Duncan 139
    Hyde, Henry 21, 135, 139
    Lagomarsino, Robert 139
    Michel, Robert 139
Housing Loan guarantees 196, 202
Hungary xvi, xvii, 3, 16, 39, 42, 44,
    52, 64, 82, 83, 90, 97, 108,
    109, 120, 125, 245, 247, 261
    US Embassy 12, 27, 40, 74, 78,
        79, 127, 145, 146, 247,
        280, 287, 291, 307
Hussein, King of Jordan 204
Hussein, Saddam i, xv, xix, 7, 95, 96,
    97, 98, 114, 115, 147, 155, 156,
    157, 161, 162, 167, 168, 170,
    174, 176, 177, 178, 179, 180,
    183, 184, 185, 186, 187, 188,
    189, 190, 197, 199, 204, 207,
    232, 233, 246, 247, 248, 258,
    260, 300, 302, 356, 362
Gulf states xix, 121, 156, 158,
    181, 187, 303
Iran 21, 134, 155, 156, 157, 183
Kuwait i, xv, xix, 7, 95, 96, 97,
    114, 115, 121, 122, 147,
    158, 159, 160, 161, 162,
    163, 164, 165, 166, 167,
    168, 169, 172, 173, 174,
    175, 176, 177, 178, 180,
    181, 182, 183, 184, 185,
    186, 187, 188, 189, 190,
    197, 198, 199, 204, 232,
    238, 246, 254, 262, 266,
    302, 313, 356, 358, 359
Revolutionary Guard 185

I

Intercontinental Ballistic Missile (ICBM) 218, 225, 233, 364, 367
Iran–Contra
   Casey, Bill 21, 133
   Contra affair 127
   North, Oliver 21, 133
Israeli officials
   Arad, Moshe 193
   Arens, Moshe 200
   Levy, David 174, 198, 362
   Modai, Yitzak 202
   Peres, Shimon 196
   Rabin, Yitzak 210, 303
   Shamir, Yitzak 192, 193, 324, 362
   Shoval, Zalman 202, 363

J

Jackson Lake Lodge 28, 29, 130, 219
Jackson-Vanik Amendment 25, 108, 109, 116, 120
Jamieson, Jim 116
   YPO 116, 307
Japan 2, 156, 167, 171, 175, 176, 191, 313, 360, 361, 376
   automobiles 2
   Gulf war xix, xxi, 155, 172, 185, 191, 199, 202, 203, 205, 206, 233, 293, 313, 326, 357, 359, 362
Jesuit priests 142
   Universidad Centro Americana (UCA) 142
Journalists xxii, 7, 16, 17, 59, 71, 73, 74, 87, 89, 95, 164, 203, 339
   Brokaw, Tom 29, 336
   Donaldson, Sam 87, 338

Friedman, Thomas 11, 333, 334, 363, 364, 365, 366, 370
Hoffman, David 25, 336, 347, 350, 357
Kondrake, Morton 72
Novak, Bob 1
Oberdorfer, Don xi, 23, 322, 328, 334, 335, 336, 341, 346, 356
Safire, William 72, 92, 262, 344, 347, 355
Trimble, Jeffrey 308
Will, George 87, 95

K

Karpov, Victor 219
Kelly, John 7, 155, 194, 203
Kimmitt, Robert, Bob xi, 7, 160, 308, 332, 359
Kissinger, Henry xvi, 3, 4, 50, 82, 212, 219, 323, 332
   Trilateral Commission 4
Kohl, Helmut xiv, xviii, 26, 39, 46, 214, 241, 299, 307, 308, 319, 340
   Bankers 103, 104, 113, 248, 251, 288
   Ten Points 48, 49, 198
Kozak, Michael 143
Kozyrev, Andrei 270, 285, 307
Kravchuk, Leonid 281, 290
Kurds 156, 185
   Baker's visit 257
Kurtzer, Daniel xi, 328
Kuwait i, xv, xix, 7, 95, 96, 97, 114, 115, 121, 122, 147, 158, 159, 160, 161, 162, 163, 164, 165, 166, 167, 168, 169, 172, 173, 174, 175, 176, 177, 178, 180,

181, 182, 183, 184, 185, 186, 187, 188, 189, 190, 197, 198, 199, 204, 232, 238, 246, 254, 262, 266, 302, 313, 356, 358, 359
Sabah, Emir al- 168

L

Landsbergis, Vyautas 83, 86, 226
Lavrov, Sergei 67, 322, 344
Leffler, Melvyn xiii, 320
Lilley, James 72, 320, 344
   Baker 74, 76, 79
   Tianamen xix, 71, 72, 73, 77, 78, 81, 84, 267, 302
   United airlines 76
Li Peng 73, 75, 302
Li, Shuxian 78, 79
Lobov, Vladimir 274
Lubbers, Rudd 260, 371
Lugar, Richard 235, 278, 321, 367

M

Macedonia 249, 256
Malta Summit 50, 51, 108, 110, 174, 222, 223, 323, 337, 365
Matlock, Jack 11, 13, 65, 333, 337, 343, 346, 374
   Rebecca 12
   Spaso House 12
Mikhailov, Victor 295
Miller, Aaron David 204, 308, 321, 361, 363
Milosevic, Slobodan xx, 300
Mitterand, Francois
   Bush 14, 28, 45, 48, 53
   Walker's Point 74
Modrow, Hans 51
Momper, Walter 43

Mosbacher, Robert. Bob
   Business Delegation 116, 117
Most Favored Nation (MFN) 25, 76, 93, 100, 104, 108, 109, 116, 120, 236, 345, 351
Mubarak, Hosni 168
Mullins, Janet 6, 139, 308
Mulroney, Brian 9, 153, 240
   Gorbachev 9, 10
   NAFTA 153, 300

N

NATO ii, xv, xviii, xix, xxi, 11, 14, 25, 26, 27, 28, 36, 39, 42, 44, 45, 48, 49, 53, 55, 57, 58, 59, 60, 61, 62, 63, 64, 65, 66, 67, 68, 69, 98, 112, 113, 155, 168, 169, 171, 191, 197, 213, 214, 215, 216, 217, 223, 226, 227, 228, 231, 236, 240, 253, 259, 260, 261, 268, 291, 301, 302, 307, 317, 319, 321, 324, 332, 336, 340, 342, 343, 344, 357, 370
Negroponte, John 144, 152
New World Order xvii, 170, 173, 179, 206, 265, 330, 363
Nickles Amendment 249
Noriega, Manuel 143, 327, 353, 355
North American Free Trade, NAFTA 152, 153, 300
NSC advisors 40
   Blackwill, Robert 55, 58
   Burns, Nicholas ii, xi, 307, 327, 352, 373, 375, 376
   Haass, Richard 157, 193, 205, 318, 356, 361, 362

Hutchings, Robert xi, 40,
  50, 307, 316, 318, 338,
  340, 341
Pryce, William 144, 328,
  353, 354
Rice, Condoleezza xxii, 40,
  58, 327
Nunn-Lugar initiative 279, 321, 374
Nunn, Sam, Senator 135, 177, 239,
  276, 324, 373, 374

O

On Site Inspection Agency
  (OSIA) 292
Open Skies Treaty 301
Organization of American States
  (OAS) 145, 146, 149, 354

P

Palestinian Liberation Organization
  (PLO) 170, 192, 193, 194, 195,
  199, 204, 207, 208, 210, 303,
  360, 362
Panama 143, 144, 145, 146, 147, 148,
  149, 313, 353, 354, 355
  Panama Canal Treaty 144, 148
  Panamanian Defense Force 145
Perestroika 15, 16, 18, 19, 23, 30, 35,
  38, 83, 85, 93, 100, 105, 106,
  108, 110, 115, 134, 137, 138,
  197, 221, 223, 266, 309, 310,
  317, 337, 364
Pickering, Tom 159, 166, 308,
  356, 357
Polish leaders 53
  Jaruzelski, Wojciech 39
  Walesa, Lech 3
  Wojtyla, Karol, Pope 34
Pope John Paul II 149

Powell, Colin 164, 235, 320
Presidential Nuclear Initiative (PNI)
  274, 275
Primakov, Yevgeny 161, 167, 226
Prunskiene, Kazimira 226

Q

Qian Qichen 180
Quayle, Dan xxii, 72

R

Reagan, Ronald xiii, xiv, xv, xxi, 2,
  5, 9, 10, 21, 22, 26, 37, 43, 46,
  71, 212, 214, 258, 319, 320,
  321, 331
  Central America xiv, xv, 2
  Governor's Island 8, 134
Rice, Condoleezza xxii, 40, 58, 327
Roberts, Adam xiii, 310, 331
Roedder, Andreas 68
Ross, Dennis 6, 9, 17, 19, 27, 28, 55,
  62, 65, 106, 155, 157, 160, 161,
  183, 192, 203, 204, 286, 308,
  322, 323, 333, 335, 336, 337,
  342, 343, 360, 363
Rostow, Nicholas 145, 328, 354
Roy, Stapleton J. xi, 6, 27, 43,
  308, 345
Ryzhkov, Nikolai 101

S

Sajūdis 84
Salinas de Gortari, Carlos 152
Sandinista 16, 20, 22, 23, 132, 134,
  135, 138, 141, 150
Schmidt, Helmut 213, 251
Scowcroft, Brent xiv, xxii, 3, 8, 13,
  34, 78, 212, 247, 314, 324, 331,

334, 335, 336, 337, 341, 352, 364, 370
Seitz, Ray 27, 58
Senators 71, 93, 118, 120, 123, 158, 184, 235, 237, 263, 278, 279, 280, 283, 300, 347, 358, 374
    Baucus, Max 120
    Bentsen, Lloyd 118
    Biden, Joe 81, 235
    Bradley, Bill 96
    Byrd, Robert 96
    Chafee, John 120
    Danforth, Jack 120
    Harkin, Tom 176
    Helms, Jesse 133, 236, 367
    Humphrey, Gordon 93
    Moynihan, Daniel 120, 351
    Nichols, Don 249
    Robb, Chuck 135
Sharaa, Farouk al- 170, 209
Shevardnadze, Eduard xiv, 4, 28, 95, 181, 232, 266, 311, 324, 334, 337, 356
    Baker xiv, 13, 14, 15, 17, 20, 28, 29, 30, 34, 44, 51, 56, 61, 62, 63, 69, 80, 83, 87, 91, 92, 95, 105, 110, 141, 161, 162, 163, 166, 175, 179, 180, 181, 182, 219, 220, 223, 225, 226, 227, 228, 230, 264, 266, 272, 342, 343
    Bakers 105
    Gorbachev 13, 18, 30, 44, 53, 63, 67, 80, 83, 87, 92, 113, 141, 161, 162, 174, 225, 226, 228, 229, 235, 266, 322, 334, 344, 350
    Nanuli 17, 18, 106
    Patriotic war 61

Resignation 5, 46, 69, 95, 96, 268, 314, 376
Shia marshlands 156, 185
Shultz, George xiv, 2, 6, 15, 17, 26, 136, 162, 192, 335
Shevardnadze 162
Silayev, Ivan 271
Slovenia 248, 252, 253, 256, 257, 259, 300, 317, 369
Solidarność 39, 41, 45, 261
Soviet economic advisors
    Abalkin, Leonid 101, 117
    Aganbegyan, Abel 102
    Avrorin, Yevgeny 295
    Gaidar, Yegor 271, 281, 316
    Petrakov, Nikolai 101
    Shatalin, Stanislav 101
    Yavlinsky, Grigory xxi, 123, 304, 327, 351
Strauss, Robert 289
Sununu, John 34, 130, 149, 289, 355, 375

T

Tarasenko, Sergei 28, 62, 106, 161, 272, 336
Teltschik, Horst xiv, 44, 48, 49, 214, 308, 325, 339, 340, 341, 342, 344
Thatcher, Margaret 26, 39, 46, 53, 308, 325, 336, 347, 356, 358
    Acland, Anthony 55
    Howe, Jeffrey 27, 217
    Hurd, Douglas 55, 240, 268
    Powell, Charles 26
Tiananmen Square xix, 71, 72, 73, 77, 267, 302

Treaty on the Final Settlement with Respect to Germany 68, 325, 344, 350
Tutwiler, Margaret 6, 24, 44, 75, 92, 139, 158, 232, 256, 294, 333, 345, 363, 370

U

UN Security Council Resolutions 174, 184, 187
   660 161, 167, 172
   665 167
   670 167, 172
   672 174
   673 174
   678 172, 178, 180, 183

V

Vnukovo airport 163, 174, 182
Voice of America (VOA) 37, 157

W

Walters, Vernon 41

Warsaw Pact xxi, 20, 39, 45, 50, 52, 57, 59, 61, 63, 64, 67, 68, 133, 213, 215, 236, 261
Wolfowitz, Paul 201
Woolsey, James 235

Y

Yakovlev, Alexandr 372
Yeltsin, Boris xx, 102, 115, 239, 267, 268, 270, 271, 281, 282, 283, 305, 307, 321, 349, 352, 375
Yugoslav Federation 247, 248, 250, 251, 252, 255, 257, 300, 303
   Kucan, Milan 257
   Markovic, Ante 256
   Tudjman, Franjo 252, 256
Yugoslav National Army, (JNA) 246, 252, 257, 259, 370

Z

Zhao, Ziyang 74
Zimmermann, Warren 370
Zoellick, Robert 6, 135, 153, 308, 342

CPSIA information can be obtained
at www.ICGtesting.com
Printed in the USA
LVHW091609280321
682530LV00012B/9